THE ENCHANTED GLASS

Tom Nairn was born in Fife, Scotland and now lives in the Czech Republic, where he works at the Central European University in Prague. Previous books include THE BREAK-UP OF BRITAIN (1977 and 1982), and THE LEFT AGAINST EUROPE (1974). He has also worked in television for some years as writer and consultant, and his productions included *Borderlands*, a six-part Channel 4 series on post-1989 frontier peoples and problems.

THE ENCHANTED GLASS

Britain And Its Monarchy

Tom Nairn

Published by Vintage 1994

2 4 6 8 10 9 7 5 3 1

Copyright © 1988, 1994 Tom Nairn

The right of Tom Nairn to be identified as the author
of this work has been asserted by him in accordance
with the Copyright, Designs and Patents Act, 1988

First published in Great Britain by Radius, 1988

Vintage
Random House, 20 Vauxhall Bridge Road, London
SW1V 2SA

Random House Australia (Pty) Limited
20 Alfred Street, Milsons Point, Sydney
New South Wales 2061, Australia

Random House New Zealand Limited
18 Poland Road, Glenfield,
Auckland 10, New Zealand

Random House South Africa (Pty) Limited
PO Box 337, Bergvlei, South Africa

Random House UK Limited Reg. No. 954009

A CIP catalogue record for this book is available from
the British Library

ISBN 0 09942 441 X

Printed and bound in Great Britain by Cox & Wyman,
Reading, Berkshire

Contents

For Christine

l'amata del tempo delle colombe.

Ma dal profondo tuo sangue,
nel giusto tempo umano,
rinasceremo senza dolore.

I am grateful to Ernest Gellner and his Centre for Research into Nationalism at the Central European University, Prague, for support and research facilities in producing this farther edition of the book. Also to David McCrone and the International Social Science Institute of the University of Edinburgh, where part of the work was done. A good deal of it was also done at home, where I must acknowledge many other kinds of help from Millicent Hendry, Greig and Rachel.

INTRODUCTION

'Verdict on Royals: No More Cash'. With this headline the *Observer* greeted its customers on December 26th, 1993. Still sagging from Christmas, they learned that –

> According to an overwhelming majority of people interviewed in an Observer/ICM poll, the Royal Family should get no financial support at all from taxpayers. Only one in five believes the Exchequer should continue to finance the monarchy.

True, about two-thirds of those questioned thought Britain should go on being a monarchy. The other third of (mainly) new republicans were apparently divided between electing a President (20%) and promoting the Prime Minister to Head of State (10%). But that verdict had been delivered earlier in December, after a long period during which the general reputation of British politicos had sunk to the 'All-time Low' beloved of British sub-editors. Also, by publishing her memoirs in the autumn Mrs Thatcher had reasserted her authority as Britian's unofficial President, a fact sufficient in itself to keep incalculable numbers of waverers within the monarchy camp. And there must have been other doubters too: those simply unable to imagine John Major as Head of State for instance. Add up all the 'don't really knows' and a ghostly republican majority could be glimpsed lurking within the newspaper's quota sample of '1,106 adults aged 18 and over, face to face, in 52 randomly selected constituencies across the country'.

A week later came the New Year Honours List. It was to be

a long-postponed fanfare for the British common man and woman – the first 'classless' bestowal of titles and medals. Nominations had been sought from the general public for worthy recipients. In 1993 thousands of forms had gone out from the Honours committee in Downing Street. 11,000 were requested. 10,000 were returned and (allowing for duplicate recommendations) about 7,500 people were suggested. In the 1988 account of the Honours system given below (pp.311–14, see also pp.83–4) I pointed out that it depended upon the prestige of Royalty, that its main function was distributing routine awards to stuffed shirts, and that its only justification lay in the somewhat haphazard 'recognition' bestowed on a few citizens who had served communities or causes well. It was to try and strengthen this last element that Mr Major had launched his popular nomination process. For ages people had been saying: 'If only *I* could tell them who deserves a medal' – now they were to be given the chance. At the same time, the Prime Minister announced his government's intention to cut back heavily on the quota of 'gongs', or Honours bestowed purely for reasons of hierarchy and age (i.e. long and generally undistinguished service to the Establishment).

On 1993's last day the fruits were disclosed: four more gongs than in the previous List. The Foreign Office had done particularly well, upping its tally to 141. As for the democratically nominated, these came to only 70 out of 970. Worse still, it looked as if only a small part of the people's choice had been seriously examined at all. *The Times* noted severely that: 'It is thought that nearly 7,500 nominations were received, *of which only 500 were scrutinised*. The rest will now form part of a serious backlog, which will swell further when the counter opens for the next list...' In other words, the people had taken the whole thing too damned seriously and as a result money might have to be spent to keep them happy.

Also, 'The Cabinet Office declined to state which of the 970 had been nominated by members of the public, saying that it did not wish to create two tiers of honours...' (*Daily Telegraph*, 31-12-93). Apart from this staggering remark (to which I will return below) even the Tory *Telegraph* found it hard to opt out from the general derision which greeted the new list. 'A surprisingly small proportion of MBEs owe their preferment to the new system of recommendations from members of the public', sniffed its editorialist, 'The top of the list is a degree duller than it was, but essentially the same... If this Honours List is anything to go by, the classless society is likely to prove a rather dull place.'

After the Fall

I mention the first of these two incidents from the last week of 1993 for the simple reason that it was quite unimaginable in the spring of 1988, when *The Enchanted Glass* first appeared. It indicates how much things have changed – a sea-change of popular opinion and sentiment around what then still seemed a sacred and resistant institution.

The second event, by contrast, suggests how at another level things have scarcely altered at all. There may have been an earthquake in the depths. But Ukanian government continues its traditional bucket-and-spade operations around the edges – in this case, trying to inject a craintive populism into a system of hopelessly starched hierarchy, the aim being (as ever) to make the latter more acceptable without changing things too much.

It would (e.g.) have been 'too much' to bring out a two-tier system where democratic nomination risked colliding with Establishment patronage and due preferment. British Honour-tossing is intrinsically a matter of scalable and multiple tiers and grades: from the supreme, the exalted and the reasonably grand down to the modestly worthy. So why should a mere *two* new tiers suggested by these arrangements be avoided? Because one of them might get out of hand. If those honoured by acclaim came to smell like the people's wish *as against* the stuffed-shirt rota and political bribes, then the whole structure would be fatally endangered. Hence Official Secrecy is deployed from the outset to prevent the public knowing just which 'tier' it has elected and which is still being selected by the ancient norms. Otherwise two very different kinds of trip to The Palace might soon be occurring: those perceived as really (and identifiably) 'deserving' it as distinct from those whose turn it happens to be – or who have happen to have done some favour to power, party or Prime Minister.[1]

This book tried to describe Europe's last feudal system from the vantage-point of its soul, the Monarchy. Six years later, that soul has gone. The outer casing is still in place, of course, as is the Honours List, the Palace of Westminster and all the rest. But all this means is that nothing has yet replaced them. The living dead are defending the cemetery quite well. A social structure is not institutions but what animates them – a set of allegiances, stresses and tensions, all now functioning rather differently from the way they did in 1988. At that time, in 'Two Villages', a Channel 4 TV series contrasting two villages in France and England, the people of the Dorset township explained solemnly how central Royalty was to their identity, how it confirmed their intimate sense of Englishness – of being distinct from the rest of Europe. Nowadays, apparently, the Crown is costed and found wanting.

But may it not be that in reality it is found wanting because it is costed? May not the soul have depended upon exemption from the ledger-book? In the first edition I see I took a rather snooty view of old-republican complaints about the cost of Royalty. The theory was that most people were really unmoved by such moans since they felt there was something priceless about the Queen. Where so much national dignity was at stake it scarcely mattered what the Royal Yacht and Train cost, and protesters on these grounds risked looking like grudging cheapskates. In fact an only mildly perverse pleasure in the expense was sometimes in evidence – as if only a people of natural aristocrats could be guilty of such heedless excess. There were also the usual more dubious arguments about how much the Royal show 'brought in' to the nation every year from bedazzled foreign tourists.

I am not sure that the theory was mistaken then, but events since have certainly made it absurd. When personal and

---

[1] In this case these included Mr Francis Coulson, MBE, proprietor of the Sharrow Bay Hotel in the Lake District, where (as the *Guardian* acidly observed) – 'Mr Major and his wife Norma unwound after his testing speech to the Party Conference in Blackpool last October... In the 1993 *Good Hotel Guide* Mr Coulson loyally echoes the Prime Minister's philosophy of classlessness: 'Tipping is a feudal system and degrades both giver and receiver'.

incendiary disaster struck in the early '90s it became clear that pricelessness was already history. A nation which had succumbed to aggressive cost-effectiveness could no longer avoid applying it to the Head of State. But the very fact that this happened meant that aspects of the institution would be found wanting. If certain things like HMS Britannia, Queen Elizabeth's personal wealth, or the price of Royal security operations are seriously interrogated at all – rather than gaily brushed aside – they were bound to appear dubious or preposterous.[2] Here the downside of Thatcherism's emancipation was a certain sourness, a crabbed unwillingness to go on being had – particularly by 'Them', the old class regents of the national soul. But there was no middle way here: once They were no longer given the benefit of the doubt, then They could only get it in the neck.

The Queen then made matters worse by opening Buckingham Palace to the public and charging them for entry. She 'meant well', of course – as with the previous decision that the Royal Family should start paying income tax. Both moves were thought of as modernisation, or 'opening up'. But in fact they could only be opening down, levelling things monarchical into a society going through a fit of cankered and lop-sided modernisation where greed had eclipsed class. All that was sacred could but be profaned – and no less so, actually, when the idols asked meekly to be costed and tried to put their own price on the mysteries. What they were encountering was former subjects who have unintentionally half-mutated into citizens – but all this in a society still unprogrammed for citizenship. In that context, without more drastic changes, the new is condemned to stagnate alongside the old.

An outward institutional order does not immediately collapse when its inwardness is transformed. Entropy merely increases – the inert persistence of a régime whose special bent has long been for *bricolage* rather than building. The 'reformed' Honours List is a perfect specimen: a token readjustment intended to keep the unspeakable in being with a small improvement to its performance. This book is full of

[2] On this theme the most careful research and judgement has appeared in Anthony Holden's *The Tarnished Crown* (1993).

earlier examples of the craft, from a time when Britishness was healthier and 'social engineering' more than a nostalgic joke. But at the close of 1993 we see it still being practised, accompanied by the same broad spectrum of reactions around the same crucial dilemma – how to appear a bit more democratic while avoiding the damnable inconvenient rudeness of the real thing.

I know one has to be more careful about 'tokens' today. Political Correctness has also disembarked since 1988, with its tendency to identify any and every change as conspiratorially trivial. Were time-travel possible, there are now those who would dismiss the taking of the Bastille and the execution of Charles I as tokenism. But it should not be concluded that actual tokens and surrogates do not exist, or cannot sometimes be distinguished from reforms and revolutions. No: tokenism lives, and the Brits are its experts. A petrifying social order over-burdened with customs and symbolism is particularly exposed to its risks simply because it has, like Alice in her Wonderland, got away for so long with causing things to mean whatever it wants them to mean. The traditional assumption is, therefore, that there can be no reason why a new range of elected and approved Honours should *not* mean the enhanced popularity of Honours as such – of The Bath, The Garter, the Royal Victorian Medal (Silver), and Companions of Honour alongside these 'humble' do-gooders of suburb and shire. Damn it, the whole thing was only British Parliamentarism in a nutshell! Let the Royal Fount of Honour flow more broadly and be sweeter unto the multitude, while disturbing neither Prime-Ministerial whim nor Established interest. As a tongue loses its sense and declines into babble it becomes more, not less, important to decree the meaning of every syllable.

Only one problem: the Royal Fount itself has dried up. For about two years it has disgorged little but a daily trickle of petty scandals and scabrous speculation. There is no need to reiterate here what every newspaper in Ukania has been churning out, from the Prince's pillow-talk to the impending Divorce, from *annus horribilis* to the twelve-year-old Prince William's prospect of short-cut accession. The fact is that in that spiritual or ideological sense which the book's main argument saw as crucial to the way British identity functioned, the House of Windsor is dead. It may continue in a moribund and more or less festering condition for as long as Queen Elizabeth lasts. But this only confirms the sentence. For every year she endures on the Throne with no salvation appearing elsewhere from within this dynastic *chienlit*, the verdict will grow more final and the chances of a Republican solution stronger.

As the poll cited above and many other instances suggest, what counts is that people feel differently about it all. They have turned what would once have been called 'bolshie', but now has to be 'Thatcherite'. Is this aggravation, or adulthood –or some weird new mixture of the two, as yet unfathomed? They simply will not trust the way they used to. The same *Observer* poll that showed people so distrustful of Royalty revealed them as even more distrustful of government, the judicial system and the civil service. After two and a half years of Majorism, only just over one third of Conservative voters confessed to any trust *in their own government*. In the North of England (and hence, most likely in Scotland and Wales too) a majority is now opposed to Prince Charles succeeding his mother.

It is as if the very context of authority has changed, in ways which render traditional face-lifting manoeuvres like the new Honours System nugatory. As nugatory as have been (let us say) the Citizen's Charter, the pseudo-reform of Official Secrecy, the deregulation of TV franchises, the 'Back to Basics' campaign or the second Great Reform of Local Government. Over the latter I must admit to frank *Schadenfreude*, since the theme was mentioned more than once in the first edition: 'energetically and expensively futile reforms of the unimpor tant and the secondary, in search of that energising modernity which had somehow eluded the grasp of one Ministry after another' was one rather long-winded phrase I thought up for it. In 1994's bedlam of disappearing shires and regions, resurrected districts and amoebically-multiplying quangos some readers may have forgotten there was an earlier round. But there was, and all that has really altered is the expense factor. In the 1960s cosmetic modernisation was at least decently paid for. Now everything has to be on the cheap. One consequence is that no new administrative caste with a strong vested interest in the system will be created, and no-one will seek either to make it more popular or to defend it against central power. It might as well follow the Greater London Council into oblivion.

This does not even qualify as 'regressive modernisation' – Professor Stuart Hall's now classic term summing up first-stage Thatcherism. 'Pretend post-modernisation' would be more like it: the addled persistence of antique rituals (including the ritual of pretending to be less ritualistic) after a Fall in which most of their historical meaning has evaporated.

The Shattered Glass

But this returns us to the main problem. What was the Fall? Why did it happen so quickly? Why did so few (including the author of this book) see it coming? Today I find it embarrassing to read the concluding section of the book, 'Endless Dream-time?', with its cumbersome straining after silver linings. Even after all had been said about the cracks around its edges and the tarnished gilt, the Royal identity-mirror was still intact in 1988 and the folk of four nations were still entranced by it. It was duly noted that the *Geist* of Thatcherism posed a real threat to the identity-structure or 'soul'; but not that the end was nigh. Whatever they said in public, most Republicans felt instinctively that the apparatus would last for a long time yet. It seemed more likely to run down into desuetude within the new European context than to collapse for internal reasons.

In truth the reasons were not simply internal but, in a sense, native. It was observed below that 'glamour' is what matters to Monarchy, and that this lies as much in the eye of the beholder as in the features of the glamourised object ('The Mystery', p. 79):

> While the spell endures, there is absolute resistance to interruption, the dreamer resents and fears recall to reality. Yet when it is broken he or she may also be restored in the (literal) twinkling of an eye...

That sudden switch of deeper attitude took place around 1990, not quite from one day but certainly from one year to the next. The sign-posts now mainly recalled are the Queen's decision to start paying income-tax, the Windsor Castle fire, and the breakdown of the two most important succession marriages, those of Prince Charles and his brother Andrew, Duke of York. These happened in 1992–3, and it was the reaction to them which disclosed something like a new state of public opinion on Royalty – an outlook of which the *Observer* survey eighteen months later is only a continuation. However it seems safe to assume that much of the feeling shown was already there before the events and must, therefore, have been accumulating in the later 1980s and the start of the '90s.

The problem then becomes, what lay behind that? The most popular candidates for blame are still Royal misbehaviour and the British tabloid press. Obviously nobody would deny these were necessary conditions of the shift – or at least, of its assuming the form it did. Had there not been a salacious and intrusive press and plenty of Royal tit-bits awaiting disclosure, then things might not have accelerated as they have to produce what A.N. Wilson calls *The Fall of the House of Windsor* (1993). Yet it remains very doubtful whether these necessary conditions amount to the sufficient condition of such a startling change. As many commentators have also pointed out, Monarchy has always been fertile in scandals and people have always adored gossiping about them, usually without damage to the institution's deeper prestige. For most of its history the pervasive British media have sought to praise Royalty rather than to bury it – and would do so again given the chance. The one thing sweeter than rabid denunciation is mawkish forgiveness and a hearty 'God Bless You!'. In a stable world where other continuities persist, this one might have surely been restored.

But there's the rub. Somehow the framework has altered at the same time, rendering fatal what might otherwise have been merely a series of gaffes. The ground seems to have moved beneath the feet of Royal performers and *paparazzi* alike. To what can that alteration be related in terms of theory, or elsewhere in Europe or the world? When I said it looks like a 'native' reaction, the implication is that this looks something like an emergent nationalism, in motion but not yet fully conscious of its name and nature. The rejection of Monarchy in the old simple-faith sense analysed below was certainly not a self-conscious striving for a new or different national identity. Yet maybe it was moving in that direction: an unselfconscious impulse which, if persisted in, can lead only to some kind of reformulated nationalism – whether British or more narrowly English is another key question, to which I will return later on.

The most obvious thing it can be related to is what was happening around it. The year after *The Enchanted Glass* was published a series of revolutions shook Central and Eastern Europe, and brought with them a striking general renaissance of political nationalism. Country after country shook off what was left of its communist command-economy and adopted capitalism, but the route to the latter always took a national turning. Some peoples recovered their old national states, others tried to invent new ones, while still others (like Russia) had to begin reformulating a national identity within old or shrunken borders.

As any reader can see, one presiding influence on the original 1988 text was Ernest Gellner's *Nations and National-ism* (1983). He leads what one might call the 'modernist' wing of nationality-theory in the social sciences. The gist of this argument is that what we really mean by 'nationalism' – its general or '-ism' aspect, its inescapability – derives more from modern tensions than from ancient instincts. 'Blood' is a modern myth-process, not the rediscovery of inherited truths. The reason why national*ism* was never heard of before the 18th century, but has been universalised since then, is simply industrialisation. It is Progress itself which has created that other visage in whose name nationalism is so frequently condemned – the concrete, sometimes backward-looking face which was invariably to accompany the formation of modern economies and every known transition from an agrarian to a market-dominated society.

The original *Encyclopédie*-style blueprints of Progress had left such factors out. But all that such metropolitan omni-science concealed was a naïve conviction that the world's other peoples were really Frenchmen in odd ancestral disguises.

They would soon discard the ethnic rags, however gorgeous. Or if reluctant to do so they would be persuaded – or where absolutely necessary, forced – to put these away along with mankind's other childish things. Simultaneously museums were being invented for that very purpose. Later the British, Americans and other metropole-centred cultures found the same delusion irresistible. It was one of the materials 'imperialism' was made of, and unfortunately much of it was preserved by the strange forty-year twilight of the Cold War between 1950 and 1990.

It seems to me now that the last full age of the British Monarchy – 'Ukania' as the book labelled it – was part of that twilight. I could see in the '80s that Royalty was an odd form of nationalism all right. It expressed certain characteristic motifs of political nationality, and performed many of its standard functions. Yet there were others which it repressed altogether, notably those with any ethnic content. However bizarrely, a pure genetic myth – Protestant, aristocratic consanguinity – had been made to stand in for the usual collective ideology of popular nationhood. A dazzling folklore from above had replaced the more usual kind 'from below' promoted by most nationalism. It was also easy to see why this suited an ex-Imperial and multi-national state. Defining its peoples in terms of allegiance to a single symbolic family restrained them from too openly resenting one another, and so resorting to separate mobilisations of identity.

Admittedly this was a solution which found an uncomfortable nemesis in one particular people, the Protestant community of Northern Ireland. There, 'Loyalism' had turned into a separate and violently exclusivist variety of ethnic politics, more or less the contrary of the official mainland myths. However, Protestant nationalism which could under no circumstances whatever declare its name was also one oddity growing out of another. It seemed at the time to affect the parent body extraordinarily little.

In Gellnerian terms the mainstream Royal-British identity could (therefore) still be presented as an eccentric variant of modernisation. It corresponded to 'restrained' post-imperial multi-nationality, the breath of a 'stalled' industrial society sentiments or reflexes of 'being British'. The reader shouldn't take my word for it, let me refer him or her at this point to Mrs Thatcher's heir-apparent, Mr Michael Portillo. In an instantly-famous speech of January 1994, he described the Crown as follows:

> Nihilism has transformed every British institution into an object of ridicule. The Royal family provides the clearest example... We have had popular kings and queens and unpopular ones. But the point of the Monarch is that it is a national focal point. It's the source of the authority and legitimacy of government yet above politics. Above all it is the personification of the nation. It's an institution vital to our national well-being.[5]

When the political end of this spectrum fell into such ridicule, the rest was certain to be affected in some way. National identity is not a single or simple entity, of course, and blows in one area will not cause the whole structure instantly to 'collapse'. However, the sense of all identity-formations is to unite, to make the contrasting elements of civil society cohere. This makes them inherently susceptible to shock-waves and reactions. As Portillo notes, the British version had particularly prized 'consensus', with a moral-personal intonation powerfully symbolised by the Monarchy. But Mrs Thatcher (and presumably her heir-apparent) despised consensus above all else, and she actually succeeded in demolishing a good deal of it in practice – which in turn could not help rebounding upon the main symbolic edifice of Establishment reasonableness and acceptability, the Royal Family.

The 'Thatcher revolution' Mr Portillo wishes to continue set out to restore British grandeur. What it actually did was to break the back of British identity. That was the source of the 'nihilism' which he now denounces. Thatcherism was a contradiction in terms: liberation of a civil society with no change to its political state. The contradiction could in practice be 'resolved' (not quite the right word) in only one way – by

---

[5] As cited in the *Independent*, January 16th 1994, p.2: 'Poison of a New British Disease'. The speech was Mr Portillo's riposte to some remarks by Prime Minister John Major earlier that week, quoted in the *Sun* as 'I'll f****** crucify those right-wingers' after the tribulations of his 'Back to Basics' crusade.

others. The folklore from above greyed-out that from the lower depths. It made ethnic character into a mixture of joke and threat: a joke for we civilised people, a threat among humourless foreigners (especially East of the Elbe). Yet there remained this uncomfortable difference: Protestant Ulster apart 'Britain' usually felt too shallow and 'England' too deep.

Since the Fall it is as if things are reversed. The Monarchy and what it means have turned grey, like a range of now abandoned options. But unfortunately the alternatives are not yet clearly high-lighted: for the time being there is only grey on grey. The old mirror-image has shattered and the glamour of 'Britain' has effaced itself. However, no other convincing image yet presents itself to the formerly enchanted.

Identity-breakage

Who threw the brick? 'Thatcherism' is by far the most likely culprit. For a decade beforehand it had been breaking the rules. In 1979 someone had arrived in power actually (rather than rhetorically) determined to 'reverse decline'. She decided to foster a new society, the enterprise culture, to replace gentility and class. Unlike most of her party she really was irreconcilably impatient with both socialism and the old order of things, seen as obstacles to individual prosperity and getting ahead. Popular energies and resentments were 'unleashed' as part of that, over a much longer period than ever before. There was supposed to be an American society waiting to be released inside the declining British one – vigorous and naturally market-oriented, a nation of small capitalists. Mrs Thatcher's view was that the 'management of decline' since World War II had held back and oppressed this alternative nation. Now, a sustained bout of radical populism was needed to free it. The government's task was nothing less than national liberation. Of course Tories had always spoken about 'setting the people free', but the club rules of the post-war consensus had effectively stopped them doing that.

If one rehearses this familiar account of the Thatcher idea-world within the broader context previously outlined – the end of Communism and the explosion of new nationalism – then I think something immediately leaps to view. With the slightest shift of focus, all the distinctive themes of Thatcherism can be given a sense quite different from their author's intention. It is easy to read them as a manifesto for revived nationhood, and not just for a revivified economy. One small adjustment of the lens, and the former may be uncannily glimpsed hiding behind the latter: a half-explicit nationalism whose substance was English rather than British.[3]

What concealed this new nationalism was the old. Rebirth was imagined as occurring entirely within the ancient carapace of Monarchy, Westminster and the unitary state. Like Enoch Powell before her, Thatcher left all ruthlessness behind at the gates of Buckingham Palace. The Constitution had to be untouchable. Thus, paradoxically, a revolution was promoted inside unchanging parameters of history. It was believed that an economy could be transformed, a class élite demolished and a people freed with no damage to the outer shell of allegiance and state authority. Without damage (either) to the identity-mechanism which those forms of authority had so long sustained – that is, the idea-system of Britishness as an extended family metaphor reconciling other and potentially competing national definitions.

When the 1980s Eastern leaders sought to promote ana-logous socio-economic 'revolutions' without damaging Com-munism and one-party power, that was always denounced as hopeless contradiction. Liberty is indivisible, it was said: free

[3] The most persuasive argument here is Professor Shirley Letwin's analysis of the Thatcher Decade, *The Anatomy of Thatcherism* (1992). She maintains that the foundations of Thatcherism lie in early-modern English social history rather than in the problems of British economic decline. The native English character is 'distin-guished by vigorous virtues (and) offended by attempts to treat them as children or invalids, who want to pursue their own projects in their own way, within the framework established by the law of the land...' (p.35) President Tudjmann of Croatia could not have put it better – nor any other post-communist ideologue. Hence the curious double resonance of Mrs Thatcher's '-ism': on the one hand a Churchillian will to put the 'Great' back into Britain, on the other an underground redemptive appeal to ancestral factors rooted in Tudor-period nationhood – the formative epoch of the English (but not the British) state. Letwin's ideas derive partly from the English Tory empiricism of the philosopher Michael Oakeshott, and also resemble the preoccupa-tions of English revisionist historians like Alan Macfarlane and Jonathan Clark. See Andrew Gamble, 'The Entrails of Thatcherism' in *New Left Review*, No. 198 (March–April 1993).

market economics demanded a liberated state and culture. But if as I am suggesting one looks in the other direction – from East to West as it were – then the same question can surely be put the other way round about Great Britain. How did the latter's dictatorship believe that it would radically modernise a backward economy while leaving intact an archaic Monarchical state and a pseudo-feudal hierarchy of class power?[4]

At the time there were certainly a number of reasons for thinking it possible. I mentioned one already: the delusive fixity of the Cold War twilight, with its false security of permanent equilibrium and untouchable statehood. It was the British custom to delude themselves that they were far more important in that order of things than was actually the case. Its intangibility seemed to support their own. Mrs Thatcher was of course an ardent cold warrior and a fulsome protagonist of the American side of the Western alliance. Her rigid enthusiasm for President Reagan was more than embarrassing to pro-European Tories – it led directly to all her principal political difficulties of the mid-'80s, and paved the way for her overthrow. Yet her recently-published memoir *The Downing Street Years* (1993) shows no second thoughts about such faith. Rather the opposite: the way she was lionised in Eastern Europe convinced her it had been absolutely justified.

However disastrous, that faith should not be seen as blind. Part of the book's original argument was that Britain's old extra-territorial dimension – the Commonwealth, the City, the racism of 'kith-and-kin' fantasies – was congruent with retention of the sort of overblown Monarchy we have. After 1948 the Cold War and servile pro-Americanism were added to this armoury. By underlining the changelessness of statehood and the self-importance of Britain's political élite they also

---

[4] If 'dictatorship' seems too strong a term for Mrs Thatcher's concentration of power and reverse-command economy, let me refer the reader to another theoretical perspective, that of Professor T.J. Pempel in his comparative study *Uncommon Democracies* (1990). This is a study of 'one-party dominant regimes' where a guided or authoritarian democracy adopts certain aspects of totalitarianism, alters the underpinning of a parliamentary system and castrates opposition in order to prolong its stay in office. Though the book did not deal with Britain, I have argued elsewhere that Thatcherism fulfils every condition of the model and may even end as its most remarkable example – *see New Left Review* No. 200 (Sept–Oct 1993)

quite naturally endorsed its talisman. Here was a country whose real distinction had been to lose an empire without trauma: even the Imperial Monarchy had been conserved intact to serve another age.

An internal rigidity matched the external one. The spell of the Crown involved a parallel magic belief in the Crown Constitution. The latter need never be changed because it is flexible enough for all conceivable political purposes. Mrs Thatcher alone should not be blamed for clinging to this superstition, since nearly everyone in British government did. Only later – about the time the Monarchy crumbled – did ideas about reforming or replacing the Constitution become more widespread and urgent, and begin to affect many members of the ruling parties. In the meantime, central power had greatly increased in Britain. The 'unchanging' constitutional parameters did allow developments, but in one direction alone – that of a return to origins and innermost nature. This implied an effective autocracy which destroyed or down-graded every barrier between itself and the individual. In contradistinction to most other European countries, regional and local government were deconstructed into executive agencies of state policy.

Thus socio-economic liberation was to be by command, and from a single source – the state. Since no intermediate authority was allowed to interfere or qualify that influence, resistance could assume only the form of mutiny. This was exactly what took place in the struggles over the Poll Tax which were beginning when the book went to press: individuals simply refused it in numbers which rendered its imposition futile – with very little help from the weakened local government they were supposedly paying for, or from a political opposition still crushed by Constitutionalism in the old British sense (where democracy always defers to legality).

But there were bound to be unintended consequences. Crown Constitutionalism was not just a set of Parliamentary conventions and administrative habits: it was an ideology. It was in fact *the* ideology of United Kingdom statehood, in the sense of the emotive tissue which connected political rules and the higher institutions to everyday life and instincts – all the sentiments or reflexes of 'being British'. The reader shouldn't take my word for it, let me refer him or her at this point to Mrs Thatcher's heir-apparent, Mr Michael Portillo. In an instantly-famous speech of January 1994, he described the Crown as follows:

> Nihilism has transformed every British institution into an object of ridicule. The Royal family provides the clearest example... We have had popular kings and queens and unpopular ones. But the point of the Monarch is that it is a national focal point. It's the source of the authority and legitimacy of government yet above politics. Above all it is the personification of the nation. It's an institution vital to our national well-being.[5]

When the politcal end of this spectrum fell into such ridicule, the rest was certain to be affected in some way. National identity is not a single or simple entity, of course, and blows in one area will not cause the whole structure instantly to 'collapse'. However, the sense of all identity-formations is to unite, to make the contrasting elements of civil society cohere. This makes them inherently susceptible to shock-waves and reactions. As Portillo notes, the British version had particularly prized 'consensus', with a moral-personal intonation powerfully symbolised by the Monarchy. But Mrs Thatcher (and presumably her heir-apparent) despised consensus above all else, and she actually succeeded in demolishing a good deal of it in practice – which in turn could not help rebounding upon the main symbolic edifice of Establishment reasonableness and acceptability, the Royal Family.

The 'Thatcher revolution' Mr Portillo wishes to continue set out to restore British grandeur. What it actually did was to break the back of British identity. That was the source of the 'nihilism' which he now denounces. Thatcherism was a contradiction in terms: liberation of a civil society with no change to its political state. The contradiction could in practice be 'resolved' (not quite the right word) in only one way – by

[5] As cited in the *Independent*, January 16th 1994, p.2: 'Poison of a New British Disease'. The speech was Mr Portillo's riposte to some remarks by Prime Minister John Major earlier that week, quoted in the *Sun* as 'I'll f****** crucify those right-wingers' after the tribulations of his 'Back to Basics' crusade.

sharply accumulating central power, by a creeping authoritarianism which would issue in the outright moral reaction of 'Back to Basics' in the winter of 1993–4. Thus the cost of whatever liberation occurred was its opposite – the intensification of a command-state buttressed by secrecy, quangos and the liquidation of all intermediate and corporate authorities. Its ethos was the opposite of what the Monarchy had symbolised – 'consensus' based on such authorities, and articulated by the familial metaphor-system described below. So it is not really surprising that Thatcherism brought the effective end of the Monarchy, and the onset of struggles to replace it with something else. But of course nothing can 'replace' the Crown in the complex historical and evolutionary sense described below – a *sui generis* formula for reconciling four different nationalities within a single imperial state. However much better a modern written constitution might be, miracles should not be expected.

Levels of Identity

As the second of the *fait divers* I quoted to begin with shows, on one plane Ukanian existence trundles ahead much as usual. The musclebound philistinism of Westminster still prevails, not as yet unduly disturbed by Black Wednesday, the implosion of 'Thatcherism', mass demonstrations like those against the pit closures and the Poll Tax, or the Windsor mess.

However, this may be partly because the wounds inflicted on Britishness have occurred at such a deep level. The changes in Southern-English attitudes affect the zone so consistently aimed at by Thatcherism, that of micro-economic or daily and family living. 'Loadsamoney' lunacy had little effect on who owned what at the upper levels of British finance and business but it seems to have transformed popular attitudes. There never was an American or German industrial genie slumbering within Britain's bosom, waiting to be released by the appropriate policies. But what the latter did do was destroy deference and the ideological community which, under the Royal insignia, had made up the 'bosom' itself. By the time Mrs Thatcher was overthrown in a party coup worthy of any old Eastern state, few in Southern England were still attending that tea-party of the mind which formerly embodied the national decorum of British Monarchy (see pp.84–88 below, 'Tea With the Queen').

A psychological transformation like this occurs below the plane of existing policies, and is likely to make little initial impact on the upper story where political life is fossilised into strongly traditional patterns. In the East it certainly did. But the Eastern régimes were forty-year-old upstarts in charge of a process of desperate, forced-march industrialisation. When their imposed state-identities crumbled away there was nothing to fall back on but force. By contrast Great Britain celebrated the three-hundredth anniversary of its revolutionary origins in 1988 with extraordinarily complacent all-party rituals intended to signal farther epochs of evolution and achievement. By that time (in rueful hindsight) the rot within was already deep, visible and probably incurable. And a significant new opposition had arisen, with a title reflecting Eastern inspiration: 'Three Hundred Years is Enough!' cried the reformers of Charter 88 at that time, a slogan which would steadily gather meaning and support during the 1990s. However, no popular movement was ready to carry these impulses into a demolition attempt against state authority as such.

On the other hand, it seems to me that manoeuvrings towards such a demolition are well under way. The old continues to cloak the new, of course, as it did in Mrs Thatcher's decade (which is only another way of saying that revolutions imagine themselves as traditions). The decisive indicator is the unstoppable slide of the Monarchy in both popular and political estimation. It is carrying the whole conservative edifice of British identity with it, and leaving behind a vacuum which only some kind of ideological civil war can fill. All the post-'89 debates about Eastern Europe have made much of the 'void' left by Marxism's humiliation, and often suggested that this was what led to nationalism's abrupt triumph. The ethnic memories and patriotic motifs discredited by the old régime were the most accessible and popular reservoir of alternative sentiment. Hence it was they which revived first and rushed into the vacuum. Whatever the final verdict on the general theory is, I think that something analogous is discernible in Britain. Only it's happening in curiously slow motion.

In other words the nation awaiting emancipation by Thatcherite rebirth was Britain itself, not a second America. The rebirth has been heralded by the eclipse of Monarchy. And the real, emerging problem is whether any acceptably British solution at all can emerge from the other side. Mrs Thatcher's revolution moved the centre of gravity far more to England, and in fact to one area of England – its Southern heartland. One of the tragicomedies of her decade was a total failure seriously to change Scotland. Her memoirs chew angrily over this inexplicable debacle, attributing it to the unexpected strength of the dependency-culture there.

In fact Scotland's 'dependency-culture' also reflects a distinct national inheritance as old as Mrs Letwin's vigorous virtues or Professor Macfarlane's English 'individualism'. It has (so to speak) a corporate gene deriving partly from a Calvinist Reformation and in part from the incorporation of a Celtic sub-society. Recently this may have implied support for Labourism (which grew notably stronger while Thatcher was at work). However, its origins long predate the British welfare state and Socialism. So here too the enterprise culture was unintentionally fomenting a nationalist reaction, all the more so since Thatcherism's vast increase in central power could only be perceived there as politically offensive. Dependency was ostensibly diminished in one field only to be crassly augmented in another, by a Secretary of State representing a party which won less than a quarter of the Scottish vote.

She suffered similar if less clear-cut failures in Wales and the North of England.[6] Thatcherism used the state to reject the state. It aimed to stimulate the same sort of freedom everywhere – a homogeneity of individual and vigorous virtues, economic man ascendant and more or less identical in all places. That economic man was also English man either did not occur to her government or was dismissed as un-

---

[6] On the North of England, by far the most interesting recent debate is the one led by Peter Taylor in *Political Geography*, vol.12, No.2 (March 1993).

important. Britishness is inherently metropolitan (not 'international'). Thus the differing ethnic and communal rags were no problem: provided people behaved themselves like entrepreneurs their retention could be licensed, they might even be loved.

In such debates no-one ever says a word against regional or national variety *as such*. But that is because in one use the term 'identity' has come to signify a kind of moving false consciousness around just this point. Both under Thatcher and during the arguments over the Maastricht Treaty it was continuously employed in just that way. Its denotation became something like this: the aesthetic (hence harmless) enjoyment of customary or folkloric differences, legitimating 'pride' without negative political side-effects.[7] In the absence of the negative there is of course always more room for the positive: indifference towards, maybe even support for, the British or European status quo.

But 'identity' in that specious definition has in fact little to do with what has counted in developmental terms (and hence in the genesis of nationalism). At a deeper level, identity is more accurately described as what one cannot help being, a social inheritance transmitted through the family and various communal contexts. At any given moment, or even across long periods of time, it may be unconscious in the sense of rarely if ever contemplated or thought about, much more a configuration of the will than of the imagination – a 'way of life' which may find only intermittent and fluctuating expression in high culture. I know that nationalists often resort to genetic history to account for such transmission, but in the present state of science 'immemorial instinct' is best treated as another myth. Social history seems to explain most identity well enough.

---

[7] The intention is close to Sigmund Freud's in his notes on 'the narcissism of minor difference', a mechanism whereby individuals or groups conscious of how essentially like others they are may exaggerate minor traits in order to seem more distinct: 'A convenient and relatively harmless satisfaction of the inclination to aggression, by means of which cohesion between members of the community is made easier . . .' See *Civilisation and its Discontents* in *Complete Works* vol.21, p.114. But the habitual underlining of minor differences may also occur where major or structural divergences have been hidden or disallowed, finding no expression except trivial ones – which tend therefore to be obsessive and irascible.

Under the impact of modernisation peoples become more aware of differing identities in that sense, and a self-conscious cultivation of linguistic and other cultural differentiæ follows – often but not invariably linked to political separation and statehood. Such cultivation is broadly instrumental in its effects. It arises not because socio-ethnic variety is fun but because it seems like communal life or death.

Take one famous historical example. It would never have occurred to the most dead-pan of Thatcherites to think that the plays of William Shakespeare had been harmless identity-gymnastics good for keeping the English ethnos happy while the Hispanic Empire busied itself assimilating the British Isles to its version of anti-enterprise culture. No: these had manifestly 'helped to steel the nation's will' (however much fun they also contained), to build up an exemplary 'national character', and so on. The King of Spain had a radical-metropolitan, Madrid-centred plan for the evening-out of civilised development in the Old world as in the New. By contrast the Queen of England stood for uneven development on the basis of recalcitrant native identity, with naval sea-dogs and all available cultural weapons to hand.

It is metropolitans who naturally perceive culture as ludic and identity-variables as some sort of museum-display. No less naturally the dissident or peripheral societies of any given time will tend to see culture as a life-line and identity-definition as a form of salvation – the precondition for equality of status and more advantageous socio-economic development. In Britain the metropolis itself formerly possessed a highly effective ludic display-system, the Monarchy, which reconciled the main body and its dependencies. The latter's identity-games and dilemmas were in a sense contained or partitioned off by it, like so many native reservations within a larger theme-park. As in Eastern Europe, when the broader system collapses its composite parts are bound to be released to find their own paths.

The Original Model

To some extent they already have. The fact is sufficiently

obvious in the outer reservations, where Welsh, Scottish and (inevitably in a different way) Ulster-Protestant redefinitions of identity have accumulated their pressures on the centre since 1988. It is still somewhat shrouded in England itself. There, a post-imperial and (now) post-Royal loftiness prevails, fortified by the rigidity of a backward-looking and party-bound political class. As many commentators have written, in British politics nothing matters but party, and the parties belong integrally to a party-system which is in effect 'the constitution'. Elective dictatorship – another celebrated phrase – remains what the system is about, and all the efforts made in the 1980s to break the mould ended in failure.

Thus, identity-breakage – the shattering of the glass – is so far unaccompanied by a process of consciously national identity-reformation. Englishness has in fact been extensively and critically discussed, new genealogies for it have been uncovered and its internal problems like the North-South divide debated. However, these arguments have found practically no political formulation, or at best mockable ones like John Major's 'long shadows on county grounds, warm beer, invincible green suburbs, dog lovers and pools fillers'. The 'blind spot' of English political nationality continues to be evaded. Both on the political left and the right it is the British alibis and formulae which remain centre-stage, in a pantomime maintained by a party-run state and its administrative caste.

Yet there is a sense in which this remains suspicious, and will probably be a passing phenomenon. For the fact is that England's national identity may be older and deeper than any other in the contemporary European showcase. Indeed we should remember that it was something like the forge of the modern nation-state. 'Britishness' has been in part a myth of transcendence, ending in the conception of the English as somehow above and beyond mere nationality-politics. In its own way the Monarchy powerfully echoed and sustained that mythology. Its artificial folklore sent back an image of diffuse moral grandeur, an aureole of 'greatness' rather than a definition of locality or ethnic origins. However, Englishness preceded and has always underlain Britishness. Hence the foundering of the Anglo-British Monarchy cannot help being a kind of deconstruction of the latter's long historical ambiguity.

Since *The Enchanted Glass* was first published two remarkable studies have analysed the formation of this double-layered British identity. The first, Liah Greenfeld's *Nationalism: Five Roads to Modernity* (1992) describes the origins of English nationalism in the 16th and 17th century. Her general premise is that 'nationalism lies at the basis of the modern world'. It is the form of modernity itself and not, as so often thought, a reaction against or departure from the mainstream of social and economic industrialisation. Previous scholarship had focused overmuch upon secondary and small-nation responses to that mainstream, or else upon the pathological dimensions it assumed during the epoch of imperialistic contestation from the 1870s to 1945. By contrast Professor Greenfeld deals straightforwardly with the five major and determining forms of modern nation-state identity: England, France, Germany, Russia and America. It was the 16th century English who first brought about what she calls 'the semantic transformation signalling the emergence of the first nation in the world, in the sense in which the word is understood today, and launching the era of nationalism...' Not only was England 'the first nation in the world' but (as she goes on to argue) it was '*the only one*, with the possible exception of Holland, for about two hundred years'. Not until the 18th century did there occur a universalisation of nationality-politics in the continent of Europe, whence 'particularistic nationalism' was destined to spread at a much more rapid pace over the rest of the world.

I mention this advance in historical theory here to try and help dispel the odd yet persistent preconception mentioned before – that the English are in some way removed from post-1989 quandaries of identity or ethnic redefinition. The real distinctiveness of England in the new context is more probably the density of those quandaries, and the amount of ideological struggle which it may take to unscramble them. They derive from that original situation in which a unique confluence of factors '... conspired to favour this growth (thus) giving English nationalism the time to gestate...' –

It was allowed – and helped – to permeate every sphere of political and cultural and spread into every sector of society except the lowest, and become a powerful force which no longer needed buttresses to exist. It acquired its own momentum; it existed in its own right; it was the only way in which people could now see reality and thus became reality itself. For nationalism was the basis of people's identity, and it was no more possible at this point to stop thinking in national terms than to cease being oneself...'[8]

The original argument of *The Enchanted Glass* concentrated in a conventional way on England-Britain's economic primacy: being first prevented it from ever being typical, and had many indirect effects which would stall later stages of development. The land of the Industrial Revolution never became characteristic of industrialisation. It failed to see that something analogous might be true at a deeper level, in the prior formation of the English national identity and state. That also had the features, and then the difficulties, of a template. The 17th century Protestant English saw themselves as a chosen people. But the Chosen will almost inevitably be deselected by the later process which they have themselves launched. Leaders are bound to fall back among the also-rans. And they may quite well finish with the tail-enders.

Somewhere in this prolonged Fall, such a people will run into what Professor Greenfeld calls *ressentiment*. She takes the term from Nietzsche, to mean 'a psychological state resulting from suppressed feelings of envy and hatred (existential envy) and the impossibility of satisfying these feelings.' Such a condition produces effects similar to Durkheim's 'anomie', disorientation and impulses for renewal. *Ressentiment* is only a necessary condition for the formation (or reformation) of nationalism, not a sufficient one. Greenfeld is careful to underline this, but also concedes that in practice few other avenues are available for its expression. Modernity has been national in form too long, and too effectively, for alternatives to possess a comparable collective attraction. Individuals may chart escapes from it, but classes, parties and other larger social

---

[8] Liah Greenfeld, op.cit., 'God's Firstborn: England' p.87.

groups cannot. Indeed (a point to which I will come back) they seem even less able to do so since the turning-point of 1989–90.

The second crucial analysis of England's rapport with Britishness is that given by Linda Colley in her *Britons: Forging the Nation, 1707–1837* (1992). Much more carefully than any previous history, this book traces the construction of British statehood and ideology following the union with Scotland. The Monarchy occupies a central role in her account, as a key part of the British response to both the American and the French Revolutions. Its symbolism was indispensable to the formation of a new British nation capable of both economic development and successful warfare. Incapable of sustaining an ethnic definition, the Hanoverian state evolved an exaggeratedly Protestant and Royal one. The result was a quasi-national identity which proved far more effective and durable than most other composites – like those of the Hapsburgs, the Soviet post-1917 state or post-1945 Yugoslavia. But it has not proved eternal, as Professor Colley recognises:

> We can understand the nature of the present crisis only if we recognise that the factors that provided for the forging of a British nation in the past have largely ceased to operate... God has ceased to be British, and Providence no longer smiles.'[9]

In this way she has very well described the old image sent back by Britain's enchanted glass: a fixed smile reassuring viewers that all could not fail to end well. Monarchy was the chosen from among the Chosen, an emblem of their ultimate impunity. The Dutch and English were the first-chosen of modernity and (as Greenfeld has emphasised) much more than a single destiny was forged by the making of the original Anglo-British nation. 19th and 20th century Royalty has been a way of selecting and fixing certain conservative elements out of this very complex story: a myth of origins which stabilised the present in the name of Providential guarantees conveyed through the smiling ritual of Monarchy. As a 'non-nationalist' nationalism it worked by minimising both the politically radical and the ethnic traits important for the constitution of English (and then British) identity.

[9] Colley. op.cit., pp.374–5.

Today, however, precisely because these constitutive factors Professor Colley describes no longer operate, such traits are bound to be released back into the political arena. There is no single myth-identity waiting to succeed the shattered glass of Royalism. All that can really be expected is a struggle between contenders for a reinvented soul, hindered both by fossilised politics and what Colley diagnoses as 'national uncertainty' –

> The apprehension with which so many Britons regard increasing assimilation into a united Europe... their apparent insularity is to be explained also by their growing doubts about who they are in the present. Consciously or unconsciously, they fear assuming a new identity in case it obliterates entirely the already insecure identity they currently possess.

Anglo-Britishism tends to be metropolitan towards the peripheral countries of its archipelago, nativist towards Europe and alternately superior and servile towards America. In addition, such insecurity is often itself justified as noble indeterminacy, the posture of a people of individuals to whom any conscious collective identity is irrelevant. This has recently been given almost classic expression by the literary critic John Bayley in an attack on the new fuss about Englishness. 'A great writer like Hardy', he observes –

> ... is English without making any sort of fuss about it, and it is perhaps the best testimony to the national adjective that few other world writers make us less deliberately conscious of their nationality than the great English ones. Individuality, not national consciousness, is all...[10]

English writers (and non-writers) have not had to be 'deliberately conscious' because they were so deeply and naturally conscious, in a way their audience has rarely been able to escape. Such an awareness rendered self-awareness superfluous. Bayley thinks it was Johann Gottfried Herder who 'invented the concept of the national psyche' – a malady which 'the English never got in virulent form'. But actually

[10] 'The Blight on Blighty', in the *Times Literary Supplement* (January 21st 1994), a review of David Gervais's study *Literary Englands: Versions of 'Englishness' in Modern Writing* (1993).

Herder's 18th century discoveries came centuries after England had established a durable model of nation-state identity. That consciousness later found its correlative in Monarchy, the symbol of a quasi-national psyche which gave voice to certain features of nationalism and occluded others. And Monarchy's decay necessarily re-poses profounder questions for the underlying structure which it subsumed for so long.

Bayley perceives English identity as an aesthetic issue, in that way I mentioned earlier. In fact it is an issue of the shared reflexes and assumptions of government. At all levels and in every direction decisions must constantly be made which, if they are to have any coherence at all, need to manifest such common ground. If the class-and-Monarchy consensus has disintegrated then another will have to be reformulated. The 'sense of who we are' is not a matter of poetic musing alone, but of actions which can only be collective. The English are for that reason likely to become extremely quarrelsome again, as they used to be before the new Monarchy was invented.

One side of the battle is probably represented by Christopher Hitchens's splendid oration at the end of *The Times*/Charter 88 conference on the future of the Monarchy in 1993: an appeal for the revival of the radical English motifs and ideas mummified by the long ascendancy of Royalism. One thing he stressed in it was how mistaken had been Mrs Thatcher's reading of the Anglo-American relationship: in effect she had attempted to import Reagan's modern Republican USA straight into Britain, and forgotten all about its revolutionary origins – a left-wing Englishness which began by overthrowing the imposed conservatism of an Anglo-Britain just then assuming its Monarchcal forms.[11] Another side may be shown in the likely right-wing heir to Thatcherism, the new national authoritarianism of Mr Michael Portillo and his friends. Still another has appeared in the revived activity of an anti-immigrant extreme right, with the British National Party and similar bodies.

[11] This debate was held at the Queen Elizabeth II Conference centre on May 22nd, 1993, and is now republished as *The Monarchy Debate*, edited by Anthony Barnett (Vintage, 1994).

For a period it seemed possible that the British state might evade reimmersion in such dilemmas. During the 1970s and '80s the formation of a European policy appeared to be offering a more advanced platform within which the political dilemmas of the older national identities might be 'dissolved'. For Great Britain, after the crab-like adaption to later modernity mentioned earlier, this prospect should have been particularly significant. Its Monarchic state-identity has been both an expression and an evasion of nationalism; was it not possible for the emergent European state-identity to assume a comparable function? In that case, a kind of transcendence might have occurred. The 'unresolved' questions of Englishness and the other post-British nationalities might have been carried forward into a new and more advanced context – the force-field of European supra-nationality, where a vortex of broader struggles might have rendered them unimportant or secondary.

But another accompaniment to Royalty's eclipse has been the slackening of all these hopes. The cumulative after-effect of the end of Communism, Eastern nationalist revival and the Maastricht Treaty is almost the opposite. They have brought about a conservative stabilisation of the European project in favour of the existing state-forms – indeed making that project appear in retrospect as a formula for their coordinated survival, rather than for their supersession. After the end of this particular history there is no alternative but to conclude, however reluctantly, that even in Western Europe the political mainstream 'has not yet ceased to be national in its conditions'. Concluding a magisterial survey of today's capitalist scene in his *English Questions*, Perry Anderson underlines that conclusion as follows:

> National differences, however relative compared with conditions outside the metropolitan zone, continue to count for those who fall under them. Lives and liberties differ substantially across the range of societies that comprise the developed world – from the great pools of misery and despair in New York or Naples to the more decent securities of Oslo or Stuttgart – and no effective opposition to capitalism can morally neglect these contrasts...

But the contrasts are surely more than 'moral'. The crystallisation of national differences into nationalist myth-systems was a structural necessity, not a moral impulse or aberration. The storm of industrialisation produced it, through an inescapable machinery of uneven development and consequent *ressentiment*, and since 1989 it does not look like blowing any less strongly. Nationality-politics are beginning to look like the salty shadow of this ever-continuing actual process, as distinct from the ideal blue-prints of the economists – a permanent reality rather than a phase, modernity's forced tribute to inextinguishable variation and discord. Nationalism has always been a response to globalisation – the particular brought to life both by and against the universal. The latter's consummation in liberal-capitalist form will certainly not arrest unevenness and *ressentiment*, and may bring an even greater, more restless consciousness of such tensions and fissures. If so then the United Kingdom may soon itself fall away, as the old enchanted mirror of its Royal unity seems already to have done.

Tom Nairn
Prague
January 1994

FOREWORD

A World Upside Down

In the place where God has put you, be who you are Madam. Be
the person in relation to whom, by virtue of your legitimacy, all
things in your Kingdom are ordered; the person in whom your
people perceive their own nationhood; the person by whose
presence and dignity, the national unity is sustained.

General de Gaulle to H.M. the Queen
(1961).

There is no power to see ourselves as others see us, and like
anyone else the British look into a mirror to try and get a sense
of themselves. In doing so they are luckier but ultimately less
fortunate than other peoples: a gilded image is reflected back,
made up of sonorous past achievement, enviable stability, and
the painted folklore of their Parliament and Monarchy.
Though aware that this enchanted glass reflects only a
decreasingly useful lie they have naturally found it difficult to
give up. After all, the 'reflection' is really their structure of
national identity – what they seem to be is itself an important
dimension of what they are. Since this is the stubborn accretion
of a long and till recently successful history, short of defeat or
revolution it is unlikely to be discarded.

The British Monarchy figures prominently in the glass's
reflections. This is because – or so I will argue – it is (as De
Gaulle thought) genuinely important for British nationalism.
Indeed it is a lot more important than even he believed. Great

9

Britain is an old State-nation, not an ethnic or a republican state-formation founded on popular sovereignty. Yet it has had to adapt to and assume some of the contours of the modern nation-state world - developing a curious, composite simulacrum of nationality in order to do so. The recreation and popularization of Monarchy was a way of doing that: a patrician oligarchy's unwilling (yet for long quite functional) tribute to the plebeian nature of modernity. Farthermore, it was the *only* effective way of doing so - of preserving and popularizing the informal authority of an élite inside the more formal and bureaucratic constraints of a quasi-industrial society.

Admittedly, any diagnosis of this kind risks an obvious error. It may be taken as suggesting that the British Royal Family's popularity is essentially something which 'They' have done to 'Us'. Now, there have of course been plenty of 'Them' over the last century. In the narrow sense, this means able courtiers and stage-managers to Monarchy, media devotees like Lord Reith of the BBC or the Fleet Street proprietors, or that adroit 'shop steward of Royalty' Lord Mountbatten of Burma. In the broader sense, it implies an 'Establishment' always conscious of how the Crown's contribution to 'stability' supported its own values and interests.

Yet if the Monarchy is to be taken seriously at all, these must remain important but secondary factors. Such efforts from above would have amounted to little had society not wished to be beguiled, and found some genuine comfort in what was offered. Here is the central theme, and the true curiosity of Great Britain's dilemma. Narrow vested interests in Royalty pall before this wider acceptance and enthusiasm. Manipulation from above has mattered far less than the lack of opposition from below. It is the absence of Republicanism, of a national-popular will to do other than *go on* sustaining an identity through such self-consciously 'archaic' images which counts most. Hence, the Royal passion-play must be an expression of some underlying structures of British national existence – not just a conspiracy of the rulers against their underlings. These are (in my view) merely the structures of nationalism, in a singular variant which alone suited both the internal nature and the external reach of Anglo-British power.

'Britons' - a title whose oddity itself expresses the eccentricity of Royal nationalism – have learnt to take and enjoy the glory of Royalty in a curiously personal sense. The view taken below is that the phenomenon implies not mass idiocy but (again) a functional requirement of this solution to national identity. A personalized and totemic symbolism was needed to maintain the a-national nationalism of a multi-national (and for long imperial) entity; and 'the Crown' could effectively translate identity on to that 'higher plane' required by a country (heartland England) which has since the 17th century existed out of itself as much as in. Though profoundly averse to democracy, this version of nationality has of course had to adapt to the popular times: and one mode of such adaptation has been precisely that *rapprochement* of Royal and 'ordinary' we find so prominent in the daily dosage of British monarchism, where a nationalist emotivity informs the concrete individuality of the Sovereign, and her family has become so all-important.

This sort of thing is often described as a national 'obsession'. So it is, but the metaphor can be taken seriously too. Decipherment of a patient's obsessions would normally be expected to show central aspects of his or her personality-structure – for which, in our case, read the real structure of the nation, as manifested through the ideology of Royalism. Doesn't the latter's increasingly weird combination of worship and lunatic concern with 'what they're really like', of Stately grandeur with 'ordinariness', indicate *something* important about the society it inhabits? To deny this would be the equivalent of dismissing severe obsessional neurosis as merely a bad habit the patient ought to snap out of. And of course, judgements of this order are constantly made about the Monarchy in Britain (there are plenty of terrifying examples below). How often does one hear it said that, nice as it is, there is 'a bit too much of all this' going on for the national good?

Unfortunately, this approach to the subject of British Royalty poses acute problems of method. These have been borne in on me in stages, in the process of writing (mainly via the exasperation of those patient editors and guinea-pig readers thanked below). Its contrast with the standard models of address – whether reverential or grumbling - is bound to provoke accusations of oddity, eccentricity or worse. The point here is really that, as Ernest Gellner has written about his own work on the general theory of nationalism (much cited below), that nothing can be said 'by simply drawing on the cards already available in the language pack that is in use':

> The pack has been dealt too often, and all simple statements in it have been made many times before. Hence a new contribution...is possible only by redesigning a pack so as to make a new statement possible in it. To do this very visibly is intolerably pedantic and tedious. The overt erection of a new scaffolding is tolerable in mathematics, but not in ordinary prose...

There is no easy way round the problem (least of all with the pack of extremely well-thumbed Royal and Stately icons). It involves a kind of sideways or crab-like insinuation - 'fairly unobtrusively loosening the habitual associations' is Gellner's description – by which a different perspective can be introduced through example, until (eventually) a new context exists for the statement's meaning.

Chapter One is mainly a survey of the Stately Home itself. But though it aims to cover familiar ground, it doesn't do so in the familiar or prescribed way – from the table where a retainer or voluntary helper sells tickets, along the worn carpet between the ropes hung up in the drawing-rooms and bed-chambers, then down via the old kitchen to a back-door exit into the stable-yard. Instead, it follows a deliberately rambling itinerary from the exit back to the porticoed front, peering into dusty cellars and some carefully locked cupboards along the way. The point of view guiding this excursion has some sympathy with that of the policeman in the last chapter of Nigel Dennis's *Cards of Identity*. This satire on national identity concludes with an improvised tour of the Identity Club's headquarters, 'Hyde's Mortimer', where the real-life exhibits are dismissed as phoney – '"I expected aristocracy, not Madame Tussauds"; "My little nipper could mould a better corpse", says a second'. Then the 'visitors' (themselves phonies) all vanish without paying and the Club Establishment's elaborate identity-charade dissolves at last into below-stairs confusion and a bedraggled procession back down the drive-way to reality. After all this the policeman too can't help wishing he was in plain clothes rather than Her Majesty's drag - those *bourgeois* plain clothes 'which, in the long run, always prove to be the best'.

Chapter Two, 'The Nation', deals with aspects of the national identity emblematized in Monarchy, and its history. Chapter Three, 'The Glamour of Backwardness', looks at a number of sociological and cultural implications of Royal-popular identity. And Chapter Four, 'Quiet Republicanism', examines some more political features which seem to derive from the main body of argument. It follows from the latter that, in an immediate sense, one might as well demand a lowering of the British annual rainfall as ask for 'the abolition of Monarchy'. The aim is far more modest than that: Republicanism has been exorcised from the arena of 'respons-ible public opinion' for over a century, and it's time it was back. Such a change would mean a lot more than people think (mainly because they have been brain-washed by 'responsible public opinion' - itself a key code of the Royal-tribal folklore designed to keep English white-male-adult Public School chaps running things). The taboo on Republicanism did not originate by chance, but because it was always far more of a threat than the Royal-distributive Socialism which the British trade unions pressed for and received in the shape of Her Majesty's Loyal Opposition. Lifting the taboo so that it re-entered the public domain and ceased being a form of nuttery or a closet-conviction ('Personally speaking *I've* no time for it...'etc.) would alter the climate, and before long more than just the climate of United Kingdom politics.These are all solemn issues. But one can hardly stay clear of them once a decision is taken to pay the Windsor Monarchy the (rare) tribute of regarding it *seriously*. It is also a farce, of course. The comedy strikes a lot deeper and blacker than the broad grotesqueries of *Spitting Image*, for these are real icons of community and power, of national identity and State author-ity. Since the 1960s we have learned to titter more openly at them. But a Republican (it seems to me) also has to say: if they are absurd, we are the more so, for their glamour is no more than our collective image in the mirror of the State. Hysterical laughter within the family is one thing; inability or unwillingness to get away from it is another, and sets a strangling edge to the most virulent 'satire'. Though I hope I have not unduly neglected the wild humours of Palace life, *Kitsch* and institutionalized necrophilia, Royal jokes are also usually more than just jokes.

The idea for the book was Anthony Barnett's, and I must thank him again for this and for his ceaseless and generous help and encouragement. It's literally true that without such help it would never have got near being written. *The Enchanted Glass* had a pre-history as *The Glamour of Backwardness*, during which I got valuable help and encouragement from Carmen Callil and her editor Jan Dalley. My agent Anthony Sheil has helped throughout, and his assistance was particularly vital over what threatened to be a publishing *impasse*. After that Neil Belton and his Radius team have been superb. Gareth Stedman Jones, Hugh Brody and David Widgery read earlier versions of it and made constructive comments which let me get re-started with it again. Neal Ascherson has supplied constant dialogue and vital inspiration on the subject for years and in these times his 'games with shadows' have become very substantial for me, as for many others. Christopher Harvie let me read the still unpublished manuscript of 'The Centre of Things', a study of Ukanian politics and letters which greatly assisted my gropings in that area, and I must also thank him for the reference to John Morley's letter on a visit to Balmoral. At an early stage I was lucky to work with Anna Coote on a television programme about Monarchy, and also to discuss the subject with her later on. More recently, a similar involvement with John Osmond of HTV in the Channel 4 T.V. series 'Divided Kingdom', and with Alistair Moffat and Les Wilson of Scottish Televsion in making the film of *Enchanted Glass* has given me continual stimulus and encouragement. Jon Halliday sent me valuable materials relating to the 1969 Investiture. Hamish Henderson and Marion Blythman kindly devoted hours to recounting their respective escapes from being turned into Officers of the Order of the British Empire, and let me read the correspondence which ensued. F. Stuurmann sent me useful comparative materials on the Netherlands Monarchy.

At home many friends, relations and neighbours gave me support during the difficult circumstances which accompanied the writing of the book. I would like to mention especially Ellen Johnson, Eleanor Herrin, Mrs Ina Knight, Mary Halliday, Christopher Brittain, Doris Allan, Christine and Aileen Scott, and Roland Beyer: 'Mare Vivimus' says the old town crest – and 'Amore Vivimus', I feel inclined to add.

St. Monans, Fife, January 1988.

1

THE MYSTERY

There are elements in this Coronation ceremony which are unexpected, emotional, and difficult to explain. I had a sudden feeling, craning at my glimpse of the bare-headed Queen at her anointing, sitting motionless with lowered eyes under her gold canopy, a sensation that was like something spoken aloud: "There is a secret here"....What that secret was, I could not say. No doubt it was the primitive and magical feeling which ancient and beautiful ceremonials still evoke, in no matter how rational a breast. That tiny golden figurine was the point of light under a vast burning-glass; the vision of an uncounted multitude was narrowed down to this.

Margaret Lane, '*The Queen is Crowned*', New Statesman *Coronation Issue*, June 1953.

1

The Mystery

A People's Monarchy

Anthropologists and psychologists all over the world are studying the reactions of primitive tribes to sexual situations. There have been concentrated within the last ten days the reactions of the people of the British Empire to a sexual situation. Here in a relatively limited form is some of the material for that anthropological study of our own civilization of which we stand in such desperate need.

Geoffrey Pyke, letter to the *New Statesman*,
December 12, 1936.

In today's world the Windsor Monarchy of Great Britain occupies a special place. That place is the subject of this book - a problem more complex and less self-evident than most received ideas would suggest. But one thing about it is obvious, and unchallengeable: its popularity. Its unique place and appeal depend upon a strong popular support going far beyond mere acceptance, or the cool calculation of benefits which academic supporters of the Crown have so often relished.

Permanent and almost unshakeable adoration quite divorced from profit-and-loss accounts seems to be the happy lot of the British Crown. 'Attitudes to the monarchy are strongly in the direction of uncritical support among all social groups', comments a recently launched survey of British social attitudes. 'Least supportive of the monarchy are the unemployed', it goes on, 'yet even here just over half consider the

19

monarchy "very important" and only 15% consider it to be unimportant'. The spectre of anti-monarchism may have arisen among the unemployed, but the evidence goes on to suggest that re-employment would probably cure it. Athough a little less fervent than Tory or Liberal-SDP supporters, Labour voters remain 77% in favour of the view that continuation of the monarchy is 'important for Britain'. So overwhelming is this popularity, indeed, that the authors of the new survey concluded it was unlikely to change much in any foreseeable future: 'This question clearly need not be repeated annually.'[1]

This popularity appears to have changed little over the past half-century. More than thirty years ago, after witnessing the funeral of George VI and the Coronation of Elizabeth II, Sebastian Haffner commented:

> Whatever one may think of the status of the British Monarchy in late Victorian and Edwardian times....it does not compare with its present immeasurable prestige and grip on the national imagination. It is doubtful whether at any time in the last thousand years the British Monarchy has occupied such an enormous place in the thoughts and emotions of British citizens as at the present moment. The Britain of the early 'fifties is not simply loyally monarchist; it is monarchy-conscious to a degree which calls for some special explanation. As every editor of every popular newspaper or magazine knows, there is an insatiable demand for every scrap of information regarding the functioning of the Monarchy and the life of the Royal family. In the everyday conversation of British families, Royalty nowadays occurs with a frequency probably shared only by their most intimate relations and friends...[2]

Then as now the People's Monarchy was also distinguished by its high quotient of froth and saccharine, and by the sort of goggling adulation critics have been only too apt to label 'mindless'. But Haffner could see beyond this and asked the right question about it:

> Can one really say that the mood of the hundreds of thousands who waited their turn in the February sleet of 1952 to pass by the bier of George VI was frivolous? Every mass emotion has, of course, a frivolous fringe. But he would be a poor

psychologist who failed to notice the deeply, solemnly, help-lessly serious core of feeling in the British monarchist revival...

Some pages from Richard Hoggart's classic *The Uses of Literacy* (1957) and the relevant parts of Mass Observation's surveys are the things usually quoted in more searching discussions of these attitudes. Since it was a progressive organization founded in the 1930s to make known the people's view, Mass Observation's archives have been an especially popular source for illustrations of national enthusiasm about Royalty, notably in Philip Ziegler's *Crown and People* (1978), a work published to celebrate Queen Elizabeth's twenty-five years on the throne.

Indeed, such enthusiasm was closely linked to the origins of the organization. The three founders, Tom Harrisson, Charles Madge and film-maker Humphrey Jennings, were originally united in amazement at the popular Monarchism of 1936-7, the moment of the Abdication Crisis. It was the drama of Edward VIII's forced abdication for love which –

> ...brought to the attention of intellectuals the extraordinary hold which the monarchy still had over the British popular imagination. It had also seemed to expose gulfs between the "Establishment" and the "people", and between the news-paper press and public opinion...Late in 1936, a school teacher named Geoffrey Pyke wrote to the *New Statesman* urging that "primitive" public reaction to the abdication should be sub-jected to "anthropological study"...[3]

But by that time the group had already begun its work. The subjects covered by its teams of amateur anthropologists soon extended from Monarchy to: 'Behaviour of people at war memorials; Shouts and gestures of motorists; The aspidistra cult; Anthropology of football pools; Distribution, diffusion and significance of the dirty joke; ....' and so on. As well as *Crown and People*, other publications based on archive material relating to Monarchy include *May 12th Mass-Observation Day Surveys* (on George VI's Coronation, 1937), and *Long to Reign Over Us* (Leonard Harris, 1966).

In *The Uses of Literacy* Hoggart concerned himself mainly with the more concrete and colourful aspect of working-class views of Royalty. '*As an institution* it is scarcely thought of by the working class... They either ignore it or, if they are interested, the interest is for what can be translated into the personal...' True, he adds that appreciation is often counter-pointed by a touch of antagonism. Royalty also belongs to 'Them', a class where people are unduly well cared-for: 'They don't have troubles like us; they don't have to struggle with the kids when they're tired out; they're waited on hand and foot...', and so on.

Yet any latent hostility here is usually defused by another, equally common notion: as Hoggart takes care to underline, the Royals are always distinguished from 'Them' (the priv-ileged class) as a whole, and imagined as being at Their mercy. They occupy a quite special position, belonging neither to Them nor to Us - at society's heart, yet somehow outside the social class order. Hence, the unfair privileges are paid for by the way Royals are 'pushed around' in the name of protocol and made to sacrifice their privacy. From this perception flow such staples of British conversation as: 'I tell you *I* wouldn't have *her* job', 'Of course *they* (the Royals) can't help it half the time', and 'They would be O.K. if only they were left alone more'.[4]

Thus, 'They' as concrete individuals are distinguished from State or Establishment and felt to be O.K. So, therefore, is whatever it is They as individuals stand for - the national value-system which somehow pins together niceness, 'decency', 'ordinariness' and a vast if indeterminate train of similar ideal baggage. 'I have always had a certain idea of France' was De Gaulle's famous phrase at the start of his *Memoirs*. But what the British Royals have and daily project is a certain idea of Britain (or perhaps more precisely of 'England-Britain') which, like the General's, finds constant acceptance and nourishment in popular attitudes. Unlike his austere mysti-cism, however, the Windsor-National notion finds instant and gratifying endorsement at the most trivial level. The mere fact that a Queen or Princess is human and 'ordinary' somehow underwrites the collective soul and reinforces a feeling of community. It seems to imply a commonality transcending anything (which may mean, nearly everything) unjust, deplor-able, soup-stained and out-of-date.

Are We All Mad?

The essence of the British Monarchy is that the King, while lifted far above the nation, should also be the nation itself in its most characteristic form.

John Buchan, *The King's Grace, 1910-1935*, pp. 276-7.

Thirty years after the opinions quoted above, the machinery they describe seemed quite intact, if not stronger, at the 1986 wedding of Prince Andrew (now Duke of York) to Miss Sarah Ferguson. Earlier, when the Prince's engagement was announced, Alexander Chancellor pointed out in the *Sunday Telegraph* the media assumption that 'There is at present nothing else in the world of such consuming interest to the British public':

A question arises (he goes on)...Are we right, or are we mad? If we are right, are you then mad? Or are we all equally mad?...A friend of mine walking down Piccadilly on the day the engagement was announced saw three middle-aged ladies burst into tears of joy as they read the news in the evening paper.

It is quite true that in most countries (including Monarchies like Sweden) this kind of public behaviour would be thought at best 'simple', or at worst deserving safe confinement. Chancellor opts for the former diagnosis: 'It is perhaps rather mad, but I can see no great harm in it'. However, it was obvious both then and at the wedding in July that the hysteria of such moments is more than 'harmless' (in this context an English code for 'Do Not Touch' or 'Not to be analysed farther'). A new, long-awaited bud suddenly disclosed upon the Royal totem-tree also means something like: '*It* will all go on and on' – where 'it' surely, is, taken to signify more than the Royal Family itself. What is meant seems to be something more like the tree's whole environment, its conditions of life: that same omnipresent baggage-train of sentiments and notions mentioned before.

On the same page as Mr Chancellor's ladies there were some more probing reflections on the event, of the kind invariably found in attendance on significant Regal events. The Prince's nuptials would of course be another welcome act of *moderniz-ation*: 'The Royal Family, *our* Royal Family, are steadily formulating the style of a whole new generation of royals – a generation that will take us into the next century, God and the people willing', wrote Anthea Hall. Not that there's much doubt about the people since (she continues) –

> The British, despite the notional appeal of the progress from rags to riches, prefer additions to the Royal Family to come from the nobility and the gentry, who are already acquainted with the principles of *noblesse oblige* - not jumped up and parvenu...A closer-knit and more British Monarchy, with two modern-minded young wives as new recruits, whose fresh approach will clear away the last, dour Germanic remains of the Hanoverian line augurs well.

All too plainly, what this sort of think-piece counsels is like the indirect worship of ourselves: '*our*' Royal Family merges into an elderly nation apologetically yet triumphantly set in its ways, one of which is the disposition to modernize with dignity, moved by *noblesse oblige* rather than bourgeois crassness.

The broader context of this 1986 verdict is worth remember-ing too: it was made after Mrs Thatcher's now legendary seven years of radical strivings to unsettle the old ways. Yet this journalist could safely conclude in the Tory Party's Sunday paper that the reaction to 'Andy and Sarah' proved that 'the nation which gave the world *Brideshead Revisited* is more in love with class than ever...' The Prime Minister's ardent wish to make the 'appeal of progress from rags to riches' less notional and more a matter of popular fact seemed, like all its predecessors, to have sunk helplessly into the quicksands of Royal identity.

Prompted by Ms Hall's reflections I looked back through a notebook of Windsor Moments to find the following fairly recent entry:

> John Cole, BBC Newsafternoon prog., Feb.13, '86 - Mrs T's "depression", reported as basically due to feeling that after all she and govt. have done, British society has failed to respond!

The Prime Minister's bout of melancholy came after the

Westland affair, when it looked as if her party had had enough of the Resolute Approach and was shuffling back towards the ancestral terrain of set ways clad in a less frantic style of modernization. Some days before this moment of intuition the trend had (I noticed in the same jottings) been re-baptized by the apostate Michael Heseltine as 'caring capitalism'. Having once more failed to respond - in short - 'British society' then seemed to be settling down to enjoy a Spring and Summer of old-time, pre-Resolute events. These were to include the Queen's 60th birthday and the Queen Mother's 86th, as well as the Princely engagement and wedding. Later, Mrs Thatcher would recover her nerve and try to restore the counter-revolution's momentum; but what we should notice here is the contradiction between these two attitudes, a theme which will constantly recur.

In the same connection, it is also worth noting how the mood of spiritual resettlement after the discomposures of Thatcherism was most ably summed up by the leader of the Labour Party on the wedding-day itself. It was a glowing Mr Kinnock who emerged from Westminster Abbey to tell the media that amidst all the starch and pomp the Duchess of York had smiled like any ordinary girl: 'That smile was worth all the rest of it!', he laughed - the emblem of an ordinariness and somehow Labour-like decency and sanity ever resurgent against Them, and indicating how, despite the rituals of Establishment, all was really going well for the people.

Mystic Significance of a Small Bald Patch

Fetishism: a sort of lower idolatry in which the idol is rather the embodiment than the symbol of the associated spiritual power.

President C. de Brosses, *Du culte des dieux fétiches*
(Paris 1760).

If we aren't all mad, what are we? To take this important question farther, it may help to look at one example of popular media Royalism. No paper is more assiduous with its Regal pep-pills than the *Sun*. '*Oops, Charles! There's a Patch on Your*

Thatch!' yelled the front page of June 9th, 1977. A 'bald spot the size of an egg' had just been noticed on the future King's pate by a laser-eyed Royal-watcher, 'as he sped away after a game of polo in an Aston Martin open sports car'. 'The Prince was last night on Hair Majesty's Service, attending the mammoth fireworks display on the River Thames,' the accompanying text goes on, 'But...*noone turned a hair at Charles's secret!'*

The display on the Thames, incidentally, was part of that year's Royal Jubilee celebrations commemorating the Queen's twenty-five years on the throne. Only two days before, colossal, crowds had been drawn to central London for the official Golden Coach Procession to St Paul's and the Guildhall. In spite of fears of apathy earlier in the year, they had demonstrated Royal popularity to be much the same as a generation before. It was a summer of constant fête, sprinkled with loyal street-parties and pageantry, where the revelation that the Prince of Wales – as yet unmarried - might well be bald as a coot before turning into Charles III provoked little real trepidation among *Sun*-readers. Quite the contrary: a mildly drunken feeling was in the air which somehow accentuated the *drôlerie* of Princely depilation.[5]

Now, the point is that this vein of fun-gibberish *in extremis* is not just an amplified version of the kind of attention paid to idols of the screen or rock and roll. Sometimes the British Royal Spectacle gets dismissed all too easily into that category. Diana Simmonds' entertaining *Princess Di, the National Dish* (1984), for instance, saw the Princess as a Hollywood-style creation of media determined to distract popular attention from national bankruptcy. 'The presence on the throne of the Queen, with her Dutiful Son and his Beautiful Wife waiting at her side is the one thing that really stops little England from facing up to this ghastly reality...'(of being 'a small aircraft carrier for the USA').

It's quite true that the same papers publish vaguely similar stories and pictures about singers, actors, and even politicians. Abroad, rough-trade dailies and weeklies also indulge in salacious tit-bits, freely divorcing and coupling personalities of the Royal *ménage* in their pages. But though there is some coincidence of both form and content between popular media-

Royalism and other kinds of sensationalism, it does not follow that the former is merely one branch of the latter. The Royals may have to be media stars these days; but the appeal of media stars as such is not Royal. In Britain at least, the Queen and her family are never merely stars, or celebrities. They possess in addition a 'secret' (in Margaret Lane's words, quoted above): an element of mystique whose glamour is in the end far greater than that of any media personality.

It is precisely this mystique which concerns us here: the 'glamour' (in an originally Scottish sense) of persons and symbols ordinary in appearance but quite super-ordinary in significance. In a far more extensive, emotionally-powerful manner than any of the other surviving monarchies, Britain's Windsors are like an interface between two worlds, the mundane one and some vaster national-spiritual sphere associated with mass adulation, the past, the State and familial morality, as well as with Fleet Street larks and comforting daydreams. But just what this mystique *is* is itself mysterious. As we will go on to see, few have bothered to ask and their inquiries have not gone very far.

In any case, reflection shows that no comparable front-page splash to the one mentioned *could* have been done on, say, Larry Hagman or Boy George. It would have lacked that special something deriving from a Kingly blemish and the tinglingly absurd notion of a totemic cranium exposed to common draughts long before the supreme moment when St Edward's Crown is lowered on to it. The *ordinariness* of looming middle-age is made risible purely by association with the super-ordinary, a totem or wonder-laden figure who *also* has to comb his hair to hide baldness. The special something, in other words, is associated with a dialectic of the normal and the (utterly) extra-ordinary far more compelling than anything found in stardom and the realms of hype. This dialectic is inextinguishable too, fortunately for Britain's popular press. Thus nine years on we find (for example) the *Sunday Mirror* of September 21 1986 titillating its readers with 'Twenty Things About Charles's Baldness'.

In *Lies, Damned Lies and Some Exclusives* (1984) Henry Porter has farther underlined the weird freedom prevailing in the world of media comment on the Monarchy. Within very elastic limits journalists write what fabrications they please, because –

> Fleet Street royalty-watchers are peculiarly unfettered by the restraints that apply in all other fields of journalistic endeavour. The Royal Family has only once this century resorted to the libel laws in response to a damaging fabrication and it is unlikely to do so again...

That one time was in 1911, when action was taken against a Republican journalist who claimed that George V was a secret bigamist. Although the action was won, it was realized that this kind of publicity is deeply counter-productive: George's personal honour was vindicated at some cost to the *institution* of Monarchy. Since then the press has mostly been allowed its head. Most of the time a form of self-censorship has kept it within bounds; but when this has been transgressed (increasingly since the 1960s) the Royal Establishment has assumed an attitude of somewhat forced amusement and disdain (with occasional public rebukes, or pleas for privacy).

This observation confirms, surely, the underlying difference of status between Royalty and media stardom. 'Taking action' against the fantasists Mr Porter describes would undermine that distinction: being above that sort of thing (or 'not being able to answer back') remains essential to the mystique. This is true above all of legal moves which might involve court appearance. For there they would be 'answering back' on a level with the accusers, as ordained by Law. The myth of Equality before the Law may be at the heart of Free-born England; but in this particular case, best not insisted upon. After all, the British Sovereign is not even first among equals: she is (as one legal journalist has put it) 'quite simply "first"...No one in the entire realm is legally her equal. Because the Queen is legally the fountain of all justice – the courts are her courts, the judges are (as their official title does indicate) "Her Majesty's Judges" – she cannot be prosecuted or sued.'[6]

Quite unwittingly, the most vulgar joke may connect in this sphere with antique mysteries. In his exhaustive study of the symbolism of mediaeval Kingship, Ernst Kantorowicz concluded that England's peculiarity had always been recognition of 'the King's Two Bodies' – that is, a relationship between the corporeal frailty of the man or woman and the undying mystique of the Crown. In this 'Royal Christology' there were always 'two bodies but only one person'; the transient, often absurd earthly creature translated a 'body politic' ('the Dignity which does not die') into visible terms. Thus, 'Charles's secret' is both the bald patch *and* the fact that here is the personage who will be reborn as King the very second Queen Elizabeth draws her last breath, forty-sixth in line since William of Normandy's conquest; his flaws and quirks are both just like everyone else's and yet – inevitably – utterly different. [7]

Even if he learns polo and gets a different open Aston Martin for each day of the week, no pop idol can acquire *this* dimension of glamour. Decades of exposure and effort may bestow a shadow of 'charisma' (in Weber's original sense) on some exceptional figures like John Lennon or Bob Dylan. Prince Charles, alas, unfairly acquired the real thing merely by being born.

Royalty and Fashion

When a man ceases to be an anti-dandy in England, he tends to swing right round, to become a dandy.

Martin Green, *Children of the Sun*
(1977) p.483.

Another example of what is really the same distinction can be seen in the Royal wardrobes. Court women are the focus of voluminous comment about their clothes, and maintain a respectable cottage industry of couturiers and seamstresses. In any one year the Queen chooses and buys more clothes than most of her subjects do in a lifetime, and the Royal wardrobes have probably always accounted for more column-inches than any other single item in their repertoire.

If there was any doubt about this before Princess Diana's arrival in 1981 there can be none now. Her wedding gown was the most raved-over of post-war garments and brought to instant fame the young couple who made it. The wearer had some natural advantages for the modelling business. As Di

Simmonds points out: 'Being a 5'10" size 10 is the ideal for a photographic model and is thus the impossible image which every woman is taught to believe is perfection and which gazes out with assured arrogance and disdain from posters and hoardings the Western world over'.[8] Also, she is said to have got help from the editorial staff of *Vogue* magazine itself in cultivating the new image.

Yet this identification is, as suspect as that of Royals with pop-idols or film-stars. Again we see a partial coincidence of appearance and treatment which hides a more significant difference. After all, no future Queen can actually project 'assured arrogance and disdain' through her photographic image, or risk that blatant symbolic seduction of the audience which is the professional model's function. The model's body is a kind of sexual abstraction, an instrument of the fashion code: Roland Barthes' analysis in *Système de la Mode* picks up the inversion at work: clothes normally give meaning to the body, while her body has to give meaning to clothes.[9] Its anorexic 'unreality' mirrors this function (shown also in the way one model-body or face can itself be in or out of fashion among the image-makers).

By contrast, the Royal rag-trade works with sacred personalities, not mannequins. It has to create 'niceness', acceptability – an asexual charm free from the sharp edge of real fashion. But this need pulls in a direction opposite to fashionability: modes *have* to be transient, both commerce and the type of allure they aim for mean that 'in' and 'out' are vital. Regal femininity has to be permanently 'in', however; and what is always in fashion can never be truly fashionable. It tends in fact towards a sort of fluorescent tedium exemplified for many decades now by the Queen's own public wardrobe and what this represents is a *sui generis* 'style' which can make little more than periodic gestures of alignment with the styles unfolding in the market-place. These inflections are invariably noticed as miraculous evidence of Royal sensibility to what's going on: yes, they *can* be just like us. Not to the extent of being caged in by the 'whims of fashion', though : more like an occasional prison-visit to console the inmates.

The inexorable limits to Regal pseudo-fashion are set by the function it performs. In Andrew Duncan's words, Royal appearances are like 'an everlasting wedding photograph', and what this calls for is a special kind of theatricality. What it demands is totemic exhibitionism rather than *chic*.

> All royal designers, from Hartnell on down, have had to learn one basic lesson' (writes Colin McDowell in *100 Years of Royal Style*) no matter how beautiful, original or memorable a design, it is a good *royal* design only if the person wearing it is able to fulfil her role with absolute smoothness, precision and efficiency. This is what the endless time and trouble taken over royal clothes is about. The dictates of fashion, the whims of the designer and the taste of the royal client are all secondary to the overriding requirement: a design which is suitable for its function...[10]

Noone can (for example) have failed to notice the astounding colours of so many Queenly garments: shrieking turquoise, retching pink, acidulous lemon-yellow. But as McDowell points out, these are really prescribed by the demands of visibility - she can never sport a 'a shade that would tone in and get lost among a large crowd' and thus destroy the wedding-photo effect. Each Royal manifestation must be in some degree a renewal of the Coronation marriage vows.

The Queen Mother has long been an epitome of this Royal anti-*chic*. After becoming Queen in 1936 she was launched by Hartnell with a '*robe de style* of gleaming silver tissue over hooped *carcasse* of stiffened silver gauze with a deep *berthe* collar of silver lace encrusted with glittering diamonds', and never looked back. The permanent effigy-look (topped by one of her celebrated crown-substitute hats) varies only slightly with time: each new season's offerings from her designers will include one or two timid 'fashion-of-the-year looks', normally rejected with polite horror. Nothing should interfere too much with what Cecil Beaton called 'The unreality of a spangled fairy doll on top of a Christmas tree...' with its dazzling effect upon 'devoted but dazed beholders'.

For a year or two after the Princess of Wales's arrival it seemed this might be less true. The combination of novelty, her looks, and the use made of new designers like the Emmanuels and Bruce Oldfield suggested a much stronger Royal link to (relatively) vanguard couture. But time has begun to tell. On a recent trip to Italy her appearances were, wrote McDowell, 'a fashion non-event, because the Princess's clothes were so totally uneventful'. He went on to underline the dilemma:

> This is the problem. We have a fashion-conscious Princess who cannot wear fashionable clothes. Good fashion design is either foreign or too strongly cocking a snook at accepted fashion taste. What we have seen in Italy is the result of too much respect, and too much hard work...The results were staid...If it is any consolation her mother-in-law had precisely the same problem when she was young: "lamb dressed as mutton" seems a recurring Royal problem.[11]

There is of course no consolation at all to be found in the direction Mr McDowell indicates. As far as Italy was concerned he was reduced to warning Princess Di against wearing any more of those hats: 'The quaint designs paraded in the past ten days should make the Palace think again about the wisdom of dressing a young Princess too formally....'

But this is the nub of the whole problem. What do 'those hats' represent but the self-castration of fashion in the face of (inevitable) Palace formality? This is a terrain where in the long run dullness frilled by jocularity represents the highest attainable mark. While maturity alone can bring the full matronly grandeur catered for by the Hartnell tradition, the Princess is clearly making progress. In other words, to enter the Crown's magic circle is to leave fashion glamour for another kind, and while the two may remain interwoven for some time the balance can't stay equal.

A revealing second twist to the philosophy of Regal vestment is provided by the special features of contemporary British fashion: the business of 'cocking a snook' at Established modes of grandeur. Britain has been prominent in this kind of anti-fashion: iconoclastic street modes are its sole claim to inventiveness. Yet nothing could be more completely at odds with the rules of Royal wardrobery. A *punk* Princess of Wales? - the question answers itself. British clothes trends manifest something important about the social order, and their theatre of Establishment and street-wise anti-Establishment reflect the very truth which it is Royalty's prime function to consecrate and maintain. But that function can only be exercised *in the end* from one side: above. A kind of moral-spiritual authority is at stake which allows – indeed, prescribes – visits to the lower regions and enthusiasm from the denizens, but absolutely prohibits going native. There is simply no long-term way of keeping a foot in both camps.

The point can be underlined again by the obvious analogy of rock-culture. That too derives its sting from the open wounds of class: British prominence in the field has in part been a cry against the cultural apartheid and sludge-like immobilism of the Old Régime. Like street-fashion it has sought a destructive escape from repression through counter-fantasies of love or dread, and created an international commerce for these essentially anti-Windsor products. Yet the garish antithesis coexists on the whole quite well with Royal officialdom – rather in the way that the products of some unusually creative Indian Reservation might be said to testify 'in their own way' to the richness of a national culture.

In a chapter on 'Oppositional Dress' in her *Adorned in Dreams* (1985), Elizabeth Wilson brings out some other implications of what so many philistines have sneered at as 'mere fashion' (in the same way as the Monarchy may be labelled a 'mere symbol'). Certain British street modes of the 1970s can also be seen as a form of aesthetic *modernism*, all the more striking for their expression of a spirit largely suppressed from the official political and literary culture of 20th century Britain. The latter of course seeks always to clothe or reclothe the national essence in one or another 'natural' or natural-seeming tradition - forever re-reading the 'Unwritten Constitution' into the fabric of everyday life, so to speak. The punk style by contrast –

> ...radically questions its own terms of reference, questions what fashion *is*, what style *is*, making mincemeat of received notions of beauty and trashing the very idea of "charm" or "taste".[12]

It may also be a 'way of creating identity in a shocking and deviant way' which contrasts with the 'generalized pessimism' of a foundering British existence. Royalty, on the other hand, seems to be an essential factor in the standard identity-kit of that existence itself. It is a vital part of 'Who we are', in the staple sense prescribed by the mainstream forms of popular cultural nationalism – a communal reality always more significant in the end than 'Them and us'.

Royalty versus Celebrity

> We must call up battles and banners and many ghosts and glories before we see whatever it is that we do see in the picture of a princess feeding a bear with a bun.
>
> Virginia Woolf, 'Royalty', *Collected Essays*, vol. IV (1967).

The very fact that the public palate never seems jaded by Royal display itself serves effectively to mark off the Royal obsession from interest in media personalities. Stars have some relationship to fashion, they 'take off' or are launched, and more often than not enjoy a season of popularity before fading. Even long-lived idols generally have ups and downs in their careers, and may be eclipsed for periods before 'rediscovery' puts them back in favour. In modern times at least, British Monarchy appears to have won near-immunity from that kind of favour and disfavour. Yet if change is slower in such a highly visible aquarium then (one might think) the viewers ought to tire of it sooner. It is after all competing with these other public spectacles – popular music, the rag trade, T.V., and so on, where change is notoriously rapid and failure to feel a rising new pulse is death.

But the point is that there *is* no such competition. Monarchy dwells in a category all its own, where in some enigmatic way appetite feeds off itself and is never sated. Every tiny Royal 'concession' to fashion or trend is therefore greeted as an amazing Grace, breathless evidence that They are open to (even *interested in*) the experience of humdrums. But this is only because They (as distinct from they) do not have to make such concessions at all. George V, a sartorial obsessive who never showed a flicker of concern with new trends, succeeded nonetheless (and partly through such unconcern) in consolidating his image of National Dad. He remained, as Kenneth Rose notes, wholly fixated on the style of what had been the day before yesterday when he was a young man, while the unfortunate Queen Mary had no option but to surrender to 'the King's almost oriental requirements' for unfashionability.[13]

Hence a more general observation is also in order: the British Royals are never *just* 'celebrities'. Or rather, while they have of course had to become celebrities in recent times, what really matters (and is really puzzling) about them is that they remain something more as well. The point may be obscured abroad - for example, in the recent tours of the Prince and Princess of Wales among the American super-rich of Florida and Texas, where they could not help appearing as exotic super-stars. But it is rarely if ever obscured among their own subjects. Here it's the 'something extra' which has always counted – and which both justifies and discounts the public-relations glare that accompanies them everywhere.

Daniel Boorstin gave a famous definition of celebrity in his chapter on 'Human Pseudo-Events' in *The Image* (1961). It is, he claimed, the 'new kind of eminence' characteristic of our times, and overshadowing all earlier types of fame. Associated exclusively with the rise of the contemporary media from the mid-19th century onwards, the celebrity 'could not have existed in any earlier age': he or she is *'a person who is known for his well-knownness'*. Celebrity is measured not by any moral or personal qualities but by the weight of accumulated press-clippings and moments of 'exposure':

> The hero was distinguished by his achievement; the celebrity by his image or trademark...The hero was a big man; the celebrity is a big name...

Hence the passage of time made heroes, but destroys celebrities – 'one is made, the other unmade, by repetition'. This is why (for example) President Roosevelt –

> ...was careful to space out his fireside chats so the citizenry would not tire of him. Some comedians have found that when they have weekly programmes they reap quick and remunerative notoriety, but that they soon wear out their images. To extend their celebrity-lives, they offer their images more sparingly - once a month or once every two months instead of once a week.

It has quite often been thought that the British Monarchy must eventually fall foul of this law. For example, broadcaster David Attenborough is reported to have said after seeing the TV film *Royal Family* (1969) that trouble might ensue because once the tribesfolk had seen inside the headman's hut the mystery was gone, and they would tire of seeing it repeated. So far all such fears have proved utterly groundless. No quantity of 'exposure' appears to do anything but create demand for more. The Royal glamour has appropriated and used the world of celebrity, not vice versa. Hence, far from being definable in its terms, the problem of what Monarchy's mystique is really about is simply re-posed by them.

The only plausible explanation (or beginning of an explanation) is that the tirelessness of the Royal Romance lies somewhere else. That is, not so much in the trivia themselves as in their relationship to whatever lies behind. Essentially, they must be facets of some underlying Thing which – however vaguely apprehended through the daily parade – is felt as great, and inexhaustible. Only this obscure relationship makes it all bearable. Yet, as everyone knows, it does in fact make it endlessly bearable, and indeed loved, no matter the degree of pettiness, cosiness, 'mindlessness', vulgarity, sanctimony and repetition.

In the Doll's House: Crawfie Lives

> The King also would talk to his eldest daughter more seriously than most fathers do... It was as if he spoke to an equal. Since he had become King the shadows were closing in on England. They were, I think, realized in the Palace before they fell over, the Streets outside.
>
> Marion Crawford, *The Little Princesses* (1950) p.52.

If the popular media imagery of Royalty is like a strip-cartoon in primary colours, respectable portrayals are like a book. More exactly, like any one of the stack of Royal volumes to be found in any decent-sized branch of W.H.Smith or John Menzies. Though reading is more popular in Britain than many other comparable societies (thanks to the Public Library system) the buying and giving of books remains a bourgeois preserve, and one would expect this Royal bookshelf to mirror respectable views fairly well.

Each year for many years now twenty or so new titles have been added to the pile. These range from mainly pictorial tributes around a single event (wedding, Royal visit, etc.) to massive official or semi-official biographies. The last time I checked, in 1985, National Library catalogues showed a grand total of one hundred and thirty-seven available titles devoted to the Queen's family alone (not counting Royal Dukes and other relations). A reliable survey-point for this terrain can probably be located in the typical, chatty, illustrated, informal book about almost any member of the extended Royal Family. Take for example Christopher Warwick's recent biography of Princess Margaret, which highlights some interesting features of the genre.[14]

Familyness is important to contemporary Monarchs and crucial for the sort of national-popular identity the Windsors purvey. But to express this demands a real family – an extended unit numerous and varied enough to constitute a fictive world of its own. And as many media critics have observed, nothing is more vital to such narrative than suitable villains, or at least bad eggs. The mightiest case of this is of course *Dallas*, whose universal appeal derives almost entirely from the machinations of Devil-figure 'J.R.' In milder fashion the unfortunate Princess Margaret has undoubtedly been cast in a similar rôle. The fact is reflected in the titles of previous portrayals: *Margaret, The Tragic Princess* (J.Brough, 1978), *Margaret: Princess Without a Cause* (W. Fischauer, 1978), and Nigel Dempster's *Princess Margaret: A Life Unfulfilled* (1981).

An extra tinge of ghoulishness is given to these saurian laments by the fact that all do little more than elaborate one primal image: that provided by the timeless nursery tales of Marion Crawford's *The Little Princesses* (1950), and quickly followed up by her even soapier *Princess Margaret* (1953). These compilations of mawkish tit-bits made 'Crawfie' into an international legend. Most recently they have provided inspiration for A.N.Wilson's verse celebration of Queenly childhood, *Lilibet* (1984): a *Kitsch* epic worthy of both source and subject. Since she had been governess to the Royal sisters for seventeen years, her 'unauthorized' portrayal inevitably had some authority.

Its main point was the intriguing contrast of personalities between the two Princesses. Elizabeth was good enough to worry even Miss Crawford:

> At one time I got quite anxious about Lilibet and her fads. She became almost too methodical and tidy. She would hop out of bed several times a night to get her shoes quite straight, her clothes arranged just so...

Margaret on the other hand was full of mischief, and this worried her sister from an early age: 'Though Lilibet, with the rest of us, laughed at Margaret's antics...I think they often made her uneasy and filled her with foreboding'. The Queen-to-be (in Warwick's words) 'emerged whiter than white, an irreproachable angelic young woman, while Princess Margaret, on the other hand, was made to appear wilful, spoiled, and resentful of the office her sister would one day inherit'. His new biography was meant to be a belated repair-job on this now almost ancestral 'bad sister' myth (fortified, in the intervening years, by the Princess's many and well-advertised personal turmoils). Its intention was of course underlined by the editorial imprint upon the volume: that of Lord Weidenfeld, Britain's quasi-official Royal publication house which ought long ago to have been granted the 'By Appointment' Coat of Arms over its front door.

More generally, Royal biography seems to be a weird craft with rules and punishments all its own. The writer has to make his way through a decorative maze sown with land-mines. Trailing too supinely between the crisply-trimmed hedges leads to unbearable dullness; yet forays into the weedier-looking dead-ends involve the near-certainty of booby-traps and outrage. The Bloomsbury intellectuals of pre-war days like Virginia Woolf and Harold Nicolson derided the official *genre* of 'fat volumes' on Regal subjects 'noble, upright, chaste, severe....above life-size in top-hat and frock-coat'. And one of them, Lytton Strachey, mounted a famous attack on it with *Eminent Victorians*. Yet when he turned his attention to *Queen Victoria* (1921), the result was quite a mellow appraisal.

For all his own sins Nicolson was to end up as official biographer of George V, an ordeal which made him think more highly of chaste predecessors like Sidney Lee, the chronicler of Edward VII.

For example, one of Edward's many disagreeable characteristics was gluttony. From earliest youth, writes historian David Cannadine, the fact is that –

> He had acquired a passion for very large amounts of very rich food. Age only augmented both his appetite and his waistline...he ate anything and everything; and he ate it very quickly. All day, every day, day after day, he ate ...Somehow, it was altogether appropriate that the man known as "Tum-tum" should have to postpone his coronation because he was suffering from appendicitis.[15]

Sir Sidney's single-phrase rendition of this gannet-like voracity deeply impressed Nicolson. It sums up the whole problematic of Royal biography. The King-Emperor, he wrote, 'never toyed with his food'.[16]

All Mr Warwick's efforts on behalf of Princess Margaret show, unfortunately, is that in the present climate such problems remain quite insuperable. To 'put right' so many malicious slanders and unworthy attacks is not to get at the truth, but merely to restore the image (or something of it). For instance, red-eyed survivors of the Princess's mature passion for all-night parlour-games and charades have been driven to complain in at least semi-public of the awful experience: for decades noone dared go to bed or even indulge in a nap until, often after dawn, the last Royal cigarette had been stubbed out and guidance offered to the Bedchamber. Well, does this mean that she *is* spoiled, petulant, wilful and resentful, or not? Or – if she is also charming, warm, loyal and 'one of the most fascinating women I have ever known' (p.1) – then how are these traits related to the others? There is, after all, an interesting literature about 'bad sisters' (and brothers), *doppelgängers,* and so on: is it impossible to bring any of this to bear? The very fact that the wart and scandal count is so high in this case might lead one to hope for something actually interesting about - for example - the conflicts between a refractory personality and the pulverizing boredom-level of the Royal Household stereotypes. She tried to get out of it through marriage and other escape-routes, but failed: ought she to have tried harder? Or like her 'Uncle David' (Edward VIII), got out altogether? 'Biographies' of the present Ruler and her Consort, who have given themselves so wholeheartedly to the task of being effigies, will by definition be tedious panegyrics. But what of somebody who has so regularly collapsed on to a more human level?

Normally biography entails weighing up such claims and speculations, and reaching some verdict independent of self-image and rumour – even if it should be hurtful. It also involves some critical judgement of the subject's milieu, and of its influences upon her or him. Good biography has to be history and sociology, as well as the psychological portrayal of an individual. But in the case of Royalty, this is even more difficult than objective verdicts on the person: it is above all expected, and indeed demanded, that the author be acceptive of the infrastructure of Monarchy as well as of the subject's essential merits. Warts and blemishes are indeed carefully mentioned these days; but only to throw the merits into higher relief. Tongue-in-cheek attitudes have grown more acceptable - provided the tongue remains glued to the cheek and won't stick out straight again.

Thus, after quoting at length her refutations of the worse calumnies and heavily underlining the Princess's roster of visits and tours, what is Mr Warwick's conclusion?: 'Ultimately, duty has demanded of Princess Margaret rather more than privilege has restored....' Though often deeply afflicted in both body and soul, she never gave up; she may have played rather too hard, but she has worked jolly hard too. Two whole grovelling editorials (one titled 'Qui mal y pense') are quoted from the *Daily Telegraph*, whose sword has so often leapt from its scabbard in 'P.M.'s' defence. In this tide of thoughtful commiseration, all the interesting questions about the Princess turn somehow into preserved sweets: one suck, and then the reader is hurried onwards to still another list of official duties and noble impulses.

The task of true Royal biography is in fact *to say nothing*. That is, nothing 'interesting': nothing salacious (of course), but also nothing too denigratory of the individual or (above all) too disrespectful of the institution. Nothing – in short – of the sort of thing which normally drives people both to write and to read biographies. For all its artless awfulness, *The Little Princesses* did say something. This is why it aroused so much distress and has remained so influential. Marion Crawford was the Peter Wright of the 1950s Court – an ultra-loyal underling who spilt the beans for love as well as money. Its coy cosiness and naiveté were too perfectly in tune with one aspect of Monarchical public relations to be refutable and her 'revelation' could never be undone (certainly not by strained cover-up jobs like Mr Warwick's biography).

Isn't it possible to be both appreciative *and* 'interesting'? The history of the craft shows it to be, at least, extraordinarily difficult. Edward VIII was an exception, obviously: but this is because the system rejected him like a dud coin, leaving the way open in principle for less inhibited investigation (it should be noted, though, that the practical problems proved enormous: half a century after the Abdication it is by no means concluded). Apart from Edward, a century of padded eulogies has so far produced extremely few volumes approaching the norms of ordinary biography. The best recent example is undoubtedly Kenneth Rose's *King George V* (1983). Mr Rose's approach is wry and witty on one level: he cannot help noticing the absurdities of both the man and – more important – the father-figure role into which he was type-cast more effectively than anyone since his ancestor George III. Yet such acerbity is (as it were) constantly redeemed and compensated for by the stuffy arch-conservatism of the author's wider view.

Thus, commenting on the 1936 funeral rites, he observes how this ceremonial 'seemed to reflect...an order of precedence remote from the realities of power: titles and places, it might be supposed, that the reforming zeal of the Prince Consort had failed to sweep away almost a century before'. One may indeed suppose this. Prince Albert was both the first and the last genuine modernizer in British Royal history. But the impulses represented by the Crystal Palace and the Great Exhibition were exactly what Great Britain was destined not to turn into - in fact, what it refused and down-graded in order to sweep back a world of hierarchy and title, the Crowned subordination of the modern to the traditional.

But the point is that nothing like this *is* really supposed by Mr Rose: the remark is only offered as a characteristically amusing aside. He hastens onwards at once to declare that 'the England which George V bequeathed to his son was indeed a demi-paradise' by comparison with the rest of Europe ('England' - rather than pedestrian-synthetic 'Britain' – is of course made obligatory here by the Shakespearian allusion). Thus, a moment of British history now most often classed as politically and socially shameful even by conservative historians, is given a retrospective glow by the rosy illumination of George V's passing, amid a 'triumphant litany of death', gun-carriages, vast crowds, and so on. All the author's shrewd, abrasive or penetrating observations are in this way gathered up to be blanched and enfolded in final prayer. That somebody so grotesque and limited could mean so much simply renders the Royal demi-paradise *even more miraculous*.

Or again, in his treatment of Queen Mary's famous doll's house, we find the same bluffness standing in for what might have been an uneasy perception of significance. George V's publicly awesome Queen was (Rose notes) 'captivated by the diminutive, a taste shared by most of the crowned heads of Europe'. Her passion for the little was comparable to her husband's absorption with the British Empire postage-stamps bearing his own portrait. Princess Marie Louise (1872-1956, a grand-daughter of Victoria) had the idea of flattering her childhood friend's obsession with a very special gift. She asked the architect Sir Edwin Lutyens to design a doll's house for her. At first 'rather taken aback' (he was busy building New Delhi just then) the great man came round to the notion and said (in Marie Louise's *Memories* at least): 'Let us devise and design something which for all time will enable future generations to see how a King and Queen of England lived in the 20th century, and what authors, artists, and craftsmen of note there were during their reign'.[17]

The result was the celebrated miniature Palladian mansion now shown to the public at Windsor Castle: the country-house, anti-Crystal Palace England of 1923 forever shrunk to the scale of a baby's dream, complete with tiny shot-guns (which can be broken, to take microscopic cartridges), a library holding 'two hundred volumes the size of postage stamps each written by a contemporary author in his own hand', real water coming from the taps, bed-linen it took fifteen hundred hours to weave, fingernail-size bottles of real vintage wine in the cellars, and 'the gramophone in the children's nursery playing "God Save the King" '. Max Beerbohm's volume for the library began: 'For as long as I can remember, I have alway wanted to be very small'. There was even a stamp-album like King George's, filled with a collection of practically invisible stamps. When told she was to be given this disconcerting object, the Queen 'made only one demand on her benefactors. She asked Lutyens to ensure that she could open the doll's house at will, without needing to summon servants. That was the measure of her secret delight.' Unwilling to risk comment about either the Royal fixation on smallness or the obvious National willingness (especially pronounced among authors) to shrink, Rose writes merely: 'It was all the greatest nonsense and the greatest fun'.

What are They *Really* Like?

Only the British sovereign is expected to act as if there were some sacred or magic quality in a monarch which required a loyalty to his very person.

Donald Horne, *God is an Englishman* (1969) p.80.

Both respectable effigies and the demented cartoons from lower down agree on emphasizing the all-importance of Royal *personality*. This is a fundament of the modern Royal ideology: the institution is almost eclipsed from popular view by the (imagined) personal nature of the Monarch, her dependants and her ancestors. Servicing this obsessive interest is the main task of the Royal book business and Fleet Street's pack of Court Correspondents. Since Crawfie led the way there has been no stopping the cumulative process: one 'revelation' after another, each biography or news item claiming to snuggle closer to the real truth than its unduly respectful predecessors.

In the later 1960s the Court finally caved in to the mounting pressure and produced its own vision of 'What They're Really

Like', Richard Cawston's film *Royal Family*: an official version of the frank and unofficial truth. What We're Really Like turned out to be (as Antony Jay's script put it) the 'job-definition' of Monarchy over a year: their own succession of humble tasks, with some glimpses of leisure activity. There They were scorching sausages at a boring lochside barbecue like any other posh family; watching the telly and laughing together; She at a desk answering mail, then receiving Harold Wilson on a Tuesday evening ('The moment when Democracy and Monarchy meet...'), then meeting Nixon ('World problems are *so* complex, Ma'am...'), then saluting a goose-stepping military parade in a 1968 Santiago de Chile. This act of determined self-exposure had no effect, except to feed the appetite. However, such a consequence is in the nature of the appetite itself, which is really less of an urge to know than to worship. It is national devotion, deluding itself with the goal of an unobtainable (and in any case irrelevant) intimacy.

A normal curiosity about important or hidden facts can in principle be satisfied. Thus – to take an example from the field of historical studies of Royalty – Neal Ascherson's account of the Belgian King Leopold II's activities in 19th century Africa shows how these were used to try and 'reverse the historical victory of the middle classes over their kings' – to forge a 'new path to absolutism' at home in the context of imperialism abroad.[18] This *was* what lay behind the 'Heart of Darkness' in Joseph Conrad's famous story: a Constitutional Monarch trying (and finally failing) to win back more leverage than the constitution allowed him, by building up an immense private fortune drawn from colonial super-exploitation.

But the sort of 'revelation' that features in the British Cult of Personality has nothing whatever in common with this approach. It is a religion demanding the *appearance* of ever-closer knowledge, the expanding mass illusion of intimacy. The aim of such 'knowledge' is not, of course, to see through the veils and be satisfied: that would entail loss of interest and subsequent indifference - the very things the Cult strives to avoid at all costs. The 'obsessional' character of the curiosity means just this: it is in a literal sense unthinkable that discovery or understanding of certain facts about the individuals in question should end in normal classification and relegation from the forefront of attention. One is precluded by this dream-logic from ever reaching the point of saying: 'Ah, so *that's* what they're actually like' – so that, the wonderment dispelled, one can go on to worry about something else.

The inner meaning of the belief that 'They're just like us' ('ordinary beings', 'got their own problems', etc.) is the certainty that they are not, and cannot conceivably be just like us. Noone really compares them to the Robinsons down the road, or that funny lot round the corner (who became understandable when one heard about the Lebanese granny and the son in prison). The actual sense is more like: 'They're just like us *in some ways* (and what *this* implies is how absolutely extraordinary - unlike us - the rest must be)'. Thus – since what's marvellous about them being like us is that it shows they aren't just like us - each new glimpse or revelation can only reinforce the glamour rather than dissipating it, forever sharpening the appetite for more.

The general assumption which sustains the circular logic must (naturally) be that They are Nice. However, this can also be fed by salty rumours (and even the occasional fact) indicating lapses from Niceness. A dose of naughtiness, tantrums, fainting fits and familial squabbles feeds the appearance of intimacy without really threatening the faith. To be so like normal mortals in this way means that it's even more wonderful that They are who They are, do what They do, and so on. Thus – in the example above - the fact that Princess Margaret has endured a lifetime of being second, kicked over the traces, and yet still carries on must show something really big at work: or as Christopher Warwick says, the stout magic which there simply must be behind such a 'royal stiff upper lip'.

The situation would be different, obviously, were some fearless investigator to uncover a Leopoldian-scale scandal with irrefutable evidence; were it to be shown that (for instance) part of the Queen's huge and secret private fortune was invested in the heroin trade or that an establishment devoted to *le vice anglais* or under-age sex had been flourishing for years in the Buckingham Palace cellars. But because revelations of this order are vanishingly unlikely we have to make do with naughtiness and indiscretions. And these are a different matter altogether. The disclosure of peccadilloes in an unusually boring extended family simply makes them look more human. And this 'look' is the whole point.

Taboo-supported Niceness

The length of time taken over a hat, and hence its price, varies according to the Queen's movements. ... From June to October is not an uncommon length of time for the making of a hat. This is time well spent, for, in the iconography of dress the hat is surely the most important item. It not only denotes authority, it is, in Royal terms, a substitute for the ultimate symbol of power: the crown.

Colin McDowell, *100 Years of Royal Style* (1985).

Beyond this positive function lies another: the repression of criticism. Because what is actually a State magic has been concentrated into persons, all dislike of the institution is easily turned into an attack upon the individuals themselves. And this, of course, is 'unfair' or even 'ungallant', since (*not* being just like us) 'They can't answer back'. Resentment of Monarchy is turned into 'What have you got against *her*?' ('perfectly decent person', and so on). Only a cross-grained egg-head would want to do *that*, probably under foreign influence. It makes normal chaps want to draw their swords, as Edmund Burke imagined them doing in 1789 to save Marie-Antoinette from the simian clutches of the revolutionaries.

The critic is of course free to say he doesn't have anything against them 'as people': what *he* minds is the institution, the symbolic pomp and circumstance. Yet with the switch a vital part of the front is evacuated and defeat looms already. For of course any opposition worth its salt must surely *to some extent* object to them 'as people' – or object, at least, to the way in which (and the reasons for which) a synthetic image of their personality is so inescapably thrust upon us. Institution and personality have become fused in ideological practice. This ceaseless personalization is a great part of how the institution now functions, and 'They' have lent themselves ever more compliantly to the process, albeit with well-publicized pleas for privacy. For several generations now, all 'Royals' have in fact been formed as individuals by these pressures (with mounting success, except for the incorrigible Edward VIII). Any critic is quite justified in resenting *this* and should say so – the point is, it's nothing like disliking a neighbour or indeed anybody known in the flesh, and only ideology makes it seems so.

The barb of the accusation is that the critic attacks them 'as people' *apart from* the show and public function. This is nonsense. Neither the Republican critic nor 99.9% of Royalty's defenders know the Windsors 'as people' in that sense. How could they? Shaking the Regal hand once and exchanging the ritual few words on some Visitation counts for extremely little in this context.

An illustration may be useful here. In May 1984 the new Thames Flood Barrier at Woolwich was inaugurated. This rare and admirable example of modern public enterprise was the work of the Greater London Council, one of the big-city democratic authorities shortly to be dissolved by governmental decree. Its socialist leadership had at first wanted to stage a new, anti-official opening ceremony where representatives of the workers and ordinary Londoners would do their own honours; but this radical notion was subverted by the workers themselves. They wanted the Queen. She came. The *Times* front page next day (May 9) showed Ken Livingstone bowing to the Royal presence, his own small bald patch exposed several inches below the astounding hat chosen for the event: a lime-green dome overhung by a spray of wobbling baubles ('some form of royal bird-scarer?' conjectured the *Times* reporter). Now, there may have been all sorts of sound tactical reasons for this uneasy moment of alliance between Municipal Socialism and the Crown. But what concerns us here is Mr Livingstone's verdict: 'I have always thought' he declared within earshot of a *Times* reporter, 'that the Queen is a very nice person indeed. Today confirmed that view'.

It is no reflection on his politics or on the day itself to point out that (like the hundreds of others in similar situations each year) he had no basis whatever for this observation *in the normal sense* of the words. But the point is that here this sense does not apply. What is endorsed is the symbolic, cult-idea of Royal niceness (and of society's prostration before it as a moral talisman). As long as they don't actually undermine such rituals, Elizabeth Windsor's personal attributes are irrelevant (and of course, well-shrouded by all the disciplines of professional niceness and good background briefing).

What the theatre of Royal obsession sustains is not (real) personality, therefore, in the ordinary sense of individuality or idiosyncracy. It projects perfectly *abstract* ideas of 'personality', which are received and revered as some kind of emblem. In other words it is an abstract cult *of* the concrete - an ideology of the (supposedly) non-ideological, never stronger than when casually endorsed from the Left. There is something deeply and recognizably English about the performance. This too is not a quirk (as I will go on to argue) but a quite decipherable and rather important aspect of national identity. Though deviating from standard models of nationality, idea-impermeable Anglo-Britishness can also be seen as having made resounding historical sense in developmental terms. And we can see right away that as a belief-system it has at least one extraordinarily useful feature: it is fuelled by addiction to trivia. Hence it does not require Academies of Royalism, school indoctrination-courses, the attention of sociologists, or Ph.D. theses on ticklish points of Monarchical Philosophy. Quite the opposite: a characteristic of the Monarchic trance is automatic repulsion of inquiry from the overflowing cup of darling details and throbbing personalized emotion.

As we noticed before, within this flood rumours about non-niceness serve merely to endorse an underlying acceptability. 'It's crucial, of course (as Clancy Sigal has written) that there be some fallings-off – and not just from polo ponies: Prince Andrew's romp with Koo and others, for instance, the Duke of Edinburgh's fits of bad temper, or Princess Margaret burning the candle at both ends.' What these do is lend a touch of verisimilitude to the reigning myth so that, as Sigal puts it, 'Somehow the aura of royalty is enhanced rather than diminished by this adaptation of its mediaeval mystique to the global media'.

For the same reason true or really wounding insights into any aspect of 'what they're really like' are very rare in print.

Sigal himself has provided a remarkable one in an otherwise obsequious volume of essays published in 1986 to salute the Queen's 60th birthday.[19] This uncommon and thoughtful account is worth quoting at length:

> I remember precisely when I fell out of love with the British Royal Family and stopped having dreams of wrestling their would-be assassins to the ground in single combat in Pall Mall. One night I was sitting in an audience at the Dorchester Hotel ballroom entranced by a performance Marlene Dietrich had just given. One of the royals was sitting at a nearby table. A well known but "tired and emotional" actress wobbled shakily over to attempt a curtsy. The actress was American, and I completely understood her spontaneous attempt to pay her form of tribute to British hospitality and all the other graces that keep us here but are hard to put into words. Inadvertently the actress touched the royal presence as she nearly fell down in her effusive, inelegant bow. I will never forget how chillingly, killingly, the affronted royal personage froze that poor drunken woman with a stare that would have petrified an SAS man. That may be "Royal" behaviour but it isn't very royal.

Whether or not such incidents are rare, they are very rarely registered in this way. But another aspect of the story should be noticed. Both the well-known actress and the writer are American - one outsider afflicted by the puzzling 'graces' of a Royal culture (as well as by drink), and the other an outstandingly frank and penetrating socialist critic and novelist (whose dream-life none the less often focused on helping Royalty out of a mess). It can be doubted whether two insiders or true-born subjects would have dared – either to intrude or to describe an infringement of taboo with this degree of energy and disillusionment.

But apart from such rare moments Royalty is pretty safe. Safe, that is, once exonerated 'as people' and discovered to be very nice. The sour-faced critic is left attacking only what they 'stand for', the ritual, the accoutrements of Majesty, the mock prostration, the hangers-on, etc. However – going back to Richard Hoggart's observations – the philosophy of British daily life has a strong defence ready on precisely this point: all that is either 'not their fault' or *doesn't really matter*. It's just show, a bit of harmless colour which only prigs could find objectionable. The Republican is already standing in the classroom corner, defined as (at best) a well-intentioned crank whose wish to save the next generation's teeth means closing down the village sweet-shop. But he may also be the sort of thoroughly bad apple who's against *everything*. Either way, he can have no sense of humour.

Taboo and Idiot-theory

Now that the mystical unreality of the royal family is so firmly established, there's no political mileage to be gained from attacking the Queen's exemption from tax. How can you tax fictional characters?

> John Rentoul, 'The Royal Family: a greed example', in *The Rich Get Richer* (1987).

Delegitimated in this way, the opponent of Great Britain's Royal shroud is forced back into characteristic defensive postures. The trouble with these is that in practice they amount to little more than farther legitimations of the ruling idea. Few things reinforce belief more than an obviously weak, embarrassed and self-immolating opposition.

Conscious (for example) that the sheer dimensions of popular Royalism demand far more than grumbling about costs and snobbery, those who oppose Monarchy have found it difficult to manifest a credible counter-outrage. They tend to founder into inarticulate rage. This hatred unable to speak its name boils over internally, uselessly. Sometimes it ends in the stern and predictably futile resolve never to devote one more second's attention to Them as long as life lasts. In one defence of Monarchy by political journalist Henry Fairlie there is an amusing portrait of this familiar stance:

> I have a friend who cannot bear the sight of Princess Anne...Although he is otherwise a self-controlled person, a photograph of her, especially if she is giving that condescending little wave, or stir, which has become one of the inherited graces of the British Royal Family, moves him to a hysterical rage. I have known him spread out, on the floor in his office, every

morning newspaper which carried a picture of her...solely in
order to feed his consuming indignation. I have seen his fingers
quiver as he points at her haircut, his lips go pale as he rails at
her coat, her hat, even at her shoes. And this is a man who, from
time to time, sees fit to lecture the British people for taking the
Monarchy too seriously...[20]

Such incoherent fury is in its own way merely another tribute
to the taboo, and so to the radiance of the Crown. Trivial
carping and foaming impotence alike help to underwrite its
inevitability, its easy occupation of the public spiritual arena.
As objections, fretting about the cost of the Royal Yacht or the
exact amount of the Civil List are too trivial; yet unfocussable
rage about the whole system – the nation of meaning implicit in
the 'condescending little wave' – is bound to be too much.

Regrettably, trivial carping has been a speciality of Britain's
best-known Republican, William Hamilton, and of a few other
Parliamentary colleagues. Chapters 2 and 3 of Hamilton's
book *My Queen and I* (1975), 'The Price of Monarchy' and
'The Crown Estate, the Duchies and Other Matters' recapitu-
late his complaints about Royal extravagance over the years.
He is of course especially severe on the annual State allowances
paid out to members of the Royal Family, the Civil List. 'The
Civil List and I', a considerable chunk of these memoirs might
well be called, dealing as they do with the M.P.'s labours on the
Parliamentary Select Committee which reorganized Civil List
payments in 1971.

He laboured in vain. But the point of the dreary chronicle is
not this. It shows that the Committee's recommendations for
increases, and for a new system even less dependent on
Parliamentary control, were perfectly inevitable. His Parliamentary colleagues were either indifferent or, more often,
inclined to imitate Harold Wilson: the ex-Prime Minister
'showed himself to be a firm ally of the Tory and Royal
Establishment throughout the battle over the Royal cash...'
Public and press opinion acknowledged Hamilton's strictures
about the unseemliness of large Royal pay rises; but invariably
re-emphasized their profound Loyalty to make up for it. The
Daily Mirror ran a poll of readers and found a majority against
the new financial arrangements. *But* (its editorial went on):

This doesn't mean that *Mirror* readers want a republic: perish the thought! When they were asked their views (the same citizens) were 9 out of 10 in favour of monarchy in the United Kingdom!

In other words, while (of course) unlikely simply to approve in so many words huge new hand-outs to the Royals, they didn't really mind. The mildly pleasant, grumbling feeling that 'They could do with a bit less!' or 'Make sacrifices like the rest of us' is a part of popular Monarchism, not opposition to it. And it is absurd to think that with the right leverage it could somehow be geared up into genuine Republicanism.

Yet Hamiltonian anti-Monarchy amounts to little more than this hope against hope. While at the same time such prominent grumbling on the sounding-board of Westminster adds something valuable to the effects of the Royal orchestra - a tinny triangle, as it were, whose rattling contrast can only end by deepening the resonance of the massed string section. It is one thing to be a Republican; another to be the kind of Republican all true Monarchists love to hate.

Nor is this all. There is an uglier, more desperate fellow skulking behind such one-legged Republicanism. No amount of fulmination about the immorality and cost of the system can hide a basic truth: it is an expression of mass conservatism. Mr Hamilton's curses at his own party's supine Royalism dissolve into helplessness, since he is honest enough to admit that they can't help it. Whether 'National Character' or poisoned media are to blame (he oscillates between the two) the stubborn fact of Monarchy's popularity will not go away. But what follows from this?

The Royal taboo's implication is that disloyal opponents are not just a minority but (almost) a minority of alien beings. Under the electoral machinery to which Hamilton owes his own public position (and which he never criticizes) such minorities can find almost no expression. And it is, unfortunately, a short step from being an oppressed minority to feeling like an *élite*. Popular conservatism begins to look like self-evident stupidity. The minority by contrast shines with the light of an equally self-evident superiority. The diaphanous line is crossed between being a minority that actually knows better (an uncomfortable but hardly disastrous plight inseparable from most of history so far) and *élitism* – the sad, sinking conviction that 'human nature' may have a hand in the matter, and that the majority may be irredeemable. Then it seems to follow that the knowing few are history's sole justification and salt: what better proof of such a dismal point than Mass Monarchical silliness?

It should be noted also that media-conspiracy is really only a sub-clause to this kind of warped theory. Either they're idiots, or (more palatably) they are being made into idiots by evil forces. Stupidity is manufactured by media barons and the Establishment in the interests (respectively) of making money and conserving privilege. But – without denying for a moment that Monarchy is Fleet Street's golden egg, or that something important is conserved by the Royal ideology – as 'explanation' this is hopeless. For what can it be that has made the majority so vulnerable to this kind of exploitation? It is circular non-explanation to blame it all on poor education and exposure to garbage. No doubt if schools were better and the present generation had inherited less ideological nonsense it would be more discerning; but this is only truism. The assumption continues to be that the mass is a passive, wholly manipulable entity: not just plain idiots but fooled (or poisoned) into idiocy or (another favourite) 'mindlessness'.

Yet the awkward fact which pseudo-Republicanism tries to exorcize with this kind of bad faith is of course that popular Royalism is visibly *not* passive and mindless. It has something highly positive about it – an apparently inexhaustible electric charge. This is what makes media and Régime exploitation so easy and effective (and opposition feel so hopeless). People enjoy the Monarchical twaddle, and show very little sign of being robotized or 'brain-washed'. They relish the weird mixture of cheap fun, exalted moments and great spectacles, and come back for more. Whatever it all means, that meaning is sustained and (apparently) continually refreshed by a genuine, positive will more significant than any amount of peevish grousing about cost.

The only idiotic factor in this landscape is, in fact, idiot-theory itself. Republicans are edged into such an absurd cul-de-sac because there is no effective space for them in the public arena – no respectable or dignified corner to be occupied and held. There is no serious Republican campaign or movement, no Republican press, and no recognized or avowable anti-Monarchic stance in everyday argument and debate. It is this climatic fact that defines Republicanism from its first syllable as posture and wilful eccentricity. The would-be Republican's words are frozen into absurd shapes in this air, and he or she can only retreat inwards - to the equally familiar closet-stance of: 'Well, *personally* speaking I've no time for it'. Some private dignity is apparently saved in this way. But what's the cost? The Republic – *res publica*, which ought to be the essence of the public or common thing – has been magically converted into a defiant form of eccentricity.

Yet even this is but the penultimate humiliation. Republicanism's *via dolorosa* is then completed by another interesting facet of the Royal culture: the comfortable place which it has traditionally awarded to eccentricity. The 'determined Republican' is not even allowed pariah-status: rather, he finds himself classed alongside dotty squires, mad professors and believers in ley-lines. Can his belief really be the great political philosophy of Antiquity, revived by Machiavelli, embraced by John Milton and died for by Commonwealth-men, then carried forward into the revolutions of modernity? Yes, alas: but somehow a Monarchic culture's combination of the romantic and the 'empirical' has reduced this noble inheritance to the equivalent of food-faddism or an obsession with steam trains. The 'ordinary' of a Royal culture and poetry has as complement the extraordinary or numinous - a glamour into which the dank or mundane is uplifted and by which it is justified. Outside this dialectic there can only be the sideshow of eccentricity: an endearing limbo of bees in the bonnet and notions rendered quaintly palatable by their irrelevance.

Once entered, such a definition is then virtually impossible to escape from. Defenders of the Régime can point all too easily to a certain pathological and wilful aspect, uncomfortably like a wish to be different 'for the sake of it'. And in the ambient circumstances of Great Britain that wish *is* difficult to avoid. Opposition is frog-marched into hopeless élitism and left there to rot. Republicans, in short, are intellectual wretches unable to satisfy themselves within the liveried womb of their mother State; but powerless, fortunately, to summon the midwife who would have us all out in the cold.

Royalty and Civilization:
the Mystery Deepens

Public opinion, the last resort of all English public life, is largely formed by English society, whose acknowledged head is the King. Any social group or individual whom the King distinguishes with his notice receives thereby a *cachet* that disarms all criticism in the country of snobbery.'

Wihelm Dibelius, *England* (1922).

Those who have not studied the tragic evidence accumulated (often unwittingly) in *My Queen and I* may still think the situation less stark than I have depicted it. Is it really unthinkable that some energetic reforming administration should one day decide to legislate the Crown away and pension off the Windsors?

But here too the press may come to our rescue. From a century or so of possible examples, take the response of the *Times* newspaper to a fairly recent Royal incident. On March 20 1974 the Queen's daughter Anne attended an equestrian charity function with her husband Captain Mark Phillips. On the way home their car was held up in the Mall by an armed man. He intended kidnapping the Princess, but succeeded only in wounding an accompanying detective and the chauffeur, as well as a policeman and a journalist who tried to intervene. The Lord Chief Justice of England later found him to be mentally ill and ordered his permanent detention.

This was the most serious of modern physical assaults on the Royal Family. There have been others (all involving deranged individuals) but none so squalid and frightening, or so potentially lethal. So a certain amount of outrage was in order next day. Before routine suspicions arise about the popular press, however, it should be said that the *Sun* and *Mirror* were definitively outclassed by that old megaphone of élite authority, the *Times*. As if numbed by the event, the Fleet Street populars managed only rather sub-standard shock-scandal front pages and leaders on the 21st of March. At Printing House Square by contrast the Editor (then Sir William Rees-Mogg) had seen and leapt avidly upon the national, and indeed cosmic, significance of the shootings.

His Editorial led with a straight right: 'The Crown is the symbol of the nation and of the standards which Britain has lived by.' The previous day's attack, therefore, was not on two individuals - however special – but on 'the idea of Britain'. That is, on symbols of 'order and grace', later amplified by the text into 'a whole world of tranquillity and decency' comparable to a Vermeer painting (it so happened that a Vermeer picture had just been stolen from the Greenwich Museum). Who could do such a thing? Easy: 'There are people about who hate civilization because it exists, the enemies *of the inner spiritual essence of our national life*' (my emphasis). More is aimed at here than the crazed person responsible, obviously. 'They hate us very much', went on the Editorialist, 'but most of all they hate anything good about us', so of course 'they' think first of smiting the symbol of everything good about us, the Monarchy. All the more so because they are active elsewhere too, in lands less well endowed with order and grace. 'The vanguard of anarchy is indeed at loose in the world...' transforming (in this case) an incident of mania into 'a sign of civilization in regression, turning back from achievement to a neobarbarism'.

To attack the symbol is to attack 'decency': no word is more redolent of this England ordered from above, not by bureaucracy but through the operations of the national spirit-essence. Decency is conveyed in the usual Orwellian fashion, as a superior island way of arranging things *not* involving guns, clubs, sadists and fanatical theories. Hence the significance of the Mall incident: a sign that 'violence' no longer begins at Calais, that we have grown less immune from 'their' social arrangements.

In case any readers should think such notions peculiar to Rees-Mogg, or only at home in an old-style *Times* sermon, it should be pointed out this is not so: all the evidence indicates that they are very widely held. Nearly twelve years after the Mall incident I took part in a live-audience broadcast about Royalty where most of the public expressed exactly the same views in less florid terms. The records of the 'phone-in' accompanying transmission list remarks like: 'We need someone to look up to', 'Queen is First Lady of the world', 'Royal Family represents majority in this country – hooligans represent the minority', 'Royal Family is what keeps us all together',

'They stand for everything decent about this country', and 'Royal Family conduct themselves in a civilized manner - unlike people on this programme'.[21]

Breathless after so many twists of his spiritual knife, the *Times* leader-writer then subsided into a paragraph of humdrum condolences with those injured in the Mall. A measure of exhaustion at the paper was quite understandable just then. The agèd organ had had to swallow a successful miners' strike, and then the fall of Heath's Conservative government at the general election in February. But making every allowance for this, its reaction remains astonishing, and revealing.

Suppose that by misfortune the Royal couple had been shot, or even shot dead. Would this really have signified the imminent triumph of a new barbarism? They are – in the article's own terms - 'a symbol' of British national decency, not this quality in person. Can our 'inner spiritual essence' now be so vulnerable that removal of an emblem is liable to crush it? Queen Elizabeth's Royal Family is a large and rapidly-growing greenhouse of symbolic personages: however regrettable or appalling in its details, the loss of one or two (a common occurrence in all past dynasties) would surely mean something less than national spiritual catastrophe? Particularly when the assailant was a quite unpolitical lunatic dazzled (as in some other similar cases) mainly by the Royal public-relations glamour which the national media project so incessantly?

Such obvious considerations were beside the point. The spiritual point of the outburst was precisely that our inner essence *is* somehow over-invested in symbols like Princess Anne and her husband. They actually have become national decency (or, looked at another way, our decent nationalism) 'in person'. This is the only reason why the outrage could be presented in such an amazing fashion – amazing but (one must assume) quite plausible to most *Times*-readers. With only slight re-translation that morning's message read: True Civilization is Great Britain; the pure and consummate expression of that Nation is its Monarchy; hence an attack on the latter is a Devilish insult to Civilization as such. Let *this* symbol be destroyed, and nothing anywhere will be safe.

We learn something of the content of the symbolism, at the same time. However preposterous, the reference to Vermeer underlines the *gentility* of 'grace and order'. The Old Master's calm splendour is travestied into what one can only call call 'niceness': the finely contrived, tranquil decorum of a Royal visitation, taken as a master-image of social and moral order. In all such performances human nature emerges as perfectly tamed and regulated, spontaneous motions being limited to such tiny delightful details – a laugh or a frown, a child's confusion, a dropped bouquet, sudden rain – as serve to confirm underlying reality (and so graft on the symbolic meaning more securely).

A tangible dose of old-fashioned religious Grace is lurking somewhere in this vision. Also prominent in the *Times*'s sermon is a degree of *resonant abstraction* absent from the frolics so loved by the *Sun* and other front pages. For Top People, clearly, the Monarch *is* an 'institution' - close indeed to being *the* institution when questions of soul and national essence arise. Under threat, it is not just the individuals but what they *mean* that counts: the abstract, sacred thing somewhere in the background. It is a matter of everyday observation how often such attitudes crop up in middle-class conversations. Rarely with the pompous extremism of the *Times*, admittedly, but this was a limiting and defining example corresponding to a supposedly extreme peril.

Now - returning to the question posed earlier - it is, surely, extremely difficult to imagine any government legislating away *this*. Within the existing consensual system - the old Constitution supported by nearly all Westminster parties - can one really conceive of the head one day calmly ordering such a heart-transplant? Some Labour Premier deciding, after much Committee work and intensive Cabinet deliberation, upon new arrangements for the national spirit-essence and Civilization as such?

In fact, attacks upon the British Crown arouse what one might call identity-rage: the everyday taboo generates an instant and furious counter-attack. The point seems to be that the National Soul is threatened. Whatever this sacred abstraction is, we are supposed to live by it. They (the Royals) are not just nice; they represent and embody Niceness. The latter quality is our special, inherited capacity for civilized conduct – our moral identity so to speak. Without this heart we would sink down into the heartless, modern world alongside everybody else. Another prominent aspect of instant popular reaction to criticism of Royalty (like the phone-in I mentioned before) is normally the implied awfulness of elsewhere: the Queen 'saves us from dictatorship', 'It's better than a President, and costs less', 'Would these disgusting critics prefer General Franco or Juan Carlos?', 'Would they prefer Reagan or Gorbachev as Head of State?' There was one caller who wanted to stress that the Windsors are descended from the Pharaohs of Ancient Egypt; but the other who claimed that only a studio full of 'foreigners' would denigrate Monarchy was closer to the popular sentiment.

Respectable and Popular Monarchy

Royalty can't, like the politician or industrialist, be blamed for their rôle in society; and our acceptance of *their* place tends to carry with it an acceptance of our own.

Judith Williamson, 'Royalty and Representation',
in *Consuming Passion* (1986).

Sometimes would-be Republicans have been tempted into taking comfort from the robustness and irreverence of popular or working-class views (apparently not too different from their image of pop-music or other stars). Such comfort is misplaced. There is nothing surprising about these striking varieties of attitude, in a society still so markedly divided in so many other ways. On the contrary, the single and vital unifying ideology of British Royalism *must* be able to offer itself in suitably varying modes to its believers. Historically, great religions have always acknowledged this necessity: there has always been (to take an obvious example) a Catholicism of the intellectuals and another, simpler version for the poor or the illiterate. Vulgar superstitions may subvert the authority of learned superstitions, but not the régime of superstition itself. Such distinctions testify to the power of an ideology, not to its weakness or mutability. If the lower orders were *not* able to see what they want in the dominant symbol, then the Crown might become dangerously distant: solely a matter for 'Them' to bother with. In which case, one might as well be without it.

British Monarchism is therefore a common language spoken in widely differing dialects. But such dialects cannot be equal. Though a romanticism of the Left sometimes pretends otherwise, these various idioms derive their present-day sense from a common culture.

> Culture is no longer merely the adornment, confirmation and legitimation of a social order which was also sustained by harsher and coercive constraints; culture is now the necessary shared medium, the life-blood or perhaps rather the minimal shared atmosphere, within which alone the members of the society can breathe and survive and produce. For a given society, it must be one in which they can *all* breathe and speak and produce; so it must be the same culture...[22]

Inside such a culture there has to be a variety of sub-cultures and counterposed forms, but these are also joined up (often in tacit or less than obvious ways) by a degree of structural unity. *One* mode has to dominate, at least where any clash occurs, or where some kind of crisis forces a stronger assertion of identity.

Just as in spoken English the *Times*-BBC-Home County 'dialect' constitutes the official or commanding idiom so, with the Royal cult, it is the respectable version which really defines the true aim and form of worship. This may be clearer if one remembers that there are more than two dialects. As well as the middle-class and working-class idioms we've looked at, subgroups within or even outside these are allowed their own tongues. In his chronicle of the contemporary underworld Laurie Taylor has shown for instance how criminals (generally very loyal) have a distinct perspective on Monarchy. They regard them as the supreme rip-off artists currently at work. One of his confidants remarked:

> Look at the Royal Family....It's marvellous they way they kid people. Honestly, it's incredible. I watched the Duke of Edinburgh the other night talking about the Royal Yacht. Fucking *yacht*. Fucking *yacht*. It's an ocean-going liner...

This is an ideology which clearly reflects the speaker's relations of production. The Royals are not merely 'doing a good job' but putting one over on the humdrums or 'wallies' (i.e. everyone in between crooks and the real upper crust) –

> Honestly, this country is run by some of the most clever sophisticated heads that it's possible to have. And what's so incredible is that very few people tumble. They just don't know...

What they don't know is that the Queen and her lot are on the game, getting away with it on a gargantuan scale, *and* being loved for it. What style! This view too is one ingredient of the Royal U.K.'s 'minimal shared atmosphere'. Its element of disrespect doesn't contradict the latter; on the contrary – in its own way it adds to the mainstream of atmospheric nourishment.

What is at issue here is a focal point of British culture, worth insisting upon. We're concerned with Royalty, one of the obsessive strains in that culture; but this obsession has a remarkably direct structural link to the second universally acknowledged fixation of our 'necessary shared medium' – 'class'. Monarchy may be relayed to a British mass audience through an endless strip-cartoon of jokes, scandals, smut and *Schmalz*, from which 'the idea of Britain' seems remote. But in fact - though both are necessary – the former depends logically upon the latter and it is the latter's triangulation-points which compose the overall map: that is, the structure of *authority* which defines other speech, conduct and people as (for example) merely those of a class or region.

Such authority is often dismissed by philistines as simply that of verbal inflection, manners, or customs – 'social history' in a trivial and unpolitical sense. But this is only the glum union of bourgeois common sense and scorbutic Marxism that weighs so heavily upon British culture's theoretic dimension. In fact, 'manners' embody (rather than 'reflect' in an erroneous mirror analogy) the deeper structures of a society and State. All societies and States rely on such social customs and concrete verbal and body languages in reproducing themselves; but it is not just this truism which is at stake here. What the extraordinary ideal prominence of Monarchy suggests is, surely, a social formation in which such concrete features play a bigger than usual rôle in these processes of transmission and cohesion.

Cultural disparities at once maintain and conceal or bind up real disparities within society. The point here is their functional ambiguity: in the Anglo-British case we find especially prominent, parochial divisions of the class-structure whose ostentatious and stultifying birth-marks *at the same time* serve to confirm an equally prominent over-arching unity - the inherited, transcendent, and non-ethnic culture of the Crown. The variety of the former serve also to emphasize the unified grandeur of the latter. The glamour of Royalty and the neurosis of 'class' are the two sides of the single coin of British backwardness. The successive and futile formulae of modernization proposed by British governments since 1945 have aimed at a more 'classless' and homogeneous nation-state. But were this realized, the miraculous oneness of the traditional Royal identity would be sharply diminished: there would be more, and more open, conflict, not less. Unity would still be needed – naturally – and a Monarchical (rather than a Presidential) symbol might still be preferred under such conditions, as in some other European countries. But that's not what we're discussing. The issue here is the *miracle* of the Old Royal Régime: obsessive Monarchism and its social roots in the inherited nature of the British economy and British Statehood.

Queenspeak

All speech is a form of customary behaviour, but, likewise, all customary behaviour is a form of speech.

Edmund Leach, 'Ritual', in
Encyclopedia of the Social Sciences (1968).

'I heard this *voice* asking for stamps in the next queue at Notting Hill post office', a friend once told me, 'and wondered for a second if I was dreaming'. But it wasn't the Queen, only a mutual acquaintance famed for the numinous purity of her Home-County intonation. My friend had heard the voice of a class, and of upper-England, resounding with such confident loudness that her imagination was irresistibly carried to the main practitioner of our Received Pronunciation.

In a celebrated – though really very mild – attack on the Monarchy a quarter of a century previously, John Grigg had written: 'The personality conveyed by the utterances which are put into her mouth is that of a priggish schoolgirl, captain of the hockey team, a prefect and a recent candidate for confirmation'. His gentle strictures on the Crown amounted to no more than a suggested modernization of the Royal Household and personnel, away from a monopoly of 'the tweedy sort' and towards more recognizable or ordinary beings. Yet this incautious remark on Queenly pronunciation has somehow stuck in common remembrance, long outlasting other details of the scandalous episode.[23]

Intentionally or not, Lord Altrincham (as Grigg then was) had struck into the quick. The Royal diction does indeed convey an authority, a national world of meaning in which the sporting spirit, a certain style of education, prefectorial charisma and echoes from an Established Church all play their parts. And it does so independently of content: Grigg was mistaken in imputing the fault to whatever had been written down for the Queen to utter - thus transferring blame in familiar fashion to 'them', speech-writers or advisers. 'Like her mother (he went on) she appears to be unable to string even a few sentences together without a written text'. But in fact it was the utterance itself which mattered, more than what was written: the quick of pronunciation, and its instant command of the listener's cultural reflexes.

What such immediate entry and spiritual obedience reflect is an informal yet very powerful authority-structure. Informal because manifested in 'pronunciation', in the symbolic mode of person-to-person rather than through a written discourse; powerful because removed by this very modality from the formal or abstract rationality – and hence the potential critique - which the mere content of any written text would be likely to invite. The 'person-to-person' mode does not of course have to be literally that nowadays: modern media can put one voice or manner face-to-face with millions.

As with many other aspects of contemporary Monarchy, it was the reign of George V which saw the first significant steps towards this *rapprochement* with subjects. In 1925 an estimated audience of 10 million heard him open the Empire Exhibition at Wembley. Seven years later the BBC's Director-General John Reith got a Christmas address out of the King after long and patient manoeuverings, and recorded in his diary for December 25 1932:

> After lunch we listened to the Empire broadcast, which was most impressive and excellent. The King was evidently quite moved and spoke more personally and effectively than I had ever heard him...[24]

The text was composed by Rudyard Kipling, and spoken in what A.C.Benson called the King's 'odd, hoarse voice, as if roughened by weather'. In spite of the event's success it did not automatically become the institution so many people now recall. George himself was unwilling to repeat the experience, and fears were expressed then (as on all comparable occasions) that greater familiarity might breed contempt. It was only when a Minister in Macdonald's National Government, the working-class J.H.Thomas, showed him the appreciative letters which had come in from all over his Empire that he agreed to continue.

A few years later Reith visited Macdonald's successor as Prime Minister, Stanley Baldwin, and noted in his diary (*à propos* King George's terminal illness) –

> 18 January 1936...Worried about the King dying as things were so critical. Agreed that kingship never stood higher in this country and that broadcasting had a lot to do with this – that, as I said, it had brought the solicitude of fatherhood in where before was the aloof dignity of the throne.

Thus was the Royal voice and pronunciation literally brought home to the people. It is also relevant to remember something of the context, in the shape of Reith's BBC. The massive emotional impact of the nation's rough fatherly voice is tellingly contrasted by one American historian with the fact that, during this era when 'things were so critical'-

> ...The kind of free-wheeling political coverage practised by the American networks was impossible in Britain. The BBC

charter was a careful compromise among major parties designed to keep radio out of politics. It guaranteed that while the BBC would not become the mouthpiece of a particular government, it would remain the creature, albeit thinly insulated, of government. To be sure, an independent Board of Governors made day-to-day policy and hired a director to carry it out. But as was typical of all mass media in Britain, those in charge were so close to the Establishment that direct censorship was rarely necessary: they censored themselves.[25]

Defending himself against the tidal wave of recriminations in a subsequent issue of his *National and English Review*, John Grigg pointed out he hadn't meant to discuss Queen Elizabeth's voice in a merely personal sense. It was her *'style of speaking'* he had objected to, or the 'synthetic character which her speech-writers are trying to create' (as distinct from her actual, or idiosyncratic character). He was trying to put his finger on an elusive yet crucial distinction here. The Monarch's 'real character' must of course lend itself to the synthetic or class character thus projected. Nor is there anything surprising about this, in a 'county and horsy' aristocrat who likes defleaing corgis and ('were it not for my Archbishop of Canterbury') would be off to Longchamps every Sunday to be herself with bloodstock horses.[26] Yet in the fusion of personal and hieratic which her speech must attain, only the class character truly counts: the language of 'insulated' (or defactionalized) authority, and of a pure parental solicitude refracted from above into minds pre-tuned to a personal communication rather than a message from the State.

'Language' in this context means a lot more than words, or modes of speech: it means something like 'culture' in the sense made famous by Raymond Williams' *Culture and Society*. So what cultural-linguistic presuppositions have given Royal-speak its devastating efficacy? The important one, surely, is that there is no other social formation known to history in which *speech-accent* occupies such a crucial and regulative function: it is by this mechanism that osmosis of the Royal can so easily take place into the humblest and least conscious parts of the body social. In the most recent general survey of British-Isles English A.C. Gimson writes –

It is a remarkable fact that, for at least four centuries, the English have cultivated a concept of a form of pronunciation which has been considered more correct, desirable, acceptable or elegant than others...(the idea that) in fact that standard already exists, and is the norm unconsciously followed by persons who, by rank or education, have most right to establish the custom of speech...[27]

He is quoting from a previous authority of 1869 here, A.J.Ellis. Ellis was worried because he thought the lower orders would just never have the chance to acquire the speech of 'the metropolis, of the court, the pulpit and the bar'. 'Real communication between class and class is all but impossible', he ended gloomily.

But as Gimson says, this was much too pessimistic. No revolution was needed; decently-timed reform has diffused the transcendental speech-essence downwards quite well enough to keep things going. Not everyone can learn to speak like the Queen, true. But then not everyone needs to. Nowadays a wonderful vitality is commonly discerned in Britain's subordinate and regional accents, like the 'wonderful sense of rhythm' once detected among black musicians. While two contemporary Prime Ministers, Edward Heath and Margaret Thatcher, have been equally wonderful specimens of painfully-learnt 'R.P.' (Received Pronunciation).

No other nation has been crucified to such a degree by codes of pronunciation. Observers (and the victims themselves) often speak quite properly of a 'national obsession' with 'correct' ways of talking and modes of address. The implication is never far away that correct speech leads into correct conduct, character, and style of existence – manner of pronunciation is (or is the best guide to) manner of life, general level of civilization and culture. In other words, pronunciation leads straight into the spiritual structure, the very soul of Regal-British society: 'class'. What the term denotes is not *lumpen* stratification, the beloved categories of philistinism, but the style and embodied assumptions of authority – of a live and heeded hegemony. Royal 'class' is of course hierarchical in essence: it can only be constituted from above, by a moral-spiritual (or in today's terms, an 'ideological') authority whose indispensable locus is the Crown.

'Correct' partly overlaps with 'educated', but this over-printing leaves out one all-important and English distinction: the vital thread of Royalty, neglected at one's social peril. The 'correct' is (or at any rate ought also to be) the *natural*. For those not born to such a nature, then the acquired culture ought at least to *seem* natural. The whole point of an irrefutable, central model has to be its naturalness (or as Ellis put it, its *unconscious* character) - the fact that some people just do possess the mode and what it entails without fuss or effort. Others can approximate to this via education, and doubtless all who wish not to be categorized as boors or rustics ought to do so; but (as with Mr Heath and Mrs Thatcher) the approximation will just never be the same thing.

Under the inescapable title of 'The Queen's English Society' there exists an Association whose aim is to consecrate and intensify speech-obsession. It engages in both guerrilla and strategic warfare against what is regarded as the rising tide of dialect and populist laxity, and its pundits, like Professor John Honey of Leicester Polytechnic, accuse both liberal and regional educationists of treason against 'Received Pronunciation', which they like to describe as the standard speech of 'the South-East of England'. This label gives the speeches at annual meetings of the Q.E.S. a harmless, rational air. After all, other tongues too have standardized forms taught in schools, and as a rule these derive historically from one or another dominant region (e.g. the standard form in Italy is known as 'Tuscan' Italian). We saw earlier how a recognized 'high culture' seems to be a prerequisite of modern nation-state existence, and literacy in this sense implies a common tongue to be literate in. So, what can really be so pernicious about a practical necessity - especially when (as in one of Professor Honey's recent addresses) supported by harrowing vignettes of Third World peasants, foreign scientists and air-traffic controllers all avoiding disaster thanks to the clarity of their 'R.P.'?[28]

What this argument does is conflate together two distinct (though usually closely related) things. As Gellner notes, modern nations do have to have a high-cultural language in the sense entailed by 'literacy', where the primary reference-point is writing and reading: there can be no modernity without the possession of such a minimal vehicle. What they mercifully do *not* require is the kind of face-to-face spoken version of that vehicle which is supplied by Southern-English Received Pronunciation. Here the full reality of Royal English precisely replicates the inwardness of its State and the genetic code of its history: an antique caste for long enabled by a combination of fortune and blind fidelity to its own origins to draw a fresh life from the circumstances of modernity. Thus what the contemporary Anglo-British idiom really does is to fuse literacy with aristocracy: a democratic need is at once fulfilled and nullified by the generalization of a form of class speech. Mass culture advances not on to the neutral terrain of a merely national language but into the constraining country-house garden of a tongue. It is both advanced and neutered by the already institutionalized and consecrated speech-acts of an élite.

According to Professor Peter Trudgill of Reading University 'Queen's English' is the natural speech-mode of about 3% of the United Kingdom population and its most significant practitioner is without doubt Queen Elizabeth II herself. It's also quite true that many of that 3% like to chuckle in private over the Royal way with English. What they discern is a prim over-definition of accent, a lack of proper casualness and freedom in the Windsor diction separating it inexorably from the *real* real thing. This can also be snidely pictured as another of Anthea Hall's 'dour Germanic remains' in a dynasty which (after all) hastily switched from 'Saxe-Coburg-Gotha' to 'Windsor' in 1917. But this is probably unjust: the more stilted features of Queenly diction represent merely an imperfect suture of personal and class articulation (also heard in her father's public addresses, thanks to the famous hypnotic stammer). And in any case such niggling criticism counts for little: 'R.P.' remains an undifferentiated whole for the other 97% oblivious to these in-group nuances.

Now, while Queen Elizabeth and many co-articulators do dwell mainly in 'the South-East' what they utter is hardly formed by this geographical fact alone. It is more accurately described as the slurred, allusive, nasal cawing of the English gentry. Great Britain's accepted tongue is the ultra-distilled by-product of drawing-room, shoot and London club, a faded aristocratic *patois* remarkable for its anorexic vowels and vaporized consonants. It is social geography that links this vernacular to the London-Oxford-Cambridge triangle; while the social power of the same locality which has turned it into the inevitable emblem of authority, acceptance, literacy and nationality.

'But' (watch-dogs will object at once) 'that's just the way people *speak*'. If a measure of snobbery or status attaches to it, is not all human nature prone to such ills? An ineffaceable class idiom may have captured the national tongue, so that the Home Counties are at home nowhere and everywhere. Can this stratum-mark left by history itself really be so important, given the practical needs served by today's 'World English'? Professor Honey's Japanese air-traffic controllers and Third World village folk no doubt have their own ways of coping with Received Pronunciation; in everyone's interest they would be well advised to apply themselves to American, or Russian. The more general question begged by apologists of Queenly English is the social status of speech as a part of language. The latter's complexity allows a differentiation between the abstract vehicle of literacy and its habitual, concrete mode of actualization - the *parole* or exemplification where society is made flesh, gesture and inflection, and where 'a world of meaning' may therefore be projected in a single look or intonation.

That's the point: a Monarchic Constitution and a Crown-obsessed society dwell in the *parole* rather than in a mere vehicle of literacy – in the State Coach rather than in a vulgar omnibus of modernity. We also noticed how such differences *both* assert and contain class-distinction –- for all its fun and raucousness, underling loyalty is inherently subordinate to the other kind. The semantics and phonetics of Queen's English are only another way of representing that broader speech-class configuration. And the essence of the latter is precisely homologous with what Ralph Miliband pin-pointed in his discussion of British Parliamentarism in *Capitalist Democracy in Britain*. Through it the governing élite both admits popular voice and – by the very mode of admission – reduces it to a beseeching murmur: 'The point is....to give adequate and meaningful scope to popular participation; but to "depopularize" policy-making and to limit strictly the impact of the market-place upon the conduct of affairs. Parliamentarism makes this possible: for it simultaneously enshrines the principle of popular inclusion *and* that of popular exclusion...'²⁹

As I will try to show later, the homology is more extensive than this. 'Speech' or the style of command are the nerve of 'class'; 'class' is the nerve of an 'Unwritten Constitution' where power is wielded through Majestically-descended 'conventions'; and the complex of these customs compose a traditional moral identity which is the framework of British nationalism. Miliband analysed that framework as a legitimation of 'capitalism'; but what the Royal cast of national identity really projects is something both more limited and more archaic than this broad term - a specifically early (though very resistant) form of political economy which, unable to countenance political modernization, has found it easier and more appropriate to reanimate the past.

Hegemony via such reanimation is the success-story of the 'Modern British Politics' justified in a thousand lugubrious text-books. Soon after the *National and English Review* storm, Sir Harold Nicolson detected signs of improvement in the Royal articulation: 'She came across quite clear and with a vigour unknown in pre-Altrincham days'. Also, she was now on television as well as radio. Of the various presentation-styles suggested by the BBC (reading from a script, an 'eavesdropping' image of her speaking to a microphone, etc.) the Queen herself selected 'face-to-camera delivery of a memorized speech, set in her own home'. Robert Lacey's *Majesty* continues:

> Since the quality of television recordings was so poor in the days before videotape, however, she had to broadcast live, and eat her Christmas lunch with the prospect of appearing at three o'clock before a wider audience than she had ever previously addressed. Her smile of relief to her husband when she did not realize the cameras were still focused on her at the end was worth a thousand articles on "The Monarchy"...³⁰

Since those days the Royal Christmas broadcast has broadened out from one voice to a familial symphony, under the guidance of *Royal Family* Cawston. Sometimes the whole family appears in it, behaving as if cameras were not focused on them and conveying the sublime ordinariness of an 'R.P.' deployed on babies and Christmas-tree decoration. From the intimacy of their own homes, subjects are transported for a few moments into the nation's principal stately home and find ordinary smiles and gestures there. Thus those like Tony Harrison's father, whom England has so consistently and by its inwardly Royal nature 'made to feel like some dull oaf', again discover all the redeeming signs of a traditional community beyond – and far stronger than – all the resentments of 'class'.[31]

The Royal Touch

What created faith in the miracle was the idea that there should be a miracle. It was this idea too which allowed it to survive... As for the cases, numerous enough by all accounts, in which the Evil resisted the touch of these august fingers, they were soon forgotten. Such is the happy optimism of believing souls.

Marc Bloch, *Les rois Thaumaturges* (1924) p.429.

In the mediaeval times which have not quite vanished either from the world or Great Britain, Monarchs claimed and kept possession of their realms like the most powerful of the beasts. This was the reality of the lion or the eagle who now glare and spit only as heraldic symbols. The King or Queen took possession of the territory through the prostration of all its inhabitants, at the Coronation. Then, armed with the thunder-bolts of life and death, he or she constantly reaffirmed Royal authority: 'Making appearances, conferring honours, exchanging gifts or defying rivals, they marked the countryside like some wolf or tiger spreading its scent through his territory, as almost physically part of them...'[32]

These Royal Progresses were accompanied by much popular fun and ingenious displays and contrivances, as well as by obeisances and the savage punishment of transgressors. The 1559 Coronation Procession of Queen Elizabeth I, for example, as well as the later ones to Coventry, Oxford, and Bristol: all were marked by tableaux and festivities putting the pallid ceremonials of her Windsor successors to shame.

After passing through Cheapside and the painted likenesses of all her Royal predecessors arranged in chronological order, and receiving two thousand gold marks from the City dignitaries, the Virgin Queen discovered in Little Conduit two artificial mountains, one cragged, barren and stony representing 'a decayed commonweal', and the other fair, fresh and green standing for 'a flourishing commonweal'. On the former stood a dead tree with a tramp slumping disconsolately beneath it; on the latter 'a well-appointed man standing happily', while between the hills was a small cave, out of which a man representing Father Time, complete with scythe, emerged (accompanied by his daughter Truth) to present to the new Queen an English Bible. Elizabeth took the Bible, kissed it and 'raising it first above her head, pressed it dramatically to her breast...'

At Bristol some years later, the Royal coming was signalled by a three-day mock siege on Avonside, where the armies of Dissension stormed a specially constructed fort called 'Feeble Policy'. The fort was saved by Royal intervention at the last minute, just when all seemed lost. One of the players swam the river bearing 'a book covered with green velvet' to plead for the Sovereign's aid (and explain to her exactly what was going on). Clowns, allegories, mock battles, gilt dragons, prancing nymphs and (in the background) executioners all underlined the willing servitude of province or town, and deepened the claw-marks of the Crown.

Executions in the name of the Crown have been suspended for some time now in Britain, though Her Majesty's Parliament might well restore them one day. The rest is still with us, etiolated in content but projected far more powerfully as a formal image. What modern public Progresses lack in folk-colour and baroque spontaneity they have gained in overall organization and – above all - diffusion to crowds far vaster than those piled into Renaissance alleys and market-squares. Since this sort of Royal ceremonial came of age with Queen Victoria's Golden Jubilee in 1887, it has undergone a century of regular development. The sense of reverential continuity has been part-revived and part-created since the 1870s. Timeless spectacles do require some real traditions, of course and nobody will deny that post-1688 British history has these to offer. But what the pageantry version does is elevate them into the throat-catching 'Thousand Years' of Orb and Sceptre, in order to stabilize and sweeten the present and define a people into its future.

Another feature of ancestral times was belief in the Royal Touch. Through the Monarch's fingers as they brushed against certain scabs or inflammations, a magical electric charge was thought to flow and bring healing. The faith survived – or half-survived - until the early 18th century, the last Monarch to attempt a Royal Touch being Queen Anne (who touched amongst others the youthful Samuel Johnson). Before this, the last great crescendo of Monarchic therapy had been that staged by Charles II immediately after his Restoration in 1660. It reflected 'the efforts of the Stuart dynasty to consolidate itself after the upheavals of the Interregnum', when there was a republican menace to be dealt with. Like William Shakespeare's History Plays, such quasi-medical assiduity was meant to shore up smashed traditions and a communal sensibility fractured by civil warfare and religious strife. A few days after Charles's disembarkation, six hundred were touched in a single gargantuan session. Although enthusiasm sagged after a few years, it returned in the darker days towards the close of his reign. In only eleven months in 1682 and 1683 eight thousand, five hundred and seventy-seven entries were made in the Royal 'Register of Healing'. Although (as a cynic of our own day remarks), 'swelled by patients returning for a second time', these numbers were remarkable enough to make one addict declare Charles had in his day 'touched near half the nation'.[33]

Noone today thinks Queen Elizabeth II can cure any particular ailment by laying on hands. However, she does regularly touch far more than half her nation, by more sublimated and ethereal means. Talking of the 1977 Jubilee celebrations, Philip Ziegler commented on how — 'As she walked through the crowds, their hands stretched out to her as if she were a mediaeval monarch whose touch could cure...'[34] A certain pervasive 'healing' (or at least mildly uplifting) power is more widely acknowledged and loved than in the past. Belief in individual therapy has become acceptance of a kind of *social* beneficence, an almost daily blessing of existing institutions and customs.

But there is another significant difference. Today, the mass of patients is not deceived. They return incessantly for more, not because previous contacts failed but because they, in some sense, succeeded and provided what was wanted. Somehow, visitation and touch do seem to bind society's fabric reassuringly together. They refurbish certain cohesive elements, a common identity which – since the majority still accept and cling to it - is also a personal matter.

Another important contrast is in the attitude to the past entailed by such visitations. Though of course 'traditional' in character, it is not the case that the community-feeling aimed at is against change or progress as such. It is not (as so many scandalized critics have thought) merely an appeal to about-turn and live wholly in the sentimentalized past. The synthetic traditionalism of Windsordom was not (and could not possibly have been) invented for that purpose alone. In truth, the aim is a curious and nationally specific 'modernization' consonant with the national identity which Royalism sustains. I will say more about this later; but it can be provisionally defined as the dignified adaptation alone tolerable to a 'national interest' inseparable from that of Mankind as such. The Crown stands for the easy and natural-seeming definition (and re-definition) of this interest: performed from the upper spheres, yet acceptable to those below in a theatrical ballet rehearsed by each particular Royal Visit or Tour. Thus, what is at stake is a national concern – and hence a given national identity and structure – which naturally rises towards the transcendent and remains in principle unconfinable to a merely territorial ego, a particular ethnic population. Its outer parameter is the spiritual vagueness of the Commonwealth, not the 'narrow nationalism' of one folk or one frontier-line.

Regal Walkabout

The Queen's relationship to God changes as she moves over the Scottish border. She becomes less important.

Andrew Duncan, *The Reality of Monarchy* (1970) p.271.

Three years ago the Queen and Duke paid a standard Royal Visit to my own fairly remote part of Scotland. This is the East Fife peninsula, which protrudes into the North Sea between the Forth and Tay estuaries. They started off from Leuchars, the Crown's 'prime air defence airfield'. With its Phantom squadrons, 'hardened' fall-out-proof shelters and Rapier Blindfire missile defences, the base is a key part of what has been tagged 'Fortress Scotland'.[35] The normal music of a Scottish east-coast day is the tearing scream of low-flying warplanes rehearsing Day One of World War III; but it was to be absent from this special, uninterruptable Day of Smiles.

The Royal cars drove first to the little university town of St Andrews, not previously touched by a reigning Sovereign since James VI and I vetted it for theological soundness in 1617. James's forebears had often tried to counter Old Scotland's chronic financial crisis by the sale of Charters to aspiring hamlets; now, the regalia of the incredible number of 'Royal Burghs' dotting the county had been gathered together at the Town Hall for inspection. Serious hand-shaking began there with the officials of the still unpopular entity which replaced that tradition a decade ago, the North-East Fife District Council.

Many would see this as a typical if rather boring foot-note in today's Royal Book of Hours; yet only a slight shift of perspective brings out an interesting feature. The Reform of Local Government so recently perpetrated had itself illustrated something of the Régime's underlying historic dilemma: like other anachronisms before it, it was now devoting ever more time to energetically and expensively futile reforms of the unimportant and the secondary, in search of that energizing modernity which had somehow eluded the grasp of one Ministry after another. Hence an entirely contemporary drama was also being enacted in the Town Hall rituals. The glamorous summation of everything hopelessly and enjoyably backward had Herself now appeared to sprinkle a little tradition – a sense of time-bound legitimacy - upon the dismal and still generally accursed by-products of such sixties and seventies rationalization. By its tender care of the colourful old regalia plus a Royal smile and touch, the N-E.F.D.C. for its part aspired to garner a first tremulous aura of timelessness and go up a little in popular esteem.

After inscribing the Visitors' Book Her Majesty left the Town Hall and proceeded through the cheering crowds a hundred yards up Southgate, and into St Mary's College. It was walkabout time. This term from the pidgin of Australian Aborigines is a gift of Royal commentators to the mother-tongue, meant to depict the new, less formal intimacy of a modern Sovereign with Her subjects. With a perfection which could only be unconscious, its archaic timbre does convey something of British identity's dilemma today: an accentuated tribalism labouring to salve the worsening neuroses of modernization.

Just before, smiles had erupted into hilarity. In spite of all efforts to prepare the walkabout terrain a rusting student's bicycle had remained attached to one of the trees flanking the College entrance: it was tethered to an iron tree-guard by the kind of thief-daunting padlock and chain favoured in bicycling towns. Though some metres from the likely path of the Sovereign the thing had undoubtedly become a blot. A police-van appeared and four officers tumbled out. Quick inspection revealed the size of the problem, and one of them hurried across the street and pushed his way into a local ironmonger's. The large hacksaw with which he emerged seconds later proved useless: to mounting ironic cheers and laughter, no amount of frantic sawing produced the slightest effect. 'Police faces became pink from exertion and embarrassment', noted the *St Andrews Citizen* reporter, until - with almost no time left – an assault was mounted on the tree-guard itself. This parted more easily than the chain, the bike was quickly bundled away and the railing pushed back into place, leaving the entrance clear just as the Queen came out of the Town Hall.

Little incidents like this always figure in Royal processions: people love cheering the roadsweeper who hurries along before the Golden Coach, and remember with delight the hat blown away by the wind before the wearer could doff it for the Queen. Accidents are transformed by their juxtaposition to the transcendent. They become introductory light relief, like a shoe-horn for the briefly-worn magic footwear.

The St Mary's visit was followed by a drive across the Fife headland to Anstruther, on a route omitting two Royal Burghs. Some inhabitants have grudgingly forgiven 'Them' (the arrangers of the tour) on grounds of limited time and 'You can't expect her to go everywhere'. Others never will (though still without blaming the Queen). At Anstruther, the main East Neuk coastal town, she was shown round the Fisheries Museum and met the staff and a blue lobster in the aquarium. Prince Philip went out for ten minutes in the local lifeboat, showed interest in the technicalities of launch and vessel, declined to take the wheel, but was summed up by coxswain Peter Murray as 'A tremendous guy....really good' ('reflecting on his trip to sea with the Prince', said the *East Fife Mail*).

It was now past one o'clock and the Royals reunited in the Craw's Nest Hotel. This haunt of Mason and Rotarian had been selected by the hosts, Fife Regional Council, as the most suitable venue for an official luncheon. Less loved if anything than N-E.F.D.C., the Region is the other grey inheritor of the ancient patchwork-coat of Fife local government. More dependent on the mines and manufacturing of West Fife than the farms of the East, the Region's stake in the tour was smaller. However the day was supposed to end in Leven-mouth's Labour territory, on the sad fringes of the industrial belt. By now three Members of Parliament had joined the Craw's Nest party, including George Younger, then H.M.'s Secretary of State for Scotland.

Haddock Mornay, roast beef with oatmeal stuffing, and fruit salad were followed by coffee and chocolate mints. The Queen seems to have toyed with her food, however. It has often been remarked since how admirably little She eats. Mediaeval sovereigns, by contrast, were usually admired for their superhuman gluttony (and her great-grandfather would have been at home among them).

There is an implicit lesson in decorum here. Martin Green pointed out in *A Mirror for Anglo-Saxons* (1957) how one distinction between Royal and Hollywood glamour is that the former '...remains essentially well-bred and, as it were, unconscious of the public, so that the latter gets a rather snubby lesson in good behaviour as well as the thrill it came for.'[36] This element of restraint or inhibition seems essential to modern

Royal performances. No walkabout Sovereign can be allowed to belch in public. Far from cancelling out the 'thrill', its shadow of masochism (not to say boredom) furnishes an extra and expected legitimation. The sentimental, effusive side is shown not to be mere 'mindless' indulgence by these accompanying signs of rectitude or inbred propriety. The cutlery used by H.M. was kept apart, as were the serviettes and the wrapping paper from which she had extracted her mint. They would be shown later at many Guild or Rural Institute meetings and slide-shows. As they left the hotel a piper blew them farewell along the coast road, and our Lord Lieutenant, Sir John Gilmour of Montrave, declared: 'A wonderful day and a splendid turnout!'

By coincidence the Queen's progress along our coastline was closely followed by that of writer Paul Theroux. He was making his way round Britain gathering material for a book, *The Kingdom by the Sea* (1983, 'His candid and compulsive account of a journey round the coast of Great Britain'). Discovering in St Andrews that he had arrived just after the Sovereign, he pursued her to Anstruther and (though failing to catch up) spent the night at the Craw's Nest. He noticed that it was 'as if the town had been refreshed with a blessing'. This 'royal buzz' was continued after the departure, in a party at the hotel that went on until two am:

> The racket was tremendous...hundreds of people drinking and dancing. There was a good feeling in the air, hilarity and joy, something festive, but also grateful and exhausted. It wasn't faked; it was like the atmosphere of an African village enjoying itself...

Though under the misapprehension that the notorious Willie Hamilton was our Member of Parliament (actually a Tory, Mr Barry Henderson), he left next morning with a fairly accurate consensus view ringing in his ear: 'Willie Hamilton can get stuffed!' He also reports a hotel cleaning lady as telling him: 'I couldn't believe it. It didn't seem real. It was like a dream.'[37]

Smiling is contagious, above all on a day of smiles. It was hard to resist this conclusion among the crowds along the meandering East Neuk highway (from which long-endured and teeth-jolting potholes had disappeared a day or two before). The procession sped through one village of flags and vainly clicking cameras after another towards Levenmouth. Crowd emotion is notoriously communicable, and hard to resist; people speak of being 'carried away'. The point of this sort of popular coming-together ('crowd' hardly seems to fit) is that the participants are sustained by the feeling of *doing* something. As a Canadian observer pointed out over thirty years ago, such occasions show 'reciprocal complementarity': 'The people are *themselves* on display to Him or Her – a kind of socially-sanctioned and culturally expected self-exhibition-ism'. Thus, both sides give and receive: 'The one receives status and privilege, the other the satisfaction derived from bestow-ing, supporting, and perpetuating status and privilege...'[38] Externally viewed, it may look like servility; but its inwardness is that of participation - a 'turnout' which keeps the mystery alive and healthy (and hence keeps a common identity, 'the country', going).

Sir John's cliché should be set against a perfectly imaginable situation where people had failed to appear, where spirits had flagged among the sparse attendance and no 'royal buzz' been created. In such a case, just what is it that would *not* have happened? 'When Devils, Wizards, or Juglers deceive the Sight, they are said to cast *Glamour* o'er the Eyes of the Spectator', wrote Allan Ramsay in his *Poems* (1721). The glamour was thought of as residing in the eyes, and the *Scottish National Dictionary* reports an associated verb, 'to glamour': Salome 'glamour'd Herod', or cast her spell into his eyes. But as the example suggests, the eyes have to be susceptible: they have lent themselves to enchantment, but may also throw it off. While the spell endures, there is absolute resistance to inter-ruption: the dreamer resents and fears recall to reality. Yet when it is broken he or she may also be restored in the (literal) twinkling of an eye.

A vast number of photographs are deposited by every Royal procession. Recently a newspaper had the idea of inviting people to send in their pictures of Royalty, and a selection of these non-professional snaps was published as *Private Views* (1984). But our local relics show how unrepresentative even this is: most really typical snaps have been selected out. These tend to show (for example): the back bumper of the Royal limousine over a blurred policeman's shoulder; a gloved hand or the brim of a technicolor Royal hat, lost in a crowd and just recognizable when pointed out; the Duke of Edinburgh's bald patch, more definite than his son's but hardly – at two hundred yards' distance - a personal memento of the Royal passage. Noone throws away such reminders of enchantment, though. Three years after the visit inquiry produced scores of them at once.

Imponderable Insipidities

When people who have previously believed themselves immune to the attractions of Royalty find themselves in its presence, they are often taken by surprise by the ecstasy of pleasure and appreciation they feel. The easiest way to rationalize this pleasure is to invest the royal personage with qualities that account for it – thus, intelligent people can often be found repeating with a radiant expression the most ordinary expressions of humanity, the most moderate examples of the Royal wit.

Frances Donaldson, *Edward VIII* (1974) p.113

A rather different country soon appeared through the limousine windscreens as they descended into mid-Fife. Eastern Fife appears in holiday brochures; middle and western Fife in the unemployment statistics. With its abandoned mines and defeated or problem industries it is an area typical of Scotland's economic malaise. Male unemployment (the 'official' kind, not the reality) was around one third at the time of the visit. One of Leven's old engineering firms was about to close for good, and the huge Distillers' Company warehouse dominating the landward suburbs was laying off workers because of the prolonged slump in whisky sales. Not many foreign visitors turn off the prescribed Tourist Route to see this zone of dereliction.

If they did, at that period past-shock must have reduced them to silence: where else in Europe could one find a 'High Street' quite like Methil's, not marked but blighted from one end to the other by closure and disuse? This is not aboriginal poverty, an ancient or customary deprivation. It is the wreckage of quite recent prosperity: a small, once confident world broken by its fall from modernity, and now condemned to the grey fungus of loss and second-best. Boarded-up shops, vacant lots, an almost empty harbour, lugubrious and defaced tower-blocks at what was once considered the street's 'poor end': Britain's de-industrializing culture reproduced in the miniature dimensions of the River Leven. The High Street area has been a little improved since the Royal Visit, partly by an EEC Regional Fund grant and partly by demolition and home-building. However, at the time of writing its main points of animation remain the Unemployed Centre (fronted by a friendly sign inviting passers-by in for tea), and a small automated bingo-parlour crowded on pension-days.

The Royal progress was tactfully steered round this emblematic scene. Its mission of hope was directed at a site standing near the end of the High Street ('the normally stark surroundings of the yard', in one newspaper's phrase). This was Levenmouth's only hope, the R.G.C. Offshore construction yard. It builds oil platforms for North Sea drilling work, and could therefore be said to have a stake in an at least short-term future. Inside the gates they were greeted by the living solution to Britain's economic problems, none other than Mr Ian MacGregor (then Chairman of the British Steel Corporation). At that time the yard happened to belong briefly to British Steel, but its very name ('Redpath de Groot Caledonian') indicated a chequered past history of ownership, and the hope was that MacGregor's 1981 takeover would at last secure the future.

'She's a very knowledgeable lady' declared MacGregor later, primarily because 'She understands the importance of North Sea activities'. It is always wonderful when She understands what every one of Her subjects has known for a decade. However, this is not because She or her interlocutors are nincompoops. The point is, that what occurs in such sacred situations is both above and below normal sense. In a survey of the 19th century Monarchy Roger Fulford admits that –

In most cases the conversations of ordinary mortals with royal persons are of imponderable insipidities. Subjects come away from a chat with their Sovereign with nothing more enduring to repeat to their friends than embroidered examples of their own brilliance or their own gaucheries...[39]

What is said is mercifully of small importance. Pure Communication has taken place, a blessing and thanks in the rather accidental shape of sentences. The Queen had come to Methil 'because the 900-strong workforce had distinguished itself with its good work' (continued the Chairman) so that the yard's future was bright.

Another aspect of these ritual occasions often noticed is the silence. Appearance of the iconic personage seems invariably to be signalled by a resounding hush: as if in recognition that a close encounter of an entirely special kind is imminent, and all pettier concerns must give way. At the decisive moment (one friend recalls) she found herself uncontrollably recoiling several feet from the proffered insipidity, as if instinctively unable to make contact with the alien being. The occasion was a Royal Film Première, and (she was not alone in observing, with some irritation) the five-star personages also chattered loudly and almost non-stop throughout the entire projection, as if regally exempt from both vulgar absorption and common (or non-Royal) courtesy. The explanation of this is surely that observed by 'Chips' Channon in his *Diary* for June 1923: whether blessed or not with aspirations to 'ordinariness', Royals simply cannot help *also* retaining the assumption of being a caste apart. After the aristocratic marriage-ceremony he had been attending (he wrote) – 'All the Royal Family, the King, the two Queens, Princesses, Empress of Russia, etc., stood for ages in front of St Margaret's kissing one another. Royalties in public always behave as if they were enjoying complete privacy.'[40]

Since 1982's Blessing, unfortunately, R.G.C.'s future has been less exemplary than Mr McGregor hoped. While he went on to the Coal Board, the great 1984-5 strike and a Knighthood, British Steel soon decided to sell out this particular investment in good work and bright futures. After a period of uncertainty and short orders, and a moment when it looked likely to join Robert Maxwell's empire, the firm was taken over by the most notorious of Great Britain's new robber-baron conglomerates, Trafalgar House. There are orders for oil and gas rigs for the next two years, and North Sea business is holding up better than expected. This is presumably what attracted Trafalgar House. Though still building rigs its prospects are precarious, however, both because of the forces now in charge and because the horizon of likely 'North Sea activities' is in any case a shrinking one. Lower Methil is likely to end in complete de-industrialization; the only question is how quickly or slowly.

Now, noone would blame Queen Elizabeth for Methil's chronic problems. The gentle benediction of a Royal Visit could hardly reverse an ancient economic malady, and certainly had no effect upon Mr MacGregor or his decisions. But it would be nearly as untrue to conclude that the East Fife tour had no influence at all on the people, or their reaction to events. It gave the sensation that *They* meant well, and were in some ectoplasmic way pushing in the right direction: yes, Crown and State were by no means indifferent to the needs of Levenmouth. Hence, rage or despair may be decanted on Governments, a Minister or Mr Macregor, but will go on sparing the wider state and social order -- the fundaments of acceptable conduct which 'They' stand for, signposted by family codes like 'fair', 'decent', 'playing the game', and so on. Anger is safely channelled into 'politics', in the specially narrow, padded-room sense of the United Kingdom system; and, after all these organized and tranquillizing Royal smiles, the system itself is more likely to continue receiving the benefit of any doubt.[41]

Another significant dimension of the tour lay in the fact that it was in Scotland, and across a region which in 1974 almost elected a member of the Scottish National Party to the House of Commons. Commenting on reaction to the 1977 Royal Jubilee in Scotland, Philip Ziegler noted that although nationalism didn't seem to have had too marked an effect – 'Yet it is possible to detect an indifference far more widespread than in England, a feeling that the monarch is an irrelevance, something alien to what matters to Scotland today: that Elizabeth II is, in fact, Queen of England...'[42] There was a time when many of the workers at R.G.C. thought they might be working to build up the industry around 'Scotland's Oil', and that petroleum revenues might be used for the drastic, almost revolutionary regeneration of places like Methil. I doubt if base calculations of this order figured much in plans for the visit, and the painful reflections provoked by them in 1982 were certainly absent from conversation and the printed reports. But the fact remains that the underlying multi-national configuration of the British State affects – and as we shall see, helps to explain – Royal ideology. The Monarchy is less important and popular in Scotland and Wales; and for that reason its presence there has added weight and conscious deliberation.

The other worthy causes - like the new Councils, the Fisheries Museum or the Levenmouth Sea Cadets she also visited - added to this influence. They deserve some help, get it from the publicity attending Royalty, and augment with some real reason the overall impression of beneficence. In the course of any year innumerable charities and interests serve the interests of Great Britain's worn fabric in this way, by genuinely and gratefully helping themselves.

Tea With the Queen

> I am teaching the Queen to swim: I ask her why she wants to learn. "If Britannia sinks," she says, "I must know how to swim to shore, so that I can hold the country together. That's what they tell me I'm good for..."

> Cheshire builder's merchant's dream, in Masters, *Dreams about H.M. the Queen* (1972)

The remote descendant of Charles I's sister now knows a popularity unimaginable to him or other feudal rulers. Absolute Monarchs could be loved or hated by their subjects, and while they usually preferred love it did not in the end matter very much which. They never had to be 'popular' in the contemporary sense. As long as their immediate vassals (the high nobility and clergy) were kept happy, or cowed, it was of small account what the mass of lower orders thought. Most of them, most of the time, almost certainly thought little about the Monarch or his court. Apart from occasional Royal

Progresses like those mentioned above (designed to shatter the finances of the regional aristocracy as much as to display the Royal Person to crowds) the Crown was a remote and God-like notion. Under Louis XIV, the historic epitome of Absolute Rule, most French men and women were in the fortunate position of rarely having to spare a thought for the antics of Versailles.

Extremely few Great Britons are in that position today. Only a deaf-and-dumb hermit with no T.V. set in remotest Shetland could hope to escape the daily Royal Touch. From the moment the daily paper drops on the mat until the end of late-night television the most casual observer cannot avoid bombardment by news of Regal migrations, openings, hand-wavings, speeches, banquets, romances, plans for nursery and paddock, receptions and walkabouts amid touched and won-dering crowds. Such items are rarely doleful or disturbing. The amazing health and longevity of the Windsor stock (a contrast to most past dynasties) tends in any case to keep funerals at bay.

Were departures and illnesses more common, incidentally, they would probably serve to intensify the mass cult. There is an interesting precedent here. The very beginning of the modern elevation of Monarchy was signalled by a riveting illness. In October 1871 the Prince of Wales (later Edward VII) was stricken by typhoid fever emanating from the drains of a Yorkshire country mansion. So dire was his condition that (in the words of one Royal biographer) 'the bulletins....caused the nation and empire almost to abandon hope'. Some lines were composed for the occasion which have survived recollection of the event itself:

> Flash'd from his bed, the electric tidings came,
> He is not better; he is much the same.

Alfred Austin went on to edit the *National Review* and then, as Poet Laureate (1896-1913), assumed the burden of what more recently Ted Hughes (on the point of assuming it himself) has called 'the spiritual unity of the tribe'. Temptations to farther bathos were cut short by the remarkable popular reaction, however. As the Prince began to recover, notes the same biographer (Philip Magnus), 'an elemental upsurge of loyal emotion destroyed republicanism overnight as a significant factor in British radical politics'.[43] We will look in more detail at the Republican episode referred to, later. But other accounts confirm that the self-satisfied verdict is not really mistaken.

Even with this big gun in reserve, then, Royalty succeeds remarkably in pervading and colouring the British way of life. Give us this day our daily trance: near the conclusion of every other T.V. news programme the announcer's manner and tone of voice abruptly alters, a warm smirk replacing the customary asperity. 'Come with me', it implies, into the Ukanian land of reliably good news where the worst that can befall us is a Princely chill or a presentation posy dropped in the mud. A kind of salve is gratefully administered after the usual ten minutes of jolts, truncated tragedies, M.P.'s pronouncements and tales of national failure. Most of the nation follows, like the victims of the alien intelligence in so many science-fiction movies: transported off to glazed euphoria, on a plane where troublesome emotions are guaranteed absent and all dialogue is a Royal monotone of insipidities. Any sign of restiveness at the fate is treated as neurosis: how dare anyone decry the only real, harmless, reliable pleasure ordinary folk get every day? Science fiction has made this theme familiar too. In Donald Siegel's genre classic *Invasion of the Body-snatchers*, for instance, the aliens produce pod-grown replicas of humanity. These are physically indistinguishable but lack the vital spark. Whenever they meet an 'unconverted' one they scream denunciations, and policemen arrive to explain how 'treatment' will bring the Nirvana of unquestioning assent.

People not only get a snatch of Royal Presence each day; to an interesting extent, both replicas and the unconverted seem to dream of it each night as well. 'Up to one third of the country has dreamt about the Royal Family', estimates Brian Masters, the author of *Dreams about H M the Queen, and other members of the Royal Family*. Anti-Monarchists tend to do so too, he emphasizes, usually discovering there that the Queen is after all 'an embodiment of kindness and responsible femininity'. The dominant theme is unmistakable: 'coming for a cup of tea', either at Buckingham Palace or (should she suddenly appear on walkabout) into the dreamer's modest home. There, the Queen or her Family are suddenly, miraculously, *ordinary*; even, sometimes, in need of cash or 'hopeless with money'. Occasionally (as Clancy Sigal felt) they have to be saved from snarling assassins who have it in for Civilization as such. What the dream seizes is a dialectic of the transcendent and the everyday: Royal Britain in revealing comic miniature.

In exceptional cases a lasting nocturnal rapport may be struck up, where the Queen returns constantly for tea and confidences. This is like the situation of Miss Briggs, in Emma Tennant's *Hotel de Dream*: 'Miss Briggs dreamed she was at the Royal Garden Party. As always the Queen was quick to notice her in the crowd and, pushing past the officious and over-protective equerries, made her way through the throng of eagerly waiting subjects to reach Miss Briggs's side....' She is the Queen's 'adviser from the common people', secretly helping her to restore a sense of meaning to life, and arrest 'the relentless belief in growth and science and the fading away of all the traditional values'. This dream mingles with those of the other decaying gentlefolk in the Hotel as, attended by Cridge (the resentful but equally dream-bound toiler in the basement), they await the rapidly-approaching end of their existence.[44]

I noticed above the pathological side so often visible in anti-monarchical attitudes. It should also be said that no less peculiar behaviour features in a lot of cravenly pro-monarchical situations. These seem to be moments where, in the physical proximity of a Royal person, dream and reality dissolve in a hopeless mix-up. Is the dazed subject in Ukania, or merely in Britain? A long time ago a visiting French psychologist thought he could observe a general tendency of the same sort, vis-à-vis the aristocracy:

> I had observed, under various circumstances, the peculiar sort of intoxication produced in the most reasonable Englishmen by the contact or sight of an English Peer....They may be seen to redden at his approach, and if he speaks to them their suppressed joy increases their redness, and causes their eyes to gleam with unusual brilliance. Respect for nobility is in their blood, so to speak....their passion for horses and Shakespeare is less violent, the satisfaction and pride they derive from these sources a less integral part of their being.[45]

If the verdict strikes us as a little heavy nowadays, there is surely little risk in replacing 'Peer' by 'Monarch'. Ziegler quotes a fascinating example of this in *Crown and People*:

> An eminent man of letters in the early fifties with a temperament of detached radicalism was invited to one of the Queen's informal lunches. He accepted in a spirit of mingled curiosity and ribaldry. The mood survived until the Queen appeared and her guests were presented. "Suddenly I felt physically ill", he said, "My legs felt weak, my head swam and my mind went totally blank". "So you're writing about such-and-such, Mr – ", said the Queen. "I had no idea what I was writing about, or even if I was writing a book at all. All I could think of to say was, "What a pretty brooch you're wearing, ma'am!". So far as I can recall she was not wearing a brooch at all. Presumably she was used to such imbecility; anyway, she paid no attention to my babbling and in a minute or two I found I was talking sense again...."[46]

Hard-line Republicans quite commonly discover in the dream-state what a charming, ordinary, and even insufferably attractive person She really is. But as we see even the waking state can founder into dreamland. Incidents like this 'could be multiplied a hundredfold', notes Ziegler. In another one he refers to, a youth said: 'I could barely stand the excitement of it all and every now and then had to pinch myself to make sure that I had not dreamed it all'.

Through the Wrong End of the Telescope: Ukania

That the craving for uniqueness cannot be fulfilled causes Britain's chronic crisis of identity. There is no generally accepted set of beliefs in Britain that can be effectively appealed to, to make sense of decision, *except a set of beliefs that cannot be fulfilled.*

Donald Horne, *God is an Englishman*, p.64.

So what is the mystery of British Monarchy? As we have seen, the actual realm of this 'powerless' institution is in practice co-extensive with really existing British society.

It binds the State together. Anyone who buys an elementary text-book on the British Constitution to read it (rather than pray before it) knows that the Crown is a crucial element in Constitution, Law and Government. Were it to disappear, these would require both theoretical and practical reconstruction, not a few adjustments with a spanner.

At the same time it is anything but a State institution in the sense of being confined to that plane. On the contrary, it also informs, entertains and deeply influences civil society. Since George V's time it has established a formidable ascendancy over the public imagination. Though strong and pervasive media were a necessary condition of this, it does not follow that they alone 'created' the effect. Similarly, although Royalty-obsession could only have developed like this in the era of star-studded popular culture and mass fashion, it does not follow that Monarchy can be reduced to the terms of this category. It has its own distinct features and rules. The dominant power has made use of media, stardom and fashion for its own ends; not vice versa.

The principal of these ends is maintenance of what R.W.Johnson calls 'the peculiar British political culture, characterised on the one hand by the imprint of a uniquely powerful and successful state and, on the other, by its non-inclusive conception of the popular interest...' The latter phrase (he goes on to explain) derives from the oddest feature of that culture – its lack of any notion of popular sovereignty. The People are 'Represented' at the Seat of Majesty but never in actual occupation there:

> It is unthinkable that a state like the British one can be "possessed" by its people. The very institution of the monarchy makes this plain...(and) the fact of the monarchy is again critical to this strand of culture.[47]

But the 'strand of culture' is the crucial, living nerve of the Old Régime: the very quick of its authority, and of the mass identity through which that power is wielded. Its living Word is incomparably more powerful than any competitive *Weltanschauung* which has so far challenged it: whether

Labourite Socialism or (since 1979) Friedmanite Capitalism. It is worth quoting Johnson's perspective on this at length:

> The history of the British state is like no other, for it has succeeded in a way no other state in the world has done. For nearly a thousand years it has successfully protected the nation against invasion. It created not one but two vast colonial empires, each in their time the biggest humankind has ever seen. It has since 1066 been successful in all wars where its national sovereignty was at stake and has won almost all of its lesser wars too. Other states have Established Churches, but these have resulted either from the church taking over the state, or from a concordat between equals; only in England did the state simply take over the church, prescribing it new doctrines in the interest of the state. This state fathered the world's first industrial revolution. Despite its small size it became the greatest power in the world, both economically and militarily, for a century...At home this state was immune to revolution, even while all others succumbed...For it knew that it was not just "the authorities", but Authority itself. It even refused, uniquely, to subject its absolute sovereignty to a constitution. It developed an immense conception of its own dignity and solemnity. And, of course, so majestic a state requires nothing less than a monarchy at its head, even in an age of republics...

There is another significant dimension to this quasi-religious nationhood which the author passes over too lightly. Though quite true to say it centres on a sense of 'State' grandeur and continuity, this has never been the abstract or impersonal apparatus which post-Absolutist Republicanism fostered in Europe (and subsequently in other continents). On the contrary, the salience of Monarchy indicates exactly the low profile and prestige of all those aspects of state-life. And this is why (as Johnson admits) 'the state, its Establishment and its institutions have come to be regarded as synonymous with the nation itself. Without its monarchy, peerage, Houses of Parliament, Britain would literally not be Britain at all for many of its people.' Its awesomeness and 'near-hypnotic impact' depend upon this ostensible identification of State with society: what one could also call – in a phrase I will try to analyse later on – the metaphorical family unity of a Shakespearian (or pre-modern) *nationalism*.

Within civil society (we have seen) each class enjoys its own Royal Family: an appropriately-tailored stock of images and myths, delivered in the correct class-idiom. But these are of course not equal in content or import. Hierarchy is built in by an encompassing language-structure so that popular Monarchy supports that of the *Times* and the B.B.C. and not the other way round. 'Class', in the oneiric British sense, is both family nickname and curse – a feature of the commanding metaphorical unity inherently open to Royal sublation. The point of its sedulously maintained wounds is revealed by orgasmic moments of communion, the Great Days of the Royal Institution - Remembrances, Thanksgivings, Funerals, Weddings, Visits, and so on - when barriers dissolve into 'the Country' and Who We Really Are. A past-oriented, decorous, semi-divine unison takes over, and the rough of outrageous caste-marks is made smooth. Were the differences not so great the deliverance would not be so sweet, and so craved after: it would lack its curious, spell-binding quality, Margaret Lane's 'secret' quoted at the beginning – 'the vision of an uncounted multitude...narrowed down to this'. But 'vision' here means the glamour cast into eyes which seek beguilement: not necessarily exactly *this* magic, perhaps, but something of the kind. And in our circumstances, it is the Windsor totems that satisfy that need. They translate the State and its history into personal terms - the awesome into an apparently recognizable cosiness.

The 'mystery' that so impressed Margaret Lane all those years ago implies a kind of national spirit-essence, a land of the mind distinguishable from the mundane countries and peoples of these islands. In addition to the actual disparate spectrum ranging from Orkney small-holders through the industrial rubble of Northern river-valleys to posh London suburbs and Isle of Wight water-colourists, there is a much smaller and more homogeneous country of the mind, often referred to at Shakespearian moments as 'This small country of ours'. While philistines and strict-observance rationalists may dismiss it as 'fantasy', it should not be compared to genuine fantasy like (for example) the 'Middle-Earth' of Tolkien's *Lord of the Rings*. One can think of it rather as a set of mental map-survey points implanted in the communal psyche. These are not necessarily referred to every day but remain indispensable for knowing where one is (especially when lost, or at moments of crisis). As Walter Benjamin wrote, they have little to do with 'the way it really was' historically: here, what counts is 'seizing hold of a memory as it flashes up at a moment of danger'.[48] But to this acute observation he might have added that reorientation is greatly aided by a degree of rehearsal and spirit-maintenance - thus ensuring that the machinery doesn't rust up completely during the long periods when people think only of jobs, families and other ordinary affairs.

This spirit-country has its own curious topography, some features of which have already been singled out. The oddness of the exercise derives from two important facts about that topography. First, inquiry is normally inhibited from treating the 'inner essence' on its own by an indispensable national aversion to theory: a *pudeur* which shrinks from 'that sort of thing' and disguises the national reticence as healthy concern with measurable realities. This structural philistinism has the effect of preserving the Royal State (that is the mode of authority whose force is actually legitimized by the 'State occasions' people love so much). On a more sociological plane, it has the effect of keeping the intellectuals in their place: a 'place' of responsible sobriety and dedication, rather than that thinking disaffection which has upset so many other modern societies. The success of these effects shows (for example) in the unease that still clings to any use of the term 'intellectual' in Queen's English: the word jars because it doesn't fit. Ukania-Britain aims (and still largely succeeds) in having what Samuel Taylor Coleridge called a 'clerisy' – a Royal (but not bureaucratic) thought-élite devoted to the brass-rubbing or coining of 'traditions' upholding organic community, rather than an 'intelligentsia' gnawing at its vitals.[49]

Secondly, the very popularity of this Vermeer-Kingdom of the imagination means that it is closely interfused with social 'reality' in the canonical or measurable sense. Hence it is surprisingly hard to isolate or analyse 'on its own' (even were there much will to do so). The power and pervasiveness of British media ensure the almost daily triumph of such integration. Through Royalty, a kind of wholeness is maintained, and kept in readiness for 'moments of danger'. Also – strongly reinforcing this effect – the unity is protected by an accompanying taboo-structure whose aim is the automatic exorcism, almost the self-elimination, of any disruptive threat. One aspect of this is the court-jester or eccentric nature of British 'Republicanism': the activity of a handful of tribal 'holy fools' both exemplifies a free country and - by reaction - intensifies that country's freely-chosen and enjoyable mode of psychic bondage (or 'identity').

This spirit-essence will sometimes be called 'Ukania' in what follows: the *Geist* or informing spirit of the U.K. The name is appropriate because none of the existing handles quite fit: we live in a State with a variety of titles having different functions and nuances - the U.K. (or 'Yookay', as Raymond Williams relabelled it), Great Britain (imperial robes), Britain (boring lounge-suit), England (poetic but troublesome), the British Isles (too geographical), 'This Country' (all-purpose within the Family), or 'This Small Country of Ours' (defensive-Shakespearian). 'Ukania' also has the great merit of recalling 'Kakania', Robert Musil's famous alternative name for the Habsburg Empire in *The Man Without Qualities*. The *königlich und kaiserlich* domains of the Habsburg dynasty suffered from a comparable plethora of names, for comparable historical reasons: Austria-Hungary, Austria, the Habsburg Empire, 'the Empire', or even 'Danubia'.

It's probably most important to emphasize here how essential the Ukanian spiritual territory is to what goes on in the 'real' places making up a country. Workaday or (the appropriate term, whose meaning we have begun to explore) 'ordinary' Britain depends upon it, as well as vice versa. A modern *nation* (as distinct from a collection of localities and interests) requires a 'cultural' counterpart of this kind to function, however indifferent (or even hostile) some of its inhabitants may appear to the prescribed idiom, some of the time. Philistinism is the deluded conviction that this is not so (or, sometimes, that the existing national-culture grid could be torn up without putting anything in its place). On both the Left and the Right of the old political spectrum the conviction was supported by the family prayers of 'British Empiricism' (the theory that the British – or anyway the English – are by nature untheoretical, and either above or beneath that sort of thing). On the Left, indeed, it has been the very marrow of the Labour Party's Royal Socialism.

A cultivated instinct historically fostered to replace theory and principle, the feeling for Ukania is fed by palpable exemplifications - uncontestable images of reassurance and guidance. An anti-abstract ideology (or non-theoretical theory) is compelled to focus upon the ultra-concrete: visible things (or persons) radioactive with an otherwise ineffable significance. This poetry of national existence – intuitive decency, 'our way of doing things' – contrasts automatically and quite naturally with the foreign, the modern, the extreme, the impersonal and the noxiously abstract. The latter represent the prose (or the plain clothes) of modernity – of a disenchanted world that has menaced Ukania-Britain since the time of the French Revolution. It tends to be true that 'foreigners' are immune from this vital radioactivity. Either they just don't understand in a hostile sense, or else they fall hopelessly (and equally uncomprehendingly) in love with it, resorting – like Clancy Sigal's drunken American actress - to embarrassing blather in their efforts to voice the passion. That happens because 'Ukania' is only transmittable within the extended national family. The transmission is not genetic, although, as all immigrants can't help knowing, the resultant configuration often bears a desolate and deeply uncomfortable resemblance to something 'racial' (in other words it is anti-egalitarian and exclusive, and tends to be 'taken for granted' like a set of genuinely inherited or physical characteristics).

While the Royal personages are by far the most important of such radioactive family symbols, 'ordinary' Ukanian life is traditionally rich with them. A good example was the old G.P.O. public telephone-box. Until Mrs Thatcher's second government these stately emblems could be found all over the realm. I can do no better here than cite the loving description offered by an anguished defender, Roger Scruton, when it was announced that the G.P.O.'s capitalist successor 'British Telecom' intended getting rid of them as part of its search for a modern image:

> In every English village there is one object that stands out as the prime focus of the traveller's attention, and the fitting representative of the stable government beneath whose mantle he

journeys. This object is the telephone booth: a cast iron structure in imperial red, classical in outline, but with an interesting suggestion of Bauhaus naughtiness in its fenestration...The door, divided into three parts by its mullions, has a brass handle, set into the cast iron frame, and above the cornice a little crown is embossed, symbol of national identity, and promise of enduring government. So suitable has this form proved to the streets, countryside and villages of England that it now appears on Christmas-card snow scenes, beside the Gothic spire, the gabled cottage and the five-barred gate...[50]

The intention is to replace such symbols with 'barbarous concoctions of steel and aluminium' like those found anywhere else today – abject surrenders to modernity (as distinct from the gestural naughtiness of 'modernization' by Bauhaus touches). Scruton's idea is that they should be reclassified as 'buildings', and so become subject to conservation notices imposed by outraged public demand.

However, readers will note one or two equally Ukanian features missing from this impassioned plea. There were (for example) never enough of the old booths. Though easily findable by the village green, they were rare in the more deprived urban areas where - obviously - most likely users were located. Disguised by mumblings about cost and maintenance, this corresponded in fact to the highest spiritual strategy of Christmas-card and *Salisbury Review* Britain: it simply did not do to provide the sub-élite with over-easy, cheap, reliable communication. No, the spirit of 'class' was best maintained by a sense of solidly Crown-bestowed privilege. And where better to ram this message home than in the sensitive nodes of a public communication-system - the exposed nervous system of the lower orders?

The same spirit was fortified by an inevitable corollary of such well-mullioned charity: destructive protest. Even when found, the public telephones in working-class quarters rarely worked. If the instrument was not already 'vandalized', some fault nearly always impeded the delusively straightforward desire to 'make a call'. Their coin-boxes would often be full up, mute testimony both to public need and to the rarity of visits by agents of the G.P.O. Crown. Inchoate graffiti, ripped-up directories and smashed glass revealed the plaintive underside of stability and cast-iron government. Mr Scruton coyly mentions 'the smell of stale cigarette ash and rusting iron...like the smell of incense' but forgets the stronger odour of stale pee so often deposited by exasperated users unable to make a call on their way home from the pub.

But it was precisely those aspects of cast-iron solidity and Stately, condescending quaintness that made the old booths such a target. Quite apart from the paleotechnology and the rarity, their very semblance lent its own equally absurd meaning to delinquency. They were indeed 'really temples, dedicated to a ruling deity': hence, when the deity had once again withdrawn the privilege of call-making, sheer hate welled up with its own nihilistic logic. At this level, no equivalent to voting Labour was ever furnished by the system: the alternatives were the miracle of 'getting through' or (after a quick glance to make sure no Crown representative was in the street) the vigorous assertion of *nothing*. In the most riot-wrecked parts of American cities ghetto inhabitants have always enjoyed cheap, easy communication from unvandalized steel and aluminium payphones located on every street-corner. But the 'message' of the little embossed Crown-boxes is profoundly different: as well as stability, longevity, loyalty, decency, what they proclaimed was something like – '*You* belong to the class for which this sort of thing is good enough; but you may nevertheless, if lucky and in possession of the correct H.M. coinage, make a call here'.

Such was the real universe that *Salisbury-Review* and Royal Britain wants at all costs to maintain. The Labour Party agrees with them, while demanding that more booths be supplied and the cost of calls be kept down. Effective change has come only under Mrs Thatcher, from an abrasively theoretical Right rather than a sensible and wisely tradition-bound Left brought up to laugh at Republicanism and win arguments about the rate of economic growth and the balance of payments. The Crown finally vanished from our street-corners in the interest of capital accumulation, not that of Progress. As with so many other features of her new Régime, modernity arrived and gnawed at the vitals of the Old by substituting cash for community: 'regressive modernization', as Stuart Hall has called it, but instantly and understandably preferred by most to a public domain where welfare implied subjecthood and no step forward really took people out of 'their place'.

Seen in this light, the question of what the Monarchical mystique means is a matter of charting the surprisingly little-known (because taken for granted) terrain of Ukania, and its main lines of relationship to the humbler and more disappointing material land we live in. Crown Britain is so to speak the spiritual landlord of everyday British realities; its mortmain is thorough and (for reasons so far obscure) not just accepted but obviously adored by most of the tenantry. What is the source of this magic-seeming authority? What bias does it impart to the social body from which it springs and to which it returns with its own special, added impetus?

The reader will be able to think of many other examples of the spirit-land's topography. It is a family-country, hence ideologically 'small' in a sense having no relationship to actual geography. Its atmosphere is at once cosy (for those wanting security) and liable to seem claustrophobic (for a minority wanting greater freedom, achievement and mobility than the decorum allows). Both traditional Toryism and Royal Social-ism emphasized the cosiness; not until the 1980s were they challenged (and then destroyed) by political forces focusing on the destruction and replacement of this old fabric. But in spite of such dislocation it is still managed almost entirely by familial custom – that is, by conventions established, 'commented' upon and incessantly and footlingly modified, rather than by script and principle. This management remains in the hands of an *essentially* hereditary élite whose chief attribute is knowing how to manage: their 'secret' is knowing this secret. [51] These family elders are (as we will go on to see) either bred or the products of a synthetic blood-line schooled into a simulacrum of breeding, and thus made capable of carrying on the right (Royal) spirit.

This spirit is diffused from above downwards in a process of (occasionally antagonistic) familial articulation signposted by notions like 'fairness', 'decency', 'compromise', 'consensus', plural concessionary 'liberties', 'having one's say', 'tradition' and 'community' - rather than the humourless abstractions of 1776, 1789 and after: Popular Sovereignty, democracy, *égalité*, and so on. Ukania keeps Britain firmly in early-modern times, in other words. But since it is the posthumous times that have generalized the terms and consciousness of modern political life, this is – inevitably – also a strategy of deep dissimulation. It has required the services of a national philosophy of dissimulation and repression: 'British empiricism', or the priority of practice over theory, of conditioned reflexes over ideal principle. It has also been served by a literature devoted to mothering the same reflexes.

An important facet of such inbuilt hypocrisy is the taboo surrounding Monarchy. As we shall see, this affords a vital double protection. It shields the sacred totem of authority from direct disparagement *and* removes it even from the indirect criticism of theory by apologetic 'disavowal'. In this way the naive emotionality, instinctive rapport and regressive colour of familial relations are preserved. In politics, the distinctive pseudo-adversarial conflict of family existence is also safeguarded: dreams of flight and murder are reconciled with a daylight of consensus where the millstones of memory grind on ('Our way of doing things', better than anarchy, and so on). The Royal way of doing things may have its drawbacks, but was (at least until Thatcherism got a grip) more essentially civilized than anyone else's. In its very failures there always lay a superior moral capacity, a sage avoidance of overmuch modernity. Thus, where the millstones have ground rather fine and produced dilapidation or mess, a sort of redemption still shines forth from decay. The task of Ukanian culture (and above all of its Letters) has been essentially to detect and register these redemptory rays. They are connected by hidden spores to the great emblems of Monarchic glamour, in a single and organic community of archaic grandeur: the same Royal-National (and deeply popular) conventions which have, since the middle of this century, been collapsing through remorseless stages into a single identity of ruin - into an accumulating backwardness which became the ultimate secret of the Monarchic riddle and eventually, with Mrs Thatcher's neo-conservatism, forced its own characteristically barbed solution: blind, backwards advance, or regressive modernization.

2

THE NATION

The monarchy and landed élite tamed the indus-
trialization of England without succumbing to
it...England never became a "bourgeois order" run
by a "conquering" bourgeoisie...There was no
movement to remove the crown, the royal court, the
House of Lords, and the ascriptive public service
nobility. Despite the decline of agriculture and
despite insular security, which viated the need for a
strong military caste, the landed classes managed to
perpetuate this "archaic" political order and
culture...

> Arno J.Mayer, *The Persis-*
> *tence of the Old Regime*
> (1981), pp.10-11.

The proper duty of the Sovereigns of this country is
not to take the lead in change, but to act as a balance
wheel on the movement of the social body...

> Baron Stockmar (1846) as
> quoted in *Albert, Prince*
> *Consort*, by Robert Rhodes
> James (1984), p.235.

2

The Nation

A Special Explanation

The Queen Mother swayed in a gentle dance when one of three
steel bands began playing a lilting reggae tune. Five yards away,
swaying with her were a group of Rastafarians wearing the red,
yellow and green tea cosy hats which are the badge of their pot-
smoking set.

From the *Daily Mail*, 21 April 1983, as quoted by Paul Gilroy,
There Ain't no Black in the Union Jack
(1987) p.43.

In an article quoted earlier Sebastian Haffner argued that 1950s
Britain was 'Monarchy-conscious to a degree which calls for
some special explanation'.[1] Perhaps the survey of Royal and
Royal-related phenomena has now brought out some elements
of such an explanation. We saw, for example, how popular
attitudes imagine Monarchy as above 'them and us', at the
heart of the social order yet – despite the blatant aristocracy of
the Windsor Court - somehow outside it. The essence of 'class'
appears mysteriously exempt from its otherwise commanding
rules. Though oriented towards a mythic over-continuity with
the past, the Crown's ideological function isn't limited to that:
a portentous style of 'modernization' has been just as significant. This is revealed in the institution's own unceasing
adaptation as well as in the public speeches of both Prince
Phillip and the present Prince of Wales. Since the time of Prince
Albert Royalty has been anxious (occasionally over-anxious)

to demonstrate that its function is not that of shoring up an *ancien régime* at all costs. We also noticed how its actual function is indicated more clearly through the notion of sapient and overarching compromise: the measured and genteel adoption of modernity to which genuine *noblesse* obliges. That attitude in turn links up with a whole range of social codes: the universe of custom signposted by 'decency', 'fair play', 'moderation', 'flexibility' and many other Ukanian mysteries.

Together such codes compose a recognizable identity, which I have tried to resume (only half-humorously) in the image of 'Ukania'. There is an apparent eccentricity in this device: but it is one imposed by the curious circumstances of the case itself. Imposed, that is, by the circumstances of what is by the norms of the late 20th century political world a highly eccentric national identity. Such oddity entails problems of understanding, because in a number of ways it evades the standard political or nation-state categories. The British-Ukanian identity is a *sui generis* variety of nationalism now undergoing rapid collapse. Modern or resurrected Royalism has been a vital way of structuring and preserving that identity: as the central totem of a sign-world it is, naturally, menaced by the decline of the old conventions.

'What's gone wrong with the Monarchy?' has been the journalistic response to the change of climate; but – as the usual host of apologists has hurried to declare – there's really nothing wrong with *it*. It's *everything* which has 'gone wrong' since a process of actual modernizing change distinct from the Old Régime's noble delusions of 'modernization' began to take effect. Nor - in spite of what H.M.'s Labour Party hopes - is there the slightest chance of restoring the old system: the meaning of Monarchy has become questionable because its custom-world is breaking up, and no number of Sir James Callaghans will put it together again. Under 'modernization' anything could be flexibly altered provided nothing really changed; but modernization *is* real change (however double-edged or 'regressive') and its alterations have begun to affect the deeper levels of identity or communal psyche on which the British Monarchy has operated.

I would now like to develop these elements of the special explanation which Windsor Monarchism calls for, approaching the subject from a variety of angles and (as suggested in the Foreword) compiling them into something more like a satisfactory theory. But before embarking on this, some words about 'theory' itself are necessary. Indeed, the very nature of the Royal taboo-system imposes it. We have seen how that works on an everyday plane, by evicting and marginalizing 'serious' critique as alien, humourless or both. On a more intellectual level its operation is traditionally just as effective.

Digression on Family Pets

Nor can a corgi publish its memoirs. This short irritable beast has become her cliché – the scarred ankles of Guardsmen, the flash of knee from her well-hitched skirt at feeding time, the small Sandringham tombstone to "The Queen's Faithful Friend, Susan" – but it is also the talisman of her insistent grasp on normality.

Robert Lacey, *Majesty* (1977) p.265.

Here, the cardinal vector of evasion is a noble lie which has long held truism-status within Ukanian culture: the Monarchy is *of no real importance whatever*. Both conservative and left-wing attempts at theorizing Royalty have enjoyed suspect agreement on the point – in effect, disavowing the possibility that Crown or Ukania-Britain might be (or at least be a vital part of) 'the real thing'. And the meaning of this for the realm of theory is obvious: who wants to waste time theorizing about something utterly unimportant?

So, on one hand there is all this obviously deep and rather solemn involvement, as if some part of *us* were inextricably bound up with the birth of a new Royal infant. In another recent and memorable example some irrefutable but unkind comments were made during a Royal Tour of Canada about the Queen's wrinkles and signs of irrepressible boredom at one ceremonial non-event after another. Next day such *lèse-majesté* was routinely turned by the British media into an assault on decency as such (and hence on British national identity). Noone could really believe that the occasion for this much trumpeting and outrage was 'unimportant'.

Ziegler's *Crown and People* devotes a chapter to the letters received by William Hamilton M.P. after the publication of *My Queen and I* in 1975. They contain a lot of familiar praise for Monarchy as a 'source of glamour in a dingy world'; but the dominant overall impression is quite different, and more serious. It is, Ziegler comments, 'the extent to which people are preoccupied by thoughts of the Royal Family....these letters reveal that thousands of otherwise apparently sane and well-balanced people feel so passionately on the subject that they consider any point of view but their own as at the best absurd, at the worst vicious or treasonable'.[2] Exactly the same impression was gained in a previous analysis of Royalist hate-mail. Nearly thirty years ago, when John Grigg and Malcolm Muggeridge indulged in the bout of mild criticism of the Queen already mentioned, they were deluged with protesting letters. These were examined by Henry Fairlie, who wrote (four years afterwards): 'I still shudder at the memory of those letters, the awfulness of which cannot be conveyed to anyone who did not read them'. But apart from the abusive hysteria, he pointed out that the singular feature of the attitudes shown was their monomania, an apparently total and personal absorption in Royal symbolism as the slighted heart of a heartless world. The egg-head critics, he goes on, failed to grasp that 'personal criticisms of the Queen were personal attacks on these millions of humdrum people, attacks on their security and sense of importance. This was the real cause of the hysteria: it was an instinctive response to the threat of danger, real, deeply-felt danger...'. So strong is this response that it looks as if, for some, 'Monarchy is threatening to become the sole prop of the weak, the sole provider of emotional security, the sole cohesive force in society.'[3]

It is easy to see a rough analogy with other talismans of daily life. For example, in any household an old cat or dog can come to represent important things about the family history. These domestic gods endure through tribulations and delights, partly in our dimension and partly in their own, a focus and talking-point which helps build a myth of continuity. Relating to them is a way of relating to one another. Especially where inarticulacy tends to prevail (as in discussing deeper feelings) talking to or about them can be a way of speaking to one another. Then, the loss of a pet can seem like losing a past, and with that something of togetherness.

However, the National-Family gods must stand for something extra: whereas common experience is mostly real (though consolidated by elements of myth), we have seen how the family saga these gods represent is almost entirely myth, boosted here and there by the rarest fragments of personal or direct experience. Yet through them Ukania is imagined as guaranteeing the stuff of actual community, or social or interpersonal relations. Also, the ideological construction of such heartfelt imagery does not, in spite of its 'remoteness', lessen the feelings of attachment, outrage and so on: on the contrary, both the glamour and the fear of loss seem to be intensified. It is the taboo-aspect of the Royal-National vista which heightens the radiance, and keeps the danger at bay. Against this threat the concrete individual and the aloof symbolic personage known only by media and repute are somehow contracted into a single felt identity.

The general purpose of taboo-behaviour is to define and combat social danger. But what is it, in this particular case? 'Danger' does appear a vague notion but (as one important analysis shows) this may be just the point:

> To speak of danger is not equivalent to speaking of the possibility of defeat or annihilation; danger is not a quantitative concept, though we sometimes think of it thus today when we say that a high temperature is dangerous from a certain point onward, or that an illness becomes dangerous, takes a dangerous turn. To face danger is to face another power. Indeed, the older meaning of the English word danger is "power", "jurisdiction", "dominion"...[4]

What the taboo does is localize this fear of alien powers, and prescribe ritual antidotes. Particular 'danger spots' are chosen as the terrain of symbolic confrontation and exorcism. The whole situation can then be 'rendered free from danger by dealing with or, rather, avoiding the specified danger spots completely'. Such 'abstentive behaviour' bestows special meaning on the chosen object or institution: a magic comes to seem inherent in them. Visitors and outsiders may not understand this 'irrational' identification, because they do not share the community inwardness it represents. The point is that 'belonging' has come to be built around it, both as endearing familiarity with what is and (more significant) dread of alien forces or changes. Anything which changes it might change everything. Again, foreigners (or brittle rationalists) are liable to scorn the evident illogic of this inference: how on earth can a totem, fetish or Crown be fateful for *everything*? But what they ignore is the powerful self-fulfilling element built into such conduct: the extent to which 'belonging' and social sentiment attach themselves to some emblem itself renders the magic 'real', and threats to it correspondingly serious.

The imagined preciousness is inseparable from the dread because, unfortunately –

> It is a major fact of human existence that we are not able, and never were able, to express our relation to values in other terms than those of danger behaviour...

Preservation of a taboo makes danger – and hence the affirmation of values - more handleable. It focuses social attention and feeling upon special objects or persons whose particular features are less important than what is being focused on them. There may be illogic, even absurdity, in the particularities; but what counts is the general (abstract) need for *some* particular thing – with or without bald patch – to project the communal imagination on to.

On one side taboo-behaviour relates to dread. But on another, any critic of the Royal pageant is also immediately and constantly told: 'What's the harm in putting a little colour into people's lives?' The implication is infallibly that the critic is some sort of nose-in-the-air, hostile to ordinary enjoyment and out of touch with what people like. The display and pleasure are 'harmless', and not 'really important': a nice *divertissement* it is insensitively heavy to criticise. Foreigners too are supposed to enjoy it all in a brasher, more touristy way: what pleases them is 'the symbol of an extinct type of authority, the pageantry, the fairy-tale dresses and tiaras, the

"EereeshStetKotch", and so on...', as John Weightman also wrote thirty years ago in some 'Loyal Thoughts of an Ex-Republican'.[5] Consequently, Monarchy is *not important enough* to object to in such a long-faced and humourless manner.

Almost any Royal occasion generates a few such contradictory and *bien-pensant* reflections: communion-services of the National identity are never complete without their tincture of educated endorsement (as well as all the madness down below). An especially useful example of this pseudo-theory was provided by the *Guardian* for the Investiture of the Prince of Wales in 1969 (I have chosen it since I want to refer to that ceremony in more detail later). The 'vast crowds' expected failed to turn up at the 'most important Royal event since the Coronation'.

We have seen how Monarchy seems somewhat less crucial to the national soul in Wales and Scotland (Ireland is as usual a different case again). It was correspondingly more important to make a success of the Day, bombs or not. The *Guardian* played its liberal part by putting the Poet Laureate on the centre pages ('...You, sir, inherit/A weight of history in a changing world,/Its treasured wisdom and its true/Aspirings the best birthday gift for you.'), while the Day itself was treated to the superb 'A Place for Panoply':

> Scepticism about established things is at, or has only just passed, its peak in Britain. That the monarchy has survived this scepticism...is largely the work of the Prince of Wales in making such a fresh and positive impact on both monarchy and people...

The liberal accent here consisted in a useful delusion regularly reiterated since Victoria came to the throne in 1837. She, George V, Edward VIII, George VI and Queen Elizabeth have all in turn been envisioned as 'fresh and positive' influences who would help to shake the dust out of old customs and 'modernize' the institution with their personal, common touch. Edward VIII was the most outstanding example. Only belatedly was it grasped that over-vigorous shaking might endanger the customs themselves, since a King could be *too* 'open to new ideas' like Mrs Simpson or what was being done for the unemployed in Nazi Germany.

> As it is (the editorialist went on) the ceremony could be welcomed and enjoyed as an affair of state different from those whose greyness usually preoccupies us...It does no harm to endow the modern panoply of state with some of the beauty and dignity which an old and perhaps irrelevant piece of ritual possesses...The whole event, with its movement and its music (of which there was perhaps not enough) was enjoyable for its artistry, apart from whatever symbolism the witness cared to attach to it. That Prince Charles himself appeared less at his ease on a formal occasion than he has done on far more testing informal ones suggests again that he sees more to his future work than being a Royal Co-Warden.

The piece of ritual was anything but 'old': Lord Snowdon had reinvented it on the basis of Lloyd George's original invention of 1911, before which nobody but mediaeval historians had heard of Investiture (even then with a good deal of scepticism). But more significant than such piety was the small note of criticism, which should be underlined. By such tintinnabulations Liberalism scatters some salt over the popular mush, saving a little self-respect as well as plugging the 'modernizing' theme. Some witnesses are not bowled over by such charades. No indeed, they calmly 'attach' (but very rarely appear to withhold) a measured symbolic meaning, soberly favouring both the colourful side and (most important) the earnest and devoted *work* expected of today's Monarch. The *Guardian* also stands for what is left of Protestant Nonconformity, in which there may linger vestiges of Puritan Levelling: it is therefore consoling to insist how the Royals have to labour at their appointed tasks and enjoy them very little.

The reference to the 'Royal Co-Warden' was a literary rebuke to the writer Nigel Dennis, who in 1955 had produced a surrealist demolition of British delusions called *Cards of Identity*. What the editorial put-down unwittingly acknowledged was that work's importance: like Musil's *Man Without Qualities* in Kakania, it focused with devastating accuracy upon the personal and emotional patterns through which a moribund State sought to prolong its existence - the reproduction of archaism amid guises of spurious modernity. Among its vigorous tableaux of Ukanian life-in-death was a hilarious travesty of 'State Occasions' just like the one at Caernarvon, the tale of 'The Royal Co-Warden of the Badgeries'.

> But what a spectacle was that half-mile of pageantry! Every colour under the sun....was laid out in stripes, blotches and bands, and cut and sewed into the most fantastic forms of blouse, trouser, breech, stocking, and head-piece. Silver and gold, silk and lace, polished steel and shampooed feather - we could see nothing else behind and before and it was only with an effort that I convinced myself that I was a part of this splendour. And how strange the contrast between us superb death-marchers and the living onlookers who crowded the pavements! There they stood, gaping in their gloomy rows, with their shabby suits and abominable footwear, staring dumbfounded at the unreeling of so much obsolescence...

A symbol of ever-reborn national identity, the great stuffed Badger from the long-vanished Forest of Hertford is drawn through these spectators by liveried devotees embodying 'the spirit of English history and institutions...standing for everything whose demise is beyond dispute'.

Dennis's satire is built round the depiction of an estate called Hyde's Mortimer, and cleverly exploits the dual sense of 'estate' in Ukanian mentality. The 'estates' of mediaeval times were the fixed hierarchy of social divisions which preceded the social classes of contemporary (industrial or democratic) society. The 'cards' or codes of English identity are founded upon a synthetic perpetuation of this older system, designed to keep industry and democracy 'in their place'. But there is also the sense of traditional landed property or domain, with its accompanying fabric of lordship, deference and 'station' in life. We saw earlier how the Ukanian hologram is a familial image; yet the smallest adjustment of perspective will at once bring the nation-estate into focus around it. Captain Mallet explains what this is all about in his address to the meeting of the 'Identity Club' at Hyde's Mortimer:

> This sort of house was once a heart and centre of the national identity. A whole world lived in relation to it. Millions knew who they were by reference to it. Hundred of thousands look back to it, and not only grieve for its passing but still depend on

it, non-existent though it is, to tell them who they are. Thousands who never knew it are taught every day to cherish its memory and to believe that without it no man will be able to tell his whereabouts again. It hangs on men's necks like a millstone of memory; carrying it, and looking back on its associations, they stumble indignantly backwards into the future, confident that man's self-knowledge is gone forever...[6]

These places are known as 'stately homes', a term itself encapsulating Dennis's satire.

Discussing recent re-interpretations of British archaeology Neal Ascherson has pointed out that in the Stonehenge era there also lived rulers 'laden with gold and divine knowledge' who tried to stop the rot 'by disguising the old order with the superficial fashions of the new'. As for today –

England teems with this sort of thing. The Cathedral has a disco in the crypt, the Prince affects the language of "street credibility". Or – a favourite of mine - we have adopted the idiotic term "stately home" for huge buildings which have been centres of power affecting the lives of hundreds or thousands of people, whose function as a "home" has been in comparison trivial.[7]

The idiocy is pregnant with Royal logic, however. For Great Britain herself is *the* stately home: the State which is also Home, a power-structure which could not so convincingly be either of these things without the Crown, and a family still in residence. Where appearance is itself a dimension of power, only through them can an apparatus of authority be made to seem so profoundly homely to its subjects.

But all this – which as social critique amounts to a good deal more than either Liberalism or Socialism has produced since the death of J.M.Keynes – was comfortably placed on the great day. 'The Case of the Royal Co-Warden of the Badgeries', declared the *Guardian*, was merely - 'A pastiche of all that is most vacuous about public ceremonial...written when Britain was much more bound to tradition than it is now and when it was still both novel and useful to question institutions which had lingered on...'

This verdict's astounding concretion of literary and historical bad faith rounds off perfectly the posture of a Hyde's

Mortimer Liberalism. While the *Times* goes for full frontals of the spiritual essence, the *Guardian* muses with affected irony on keeping it up with the times. Dennis's surreal insight into the psychological kinks of British hegemony becomes a 'pastiche'; between 1955 and 1969 (as the Investiture itself demonstrated) Britain had in fact grown *more* 'bound to tradition' and to its deeply moribund institutions. And, far from 'lingering on', these were now being assiduously refurbished and re-popularized at Caernarvon (the only essential 'work' undertaken by the Prince of Wales either then or since). This 'enlightened' position merges easily into another standard justification put about by Westminster folk and their academic mouthpieces: the great 'Why Not' theory of British Monarchy. Why not keep it all forever since people love it *and* it doesn't really matter? As the inventors of sensible Parliamentary hegemony, Britons have inherited a sense of proportion about such matters. They are uniquely equipped to devote themselves on work-days to more *serious, substantial* questions (the reader can insert his or her own House-of-Commons quavers and pauses) while such unique equipment also leaves them enviably free to toy lovingly on holidays with the amusing and indeed mildly edifying relics of time past.

This is an attitude unerringly identified by Theodor Adorno in *Minima Moralia*:

> The sense of proportion entails a total obligation to think in terms of the established measures and values. One need only once have heard a diehard representative of the ruling clique say: "That is of no consequence", or note at what times the bourgeois talk of exaggeration, hysteria, folly, to know that the appeal to reason invariably occurs most promptly in apologies for unreason.[8]

'Disavowal'

'What we have is a Mediaeval Monarchy located in No. 10 Downing Street.' Tony Benn, interviewed in 'Is Democracy Working?'

(ITV, Michael Clarke), 22 August 1986.

Thus, we see two contradictory views about the real significance of Monarchy coexisting within the Ukanian mentality,
practically in the same breath: it is all-important, *and* of no real
importance whatever. The absurdity is rendered invisible by
our British sense of proportion. One finds the two notions (for
instance) cuddling up together in that article of Henry Fairlie's
I quoted earlier. After underlining the sense of insecure
personal outrage felt 'by millions of humdrum people' whenever Monarchy is denounced, he goes straight on to say:

> For the life of me, I cannot understand why people should not
> be allowed to enjoy a prettily-staged wedding, or even a
> pompously-staged funeral, without someone breathing fire and
> brimstone down their necks. Nor do I understand the objection
> to pageantry and ceremonial...

And so to an all too normal conclusion: attacks on the Royal
symbols avoid 'the real faults of our society, its lack of national
purpose' (and so forth).

Hence, something capable of provoking a nation-wide
taboo, frothing hysteria and death-threats is also an innocent,
prettily-staged ceremonial no serious British intellect need
worry about. The danger of the Crown becoming 'the sole
cohesive force in society' is, at the same time, just 'a piece of
acceptable nonsense'. It is 'the cherished symbol by which
most of us live'. One might be pardoned for thinking this a
matter of some moment. But no, not really, since it is also 'as
harmless a symbol as any human society could find'. It matters
deeply to nearly everyone and is of no significance whatever.
Grotesque self-contradiction of this order is so common in
both popular and official native commentary about the British
Royals that one has to put it down as systematic. It has the air
of something built in to the lived ideology of Royalism, and for
that reason goes unregarded. Why is this?

The only plausible explanation is that a defensive machinery
is at work, whose very success simultaneously suppresses
awareness of the contradiction. The magic emblem is displaced
by an accompanying taboo from the sphere of the criticizable,
and the act of displacement itself paralyses any critical sense of
what has been done. Then, thoroughly protected by redefinition as 'acceptable nonsense', its actual importance can go on
being accepted and enjoyed.

This phoney dismissal of Royalty appears quite close to Sigmund Freud's definition of *Verleugnung* - 'disavowal' in a psychiatric sense. This is a procedure for retaining a belief by appearing to give it up, and he found it to be most marked in the psychology of fetishism. That is, in situations governed by the fear of male castration. These characteristically result in the choice of some secondary object as the essence of womanhood, like undergarments, hair or breasts. The fetishized object then becomes a partial substitute for 'the whole woman' - the sole way in which a sufferer from the neurosis can project and enjoy sexual interest. The fetishist's 'fixation' on his object keeps him apparently normal. 'It remains a token of triumph over the threat of castration' (Freud goes on) 'and a protection against it. It also saves the fetishist from becoming a homosexual, by endowing women with the characteristic which makes them tolerable as sexual objects'.[9]

However, there has to be a degree of rigidity about his obsession: only over-investment in it keeps the peril at bay and the contradictory-seeming 'disavowal' is merely one way of foiling direct attacks upon it. There is both fear and resentment buried in such behaviour. The victim drools over his surrogate with such effusiveness partly in order to hold down these negative sensations - his dislike of confinement to a few limiting emblems. Hence disavowal (which must never be allowed to get out of hand) both gives relief by expressing a little of this negativity *and* reconducting attention quietly but firmly back to the glamour-laden object.

The possible wider implications of this are noticed by Freud in passing. Fetishism is on his account quite a widespread condition; and there are other, related forms of disavowal which can be interpreted by analogy with the clinical situation. 'In later life', he observes with an irony which came easily under the Habsburgs, 'a grown man may perhaps experience a similar panic when the cry goes up that Throne and Altar are in danger, and similar illogical consequences will ensue...'

One aspect of disavowal is not much stressed in the famous 1927 analysis of *Fetischismus* - the sufferer's pretence of ultr-normality. The neurotic rigidity re-echoes into the machinery of concealment, producing (in effect) a caricature of sober, non-perverse deportment. And naturally, the repression works best when the subject truly believes in this effect. 'The meaning of the fetish is not known to other people, so the fetish is not withheld from him', Freud comments. He can then easily and genuinely convince himself much of the time that it 'doesn't really matter', that it's merely a little added colour and magic setting off the preoccupying greyness of his (enforced) sobriety and utter reasonableness. Thus, the essence of his feeling for life is converted into a decor, harmless wall-paper around the room of quotidian existence; but in that way the room's magic is also preserved, and safeguarded against any possible attack.

The 'real meaning' of the fetish (orgasm, erection, every-thing) becomes for defensive purposes nothing: quaint pagean-try, the EereeshStetKotch with which, as world-leaders of respectable deportment, we choose to mantle our proven gravity. Established past-masters of real, serious political business, the British can surely be permitted such a gracious divertimento? What harm can a bit of cheering and feudal nonsense do? With an inner core consisting of normality itself - the original patent - astonishing charades like the State Opening of Parliament and Trooping the Colour become, indeed, nothing but so many extra testimonials to the utter responsibility, the perennial and practical modernity of the Westminster Constitution. Whether vested in the estate-managers or the workers, only a true and irreproachably club-like masculine strength could play so insouciantly with such frills, such a weirdly perverse blend of the infantile and the living dead.

What corresponds to 'normality' in our metaphor of Royal-British nationality? The 'whole' for which the Monarchical fragment is a surrogate can only be normal nation-state existence: the 'boring' standard of contemporary disenchant-ment upheld by the United Nations: written constitutions supposedly embodying popular sovereignty, Presidents, civil rights rather than the traditional Liberties of Subjects, admin-istrative law as opposed to the Supremacy of Parliament - that sort of thing. Fearing the castration of modernity, an 'infantile' (or early-modern) polity has constructed a fetish of its own retarded essence ('our way of doing things') and imposed an instinctive taboo around it. It's bad form, or in bad taste, to question the projection; while more resolute attacks upon it can be headed off by disavowal.

There are of course historical questions here which the metaphor can't take into account. What is the 'backwardness' being so fervently treasured and defended by this pseudo-nationalist machinery? How could mere backwardness have 'survived' at all in this way, when genuine or Absolute hereditary Monarchy has disappeared? What contemporary (and in a sense forward-looking) interests have been served by such a clearly synthetic cultivation of pastness? These are questions I shall return to later.

Sociology of Grovelling, Part I

> All that remains of the criticism of bourgeois consciousness is the shrug with which doctors have always signalled their complicity with death.

> Theodor Adorno, *Minima Moralia* (1951), 'Ego is Id', p.64.

Returning to the problem of theory, we now have a perspective for understanding the absence of intellectual concern about Monarchy. Middle-brow *Guardian* reflection functions to preserve the national totem-system; the sense of proportion thus expressed is then refracted upwards to the high-brow or academic sphere as simple avoidance – an integrated intellectual élite's chosen form of allegiance. Hence the remarkable result: the British Monarchy, one of the sociological wonders of the contemporary world, Europe's greatest living fossil, the enchanted glass of an early modernity which has otherwise vanished from the globe, has received next to no attention from British social theory. Even more to the point, such attention as it has got consists mainly of acts of worship rather than examination.

Since the original democratic initiative of 'Mass Observation' dwindled after World War II, sociologists have ignored the topic. As Peter Nettl wrote sourly of H.M.'s Sociology in the 1960s:

For more than fifty years British social analysis has neither defined nor solved any problems on a societal scale and has contributed nothing to the development of sociological theory...[10]

This (he goes on to explain) is because Ukanian academics have an ideological monkey on their backs: the need to keep the language 'sacred and mystical', by striving to write 'good' English. In this way 'the complexities of society can be adjusted to the procrustean demands of that mythical beast, the intelligent general reader...Our nose is grimly kept a bare inch above the squiggly furrow of facts'. Thus 'ordinary language' (which is of course also the Queen's English, or estate idiom) has won an almost unceasing 'victory of style over understanding'. Just as evocation of a sense of proportion conceals willed unreason, so the mystique of 'good plain English' suppresses all that 'clarity' - at any given point in time – cannot or will not encompass.

The one contribution which gave rise to any serious professional debate among sociologists was in fact a clever, slavering eulogy of the British Crown. In 1956 the American sociologist Edward Shils published in collaboration with Michael Young a *Sociological Review* article called 'The Meaning of the Coronation'. It was their own academic tribute to the events of three years before. They began by observing 'the careful avoidance of the monarchy's role in British life' which had for long marked both social and political thought, and ascribed this to the 'irrational' nature of the Crown's popularity: 'intellectualist bias' made Professors and Westminster pundits shy away from the subject, rather as (nowadays) they do from religion and things sacred. But 'The heart has its reasons which the mind does not suspect' and perhaps analysis of the great 1953 Coronation rites might show what these are?[11]

The essential argument was that 'The Coronation of Elizabeth II had been the ceremonial occasion for the affirmation of the moral values by which the society lives. It was an act of national communion...' These values have a 'sacred' character requiring periodic reaffirmation and celebration, and this is best achieved by ritual means – that is, through ceremonies and sentiments which, though they may look 'irrational' to intellectuals, appeal to and sustain the social heart.

Shils and Young pressed a famous forebear into service for their own explanation: in his classic *Elementary Forms of Religious Life* the French sociologist Emile Durkheim maintained that all religion is in fact a kind of disguised representation of such collective customs. 'Gods' are the symbolic embodiment of community sentiment, of the ethical standards felt as essential to society's continued existence and health. This explains both the universality and the rational or necessary element in religious observances. While Enlightened thinkers have stressed and denounced the obvious nonsense and spiritual alienation mixed up with religion, they have failed to see its covert utility. How else *could* pre-literate (or minimally literate) societies have been welded into conscious communities – into workable 'cultures' rather than groups held together by force and fear?

While the Windsors are no longer there by 'Divine Right' in the sense fought for by their Stuart ancestors, they are still sustained by such quasi-divine feelings (the article continues). Religion, in contemporary conditions, has been somehow earthed and dissociated from its original focus. But the felt need for the holy persists, and this sacred impulse looks for alternative objects. In Britain at least the Crown has become its primary focus: the moral holiness of society projected into new guardian angels, delighted in as the image of everything still wholesome and presentable about 'us', and defended by appropriate taboos from admixture with the profane (everything non-wholesome, 'foreign', abstract or over-earnest).

There is (the authors note) no aspect of modern Britain more commented on and vaunted than 'The British love of processions, uniforms, and ceremonials'. What other culture can stand comparison with the Royal Tournament, Trooping the Colour, the State Opening of Parliament and the Edinburgh Military Tattoo? Great Monarchic events like Coronations, Weddings and Funerals - 'State Occasions' - are crucial to this popular taste; indeed, without Monarchy at its core it is doubtful whether island pageantry would be (as in other European states) more than vestigial. Shils and Young insist that the fondness for spectacle is not just 'simple-minded gullibility'. It tends to be judged as either 'childish' or 'harmless', according to one's standpoint. In the Shils-Young perspective, however, both verdicts fail to register something important: 'It is the love of proximity to greatness and power, to the charismatic person or institution which partakes of the sacred' that explains the taste. It is less the thrill of uniforms and baroque ceremonial as such than 'the thrill of contact with something great' which justifies the huge crowds and the festive atmosphere.

What is the 'something' to which (in Dennis's satire cited earlier) the archaic pageantry summons the shabby-suited onlookers? It is the idealized moral essence of society. The Coronation rites, as analysed by Shils and Young, support an ethical-religious interpretation: the transformation 'from a mere person into a vessel of the virtues which must flow through him into his society'. If Mediaeval Sovereigns took possession of their society, now society takes possession of them and holds up this burnished shield to gaze at the reflection (an image less of what it glumly is than of what it should strive inwardly to become).

Even Royal devotees might feel the argument to be a trifle unctuous at this point. For example, the persons who assemble at Westminster Abbey to swear and be sworn to are not in any recognizable sense 'representative' of contemporary society. They are in fact the feudal 'estates', with pronounced emphasis upon Nobility and Church. The authors stop short of lining up with the wilder positions taken on the issue at the time: like that of Professor B.Wilkinson, for instance, who affirmed in a special pamphlet brought out by the Historical Association that the Coronation 'presents, as no other political event, a synoptic view of the whole development of modern democracy.'[12]

Shils and Young had the sense to steer clear of this kind of hysteria, no doubt sensing its dangerous implications for the nature of Stately Home democracy. They contented themselves with a humbler and more familiar statement of much greater significance than the immediate context suggests: the mediaeval paraphernalia *didn't matter*. If at the crucial sacred moment it is an enrobed hereditary Establishment that stands in for the nation - well, this is after all *perfectly harmless*: 'no more than a dramatic concentration of the devotion which millions now feel...' More significant than this mere detail of staging is what the whole show demonstrated. The very fact that such a prodigious *représentation collective* could be put on so successfully, as well as all the details of popular devotion and feeling, showed Britain to be a society with an unusually high 'degree of moral consensus'.

That it occurred when it did was also important. Between the two wars there had been a partial breakdown of consensus; the intellectuals, in particular, had grown disaffected with what they saw as a jarring combination of economic failure and imperial pomp – a ruling class on the run, soft on Fascism but determined to hold on to its own colonial loot, disguising bankruptcy with tawdry Royal charades. By the early 1950s all this seemed healed.

In another study Shils himself has commented on the drastic change of climate which war, victory and the Labour government had brought about:

> Deeply critical voices became rare. In 1953, I heard an eminent man of the left say, in utter seriousness, at a university dinner, that the British constitution was "as nearly perfect as any human institution could be", and noone even thought it amusing...Great Britain on the whole, and especially in comparison with other countries, seemed to the British intellectual of the early 1950s to be fundamentally all right and even much more than that. Never had an intellectual class found its society and its culture so much to its satisfaction....The British intellectual came to feel proud of the moral stature of a country with so much solidarity and so little acrimony between classes.[13]

Hence, the generally semi-religious quality of a Monarchic constitution was reconsecrated by these special circumstances: traditional authority and the basic moral cement of social order were strengthened together, made as one by popular participation in a key ritual celebration. If there was an 'archaic' side to the latter, concluded the authors, we should remember it is *not sociologically significant*.

The reason for this should be marked well since it is a notion which we are now familiar with: all the backward aspects of Regal soap-opera don't count, Shils and Young maintained, because 'behind the archaic façade was *a vital sense of permanent contemporaneity*'. In other words, it doesn't (in Ascherson's words quoted above) 'disguise the old order with the superficial fashions of the new': quite the contrary – it disguises what's really modern with the superficial fashions of the old, detached from their original context and carried forward as tokens of communal well-being. As such, these emblems are guaranteed harmless and merely 'colourful': not badges of inward shame and hopelessness, but the insouciant symbols of a society so confident of its modernity that it can afford to play charades with the imagery of the past.

There is no reason to think that 'The Meaning of the Coronation' had been commissioned or suggested by the Buckingham Palace press office (at that time certainly incapable of such initiative). Nonetheless, it depicted a self-satisfied country comfortably restored (after the Thirties, War and Socialism) to the colourful warmth and simple old values of Ukania. With Durkheim's help, it even gave a little theoretical gloss to Old Régime conservatism: no small feat, since the latter's anomalies have generally produced either embarassed silence or incomprehensible knots.

Sociology of Grovelling, Part 2

In the end, glorification of splendid underdogs is nothing other than glorification of the splendid system that makes them so.

Theodor Adorno, *Minima Moralia*,
'They, the People', p.28.

The perils of even this modest piece of theory were soon revealed. For all their adulation Shils and Young had been unable to avoid excess: the extrusion of a recognizable and hence attackable idea from the solid corpus of faith and everyday 'good English'. Since 1979 this kind of thing has grown familiar, but in the good old times it was unknown. Reaction to such a suspiciously egg-head Loyalism duly came in the shape of 'Monarchs and Sociologists', a reply by Professor Norman Birnbaum.[14]

A socialist linked with the New Left movement of the later 1950s, Birnbaum maintained that Shils and Young were poisoned by 'their own strong feeling of adherence to the official morality of Great Britain — and their preference for conformity to such moralities wherever they appear'. But what this conformist bias failed to confront was the fact that 'Conflict seems to be as prevalent a component of social life as order'. As for the 'moral values' which cause order to prevail and give such meaning to Monarchy, these are intolerably vague. 'Generosity', 'loyalty', 'reasonable respect for authority' and the other norms quoted can mean everything or nothing: since when has everybody agreed (even in Britain) the amount of respect for policemen and traffic wardens which is 'reasonable'?

Underlying the Shils-Young smugness, Birnbaum claims, is really their conviction that 'The assimilation of the working class into the moral consensus of British society....has gone further in Britain than anywhere else, and its transformation from one of the most unruly and violent into one of the most orderly and law-abiding (of classes) is one of the great collective achievements of modern times'. Society viewed through the Royal-left eyeglass always means 'class', in that ambiguous Ukanian sense noted earlier; and Shils and Young were asserting that 'class' was secondary, and of decreasing significance.

Not so, he continues: visitors to Great Britain are invariably struck by the 'now traditionalized and self-conscious class consciousness' of workers – by their degree of separateness and exclusion, by the glaring proliferation of caste-marks in all spheres of social existence. Farthermore, it has been *their* separate struggles (and victories) which have forged the very situation so misunderstood by Shils and Young. Monarchy arrived where it is today via 'a successive series of capitulations to republican demands'; such 'integration' as we see today came about only through a century of Labour's own class battles to 'bring *the propertied* into the national moral life for the first time'. Civilization has really been made from below, not from above. As for the Royals, in those struggles they 'had to choose between accepting socialism or unemployment' and it is scarcely surprising they opted for the former.

Neither have the two authors demonstrated the real importance of the Crown in such consensus as there is (Birnbaum went on). More 'prosaic questions' of popular sovereignty, parliament and administration should come first. Officials of H.M.'s Department of Health and Social Security are a lot more relevant to the 'basic values of the populace' than the Regal flunkeys and horses. As for Durkheim, their attempt at theory merely 'fails to distinguish between ritual and real behaviour'. Hence (he concluded) an alternative explanation might just as well run like this:

> The very absence of shared values in Great Britain accounts for some of the attention paid to the Coronation... (which) provided a measure of surcease from that condition of conflict which is more or less permanent for complex societies of an industrial type...But the Coronation was a holiday, and its connections with the daily routine of social relationships was by no means as critical as the authors imagine. In this context, the personality of the Queen and her family functioned as the object of various fantasies and identifications in a way not much more "sacred" than the cult of adulation built up around certain film stars.

Birnbaum's riposte was one of the most concise and magisterial expressions of Left-Ukanian mythology in the post-war era. The tapestry of Whig-Labour belief is all here in miniature: moral/class community, uplift from below, and achievement yet to come. Though couched in the over-respectful tones appropriate to the *Sociological Review* (where Professors accuse one another of 'not entirely escaping ambiguity' and failing to 'present events in scientific terms') there was also real rage in it. As clearly as anywhere else such justified fury shows in his remark that –

> Those who, with Professor Shils and Mr Young, argue that the tinsel revels of the Coronation holiday in Britain represent an ultimate in gratification are hardly in a position to reproach the rest of us for contempt of our fellow humans...

Like 'deeply moving' or 'thousand-year history' on the other side, 'tinsel revels' is of course a paradigm-phrase betraying to the hearer exactly where he or she is in terms of underlying attitude.

It is worth underlining how both these attempts at a theory of national obeisance agree on one crucial obfuscation. For

Shils and Young the stuffed-badger side of Royalty didn't really matter because of the State's hidden realism and contemporaneity. For Birnbaum it didn't matter because of the Nation's hidden yet commanding pressures from below – the civilizing hegemony of its working-class majority (which simply needs more time to get rid of the tinsel). Thus, the Royal taboo is recapitulated by both Right and Left in a kind of tacit consensus. For the former the ruling class is *really* modernizing, republican in spirit and so on – its symbolism of antique moral communion and familial spirit is, therefore, a sort of healthy and justified lie. For the Left it is the Labour-led people which exhibits these progressive virtues - affirmed in spite of tinselly charades and the obstructive show-business of reaction. The 'show' is judged very differently in the moral/ class sense; but there is agreement on it being just a show.

By definition a 'show' in that sense cannot reflect reality, society's truth. But even on the basis of what we have looked at so far, caution is surely called for here: Ukanian ideology is at work in the definition itself. What is being ruled out by it is the straightforward notion that an archaic institution may express something deeply and incorrigibly archaic about the society whose institution it is: that these may be the 'occasions' of a social formation itself quite authentically 'backward'. Also ruled out is the possibility that this State may in reality be uncompensated for either by an alertly modernizing élite or a proletariat capable of redeeming things from below. Such unworthy suspicion is disavowed by the fixed, deeply reassuring conviction that all *that* is mere appearance. The living onlookers *must* believe there is something other than death behind the death-marchers: were this belief lost, why, nothing would be left on the *sol sacré* – neither the resonant historical triumphs of a ruling order nor the richly unfolding moral conquests of its subjects. The Estate-essence and all its insidious glamour would be no more. The day of general secular hangover would have come at last, disclosing a sub-ordinary nation-state of ever more shabby suits and abominable footwear, Europe's Crowned but disenchanted Skid Row of the Third Millenium.

Enchantment in Retrospect

We shall treat the Whig interpretation of history... not as a thing invented by some particularly wilful historian, but as part of the landscape of English life, like our country lanes or our November mists or our historic inns... It is itself a product of history, part of the inescapable inheritance of Englishmen...'

Herbert Butterfield, *The Englishman and his History* (1944)
p.2.

Sociological and empirical theories like these do little but rehearse certain underlying Ukanian assumptions. They resemble the gladiatorial rhetoric of the Mother of Parliaments, where all rows really exist to fortify the Crown and not to undermine it. Monarchy and 'society' are counterposed in a phoney and utterly philistine manner as show and reality – a contrast from which all the factors permitting one to make sense of either are wilfully occluded. What are these? In still cryptic form which I will try to decode : pastness and national identity, History and the Nation.

Most sociological, political and constitutional views of Monarchy prefer a static-system explanation, qualified only by the hovering *Geist* of Whiggism: where change is unavoidable it will, if controlled by responsible chaps, be for the better. Yet in terms of the concrete experience so privileged by Régime philosophy, this occlusion is odd. For if one experiential aspect of the 'object of special significance' imagined, venerated and cheered on at Royal circuses stands out it is surely this: pastness. The Coronation was not (or was not only) an effigy of British society's cherished values in the year A.D. 1953 (whether its representation of these be considered valid, biased, holiday-like, oppressive or just ludicrous). It also projected history as the great prop of the performance: a legendary 'thousand years' all somehow alive and watching from the shadows of Westminster Abbey.

Richard Dimbleby's famed B.B.C. commentary on the Crowning packed the-past-is-with-us sentiment into every throbbing syllable: what the hearers were invited to revere was not their collectivity as of that moment in time, but that moment itself as the culmination of a communal collectivity which had endured since....well, the paterfamilias of Britannic clichés, 'time immemorial'. In the cinema film which followed, after a decontaminatory blast from Shakespeare, Sir Laurence Olivier's script (by Christopher Fry) went on to describe the moment of annointing - 'the hallowing, the sacring' – as so old that 'history is scarce deep enough to contain it'.

In my own modest collection of Regal memorabilia lies a booklet produced by the City of Oxford Secondary Teachers' Association to mark Coronation Year. 'The idea of monarchy is as old as history, and indeed older....' began Mr.R.S.Stanier of Magdalen College School in similar vein. Given by Divine Providence along with upright posture and the faculty of speech, the true function of Kings has always been to speak symbolically 'to the fundamental instincts of the human heart'. There was some trouble when Monarchs went beyond this and dabbled in politics: a King who does this *and* claims superhuman authority 'will be as unpopular as the man who wants to join in a game of football with special permission to break all the rules'. But when this was put right the Crown carried forward the essential spirituality of our history. All the other booklet items – Music, Heraldry, the Order of Service, - are firmly encased in this historical involucrum where all Britain's post-Neanderthal generations crowd in and explain why 'Today we all, as loyal subjects, feel our welfare, the welfare of the country, curiously bound up with that of the Queen...'

Anti-monarchists like Birnbaum acknowledge the big drum of the ideological brass band with the accusation of 'anachronism': the Royal parade is indeed the past, too much with us – an out-of-date reliquary shameful to the modern-minded and positively obstructing preparations for the 21st century. But here the past is recognized only to be discounted, or glibly replaced with an alternative mythology of history-from-below. Both tactics conjure away the felt weight and significance of its symbolism: the density of actual experience to which State occasions and Royal *Kitsch* appeal.

They ignore – looking at the subject from a different angle - how in Britain solemn moments are nearly always given Shakespearian vestment as their badge of national continuity. Shakespeare's pre-modern attitudes can all too easily be misinterpreted as sage and profoundly-rooted national resistance to the doctrinaire: what is too much democracy but the sort of mob rule which his Monarchs enjoy putting to rights? Against that there stands an apparently more human, concrete perspective. Though in fact it looked back to the middle ages and underwrote Tudor Absolutism, post-1800 apologists have made this retrospect into a 'timeless' (hence forward-looking) view. In the 'Royal Throne of Kings' Wilson Knight observes that –

> There is properly no contradiction between royalty and democracy; rather they supplement and complete each other...Royalty at its best has always functioned in unison with a willing allegiance, and has been to that extent dependent on freedom.[15]

Real democracy will exist only when 'every man is, in his own proper self, a king' - when the ordinary has become extraordinary, the humdrum been dissolved in glamour: when mortals step into the enchanted glass or its visions step down to join us. But as we've seen, this is the whole content of today's night and daydreams about Royalty. Aren't these impossible? Well, that's human nature for you: 'here we are brought up against the tragic inadequacies of mankind...' Shakespeare is all too often credited with the last word on such tragic inadequacies. Best stay with what we've got in the demi-paradise, since a republican democracy would only succumb to these pitfalls of fate..

That English culture boasted this emblem was a great piece of good fortune. The poet of its early-modern era concocted a fake-mediaeval past for his own Sovereigns; later, when the impact of democracy and industrialization inspired another bout of tradition-inventing, ideologists could evoke this great precedent - romantic pastness and anti-modernism now had their own history to go on, a real continuity of the *ersatz* solidly implanted in mass consciousness. By the time Edmund Burke and Pitt had finished in the early 1800s, synthetic pastness had turned into a version of national identity. And – as we will go on to see – Monarchy played a vital part in this consolidation. It allowed the formation of a traditional*ism* quite distinct from mere feudal or folk tradition: an 'ism' in which the past was re-synthesized as contemporary identity. And this 'identity' occupies the dimension of nationality, not that of 'society' in the limited meaning sanctioned by the warped idiom of socio-political thought our collective sense of proportion prescribes; the sense itself has been determined by the overriding national identity of the Crown.

Theoretical indifference to Monarchy, in other words, is a manifestation of blindness to nationalism. Both the prominence of the Royal in Ukanian life *and* the virtual absence of explanations for such prominence derive from incuriosity about 'the national' as a specific problematic - a set of questions or dilemmas demanding investigation. No point in that, old chap: we know who we are. It's only foreigners who have to work themselves up over that sort of thing, regularly abandoning all sense of proportion as they do so.

Monarchy and Nationalism

Genuine charismatic domination knows of no abstract legal codes and statutes and of no "formal" way of adjudication. Its "objective" law emanates concretely from the highly personal experience of heavenly grace... "It is written, but I say unto you".

Max Weber, 'The Sociology of Charismatic Authority,' *Max Weber: Essays in Sociology*, edit. Gerth and Mills (1948) p.250.

The Ukanian Monarchy is in essence a heteronomous form of nationalism: that is, a variety 'subject to different laws' from the standard forms of that ideology, and with 'different modes of growth' (*O.E.D.*). One important aspect of that difference is – as we shall see – that the Monarchy *doesn't appear to be* nationalist. It defines itself, necessarily, as being precisely above or beyond 'that sort of thing' – a stance which, in the world of nation-states, has comported both weaknesses and remarkable (and frequently under-estimated) strengths. 'That sort of thing' includes the existing political framework of the world, and much of its history since the 18th century. This is why it is only within such a broader context that we can hope to locate and decipher the mysteries of persistent U.K. Royalism.

The crucial point here is that we admit the inevitability of nation-state development *as* a vehicle of modernity. For it is the general compulsions of that mode of development which have in turn fostered the general need for 'national identity' - those kinds of collective identification and allegiance making up a national culture. The same need, by implication, has generated what one could metaphorically call national 'neuroses', 'obsessions', and so on - the deviant, regressive or anachronistic actual forms which the underlying structural necessity has so often assumed.

This point has to be underlined because of the significant weakness just mentioned - Ukanian culture's tendency to diminish or downplay a whole range of related questions, and (in effect) to dismiss nationalism as something inherently 'foreign' or alien. In reality, nationalism is the standard politico-cultural component of the modern order of nation-states. That political order itself has been mainly produced and systematized since the 18th century, and can most reliably be dated by reference to the American and French Revolutions (1776 and 1789). What it expresses is the mainstream-process of social and economic development towards today's society: 'industrialization'. As Ernest Gellner puts it in *Nations and Nationalism* –

> Patriotism is a perennial part of human life...(while) nationalism is a very distinctive species of patriotism, and one which becomes pervasive and dominant only under certain social conditions, which in fact prevail in the modern world, and nowhere else...[16]

In other words national*ism*, in the systemic sense denoted by the term's ending, arose only through the middle-class revolutions of the 18th century and later – an accompaniment of 'progress' and continuous economic growth. It was a part of the constellation of new attitudes and ideas which fought or undermined the European *Ancien Régimes* from 1688 onwards, broke through in the American and French Revolutions, and led to their ultimate collapse in 1917-18. By that time the nation-state was established as the 'natural' model of political development and lodged as such in the ideology of both the Versailles Treaty and the League of Nations.

There were two main causes for this. The first was external: 'Industrialization inevitably comes to different places and groups at different times' (Gellner also points out) so that the pioneers can't help gaining an enormous advantage over societies still cast in a feudal or agrarian mould. The advantage leads them into an 'imperial' position vis-à-vis the now 'backward' world about them (whether manifested in political colonization or in the purely economic ascendancy more characteristic of post-1945). But the under-developed must attempt to catch up, or fight back. Hence –

> As the tidal wave of modernization sweeps the world, it makes sure that almost everyone...has cause to feel unjustly treated, and that he can identify the culprits as being of another "nation". If he can identify enough of the victims as being of the same "nation" as himself, a nationalism is born...

The broad socio-economic progress typical of modernity is incapable of steady diffusion outwards or downwards from its primary sources: the Enlightenment dream of revolutionary Progress dispensed from above, and gratefully taken up below (or outside). The Scottish Enlightenment was to be the sole example of such advance, in quite exceptional conditions which vanished once a more modern political pattern had replaced the élite managerialism of the 18th century.[17]

Elsewhere, progress proved inherently antagonistic and political in nature, creating an ever-shifting frontier of resentment and combat between 'haves' and 'have-nots', between the leaders and those dragged or enticed into the forced march of development. National*ism* is one feature of this predicament: and as the predicament became universal so did the 'ism' – forging a world in which national identity inevitably took precedence over the many other historical forms of allegiance or communal feeling. From such inevitability there follows a general rationality: however dotty particular versions of the creed may be, and however pathological national identity may have shown itself during the counter-revolutionary years between 1920 and 1945, in a broader sense nationalism is a necessary condition of tolerable modernization. It is not (as so often portrayed by the modern Left's version of the Enlightenment credo) a merely atavistic refusal of the modern, or a choice of the irrational.

At the same time, certain internal traits of post-feudal society powerfully reinforced the same tendency. Here modernization entailed both a political and a cultural drive towards greater homogeneity. As industry became a primary aim, populations had to be freed from rural servitude and illiteracy: the move from field to factory or shop floor was also one from a local or dialect culture into education and a national tongue. As Gellner points out, industrialization demands social mobility; but such mobility can only occur where old caste, tribal or guild barriers are broken down; *and* it can only happen within a common medium, a standard language shared by the employers and the new urban proletariat. In old agrarian society –

> Sharp separations of the population into estates or castes or millets can be established and maintained without creating intolerable frictions. On the contrary, by externalizing, making absolute and underwriting inequalities, it fortifies them and makes them palatable, by endowing them with the aura of inevitability, permanence and naturalness.[18]

By contrast, in the 'inherently mobile and unstable societies' driven towards industrialization, maintenance of such social dams is intolerably difficult.

For them a formalized common language is a necessity. The culture this represents becomes a basic part of the social structure. As that outstanding linguist Joseph Stalin observed, language is not classifiable as either 'base' or 'superstructure' in the Marxist socio-economic sense: these are categories of bourgeois modernity, and the modern presupposes communication. Gellner's point of view here was referred to earlier:

> Culture ...is no longer merely the adornment, confirmation and legitimation of a social order which was also sustained by harsher and coercive constraints; culture is now the necessary shared medium, the life-blood or perhaps rather the minimal shared atmosphere, within which alone the members of the society can breathe and survive and produce. For a given

society, it must be one in which they can *all* breathe and speak and produce; so it must be the *same* (literate, training-sustained) culture.

This is the conjunction of external and internal pressures that has forged national-ism, the world of obligatory nation-states and national identities. Outwardly, industrial modernity took the form of a 'metropolitan' tidal wave, impacting on successive strata of traditional societies; inwardly, the response to that challenge brought a forced socio-economic mobilization tied to inescapable requirements of common language-culture and a new kind of political cohesion. The universal form of such mobilization has been the nation-state - the only possible expression of an epoch of Progress whose actual content has also been an 'uneven development' sown with hostility, competition and warfare.

In this epoch, 'national identity' is no philosophical luxury but part of the material structure of society. Contrary to much British thinking on the subject (whose peculiarities are summed up in Crown-worship), nationalism is in itself neither foreign, narrow, neurotic, merely accidental nor *dépassé*. All that such odd ideas reflect is the heteronomy of British or Ukanian nationalism itself: a national identity isolated from the mainstream of nation-building by its own history, and which now (like Humpty-Dumpty on top of his wall) habitually judges the passing parade only in its own preconceived terms.

English Nationality

During the last war, in the course of my duties as an itinerant lecturer to the Forces... I sometimes used to be invited to spend a night at Althorp as the guest of Lady Diana's grandfather Jack Spencer and his lovely wife Cynthia – herself a lifelong servant of the Crown and the perfect ideal of an English lady. They were living at the time in great simplicity; their stately home and all its treasures were under dust-sheets, and we used to eat our frugal supper of spam or some other austere wartime dish in a small room lined from ceiling to floor with tantalizing pictures of 18th. century fat cattle.

Sir Arthur Bryant, 'Royal Wedding', in the
Illustrated London News Supplement, 1981.

To clarify the topography farther, it may be worth looking at one typical view of the history of English nationalism, older but authoritative in its day. The American scholar Hans Kohn was for long the most influential figure in the field, and specialized in the comparative study of nationalist ideologies. In an article on 'The Genesis and Character of English Nationalism', we find him tracing its principal traits to the 17th century 'Puritan Revolution' against Charles I. It was that upheaval which promoted 'a new nationalism....fundamentally liberal and universal', driven on by Protestant fervour. 'Like Israel in antiquity, the English now were called to glorify God's name on earth, to achieve the final Reformation and to teach nations how to live'. While conceding the presumptuous egoism of this design, Kohn invariably underlines its 'immense liberating importance'. Milton's moral chest-beating is quoted with approval unqualified by even mild censure:

> I seem to survey, as from a towering height....innumerable crowds of spectators betraying in their looks the liveliest interest, and sensations the most congenial with my own....From the columns of Hercules to the Indian Ocean I behold the nations of the earth recovering that liberty which they had so long lost; and the people of this island are disseminating the blessings of civilization and freedom among cities, kingdoms, and nations.[19]

Was there a touch of imperialism in these commanding heights and congenial sensations? Could it also imply that people like the Irish, notoriously resistant to the Word of the Lord, were due for severe chastisement as 'lawless rebels' in the service of Anti-Christ? Minor blemishes according to Kohn, who insists that Cromwell's vision of 'liberty and fortune' was (mostly) the precursor of modern liberalism. The Puritans were equivalent to the radical Jacobins of the later French Revolution, only better (because more moral, and less intellectual). Through their influence:

> England was the first country where a national consciousness embraced the whole people. It became so deeply engrained in the English mind that nationalism lost its problematic character with the English. It is for this reason that English philosophical thought in the 19th century offers relatively little meditation upon nationalism, its theory and implications.

For the same reason (he concludes) British imperialism was 'never only power-politics' and British Socialism ('religious, liberal and humanitarian') never mere class-struggle or revolutionism.

Thus, there has been a moral, liberating kind of nationalism which was (and is) in humanity's general interest. It started in England, then moved on to America and France: the Revolutions of 1776 and 1789 were fuller expressions of the same emancipatory movement. As a liberal Zionist Kohn's hope was that the new State of Israel would join the club. This God-blessed historical trend recognized 'the essential oneness of mankind and the desirability of a rational world order'; whatever excesses the British, French and American empires may have committed should be excused for that reason. They have assumed an *institutional form* based on Enlightenment values – democratic States which promoted popular sovereignty and freedom even while occasionally (though half excusably) oppressing other peoples. Kohn thought that the indifference of later Anglo-Britain to the nationalist problematic reposed upon early national maturity - a solution already achieved and rightly taken for granted.

But it is surely possible to suggest another and less flattering explanation of such vagueness and hostility to the 'ism' side of nationalism. For Kohn – and, one suspects, for anyone taking the modern configuration of British nationality for granted - religion did what it took revolution and nationalist warfare to accomplish elsewhere, in the less 'mature' outside world where people had to worry who they were. His theory sets what is really the gist of 'the Whig Interpretation of history' within a general perspective on the development of nationalism. Yet the most striking feature of this placement is that – even on the evidence of Kohn's many other works on nationalist history - it cannot possibly be true. One may of course say that elements of identity have survived intact from the Reformation to the present: but in itself this is truism – there are no states of which something like that is not the case. But what's not true is that such survival, even if unusually complete, was unaffected by Waterloo and Peterloo, by the generation of warfare after 1793, by Empire and the renaissance of Monarchy, or by the quickening decline of this century.

The point is that on any strict or comparative definition of the term, *nationalist* history did not begin until the later 18th century. National-ism is the systematic prominence of the factors of nationality in modern development - where 'modern' has as one of its key connotations the political idea of popular sovereignty. Only when the latter broke through with the American and French Revolutions did 'nations' acquire their decisive importance as the vectors of both political and economic development. Ethnic nationality itself may be older than recorded history; but the 'nation' as an imagined primary agency of all change and progress is relatively recent (and distinctly newer than the British Crown-State, easily the oldest gentleman-resident in U.N.O. clubland). Kohn's definition of his subject-matter was therefore too vague. It has been overtaken in theory by Ernest Gellner's precision:

> The great, but valid, paradox is this: nations can be defined only in terms of the age of nationalism, rather than, as you might expect, the other way round. It is not the case that "the age of nationalism" is a mere summation of the awakening and political self-assertion of this, that, or the other nation. Rather, when general social conditions make for standardized, homogeneous, centrally sustained high cultures, pervading entire populations and not just élite minorities, a situation arises in which well-defined educationally sanctioned and unified cultures constitute very nearly the only kind of unit with which men willingly and often ardently identify...Under these conditions, though under these conditions *only*, nations can indeed be defined in terms both of will and of culture, and indeed in terms of the convergence of them both with political units.[20]

We shall go on to see in more detail just how these observations translate into the English and British cases. But first let me pose a very general interpretation. When all the blood rushed to Britain's head during its great battle with revolutionary and imperial France from the 1790s to 1815, a nationalism was indeed created along the very broad lines Gellner suggests.

However it was forged not only to express the 'general social conditions' of modernity described but (uniquely) also for the opposite motive: to pre-empt and politically arrest these conditions. The resultant Royal-conservative identity 'pervaded the entire population' all right, and forged the basis of a successfully 'unified culture' on the crucial political plane. Thanks to military and naval victory, and to command of the world market, it quite easily established a sufficient and lasting degree of 'convergence' between the political unit and its subjacent 'will and culture' – the supportive civil structures of national identity. A workable Royal-National 'We' was put in place and could later be reanimated and - when the material development of communications permitted – successfully inflated into the mass hypnosis of late-Victorian or Imperialist times.

All students of *The Making of the English Working Class* and other radical accounts of the period know how disunited, hypocritical, and brutally repressive that identity really was, and how long it actually took to impose. Only after the decline of Chartism in the later 1840s did it become unchallengeable. However, any overall judgement will depend on which factors are privileged in one's historical perspective. In the primarily social and economic retrospect of Anglo-British culture, it remains tempting to focus upon a heroism and injustice still to be redeemed: inspiration for a struggle almost by definition continuous and incremental. In the searchlight cast back by preoccupation with the Monarchy, however, I must point out that this image is practically inverted. Here the historical nature of the State is primary, and one is forced to recognize the virtually total triumph of a conservative political order. Such ascendancy was renewed by adaptation, certainly – by reforms of a type which (unlike the Absolutist régimes of the Holy Alliance) this State was able to make. And by far the most significant of these was not Parliamentary Reform but the forging of a popular nationalism - the successful early deployment of a singular but viable national identity articulated around the Crown.

Farthermore, what this production accomplished was, in a sense, to keep the real and uncomfortable kernel of nationalism permanently at bay. That is what we find registered in

Received Pronunciation's deep unease with ethnic and national discourse, and the associated idioms of race and colour. Not *really* important, old fellow (though one has to try and be nice about it). National*ism* is inherently populist: it is the conception of a people's sovereignty and innate agency, which (therefore) a national State is in principle supposed to embody and serve. But - precisely - such populism was and has remained utter anathema to Great Britain's post-1688 State. For long the most liberal and advanced of countries in a Europe still dominated by Absolutism, it grew abruptly middle-aged in the face of 1776 and 1789. As everyone knows, within a few years it had become the ally of Tsar, Emperor and Pope in opposition to Revolution.

But unlike these allies, the British ruling class was able to mobilize an at least partially modern (specifically, an 'early-modern') social and psychic structure for the great counter-revolutionary crusade. Unlike the true *anciens régimes* with which it was allied – even those which had benefited from the 18th century's 'Enlightened Despotism' - this early-modern State proved quite capable of concocting a viable popular patriotism from which the dangerous acids of populism and egalitarianism were bleached out. And from the start a vital feature of that surrogate national identity was a new emphasis on Monarchy. The Crown alone could provide a compensatory symbolic focus and give a phoney yet concrete and imaginable sense of equality - of belonging within a traditional State-family, of a community putting both gender and class 'in their place'.

Another way of describing this is to say that 'maturity' (by what became the standard canons of nationalist development) was avoided. Far from being complete by the 17th century – as Kohn thought - it was deliberately and permanently eschewed in the 19th. The United Kingdom's contribution to the spectrum of nationalism was to be a unique familial patriotism intended to suppress all the awkward and plebeian aspects of national awakening - its capacity for either a democratic or an ethnic assertiveness 'from below'. It was designed to prevent the hour of W.B.Yeats's 'rough beast' from ever coming round – the 'shape with lion body and the head of a man' whose arrival separated the falcon from its master and meant the centre could not hold. Instead, a kind of permanent *immaturity* was chosen: the cautious arm's length from modernity that suited a national patriciate defending an earlier economy and form of State – a social order now overtaken by the second wave of bourgeois revolution but still capable of defending its historical corner for a very long time. This had to be a national-popular identity composed decisively 'from above': an ideological sense of belonging dispensed by quasi-parental law, securing its unwritten authority-structure and proposing a kind of compensated deference.

Thus, it may also be said that the real question of nationalism – the question of its place as a constitutive part of modernity – was never solved in Britain, because never raised. The elements of infantilism so plainly present in the Royal infatuation derive from this history. Such 'immaturity' was for long justified – and a good conscience maintained about it - by a combination of external good fortune and the many and visible disasters of nationalism elsewhere. However, what has been decried and held at bay is not - as the Ukanian Establishment still wants to believe – just nationalist 'narrowness'. It has been to some extent also the real and in the longer run inescapable shifts of modern development itself. British society has resisted, delayed, and in some respects indefinitely postponed such moments by a distinctive set of attitudes focused and given popular resonance through the modern Monarchy. But the delay couldn't go on for ever. By 1979 its time was up.

Leviathan and Later

When Dundas tried to explain to George III in 1799 that the Coronation Oath bound him as the Crown administering laws but not as the King giving his assent to laws passed by Parliament, the King cried: "None of your Scotch metaphysics Me. Dundas, none of your Scotch metaphysics!"

Michael MacDonagh, *The English King* (1929) p.52.

As I have already noted, no notion is dearer to the Royal culture than British aversion to theory: the natural Glory of an 'empirical idiom' indifferent to loony abstraction.[21] And nowhere has such glory been more in evidence than on Royalty itself, a subject upon which until the 1980s almost noone had written an intellectually serious word since Bolingbroke (1678-1751). There is another historical fact unpalatable to this culture which it is important to stress: before the consecration of Empiricism as psychic partner of the Whig State, there was an earlier British *mentalité* which led Europe in fanatical theorization of Monarchy. The last product of that world-view, Thomas Hobbes's *Leviathan* (1651), was the most uncompromising of all justifications of Absolutism. Even such a staunch defender of post-Hobbesian conservatism as the modern Tory philosopher Michael Oakshott, is obliged to call it 'the greatest, perhaps the sole, masterpiece of political philosophy in the English language'.

For radically different historical reasons, both the Scottish and the English Monarchies found great - and finally insurmountable – obstacles to the establishment of genuinely all-powerful Kingly states. It is the English problems that concern us here. For it is their history underlaid the drive towards Divine-Right Monarchy, and decided its outcome in the twenty years of Revolution and Civil War after 1640. That end-product in turn defined the foundations of what we experience today: a political world regulated by what must be called Parliamentary Divine Right, amplified and sustained on an ideological plane by the popular glamour of Monarchy.

It was the difficulties encountered by the consolidation of British Absolutism that led to such doctrinal exaggeration - a compensation on the plane of theory that issued first in the notion of the Divine Right of Kings and then (as the would-be Absolute Monarchy collapsed) in Hobbes's secularized and materialist equivalent.

'That to the Reformation was in some sort due the prevalence of the notion of the Divine Right of Kings is generally admitted', notes the most important historian of the notion. It was an early modern rather than a feudal concept. The idea followed logically from the principles of the Henrician Reformation in England. Once the right of the Pope and his Church to override national authority had been denied, each Monarch was compelled to buttress that authority with other means.

Deity was invoked to support each dynasty directly. No longer ruling with the legitimation of a Universal intermediary, Kings and Queens could only claim an inherited Divine Right: secular power made unchallengeable by immediate sacred affinity. In its day and context this was a progressive theory, in other words, rather than the mediaeval superstition with which it tends to be confused. Its most pronounced development took place in Britain rather than in France.

Before the 1688 Fall into the Parliamentary-empirical, observes J.N.Figgis, French thought about Monarchy was normally 'less theological, less transcendental, more legal and local than English'.[22] It failed to leap with glee on the newly-discovered abstractions of Divine-Right philosophy. It did not require to. In a series of pragmatic moves France's dynasty succeeded in forging the model reality of Absolute Monarchy in the 17th century. Faced by much bigger obstacles, the Stuarts failed to do so; and the resultant theoretical furore of Divine Right was only one aspect of their long struggle for unrestricted power.

In 1603 the Scottish God-King succeeded by fortunate dynastic accident to the English throne. Although the Scottish line had twice been debarred from the succession, these Acts were now rendered inoperative by the Divine-Right principle itself: physical legitimacy too had become absolute, and unchallengeable. As Figgis observes, James's coming lent a farther and fatal edge of Caledonian abstraction to the case. Scotland's conditions were more feudal, and its Reformation had been both more violent and more learned. James's *The Divine Law of Trew Monarchies* was the result: a disastrously thorough treatise on the need for unqualified Royal power. Half a century later his son Charles paid with his head for failure to translate that doctrine into practice.

Divine Right extremism vanished for a time once Charles was gone and the Royal enthusiasts had crowded round to dip their handkerchiefs in his blood. But it was not finally defeated until a century later, on the battlefield of Culloden. To Charles's Stuart successors the same exasperating dilemma represented itself: they saw their role not merely as restorers of the past but as modernizers, in a Europe where rational and bureaucratic Absolutism appeared ever more preponderant and normal, and Britain alone was exasperatingly unable to catch up. During the Civil War and Protectorate, the same ideological urgency was to produce a great secular answer to this puzzle - an atheist's equivalent of Divine Right, finding the source of Absolutist politics in the nature of the Newtonian universe. *Leviathan* was Europe's starkest and most utterly theoretical justification of Monarchy.

Thus, a contemporary Monarchical Constitution indifferent to theoretical justification in modern times produced during its birth pangs the most stunningly abstract of all apologias for the institution: a philosophy of Royalty so extreme, and so devastatingly pessimistic, that most subsequent thought has flinched away from assumptions and conclusions alike. Hobbes's premise was the famous vision of humankind in a natural state of total insecurity and fear: an ever-menacing civil war 'of every man against every other man', the dark sub-social condition underlying all institutions, and all pious beliefs about the soul, moral goodness and 'legitimacy'. Tending always to revert to this state - by the inescapable laws of their own material nature - men move away from the realm of the 'solitary, poor, nasty, brutish and short' only through a kind of calculating selfishness. A mythology of social benevolence is erected which is on the whole (or can be made to appear) more useful to men's interests than not.

But of course (as George Sabine wrote) Hobbes was also 'summing up a view of human nature which resulted from two centuries of decadence in customary institutions', culminating in the paroxysm of the Great Rebellion and Regicide.[23] Hence his emphasis could only be primarily on the precariousness of all social arrangements and traditions, and the nearness of chaos. Against such fragility, he believed that only the most Absolute of Monarchies could provide any real bulwark –

> I authorize and give up my right of governing myself„ to this man, or to this assembly of men, on this condition, that thou give up thy right to him, and authorize all his actions in like manner...This is the generation of that great Leviathan, or rather (to speak more reverently) of that Mortal God, to which we owe...our peace and defence.

This argument was for a tyranny far greater than that of Louis

XIV, and couched in terms more extreme than those of the leading apology for French Absolutism, Jean Bodin's *Six livres de la République* (1576). The latter sought merely to extol and justify strengthened national Kingship as a source of order superior to religion and traditional customs. Hobbes presented an integral and materialist metaphysic of power that upset the supporters of Monarchy more than its opponents, and whose true realization would not come about – even then partially – until the epoch of the 20th century dictatorships. 'Probably the greatest writer on political philosophy that the English-speaking peoples have produced' (Sabine's verdict here echoes the common opinion), Hobbes's distinction was also that of producing a philosophy in most respects the diametrical opposite of everything that, after 1688, 'English-speaking' came to mean in terms of politics, ideology and prevalent social culture.

But the opposition in question was not one of ideas alone: the political world Hobbes intended to justify was moribund by the time his ideas were received. History shows no more striking example than this of Hegel's famous dictum on the Owl of Minerva - that deeper philosophical grasp which may only be established at nightfall, once reality itself has irrevocably faded from sight and it can be reconstructed in ideal fashion. Just as the most meaningful biographies can only be written when the subject is safely entombed, so the full implications of Absolute power could be exposed only in the one society where it had been checked and decapitated. This exposure was fatal to its own supposed cause, by its very detachment and relentless theoretic penetration - by the way in which, as C.B.Macpherson has indicated, it conveyed in the abstract the dread 'set up among members of the upper classes by the Renaissance encroachments of capitalism on the older society...(and by) the freeing of more classes of men from the old social bonds'.[24] Its fate was to be that of a monumental *tour de force* deprived of both serious influence and of successors within the society that produced it.

Kings at Nightfall

The anniversary of the execution of King Charles I was celebrated as normal on 30 January by the Society of King Charles the Martyr... An altar was set up in Banqueting House – the scene of his execution supposedly consecrated by his spilled blood. Much gin was drunk. All in all a funny sort of gathering for Mr John Selwyn Gummer (recently Chairman of the Conservative Party) to be found addressing, expressing his hope that the spirit of King Charles would enter the heart of the Bishop of Durham.

The Guardian, 2 February 1985.

In a memorable chapter of his *History of the Russian Revolution*, Trotsky described and compared the fate of three Monarchs destroyed by revolution: Charles, Louis XVI of France, and Tsar Nicholas II in 1917. Of all the major institutions of history, he pointed out, Monarchy is necessarily the most personalized: 'Monarchy is by its very principle bound up with the personal'. This is why the personal traits of all three Kings were more than just quirks or idiosyncracies; and also why there were such striking similarities among both them and their families – above all as regards their respective consorts, Queen Henrietta Maria, Marie Antoinette and the Tsarina Alexandra.

The three men were 'the last-born of dynasties that had lived tumultuously' –

Their well-known equability, their tranquillity and "gaiety" in difficult moments, were the well-bred expression of a meagreness of inner powers, a weakness of the nervous discharge, poverty of spiritual resources. Moral castrates, they were absolutely deprived of imagination and creative force. They had just enough brains to feel their own triviality, and they cherished an envious hostility toward everything gifted and significant...[25]

However, such emptiness itself manifested the stalemate of the old power-structure at whose apex they stood – an apparatus ever more paralysed by the mounting force of rebellions that the old ideology compelled them to misunderstand. Later, liberal historians would wonder why they couldn't have been more 'reasonable'. But 'reasonableness' in that sense – as distinct from all-powerful charity, omnipotent concession – had no place in either the old world or their own psyches. Without the resources needed for such positive initiative they could do nothing but try to safeguard and reimpose the old, in a welter of what could only appear as deceit or double-dealing to the new men. 'Indecisiveness, hypocrisy, and lying were (Trotsky continues) in both cases the expression, not so much of personal weakness, as of the complete impossibility of holding fast to their hereditary positions'.

The same underlying situation made all three men into victims of personal and household tyranny: their Royal spouses were women from foreign Royal castes who, naturally, saw only the personal weakness and apparent indecision of their partners and responded with the 'encouragement' of heightened intransigeance and moral bullying. This attitude has come down to posterity most famously through Marie Antoinette's 'Let them eat cake!' But it reached its most extreme point in what Trotsky called 'the semi-Asiatic despotism of the Romanovs', where Alexandra created the gangrenous court clique of Rasputin to bring additional pressure to bear. In all three cases the sole effect of such nagging was to isolate the court farther, rendering it still more hypocritical and irrational and increasing the despair of those (the majority) in search of compromise. Here the main historical rôle of 'individual personality' was simply to make the Monarch's ultimate fate more inevitable.

What they did best was die. This is the grain of truth in the sentimental Tory tradition of England's King-martyr. In the nobility of bearing so evident at his trial and on the scaffold there was already a living death, the imperturbable emptiness of an order now condemned to be driven from history. Forty years later his even emptier son James was to confirm the verdict with one more attempt at restoring Absolute rule, another brief round of sanguinary example, double-dealing and indecision in the company of still another conjugal dictator, Mary of Modena. That ended in 1688 with the couple's ignominious flight to France and William of Orange's invited invasion and conquest. When this Protestant *coup* had been carried through, the debates of January and February 1689 brought the English Declaration of Right and the Scottish Claim of Right – the founding documents of what was to become the British Parliamentary State.

'Parliamentary Sovereignty'

What went abroad as the concrete rights of an Englishman have returned home as the abstract Rights of Man, and they have returned to confound our politics and corrupt our minds.

Michael Oakeshott '~~Contemporary British Politics~~',
Cambridge Journal, May 1948.

Modern national societies are mainly the by-products of revolution: they have been stamped out into their contemporary forms by social upheaval, ideologically-governed warfare, or struggles against colonial domination. Since the 17th century (it is metaphorical but not meaningless to say) these new formations have carried in their heart the revolution that founded them. The 'heart' metaphor means here a distinctive form of state-society relationship – the near-indelible nexus of a political nationhood, which usually only a farther revolution or counter-revolution will remove or transform. This birth-mark may be proudly advertised or more rarely (as in England) systematically disavowed: but its shaping or formative moment will in any case go on conditioning all the later episodes and actors of a national history.

In modern England's case we have already seen how that revolution was concentrated into a few seconds on a frozen January morning in 1649. The second Stuart Monarch of Great Britain was led out on to a specially built scaffold in Whitehall, and beheaded. 'The saddest sight that England ever saw', related Thomas Herbert, a member of the disconsolate royal party whose *Memoirs* were to become the main eye-witness source for Charles's last days. Nothing could have been more appropriate than that the self-serving recollections of this stupendous mountebank and liar should become national moral law on the subject.[26]

Since then centuries of schoolchildren have wept obediently over a scene so crucial to the modern nation's understanding of itself. Charles's two shirts (to stop him shivering, lest anyone should think him afraid); that nobility of bearing celebrated in Victorian holographs where a fine-boned and languid King upstages Roundhead roughs ; the last speech made resonant by the disappearance of a hitherto prominent royal stutter, and ending with the emblematic and doleful command: 'Remember!'. The Republican Edmund Ludlow's memoirs are more matter-of-fact. After 'the executioner performed his office', he notes that Parliament continued to meet into February:

> The House of Lords becoming now the subject of consideration and debate...(and) the question being put, whether the House of Commons should take advice of the House of Lords in the exercise of the legislative power, it was carried in the negative, and thereupon resolved, "That the House of Peers was useless and dangerous, and ought to be abolished"; and an Act was soon after passed to that effect. After this they proceeded to declare, "That the office of a King in this nation is unnecessary, burdensome, and dangerous, and ought to be abolished; and that they will settle the government of the nation in the way of a Commonwealth..."[27]

A new Great Seal of Parliament was ordered to replace the Royal one, inscribed 'God with us' on the back. Thus, what had been the Divine Right to rule of a Monarch passed directly over to a militant Parliament - to an assembly of Puritan gentry and merchants representing property (as well as God). It did not pass to the people, in the later and comprehensive sense of all men (and eventually, all adults) within a given nation. The middle class abolished the Lords (temporarily) but did not give way (even on paper) to the majority of wage-labourers, servants, apprentices, women and 'those that receive alms from door to door'.

By these later 18th and 19th century standards, therefore, this was a cramped revolution still bound to social hierarchy and the mediaeval priority of religion. As Christopher Hill has noted ironically:

> 1640 was the last national revolution whose driving ideology was religious.. But God the great Leveller, who wanted

everything overturned, a God active today in Latin America, seems to have left England after the 17th century Revolution; and not to have returned.[28]

The great religious landslide that destroyed Absolute Monarchy had indeed released popular demons – wild 'Levelling' beliefs that small, ordinary people were worth as much as their landowners and 'betters'. However, a religious ideology itself was unable to translate these ideas into reality. It gave them political form, and even a kind of subordinate permanence within the nation - a stubborn half-life destined to endure into the foundation of the Labour Party in our own century. But under pressure it would always betray them, for structural reasons unrelated to the will or passions of the individuals involved. This moral and other-worldly ethos lacked the armature provided by the later evolution of bourgeois political life - popular sovereignty and nationalism. Hence its defeats turned revolt inwards, towards a profoundly collaborative and moralizing quietism balanced by other-wordly dreams. Unlike the secular philosophies that followed on with the Enlightenment, religion (Hill concludes) 'can serve any social purpose, because of the ambiguity of its basic texts'.

Though in the 1640s poor people had been enrolled in God's militant cause and seen King Charles's head roll –

> After 1660 a new ruling-class consensus formed, when God again presided over the established order. God = history = success = what happens...The Glorious Revolution of 1688 was an additional providence, another landslide like those of 1640 and 1660, another reassertion of the predetermined social order. It confirmed England's right to rule the world. Further confirmation came from the Industrial Revolution, another unplanned gift from Heaven. The secular millenarian interpretation of England's manifest destiny was validated by these providential social transformations...

It is in this perspective that the founding moment of 1649 came to be remembered. God the Great Leveller vanished after his moment of excess, to be replaced by the supremely decent chap of modern Anglicanism. Charles became a Christ-like martyr who (without deserving to be topped) had gone a bit too far. He had been carried away by ideas like Divine Right. Yet this is consoling too, since it demonstrates the alien folly of fanaticism: one should never be more than mildly stimulated by ideas. The heartier, more wholesome England he stood for returned with his son Charles II in 1660 and (after a few more vicissitudes) was eternalized by the Glorious and Bloodless Compromise of 1688: purged of its earlier extremism, the Crown became a cherished symbol of that moderation and give-and-take by which an English identity will always bestow demi-paradise upon those that receive alms from door to door.

Had all this been merely Herbert's lies and crude folk-tales, there might be some British Republicans today. But of course it isn't. What Tom Paulin calls the dominant 'Monarchist Tradition' of Anglo-British culture has been rooted in it. In modern England the world of Letters has laboured to serve the Royal-communitarian *Weltanschauung*; and it has been through this older tradition that 'the magic of monarchy and superstition permeated English literary criticism like a syrupy drug'.[29] The principal ingredient here is faith in an organic wholeness of both the social order and sensibility: 'community' in that distinctively retrograde, apolitical and anti-modernist sense crucial to Regality and the English Word. The pre-decapitation, Shakespearian world was in this mystic sense at one with itself; then severance created - in T.S.Eliot's famous phrase - the 'dissociation of sensibility' by which culture has ever since been afflicted. Afflicted, but also loyally combatted across the centuries both by the renascent Throne and by its extended cultural and academic Court.

Ludlow himself survived the Restoration in Swiss exile. He returned briefly to London after the Revolution of 1688, enjoying now the mythic status described by Macaulay: 'almost the only survivor, certainly the most illustrious survivor, of a mighty race of men, the conquerors in a terrible civil war, the judges of a king, the founders of a republic.' His name had been fortieth on the list of the fifty-nine signatories of Charles's death warrant; now that Charles's second son James had also disgraced himself and been expelled, and the authority of Parliament been finally confirmed and crystallized, would not the old man be honoured (or at least forgiven) by the State he helped into life? But he had (again in Macaulay's words, this time ringing with satisfaction) 'misunderstood the temper of the English people'. The people in the House of Commons, at least, had disavowed their collective guilt and responsibility forever: they wished to forget no other fact as thoroughly as the one which had made them. Least of all did they want to be reminded when still another reign had been so brusquely terminated, and England's historic anarchy so painfully re-evoked. The expulsion of real Divine Right Monarchy made them long all the more for a Crown - hence the illustrious Republican's reappearance seemed a deadly, practically sacrilegious threat to this compromise.

> By all (Macaulay continues)...the act of regicide in which he had borne a part never to be forgotten, was regarded, not merely with the disapprobation due to a great violation of law and justice, but with horror such as even the Gunpowder Plot had not excited. The absurd and almost impious service which is still read in our churches on the 30th of January had produced in the minds of the vulgar a strange association of ideas. The sufferings of Charles were confounded with the sufferings of the Redeemer of mankind; and every regicide was a Judas, a Caiaphas, or a Herod...The subject was brought before the House of Commons.[30]

It was of course in the House of Commons class of person, not 'the minds of the vulgar', that the real source of all the exaggerated horror and suspect piety lay. Republicanism was by now a spectre threatening this as yet insecure élite with the return of Levelling, crazed vulgar egalitarianism, military rule and (eventually, by the sort of reaction already witnessed) some other would-be Absolute Ruler. Exorcism of that spectre demanded a safe form of Kingship – Monarch*ism*, so to speak, unperturbed by a real, interfering Monarch. And that mode of Crown-rule in turn required for effectiveness the maximum of slobbering devotion and generalized religiose feeling – a diffuse and non-questionable civil worship identifying the King with 'everything holy' (or as would later be said, 'decent') about us. It needed a moral and sentimental dictatorship – not the reduction of Republicanism to a minority opposition, but its virtual extinction by taboo and spiritual censorship.

The fully developed means for incorporating the minds of the vulgar completely into this collective theatre did not then

exist. As we shall see, they depended upon the later evolution
of society and national-popular identity: it would take the
unique conjunction of an early-modern 'unwritten' constitution and modern mass communications to make modern
Ukanian Royalism possible. Still, a recognizable foundation
for the phenomenon was laid in the Revolution Parliament. It
was dreadfully plain in the short debate about Ludlow on
November 9, 1689 (by which time William and Mary were
securely on their joint thrones). Judas was not only at large on
the streets of London, complained Sir Joseph Tredenham, but
spouting his unregenerate nonsense in the company of other
known firebrands –

> To what can these persons pretend, but to bring us into the
> same anarchy as formerly? Now we are setting things in order,
> they are contriving to make us victims to their passions...I
> would address the King to issue out his Royal Proclamation, to
> command him out of the nation.[31]

In an age where so much appears alien and precarious, we are
suddenly on familiar ground. Every House of Commons
accent is recognizable and can be mimicked in today's terms -
even the pompous little joke by which a Colonel Birch sought
simultaneously to establish his credentials and to make light of
the whole matter –

> I am in a new perriwig, and pray let the House look upon me
> before I am heard... For this person to come in the face of
> Parliament, is a horrid thing, if it be so. I am curious to know
> whether he be here, or no. Pray let somebody avow him to be
> here before you make the order.

The next day a deputation delivered Parliament's unanimous
request to William III. It was led by Sir Edward Seymour, a
staunch House of Commons man who (in today's Parliamentary blarney) could certainly be accused of having 'interests to
declare': he was the new owner of Ludlow's forfeited Wiltshire
estate. 'Seymour (notes the *Memoirs* editor) is generally said to
have been the chief instigator of the resolution...and from the
fact that he presented the address the statement is probably
correct.' The King at once agreed to act on the address, but
with characteristic adroitness made sure Ludlow was out of
England again before proclaiming the banishment.

Thus was the germ of Republicanism dealt with in 1689. Nor have certain essential aspects of the drama altered in three hundred years – except that what was then the world-view of an oligarchic élite still finding its feet has been extended, popularized and nationalized into a counterfeit of political modernity. And as part of the process, Monarchy's authority has been largely (but not entirely) transferred from the administrative to the spiritual sphere. At the same time, however, the 'spiritual' (or ideological) itself has become enormously stronger, thanks to the organized 'lay religion' of nationalism; and it is in this sphere that the Crown has truly taken its revenge upon the people who cast it out in 1649. By its regicide England dealt the first and hardest blow against the old world of monarchical authority, Europe's *Ancien Régime*. Yet with its modern Monarchy Great Britain has done more than any other State to revive and re-justify Royalty: as a result of the resurrection of dynastic prestige and influence since Queen Victoria, the remote descendants of Charles I's sister now enjoy far greater popularity than he or any of his predecessors did.

As for Ludlow, he returned to his exile at Vevey and died there three years later. The French 19th century historian Guizot wrote of this hard case: 'He learned nothing from experience, but also was never defeated by it; he entered Parliament as a Republican, and he died on the shores of Lake Geneva as a Republican...And it is certain that, among the many in his own day who judged him so severely, few were his equal'. Later I will look at some episodes of later Republican history. But a dreary moral is already plain: the relatively easy defeat of modern, democratic or socialist Republicanism had an ominous precursor in the exile of Ludlow's early-modern, élitist or 'classical' version of the anti-Monarchical creed.

The Modern Venice

In at least one domain... this immature revolution had truly long-lasting symbolic consequences. *Precisely because* it was immature, and could not establish its legitimacy on the politico-institutional, national or social contents of later revolutions, it was pressed into a very heavy symbolic investment in the last 'modern' and least 'bourgeois' of domains – the domain of the land.

> Franco Moretti, *The Way of the World*
> (1987) p.207.

Classical or patrician Republicanism belonged to Antiquity and to the cluster of Antique ideas brought to life once more in the Renaissance of the 15th and 16th centuries. It is important to note here that these notions preceded the modern era of democracy and nationalism, in more than a simply chronological sense. They preceded it also at a more basic, developmental level: certain features of political modernity were absent from Classical Republicanism. Hill has underlined what these were in the text quoted earlier: popular majority rule and its concomitant - a 'nation' inherent in the people rather than belonging like an estate to its social or proprietorial élite (put in another way, nationalism rather than a patriotically managed nation).

In Hill's Marxist terminology a similar point is conveyed by saying that the English Revolution of 1640-88 was not (as so often thought by an earlier generation) the 'first bourgeois revolution' but the last Renaissance or pre-bourgeois upheaval paving the way for a later middle-class ascendancy. In one sense, admittedly, that description was almost truistic: the new urban and commercial middle classes did play an indispensable part in the Civil War, and one result of their efforts was a decisive end to the Absolutist aims of the English Monarchy. Yet in other ways the title was over-flattering and ignored too many important reference-points. Though in certain ways anticipating subsequent modes of middle-class politicization and struggle, in others the English Revolution and its 1688 State-form remained firmly tied to the epoch of the Renaissance. As events were soon to demonstrate, it remained closer to Venice and the old mercantile city-states than to post-1789 France; closer to the Dutch Stadholderate than to revolutionary America.

Though new in terms of both its scale and its impact upon the outside world, England permanently kept its structure of oligarchy: that is, it remained what we see at the end of the 20th century, approaching the three-hundredth anniversary of William's invasion – an aristocratic, family-based élite uniting landownership with large scale commerce and managing 'its' society as a cooptive estate. Certain techniques of such management - like those involved in promoting Royal charisma - may have become modern, but this is modernity at the service of 1688-style antiquity. The forms and gadgetry of later development are used to reproduce the essence of earlier development and preserve the spirit of an early modernity.

This type of government and society was already familiar on a smaller scale, and most familiar of all on the micro-scale of the Italian and German civic states of the 15th and 16th centuries. The largest and longest-lasting example was of course the Venetian Republic – a city-state ruled by a tiny and exclusive hierarchy, whose imperial territory and trading interests none the less dominated the whole Eastern Mediterranean. From the other leading Italian State, Florence, came much of the culture and the theoretical justification for their mode of life. That self-imagery was founded upon admiration for the élite Republicanism of Antiquity. The Renaissance statelets were perceived as new versions of Classical city-states like Athens, run by an enlightened caste imbued with (and legitimated by) all the wisdom of Classicism. 'In all states, whatever their type of government, the real rulers are never more than forty or fifty citizens', wrote Machiavelli - the great formulator of 'modern politics' in this sense. Beneath the 'citizens' lay the vast majority incapable of enlightenment and (hence) of serious political involvement. Occasionally this mass might erupt in frightened protest, but on the whole it was realistically deferential to its predestined rulers. The latter for their part were wise always to maintain a *governo largo* – a rule capable of some sensitivity to those below, and where necessary of adroit pragmatic concessions.

The Dutch Revolution was the other successful 17th century movement against Absolutism. The Netherlands too had shaken off feudal rule and the Catholic faith, with the help of a powerful bourgeoisie oriented towards sea-borne trade and colonization. But like the English one, this 'bourgeois revolution' remained bounded by the political culture of the recent past. It could not escape from the Machiavellian universe. Thus, discussing William III's evolution before he was invited to become King of England in 1688, Dutch historian Pieter Geyl has stressed how futile it is to read modern political notions back into such a career:

> The Regent Régime (in Holland) was an oligarchy, and it certainly was not without the vices that almost inevitably go with that system: nepotism, for instance; pride...As for democracy, it was unthinkable. The people as a rule unquestioningly respected the authority of the gentlemanly Regents and saw in them their representatives...(while)... The Regents and most of the well-to-do citizens regarded the popular movement simply as sedition – the rabble in revolt against the social order.[32]

'Revolutionary' as it had been towards Spanish rule and the Pope, this proud oligarchy needed the Prince of Orange to fall back on for protection against the mob. And in 1688 the Prince (who was also a grandson of the executed Charles I) temporarily united the two national Protestant élites without much difficulty.

William's function in both realms was the same. In England even more than in the Netherlands (Lawrence Stone writes) 'the popular movement' was due to be put back in its place:

> It became all too apparent to men of property during the disorders of the late 1640s and 1650s, and in the light of the rise of the Leveller party...that this broader concept of liberty was too dangerous a spirit to be allowed abroad. The problem was how to use it in order to transfer control from the King to the men of property, without also sharing this liberty with the middling sort of people. Almost everyone was agreed upon the exclusion of wage-labourers and women from political rights, since they were not free persons.

Only religious millenarism had bestowed rights upon those

below the 'middling' stratum. Even the professed Republicans of the revolutionary period like Harrington, Milton and Ludlow had thought only of a State founded on a limited democracy of the educated gentry.

The English oligarchy which triumphed so conclusively by inviting William on to the throne in 1688 was also ensuring a kind of permanence in England (and then in 'Britain') for this early-modern political culture. Its élite-citizen hegemony would endure for over three centuries, because no other State of that epoch had as strong foundations, or would enjoy later conditions so favourable to its mode of authority. Hence no other ruling class with this early-modern equipment entered upon a similar *longue durée* of development.

It is the distinctive political coordinates of the early-modern that provide a definable historical location explaining both the half-modern and the unmistakably archaic aspects of 20th century Britain. That location helps explain at once the indelible Whig-Labour faith in the system's capacity for progress, and the cumulative out-of-dateness and pathetic failures now so inescapable to all outside observers and critics. British Royalism, Anglo-British national identity and the United Kingdom State are indeed all 'anachronistic' phenomena. However, the past that remains so stubbornly alive in them has nothing to do with feudalism or the 'immemorial', and still less to do with folk or ethnic traditions. What it really connects with is one circumscribed era of early modern development reaching from 1688 up to the middle of the 18th century: the founding period in which England's patrician Revolution was consolidated and rendered 'British' by the assimilation of the Scottish State in 1707. What that process created was a pre-democratic class State distinct both from the Absolute Monarchies still dominating Europe and (later) from the lower-class, more emphatically *bourgeois* and nationalist régimes aimed at by revolutionaries in the spirit of 1776, 1789 and 1848.

This developmental 'location' is all-important for understanding both the Monarchy and the related misfortunes of Republicanism. It lets one see both the validity and the absurdity of the dominant ideology of British Royalism which we have been examining from different angles. The key notion here has always been that England-Britain is *really* a 'disguised Republic': the myth given (as we shall see) a decisive ceremonial vestment by Walter Bagehot in the 1860s, and reiterated in a multiplicity of forms ever since by both defenders and critics. The modest grain of truth buried here is indicated by the simple question: what *kind* of 'Republic'? It is quite true that a 'Republic' of sorts is hidden, ornamented and preserved by the Windsor Monarchy. But *not a Republic in the modern sense*: what is being conserved is a pre-modern collectivity whose essential features all look back to the early-modern and the patrician - not forward to mass democracy and popular sovereignty (never mind socialism).

Thus, the Crown can almost truistically be presented in relation to that reality as 'mere appearance', 'show', and so on. Yet a twofold problem is occluded by this alibi-statement: the reality itself, although hardly 'ancient', is old enough to qualify as an antique – indeed, with the possible exceptions of Bhutan and Nepal, *the* antique on U.N.O.'s shelf; while the Monarchic 'show', through its crypto-nationalist function (and consequent intense popularity) is vital to the functioning of the old motor (as it could not conceivably be to a modern Republic). This career of gilded anachronism did not begin with post-World-War-II economic decline and industrial failures: Tom Paine and other radical critics pointed out its ignoble and cadaverous aspects in the 1790s. But what they could not see was the later fortunate environment that would mummify such features and give them permanent power to inhibit and control the democratic movement's later evolution.

It is when this later history is brought into the perspective that the preposterous side of the 'hidden Republic' thesis emerges more fully. Yes indeed, the Windsor Crown-State is at bottom merely an instrument (though a very powerful and active one) of 'Parliamentary Sovereignty'. But Parliamentary Sovereignty has nothing to do with Republican democracy and popular power in the normal contemporary sense. It is a transmuted version of Monarchy – the 'collective Monarch' that replaced individual Sovereigns after 1688. Farthermore, it was built up as a barrier *against* democracy and people's sovereignty – as a way of keeping élite authority and a synthetic blood-line inviolate, a technique for saving the national family from the levelling disenchantment of modernity. In the post-1945 world the enormous success of this long-range operation has been indicated by one thing above all: a consistently anti-Republican Socialism reared in the profound conviction that the intimately linked questions of democracy and national identity have been (as Hans Kohn thought) in all essentials resolved forever by the Old Régime. Only on that basis could the Labour Party afford for so long the luxurious and corrupting belief that politics is about nothing but 'class' – that a British Socialism did *not* have as its primary task the redefinition of both State and national identity.

Another interesting question is partly answered by stressing the early-modern developmental location of British Statehood and national identity. We have seen how hard it is to fit the phenomena of British popular Monarchism into the contemporary political perspectives of the nation-state world. Constitutional Monarchy presents no particular problem to the latter, but an unwritten Crown Constitution based on infatuation and a taboo-structure does. However, the reason why this doesn't 'fit' is that the entire early-modern political universe of which it was a part has vanished. Ukania is a relic: but not (as so often carelessly assumed) the relic of an indeterminate 'feudalism', the phoney traditionalism signalled by today's neo-Habsburg ramparts. It is the less romantic survivor of a circumscribed transitional or early-bourgeois period concluded elsewhere with the destruction or the absorption of the city-state and mercantile Republics into larger units. They were washed away by the continental flood-tide of nationalism. Only Great Britain's premature revolution survives, as an ancestor of political modernity unassimilable by all later development, an early-modern patriciate protected by its insular geography and by overseas conquests and resources far greater than those enjoyed by any other modern State.

The Containment of Modernity

Aboard I'm doomed to stay until my final day – how sad a plight!
If only I could flee and join that scenery, in backward flight.

Karl Kruns, *Schnellzug* (Fast Train),
In These Great Times (1984).

156

The true implication of Ukania's Royalty-fetishism is not the murder but the staged emasculation of modernity: a 'modernization' compatible with British decency, the Old-Régime national identity. There is nothing new or special about the old trying to survive by adopting new techniques and ideas: such comedies of uneven development have been attempted by most of the world's *anciens régimes*. Up to 1918 the Hohenzollerns, the Romanovs, the Habsburgs and the Ottoman Sultans all strove to fortify Absolutism with the latest in technology and armament. They had varying records but were on the whole more successful than is now remembered. A recent example was provided by Ethiopia's Solomonic dynasty, where until 1974 –

> Any expenditure, anywhere in the Empire, of more than ten dollars required the Emperor's personal approval, and if a minister came to ask approval for spending only one dollar, he would be praised. To repair a minister's car – the Emperor's approval is needed. To replace a leaking pipe in the city – the Emperor's approval is needed. To buy sheets for a hotel - the Emperor must approve it....How you should admire, my friend, the diligent thrift of His August Majesty, who spent most of his royal time checking accounts, listening to cost estimates, rejecting proposals, and brooding over human greed, cunning, and meddling.[33]

As Ryszard Kapuscinski's hallucinatory account of a real feudal relic in action makes clear, the overwhelming motive that sustained Haile Selassie into his last days was not preservation of a mediaeval past but modernization at all costs. At all costs (that is) except the sacrifice of his own authority (which was of course the pillar of the Régime, and its true backwardness).

> And he kept on reforming: he abolished forced labour, he imported the first cars, he created a postal service....In the Hour of Development, between four and five in the afternoon, His Highness showed particular vivacity and keenness. He received processions of planners, economists, and Cfinancial specialists,

talking, asking questions, encouraging, and praising....A map
of the Empire's development hung in the Palace, on which little
arrows, stars, and dots lit up, blinking and twinkling so that the
dignitaries could gladden their eyes with the sight when His
Venerable Majesty pressed a button...

Had it not been for the famine disaster of 1973-4, the Lion of
Judah might still be there. The revolutionaries got their chance
and deposed him (he died the following year, 1975). Otherwise, Sir Clive Sinclair can all too easily easily be imagined
attending the Hour of Development to advise on the formation
of an Imperial electronics industry. Then, when the hour was
up the Emperor's human clock ('His Distinguished Majesty's
cuckoo') would emerge from the shadows and, by bowing
repeatedly, indicate to the Negus that it was time to move on to
other matters.

The rule behind such weird conjunctions of antiquity and
modernity is that reform must not affect or weaken the
instrument of reform: the State itself, the class or individual
whose authority is being exercised, the essence of government.
Modernization must always stop short of self-liquidation. And
in fact, because its changes are so potentially upsetting, it
requires much simultaneous reinforcement of the State-order.
In Ethiopia, as more and more of the intellectuals needed for
Development returned from their studies abroad, 'put their
heads in their hands, and cried, "Good God, how can anything
like this exist?"', the Emperor was forced to intensify his
paranoid autocracy.

Such formal resemblances between Ukania and the other
Empires in their later days are easily established. The
Habsburg realm offers the greatest number, often of a very
entertaining sort. For instance, 'muddling through' was a
prime principle of civilized motion in both. In Vienna as in pre-
Thatcher London it was acknowledged that conservative
greatness (unlike the radical kind) consisted above all in
mastery of the stylish 'U-turn': the deft command of ever-
shifting 'winds of change' by 180° turns, to keep the vessel of
State and Class on a generally safe course. In the great
Danubian Monarchy its destination had always been registered
by *Es ist passiert*, the comforting realm of 'It just sort of
happened'. The equivalent space in the British imperial sub-

conscious harboured 'Muddling through': the decently unplanned, patrician navigation of events by occasional touches of the tiller, with stylish disregard of bourgeois formalities and earnestness, and (above all) of finger-marked and germ-laden theories.

Things just sort of happening, getting by without too much reference to wearisome principle, are also linked in all traditional cultures to the notion of ordinariness: an ideological theme to which any study of Royal Britain constantly returns. It was just as familiar to Kakanians. Transported by his dizzy involvement in the Emperor's great Jubilee Campaign Ulrich (the 'man without qualities') suddenly finds himself barking like an English M.P.:

> This means, your pictures, my mathematics, somebody else's children and wife - everything that assures a person that although he is in no way anything unusual, nevertheless in his own way of being in no way anything unusual he will not easily meet his match![34]

This is too much for his intellectual pal Walter, who has become bothered about the meaning of life:

> Walter was full of unrest, and now suddenly of triumph. "Do you know what you're saying?" he exclaimed. "Muddling through! You're simply an Austrian. You're preaching the Austrian national philosophy of muddling through!"
>
> "That may not be such a bad thing as you think", Ulrich replied. "A passionate desire for sharpness and exactness or for beauty may very well bring one to the point of liking muddling through better than all the exertions in the spirit of modern times. I congratulate you on having discovered Austria's world mission..."

No indeed, the ordinary will not easily meet its match, since there is something extraordinary about it: this is no ordinary ordinariness cast into dreg-like outer gloom. The ordinary is not separate and divorced from the higher spheres but alive with their magic. Each day the humdrums touch the hem of a Royal garment, at least symbolically. A distant, fluttering glimpse on the TV screen and the warming throb of a newsreader's voice remind them all is well. Order is intact and the redeeming glamour goes on flowing downwards.

But it is in this continuum that 'muddle through' thrives, the regulator and preservative of such old-fashioned organic health and unity. 'Compromise' solves everything – that is, all such strains and aches as tend to arise naturally from the gradual, dignified onward motion of society. A compromise is a bargain struck between elements of disgruntlement and the source of authority, by which the latter is maintained. Though presented to the former as an honourable agreement between equals (or 'consensus'), its reality must of course incline to the Crown, the Established guarantor of normality and sanity, the inner meaning of 'order' itself.

These family deals may occasionally appear squalid, rigged, stultifying affairs - but only from the point of view of some abstract idea, as wielded by a *déraciné* intellectual. This is Ulrich's whole point. Such ideas must be kept at arm's length. A passionate desire for sharpness is all very well among bookworms; but society should not be expected to swallow razor-blades and die from its exertions in the spirit of modern times. No, the decent constitution of life (Royal and ordinary at once) warns one against such adventures.

The accompanying principle of 'Muddling through' is that of 'Not too much': 'moderation' in that specifically cramping, instinctive sense found in every interstice of the Old Identity. The Kakanian urge to get ahead meant (as Musil put it) 'speed of course; but not too much speed...The conquest of the air had begun here too; but not too intensively...One spent tremendous sums on the army; but only just enough to ensure one of remaining the second weakest among the Great Powers'. Under all the rhetoric of keeping up lay the fatal Kakanian longing, the wish to – 'Get out! Jump clear!...the nostalgic yearning to be brought to a standstill, to cease evolving, to get stuck, to turn back to a point that lies before the wrong fork...' The white heat of new technology? Well yes, provided one doesn't upset the Treasury or chaps concerned about the Pound too much; but in the end something reasonably warmish may have to do. An Independent British Deterrent? Of course, just as long as the sums involved don't get too tremendous; in which case something a little less independent would at least ensure one remains on the Greatness chart.

Musil was also very taken by the symbolism of trains, and described the old K & K spirit as that of 'leaving the train of events, getting into an ordinary train on an ordinary railway-line, and travelling back home'. Nothing would have surprised him, for example, about the well-remembered saga of the U.K. Advanced Passenger Train. He understood perfectly that the realm of Faery where numberless crowds swoon at a little wave from an antique coach must also strive to have the most up-to-date of trains.

Not, however, if it means *too much* expense and trouble constructing the sort of straight tracks upon which alone super-trains can run. Twenty years after Queen Elizabeth's accession in 1953, the New Age technicians at British Rail announced some superb news. Among their ranks were, in the *Times*'s words, 'some bright young men from British Aerospace'. Great Britain was to have its own 21st century vehicle, which would equal French and Japanese achievements and out-do them *by running on old-fashioned winding railtrack*. Other nations burdened by antique permanent ways would go for it: Britain would be in the lead again, by sheer damned ingenuity and style.

The inauguration of H.M.'s A.P.T., the 'sealed futuristic aluminium tube, whose lavatories can be used while the train is standing in the station', is still sufficiently well-remembered for it to be almost cruel to mention it. After many months of passengerless travel, journalists were invited aboard on the famous run when trays of drink and food hurtled to and fro like missiles, brave smiles settled down into sea-sick agony and suddenly-recalled deadlines caused exits at every stop. 'The difficulty', explained British Rail's Mr Ian Campbell in terms that Walter would have seen through at once, 'lay in the curvaceous nature of British railways'. 'APT Proves a Magnificent Machine', said one *Times* headline, 'but it Needs the Track to Match'. 'What it cannot do', explained their Transport Correspondent Michael Bailey, 'is absorb all the deficiencies of track last updated twenty years ago'. This finely-wrought euphemism meant of course that the whole purpose of the futuristic tube was defeated: the sole point of its cunning 'tilt mechanisms' had been precisely to compensate for all those deficiencies and antique curvatures. Up-dating, in the relevant

161

sense, implied nothing but the general reconstruction of tracks undertaken by the crassly insensitive French for their insufferable *trains de grande vitesse*.

Then a farther appalling possibility was grasped. Perhaps more used to thinking of aircraft in space, the B.R. design-team had failed to visualize what might happen when two A.P.T.s did not 'tilt' in perfect unison on some old curve. These came to be called 'pinch points'. A curvaceous past has left plenty of them, and the resultant chances of disaster, though of course 'extremely remote', could not, given the persistent foibles of the tilting machinery, be completely ruled out.

It was at this point that a sighing tone Musil would have greeted like an old friend began to creep into even the most patriotic of commentaries. 'This potential world-beater obstinately refuses to come right', conceded Mr Bailey in May 1981. But was there wisdom somewhere in this obstinacy? After all (it was now much more frequently noticed) the thing *would not in fact have gone any faster* than existing Intercity services, for safety reasons. And even if it had, well – would half an hour gained between London and Glasgow really have been so important? At first sight 'replacement of the A.P.T. by a hurriedly cobbled-together electric version of the existing high-speed 125 trains' might seem disheartening to Greatness-addicts. Especially since (it is not irrelevant to recall) electrification – the basis for any real modernization of services – had proceeded only slowly and spasmodically while the world-beater was being assembled. But in the end, was this result not more appropriate to our Way of Doing Things? That is, to a land where humane curvaceousness and a flexible, slithering sort of progress matches one's inherited culture, as well as one's landscape? No, there is after all little room for ruthless straightness in 'this small country of ours' (and none at all for the tremendous sums it would waste). And in the fullness of time subjects were to prove quite content with the 'Electra' (as it was then called), a modest but somewhat improved (and electrified) locomotive indistinguishable from those of Japan and France a generation before.[35]

There are endless examples of this Royal folly: without too much difficulty post-1945 United Kingdom history can up to Mrs Thatcher's advent be resolved into a succession of them.

The tale of the Royal Bomb is perhaps the best-known, and the most telling (I shall return to it later). However, such analogies may mislead as well as reveal. They emphasize one side of Ukanian identity – the paralytic grip of traditionalism and its associated self-delusion – at the expense of others. Yet it is also these others which have helped to keep Great Britain going for so long and (notably) ensured its effective mobilization in one war after another, in ways that no truly *ancien* régime ever managed.

Again, the point in broad comparative terms is the U.K.'s ambiguity: as the sole survivor of an otherwise extinct developmental phase, it exhibits traits from both the epoch which preceded and that which followed it. Viewed on their own these would lead anyone to classify Ukania as alternately 'old' (pre-modern) or 'modern' (a post-1789 nation-state). But in fact it is neither, and the only 'peculiarity' that matters is a State-form able to knot such contrasting features together over a very long period of time. The Monarchy and Royal-conservative (or familial) British identity have been indispensable symbolic tools in this operation. Only now is the knot being loosened. And as it comes undone the Crown, Parliamentary Sovereignty and all other aspects of the totem are losing their magic.

The Modernization of George III

You may have seen Gilroy's famous print of him – in the old wig, in the stout old hideous Windsor uniform – as the King of Brobdignag, peering at a little Gulliver, whom he holds up in his hand, whilst in the other he has an opera-glass, through which he surveys the pygmy? Our fathers chose to set up George III as the type of a great king; and the little Gulliver was the great Napoleon... There was no lie we would not believe; no charge of crime which our furious prejudice would not credit.

W. M. Thackeray, *The Four Georges* (1869) pp.90-1.

The Scottish and English Revolutions impacted on a world not yet ready, either theoretically or materially, for the lasting

successor to Absolutism: *popular sovereignty*, with its implications of lower-order power and ethnicity, democracy and
nationalism. It would take the Enlightenment of the century
following King Charles's defeat to produce the ideology of this
change, and the revolutionary upheavals in America and
France to show how the ideas could be put into practice. The
old British Monarchy was decapitated too soon. This is why it
was able to creep back into the void left by its departure, head
under its arm, to find permanent lodgement in the compromise
of a quasi-regal power structure.

Parliamentary victory therefore was that of one absolutism
over another. The constitution of its power was 'the outcome
of a competition for sovereignty. In spite of the failure of the
royalist quest for sovereignty the absolute stage emerged, the
privileges of Parliament came to be substituted for the
prerogatives of the King as James I had conceived them...'³⁶
The Parliamentary class seized sovereignty, and legitimized
the transfer with a myth of the Crown-in-Parliament. This is
what was finally established by the decisive second Revolution
in 1688 – a permanent power structure where, as the socialist
Harold Laski observed two hundred and fifty years farther on,
'Legally we have no fundamental rights in Great Britain; we
trust for their protection to the ordinary constitutional
machinery of the state...' Trust, in other words, to the
reasonableness of those running that machinery, and to their
willingness to 'compromise' and heed representations from
below. Complain enough, and the butler will come down with
something.

The Hanoverians were a constitutional necessity but a
popular liability. Their establishment and survival could only
have happened in a world where popularity was still fairly
unimportant. By 1800, however, that world was showing the
first signs of general crisis and dissolution. Britain had already
been shaken by the American Revolution of the 1770s. Soon
every part of the older Europe would be convulsed by the
French Revolution and the generation of warfare up to 1815.
Through the Revolution, a potentially effective political form
was given to equality, literacy and industry. While in the wars,
Clausewitz pointed out that 'no one would have believed
possible what all have now lived to see realized': through these

revolutionary and counter-revolutionary wars the 'absolute character' of warfare (previously associated with religious fanaticism or primitive tribal hatred) had re-emerged. While in the old pre-1789 days 'War was still a mere Cabinet affair, in which the people only took part as a blind instrument; at the beginning of the nineteenth century the people on each side weighed in the scale...'[37]

It was this weight which transformed the context of both nationality and Monarchy. The older insular State now encountered the genesis of a new political world. It had done more than any other society to bring that world into the light; yet very quickly it perceived the birth as monstrous, and set out to strangle it. In this gargantuan effort Britain's quasi-modern national identity was first forged, and the function of Monarchy as a popular element within that idea-system first made clear. As England became the leader of opposition to the revolutionary cause it too had to arouse more widespread popular support. While Upper England found its new anti-revolutionary visage in the discourses of Edmund Burke, the middle and lower ranks were ideologically conscripted by more vulgar means. The Gallic Stereotype was concocted, a 'distorted image of revolutionary France' whose chief intellectual components were –

> the ideas of destruction, license, abstract political thought, atheism, and impious mockery. "Philosophy" was perhaps its familiar name. Its face, or faces, were the wizened and triumphantly grimacing countenance of Voltaire, mocker of Christianity and diabolical mastermind of the Revolution, or the face of an ape, which similarly represented destruction and absolute irresponsibility. In either case, a horrible grin appears to have been central to the image...[38]

What in Burke appears as 'quadrimanous' (four-handed or monkey-like) meddling with tradition turns into the frank racism of caricature and broadsheet: a 'nation of baboons' against which Humanity itself had now to be defended.

For the first time, incipient Anglo-British nationalism was both defined and hardened by an external threat. It is quite true that in both previous centuries the English State and people had also been at times threatened by invaders (most famously in Elizabeth I's reign, by Philip II's Spain). But these occasions were before the people 'weighed in the scale' of State affairs in Clausewitz's distinctively modern sense – before they had begun to count as participants or agents. Before (therefore) they had to be appealed to and 'mobilized' for either industry or (after 1793) interminable and secular ideological warfare. Nationality and religion had of course figured in these earlier conflicts; but it was only the more modern circumstances of post-1789 that would cast them into the mould of a national*ism* and (after that) of an enduring popular national identity.

Since its 17th century agonies, the Anglo-British dominant class had ceased to be a closed nobility of the mainland kind. It had turned into a mercantile oligarchy, where landownership was linked to commerce rather than to the exclusive feudal professions of warfare. In his study of Edmund Burke, C.B.Macpherson has accurately delineated the features of this patriciate. Burke's impassioned defence of English traditions against French Jacobinism was not really a plea for the immemorial or for 'feudal' honour: that was only rhetorical and emotive colour (of the sort which would eventually become apart of the reanimated Crown mystique). A wider reading of him shows how the great counter-revolutionary prophet knew perfectly well that by the 1790s 'the capitalist order *had in fact been* the traditional order in England for a whole century':

> His genius was in seeing that the capitalist society of the late 18th century was still heavily dependent on the acceptance of status. Contract had not replaced status: it was dependent on status...Burke saw that, down to his own time, such movement as there had been was not from status to contract but from status to status, that is, from a feudal status differentiation, which rested on military capacity, to what we should now call an internalised status differentiation, which rested on nothing more than habit and tradition, that is, on the subordinate class continuing to accept its traditional station in life.[39]

In short, a largely synthetic 'traditional' social order had already been built up in Whig Britain. It associated aristocracy with an early-modern form of capitalism, commercial rather than industrial in orientation; and far from demanding a farther rush forward into modernity – a 'bourgeois revolution' – this system was, at least in Britain's favourable conditions, both stable and (within limits) adaptable.

Until 1745 it had been successfully defended against the past - the return of a Stuart *Ancien Régime*; now it had to be defended against the future – against the precipitate advance of democracy, *égalité* and an individualism hostile to all habit and subordination. Later on I will return to the vital status-contract transition, which can be viewed in other and equally telling perspectives. For the moment, what matters is the possibility of (in Jeffrey Lant's phrase) the Crown's 'mystically embodying the will' of the entire nation - something that previously would have been mocked out of existence.[40] Yet by Prince Albert's period it was quite conceivable, and by the time of the late-Victorian Jubilees it was almost taken for granted. The key to this mysterious reincarnation lay in 'the nation' itself: in the evolution around 1800 of a popular national identity more compatible with Edmund Burke's traditionalism.

The British Monarchy seems to have first acquired a distinctly (though still shakily) 'modern' appearance during the reign of George III. His reign (1760-1820) was the longest of any British Monarch, and its last twenty years are normally skipped over quickly by his many biographers. This was the period of the madness for which he remains most famous in British popular memory. Indeed a lugubrious obsession with his ailment has led to much speculation about 'what exactly was wrong'. More significant than these macabre details is the fact that during the second half of the reign it forced him progressively out of the kind of active meddling in party politics which he had formerly indulged in. The first serious bout occurred in 1788-9 at the very moment of the Revolution's outbreak. Thereafter, increasing withdrawal turned him into more and more of an effigy, a remote figure upon whom symbolic meanings could be imposed with little risk that the real, pathetic man might reappear and undermine them.

In a recent important study of the later George III Linda Colley points out how the French Revolution's impact stimulated a reactive nationalism everywhere else in Europe – either liberal (following the trend established in Paris) or 'conservative, state-sponsored nationalism' defying the revolutionaries and trying to arouse popular support for a safer variety of patriotism. In Britain, after some initial uncertainty, it was the second movement that prevailed. The Revolution's effects, explained Sir Samuel Romilly in his *Memoirs*, 'gave almost every description of persons who have any influence on public opinion an interest to adhere to, and maintain inviolably, our established Constitution and, above all, the Monarchy, as inseparably connected with, and maintaining everything valuable in the State...'[41]

The French Revolutionary principles, if imported over the Channel, would have impelled the established British compromise forward. They promised or threatened another phase of that true 'bourgeois revolution' the Levellers had agitated for in the previous century. Faced with the menace of extinction Britain's unique oligarchic polity had to go forward, or back. Nationalism comes most into its own in the shadow of annihilation. The reply could only be quick mobilization of a 'national identity' either ahead of that proclaimed by the Jacobin *Montagne*, or deliberately behind and against it - the promulgation of a distinctive counter-revolution mimicking in its own way the needs and pressures of the new era. The way the choice would go was not long in doubt. Neither was the fact that Monarchy would play a central part in this new scenario.

Only a strong ideological counter-offensive was any use. And in trying to make the Parliamentary oligarchy more popular, grand and immemorial, the Crown was an inevitable instrument. 'The chief beneficiary of this process of state-nationalization of nationalism in Britain was the King', observes Colley. This was why George III's reign brought a sudden invention of traditions – the first premonitory ripple of what, at the end of the 19th century, would turn into a great tide of synthesized nostalgia tingeing every aspect of the British Way with Regal inviolability. In 1789, a frantic search of records had to be conducted to establish just how the Nation ought properly to celebrate King George's apparent recovery from illness. Nobody living could recall popular desire to mark such an occasion, and it was feared the appropriate ritual might have vanished with the Stuarts (eventually some rather meagre clues were unearthed from Queen Anne's thanksgiving for Marlborough's victory at Blenheim in 1704). By 1797 however – when Britain's sea triumphs over the Revolution were celebrated – courtiers and ministers now knew approximately what to do, and thanks could be offered up in time-honour'd style.

As well as State occasions the same decades witnessed mammoth growth in popular tokens of loyalty: commemorative pottery, cheap prints and obsequious ballads. As Ms Colley reveals with delicious acidity, there was even a humble ancestor of today's electronic spectacle in the shape of illuminated 'transparent prints',

> Together with embroidering standards for volunteer regiments, making transparencies became one of the most widely practised patriotic accomplishments of women of Jane Austen's social status and those who aspired to it.

Later this is developed into a general comment of great interest. Even prior to the anti-revolutionary build-up George's domestic propriety had appealed to ladies of aspiring status: 'The royal *family* and not just the monarch had acquired increased currency and popularity in this period...' The 'middling classes' above all saw something admirable in just that life-style which later aroused the derision of aristocrats and intellectual cynics; while middling women, with their responsibility for hearth and children, saw a special tribute to themselves in the model household of 'Farmer George'. It was on this foundation that 'the remarkable female investment in royal celebration' of George's later reign was constructed. Wives and mothers and would-be wives and mothers (nearly all women) found the investment attractive because the restricted (or 'nuclear') family was far more important to the bourgeoisie than to the reigning aristocracy. That the élite and the intellectuals disdained poor, boring old George was another sound reason for the new passion. By its cult of King-and-family, a stolid bourgeois family 'could affirm its own values and challenge those of society's élite'.

With the recognition of this new development, there is surely no doubt about it: we are already in the 20th century. These attitudes were unknown to earlier reigns: in the world of

Absolute Monarchy mistresses and bastards aroused little real censure and were not the business of the lower orders. But in the new conditions, precisely, they had turned into 'the business' of subjects: the formation of a more effective nationalism was accompanied by a tighter unity, a pressure for moral homogeneity which turned even the deportment and personality of rulers into a kind of object-lesson for the ruled. I pointed out earlier how nowadays we take for granted a U.K. public obsessed by finding out over and over again 'what they're really like'. And we accept, equally, a strong yet elusive feminine colouration of this cult: surveys have always shown Monarchy to be (even) more popular with women, and womens' magazines – which I will look at more closely below – have sustained the cult at a consistently high voltage.

Ms Colley's thoughtful analysis guides us towards some understanding of this. The 'obsession' is a form of assertion, and within it women have had special motives for affirming their stake. Neither assertion nor motives are 'irrational' or 'mindless'. They are of course profoundly *conservative*; but the problem then becomes just what this means. We also saw how left-wing thinkers have so often resorted to hopeless diagnoses of 'instinct' and 'national character' when they see this apparently unclimbable wall looming up once more. On the contrary, Colley's study begins to indicate how the wall was built up, and why; and when these reasons are better understood we can see that, though solid, it is hardly likely to last for ever.

After 1790, George's inability to interfere with Parliament (as he had done so notably in 1783-4 and during the American Revolution) was turned into something extremely useful. Just at the time when the State urgently needed validation *as such*, in a new, urgently nationalist sense above party bickering, it became safe to worship its Crown. In this sense the King's developing madness (whatever its medical character) was one of Monarchy's outstanding gifts to England. It occurred in the very circumstances that demanded decisive separation of Crown and State from mere politics; and the result – the rapid compilation of a more conscious, apparently non-controversial national identity – was equally decisive. Now that the Throne was harmless it could be made the focus for a 'pure' patriotism perceiving the existing State as an apolitical foundation for 'everything worth defending' about Britain. It was the very decline in Royal influence, notes Colley, which –

> ...made it much easier for the public to distinguish between monarch and minister and to celebrate the former without owing allegiance to the latter....As some radical journals recognized, this growing distinction in the public mind was potentially an enormous asset to the existing order. For of course the belief that the monarch was in some way politically neutral was profoundly deceptive. The monarchy was the apex of the existing social hierarchy and the formal head of the existing constitution: attachment to it willy-nilly dictated limits to anyone's social or political disaffection...

It was these 'limits' that counted. Negatively, they drew marks against 'unreasonable', 'impractical' opposition to the régime; positively, they were the lineaments of more consciously affirmed nationality - the image of Great Britain's riposte to arid *philosophes* and Napoleon Bonaparte. Earlier, patriotism had been something associated with (in our terms) the 'Left' rather than the Establishment. This was why it had been denounced (in one of the most misquoted remarks in British history) as 'the last refuge of a scoundrel' by the Tory Samuel Johnson.[42] But by around 1810 the scoundrels had been chased out of their refuge for good: it was being made into a Royal Palace.

In reaction against this appropriation of national robes by Throne and Altar, British democrats found themselves automatically threatened with extrusion into a stance of 'internationalism'. It could be claimed of course that the Royal, conservative-national identity was fraudulent, that a *real* Britain was betrayed and disguised by it; but the claim became weaker and more strident as an ever-larger popular majority *did* show signs of accepting the imposition. The huge crowds and 'spontaneous' enthusiasm of the celebrations for George's 50th Jubilee in 1809, and then for the Centenary of the Hanoverian accession to the British Throne in 1814, showed - in ways deeply familiar today - that this could not all be conspiracy and drunkenness.

By talking of 'the foolish multitude' or asserting that '*the people* have no *will* in the matter... (it) is an act of the government', the radicals Leigh Hunt and William Cobbett were implicitly confessing the victory of the very strategy they deplored. And 'victory' consisted partly in the fact that it was not (or not only) a strategy of 'government' in the limited party sense: the point was that Government as such had been stamped with a new identity, at once more national and more deeply-rooted. A British Way was being celebrated, a 'consensus' of which thenceforth all particular administrations would be both beneficiaries and slaves: the former when they floated with the current, indulging in no more than discreet pressures on the tiller, the latter when (like Wilson in 1964 or Edward Heath in 1979) they rashly attempted compass-guided redirection of the general course. Only after 1980 was a different route forced upon the old vessel.

Some still find it surprising that in the last years of the great battle against the Revolution there were British subjects who had doubts about the patriotic cause, and quite a few who longed for French triumph. Even in the distorted, imperialist form of Napoleonism that seemed preferable to vindication of Hanover and Old Corruption (the 'unacceptable face' of Burke's Constitution of Liberty). Years after Waterloo (which had reduced him to prolonged drunken stupor at the time) William Hazlitt described how Napoleon's defeat had 'thrown him into the pit':

All we who remained were....the lifeless bodies of men, and wore round our necks the collars of servitude and on our foreheads the brand and in our souls the stain of thraldom and of the born slaves of Kings.

Had Britain not won then (they felt) democracy and equality might eventually have had the chance to find new native expression. As it was, victory was carrying the Old Régime to the centre of the world stage and renewing its soul. This felt like not just defeat but burial alive. The feeling brought with it the temptation of national nihilism: something close to a vindictive, punishing resentment against one's own Nation – and above all against its new nationalism, the popular agent of its triumphs and the cause of the Left's impotence. Thus the reinvented Royal identity inevitably bred a parochial British dialectic of the Left: a special kind of anti-nationalism 'remote from the people', pursued by a determined assertion of democracy's right to at least a share in the national-popular heritage – to resonant and unquenchable traditions of its own (which then had also to be discovered-invented and immemorialized).

It is in such ways that George III's apotheosis makes us look forward to the next century; but so does its corollary, the régime-castration of democracy to make it fit élitism and Empire. In May 1982 I met an English democrat in a London street who said, looking around and lowering his voice somewhat: 'Bad news from the South Atlantic....it's time the Argentinians got their act together a bit better than this. Otherwise *she*'ll be in power till the year 2000!' Noone could have been less likely to support General Galtieri and the Buenos Aires *Junta* as such; yet he could not help feeling that, had they won, Old Corruption might have been wounded deeply enough to expire - and that was what mattered most. Though easily paraded as internationalism, this is that same attitude so uncomfortably close to utter despair of one's own nation and national attitudes. It goes back to the origins of (in Colley's concluding words):

> The accelerating process whereby political and social radicals in Britain vacated the realm of conventional, xenophobic and complacent patriotism, and left it for the state authorities and, crucially, for the monarchy, to occupy. The libertarian, anti-imperialist mode of patriotism was very far from dead in Britain by 1820 – it was voiced, for example, by the Chartists in the 1830s and 1840s... But the second half of George III's reign forced this type of patriotism on the defensive and helped to ensure that, increasingly, the nation would be celebrated in a very different way.

However, it ought to be stressed that this way of celebration – cosy, decorous, familial, backward-looking – was *also* a form of 'modernization'. The term is often appropriated to an exclusively socio-economic use, to mean adaptation to the conditions of capitalism, or industrial growth: to 'bourgeois society' as Marx saw it, or the mobile, individualistic, selection-through-achievement world. But States and political forms also have to modernize, either by effective representative democracy *or some substitute for it*. There was no escape from the general conditions of an industrializing world. Within a short time the most remote peoples would be drawn into its whirlpool and obliged to defend themselves with whatever arms they could muster – including the crucial, mobilizing armament of a hastily formalized collective consciousness. The Hanoverian British Empire was in so many ways at the head of the storm that it is easy to overlook those other respects in which it too was 'left behind', and had to 'catch up' or modernize. Yet it is just those respects that are decisive for understanding the resultant popular national identity – and consequently, for understanding the place of the Monarchy in that consciousness.

Folklore From Above

> The discovery was made that England was, after all, an *old* country with a precious heritage in danger of obliteration... An élite separating itself from the sources of dynamism in existing society and striving to attach itself to another way of life promoted a change in collective self-image from that of a still-young and innovative nation to one ancient and peculiarly stable.
>
> Martin Wiener, 'The "English Way of Life"?', in *English Culture and the Decline of the Industrial Spirit 1850-1980* (1981) p.43.

The whole development of nationalism since the 18th century has tended towards the fusion of the two generally recognized levels of nationality: personal or 'ethnic' identification on one hand and formal or passport citizenship on the other. But in the British Isles (itself a piece of phoney geography) such coalescence is impossible. Why? Because, as in Austria-Hungary/Habsburg Empire/'Austria', the inherited structure of the State rules it out. The Royal or Britannic domain is by its primary historical definition alien from mere nationality. This is partly a matter of being a multi-national reality (long before the late 19th century era of ostentatious Imperialism). But more importantly, it reflects the developmental location which we have been examining. The Anglo-Scottish 1707 State - which already incorporated the Welsh and the Irish in different ways - was constituted before the general formulation of modern national consciousness.

This state of affairs is revealed in the small change of Ukanian conversation, with its ceaseless and skilful shuffling of the cards of identity. A similar neurosis afflicted Habsburg salons, and was another burden for the Man Without Qualities:

> On paper it called itself the Austro-Hungarian Monarchy; in speaking, however, one referred to it as Austria, that is to say, it was known by a name that it had, as a State, solemnly renounced by oath, while preserving it in all matters of sentiment, as a sign that feelings are just as important as constitutional law and that regulations are not the really serious thing in life...

In Ukania too nationality is not part of the Royal Word. The reader might be pardoned for seeing a reference here to the convoluted hypocrisies of H.M.'s 'Nationality Act 1981'; but in the Royal time-scale, unfortunately, this figures only as a single shaming moment from a history of chronic recidivism. The point is rather the qualms attending *any* introduction of the ethnic into matters Britannic. Today's Asian and Caribbean immigrants often imagine their intrusion must be responsible for the squirming (as the Jews and the Irish did before them). But this is one thing they should worry less about: the truth of the anti-racist truism about racism being 'really a majority problem' bites deeper than even they believe.

'In other countries dynasties are episodes in the history of the people', wrote A.J.P.Taylor, 'in the Habsburg Empire people are a complication in the history of the dynasty'.[43] Within the British Empire too, both 'people' in the radical, trouble-making sense and 'peoples' in the plural or ethnic sense have figured as adjuncts of the Crown: colourful and loyal complements to the Supremacy of Parliament with an unfortunate tendency to get out of hand. In a later work on British history Taylor noted the essential similarities, with typically truculent humour. 'Great Britain' was a bit of pompous myth-geography foisted upon the English by the Scots at the time of the 1707 Union: belief that the 'Great' part signifies grandeur is confined to political cretins. The English have rightly disregarded this fiction and gone on speaking of 'England', above all at intense moments. This never ceases to infuriate the letter-page of the Edinburgh *Scotsman* but accords with most international usage, except when people are speaking diplomatically, or unnaturally. Yet even 'Britain' is sometimes not diplomatic enough. A third title is sometimes required, 'The United Kingdom', which at once consciously includes Northern Ireland and sets us apart from the world's Republican *canaille*.

Thus H.M.'s subjects are given a whole kit of titles to juggle with, and learn through practice the odd art of assigning them to the appropriate circumstances and with the appropriate nuances. 'In themselves' they are of course never 'Britons' – a newspaper-headline term for disclosures like 'Air Crash: Many Britons Lost'. Yet the adjectival form 'British' is more acceptable, because more impersonal: when immigrants say they wish to be treated as 'British' this has the sense of a formal or State-definition, linked to Westminster, the Queen's Justice and standards of something-or-other - citizenship rather than nationality. As against that, *real* nationality remains a deep-cultural or personal attribute, being 'Welsh', 'Bengali' and so on. As Fowler points out in the *Dictionary of Modern English Usage*:

> It must be remembered that no Englishman, or perhaps no Scotsman even, calls himself a Briton without a sneaking sense of the ludicrous, or hears himself referred to as a *Britisher* without squirming. How should an Englishman utter the words *Great Britain* with the glow of emotion that for him goes with *England*? His Sovereign may be Her *Britannic* Majesty to outsiders, but to him is Queen of *England*...He has heard of the word of an *Englishman* and aspires to be an *English* gentleman...In the word *England*, not in *Britain*, all those things are implicit.

A recent and more definitive chart of this identity-minefield has been published by *English Today* ('The International Review of the English Language'). There, nine pages are taken up by the full panoply of 'Anglo-', 'Brit-', 'U.K.-' and their host of subordinate identifiers. '*Britannic* conveys a sense of formalized power and glory that is now archaic. British passports, however, still contain it...'; 'The *Home Counties* are not just a place. They are a way of life.'; '*Europe* - to an Englishman is still The Continent...to this day *we* are in England, and *they* are in Europe.'; '*Englishperson* is unlikely to catch on...the more comprehensive and less emotive *Briton* and *Brit* seem to be moving in to fill the socio-semantic gap' - a process notably accelerated in Ulster English. To illustrate the rather dubious cultural dimensions of 'British' the Editor quotes Anthony Sampson's *Anatomy of Britain*:

> While foreigners mocked Britain's declining standards and industry they conceded that they could not compete with British ceremonial. As the *Boston Globe* put it after the Royal Wedding: "The Royal Family pulls off ceremonies the way the army of Israel pulls off commando raids"...[44]

Subjects can sometimes be heard apologizing for the confusion (usually with tongue in cheek and ill-hidden pride in eccentricity). But in fact this sapient and chameleon-like diversity does no more than manifest the Crown-State's historic character. It shuffles with affected insouciance around a truth that can only be evaded. The point is that the world now speaks in one way, and Royal English in another.

Forms of speech derive from real dilemmas – in this case, from the fact that even in its revolt and novelty the Anglo-British State could not help remaining part of the religious and Royal world. The State's genesis preceded the main body of Enlightenment thought: the political world of Rousseau and popular sovereignty, and of the industrial revolution. But (as we have seen) nationalism was another inevitable product of these transformations yet to come: it was the combined impact of democracy and industry that awakened and bestowed urgent political form upon nationality. However, the core Anglo-British world magically pickled by Monarchy preceded this 'Age of Nationalism' just as it did that of the Jacobins and the *Sans-culottes*. It is this underlying dislocation that explains the restiveness of today's Windsor culture with the very notions of nationality and ethnicity.

From the time of the later Hanoverians to that of the post-1917 Windsors, a British equivalent of nationalism had none the less to be built up: a renovated identity more capable of both domestic discipline and external mobilization against others. The only available way of doing this is best described as 'familial' nationalism – an odd, composite identity-structure making use of the materials to hand and serving to reconcile the established State with the new popular sentiments and ideas. As Linda Colley suggested, the Monarchy proved crucial to such a structure: whenever it came under strain, the Crown - its inevitable symbolic focus – grew more prominent. When in the 20th century the pressures finally became chronic, and resistance began seriously to weaken, that focus turned into a mesmerist's charm – the medium of the mass obsession from which Britons suffer today.

The anti-ethnic features of Royal-family nationalism are best understood by comparison with Kohn's broad classification cited earlier. The principal distinction there – one which reappears in some form in every general account of nationalism – is between 'Western' and 'Eastern' national identity. Thus on one hand we see the admirable Enlightenment tradition with its principled liberalism: the advance (still under way) of individual and constitutional rights, egalitarian customs, government by and of the people, and economic progress. Here – successively in England, America and France - the popular-national consciousness of the modern age is supposed to have taken a benevolent, rational and institutional shape whose hiccups and blots deserve to be overlooked.

On the other hand, however, we find the 'bad sister' version in which nationality has emerged as a mass force without (or against) such Enlightened rules and aspirations - as aggressive self-assertion, racism or heedless ethnic 'chauvinism'. The 'East' label applied to this refers primarily to Eastern-Central Europe, and reflects the original importance of Slavic national movements against the Habsburgs, the German Empire and Tsarist Russia. But later movements in the other continents adopted a comparable style of nationalism (and it also flourished on Europe's western edge, in Ireland). A useful elucidation of the contrast was given more recently by John Plamenatz in his essay 'Two Types of Nationalism'.[45] 'Writers about nationalism mostly agree that there was little or none of it in the world until the end of the 18th century', he begins:

patriotism, or old-style devotion to one's natural community, turned into 'nationalism' only where and when peoples shared (or hoped to share) in 'a cosmopolitan and secular culture in which the belief in progress is strong'. Echoing Kohn's perspective, he shows how such a developmental culture was launched by the benign trinity of Western nation-states, and imbued with their liberalism. But its impact upon the less fortunately-placed societies next door to them in Europe, or in the overseas lands which they colonized, generated something quite different. Those second-class people outside the comity faced a drastically different problem: they were unable easily to catch up with the now accelerating pace of progress-culture. Their 'nationalism of the eastern kind' was both imitative and competitive, fuelled by the aggressive resentment of the outcast and the exploited: it couldn't afford liberalism, or the enlightened institutional superstructure so prized by the leaders. Eastern (and later 'Third World') nationality movements placed greater emphasis upon sharply ethnic and native factors: their own 'narrow' – and often mythicized – inheritance. This had to be mobilized for ideological struggle in a novel way, in the hope that the unique (even genetic) endowment of this or that people might provide the badly-needed motor of acceleration into modernity. The way to beat the West (and catch up decisively) was therefore to be aggressively ultra-nationalist and anti-Western.

It was this second-wave movement of nationality that ran wild after the First World War. Absolute Monarchy finally crashed to the ground in *Mitteleuropa* and the east, releasing successor States dominated by an aggressive ethnic particularism. But the worst effects were not among these. It was the immediately preceding 19th century 'new nations' of Germany and Italy that suffered the most: those which had (or thought they had) 'caught up' and entered the charmed Western circle, only to encounter defeat, stalemate or relegation. They collapsed into counter-revolutions intensifying everything deplorable about Plamenatz's 'Eastern'-style nationalism, and were joined by another late-developer, Japan, in a racialist crusade. This global counter-movement was aimed at defeating both 'Western' or liberal-capitalist appropriation of the world, and Communism (seen in the Nazi ideology as a degenerate by-product of liberalism).

It is out of this era (1922-45) that a convenient demonology has arisen, relevant to my argument here because of the way it has strengthened resistance to taking nationalism seriously in Britain. It reinforced an antipathy already deeply embedded in the structural context of Anglo-British statehood. And one consequence of that has been welcome reinforcement of the Royal taboo, and resistance to theoretic raids on its real meaning. The general 'odour' of nationalism in the familial culture has helped make it impossible to come to intellectual terms with our own Monarchic version of national identity. Though a nationality-surrogate, the latter flourishes best in a climate where ethnic nationality is damned or (at least) sneered at: it is in these conditions that its 'peculiarities' or differences from standard forms are most visible, and least challenged.

I am not denying that Demonology has a certain crazy dignity of its own. A wild yet coherent world-view has been constructed around it, and gained wide currency. In his personal recollection of 'the black mystery of what happened in Europe', for instance, George Steiner has described the background thus:

> Nationalism is the venom of our age. It has brought Europe to the edge of ruin. It drives the new states of Asia and Africa like crazed lemmings. By proclaiming himself a Ghanaian, a Nicaraguan, a Maltese, a man spares himself vexation. He need not ravel out what he is, where his humanity lies. He becomes one of an armed, coherent pack. Every mob impulse in modern politics, every totalitarian design, feeds on nationalism, on the drug of hatred...[46]

There is a revealing lapse in Steiner's denunciation. When originally published in 1965 he took it for granted that any sane reader would find Nicaraguan nationalism an unsavoury joke. In the 1980s the situation is somewhat altered: today anyone claiming that Nicaraguans defend their nation and hard-won identity just to 'save themselves vexation' and wriggle out of acknowledging 'humanity' would have a lot of farther explaining to do.

But of course, what this change fingers is the weakness of Steiner's diabolism as such. Its one-dimensionality fails to perceive how the 'mob impulse' may, in different conditions, become democratic and liberatory ferment: the 'drug of hatred' may also become the adrenalin of revolutionary affirmation. Nationalism can't all be Mr Hyde: Dr Jekyll has a stake in it too (and indeed, Anglo-Britain's curious variant can be seen as the ultimate in Jekyllism). 'Humanity' may lie at least for a certain period with a national movement towards identity, rather than against it. But then – how long is 'a certain period' likely to be? How many nationalisms have had or retain such a 'progressive phase'?

These questions indicate an even more uncomfortable general truth for anti-nationalist Demonology. For the last two centuries have witnessed the triumph of the national State – the making or re-making of most of humanity in the standard nationalist political shape. Can it really be the case that this whole historic tendency has had the Devil behind it? Was it not, rather, a form of progress – *generally* inevitable and beneficent in spite of the gross counter-examples of the 1918-45 era? Were Hitler's Germany, Mussolini's Italy and their allies merely a logical outcome of that process (as Steiner and so many others have believed)? Or were they breakdowns in its onward course - pathological specimens (however appalling) thrown up by one single, and unrepeatable, epoch of counter-revolution and war?

As explanation, I will assume here that Demonology can safely be put alongside cheap *Kulturpessimismus* about mass stupidity (and Steiner has contradicted his paranoid lapse innumerable times in other writings since then). Though we should return to the implicit general argument later on, for the moment I will go on looking at British identity through the less dramatic perspective suggested by Gellner and others: nationalism as structure rather than disease, and national identity as a cultural prerequisite of modernity rather than as regressive lunacy.

Plamenatz draws a contrast between Jean-Jacques Rousseau and J.G.Herder as the respective apostles of his two sorts of national identity. But it is equally important to recall that both the Rousseauian-democratic tradition and its ugly sibling shared something crucial: the conviction that modern times had borne *the people* to centre-stage. Whether as (potentially) rational voters or as the non-rational *Volk*'s blood-call for a Leader, their rise determined the sea-change. The resulting tunes might be very different; but there could be no escape from this orchestrated music of modernity. Capitalist industry and agriculture demanded the induction of 'the masses' (as they came to be labelled) into society, and could not avoid collapsing the barriers of traditional and rural order sufficiently to release a permanent ferment of unrest. The corrosive element in that ferment was the idea and sentiment of popular *equality* - whether as equality of abstract rights and opportunities, or as the deeper identity of 'blood' and an inherited ethnic spirit or culture.

The same point can be put in still another way. Nationalism in the distinctive modern sense is *always* implicitly populist in orientation. Populism is only democracy's unacknowledged bastard. However, the extension of nationalism into a world-order was largely an uneven, antagonistic and somewhat bastard process. It's not only that the illicit offspring, crazed or 'narrow' nationalism, was strong enough to threaten the parents at times and in 1939-45 almost wrecked their abode for good. Also, the parents themselves (however genteelly they may have started out) have by their own forced reaction to a process they no longer control become bastards – they have developed their own version of 'narrowness', their own national-populist identities, in a way recognizably like the once-scorned products of under-development. Nationality as an 'ism' became a global climate which in the longer run made 'Great Power Chauvinism' as inevitable (and far more lethal) than the small-country or anti-colonial kind.

But the State which has had the greatest difficulty doing this is the one usually treated as the prime mover of the whole process: England-Britain. If denunciations like Steiner's have appealed so strongly in England it is because here an unbeatable combination of factors turned 'nationalism' into something theoretically alien. There was England's pioneering role on Kohn's 'liberal' side, transfigured by the Whig Interpretation into a predestined Protestant *pavane* across the centuries - somehow inherently different from the dark squabbles of the less fortunate. There was the fact that England had evolved so early into a Great-British multi-national State, where (with the exception of the Irish) ethnic differentiation suffered early demotion to the status of jokey nostalgia. And there was the moral burden of an overseas Empire that could only be justified in the most sweeping and supra-national terms. Missionary Liberalism was the usual tool for this, and in time received an appropriate Socialist formulation from the Fabians and the Labour Party. The sole serious, non-nationalist formula was pseudo-scientific racialism: a right-wing alternative strongly cultivated in the undergrowth of the Imperialist era, and still lurking in today's British National Front and similar bodies. Also, there was that cultivated scepticism towards theory as such which I described earlier: re-enthroned from Edwardian times onwards and given new satin breeches and regalia as 'British Empiricism', this underwrote the sense of how all doctrine leads to trouble of some non-Shakespearian kind. But nationalism – like democracy, popular sovereignty and egalitarianism – does have an unavoidable (and on the whole justifiable) doctrinaire side to it.

The paradox of George III's 'modernization' and what followed under Victoria is therefore this: Britain couldn't do without a 'nationalism', in the sense of an ideological armour for coping with modernity. But it had to have a strongly dissembling one, a national identity simultaneously above *and beneath* all that – an undoctrinaire formula bridging directly from the popular to the transcendent, from the 'ordinary' to the supernally grand and ethical. This passage had at once to mimic political nationalism and to occlude its dangerous side - defusing the populist threat, as it were, by awarding its *Volk* house-room in an older or 'traditional' structure. That is exactly what the country's cultivated modern over-obsession with Monarchy has made possible: a pseudo-nationalism fostering 'community' from above and bestowing a sense of 'belonging' without the damnable nuisance of ethnic and rudely democratic complaint.

An exact indicator of how this functions is provided by another feature of Queenspeak: the automatic humour or contempt attached to 'folk'. There is of course a body of folklore and music within contemporary British culture, and a tiny minority of researchers, performers and theorists devoted to its cause. But they have always had to labour against the mainstream of Ukanian ideology. Sensible English intellectuals have always viewed real culture as being (like the Crown) above that sort of peasant thing. Sometimes historical justification is sought for this attitude in terms of the early demise of English peasant agriculture by Enclosure Acts, and the argument that a rural proletariat had less time for folksong. But little credence attaches to the idea, above all in comparative terms: in other countries where an ethnic style of mobilization was needed, popular cultures were 'revived' easily enough and after a short time few could tell where resurrection ended and invention began. The point is that in English circumstances this style wasn't ideologically needed, and the Folk were left where they Royally belong: in a tumbledown encampment well screened from the big house, the object of belated antiquarian forays and drawing-room humour rather than nationalist veneration.

Here again the scene is different in the periphery. It was noted earlier that Royalty works at a lower level of infatuation outside the English cultural nation itself. But Scotland, Ireland and Wales also accord significantly greater importance to folk-culture, and the nationalist movements in these countries have tried to rehabilitate popular balladry and rural lore on a recognizably standard pattern. The two things fit together, and we can now see why. Where populist mobilization from below appears necessary, or even possible, then the folkish traits inherited from past times automatically assume greater salience. Where that is ruled out, as in the English heartland, folkishness becomes absurd and is easily substituted for by what is in effect a 'folklore from above' – a State-centred 'immemoriality' articulated around Crown, 'stately home', the Free-born Englishman and so on. The potentialities of mythic people and folk alike vanish behind these mythic Institutions – ruling customs of such weathered gravity and soul-shaking import that noone will ever dare challenge them (and certainly not with a fiddle or a bit of Morris-dancing).

Within the modern spectrum of nationalist attitudes, in fact, Britain's variant is the only one that is *neither* democratic *nor* ethnic-populist in nature. Founded a century before the two main currents of nationalist ideology were set upon their antagonistic course, it stage-managed a strain of identity distinct from both: 'liberal' (in an antique, patrician sense) without risking Rousseauian democracy or sovereignty-from-below, and 'popular' (in a Shakespearian-patriotic vein) without falling into popul*ism* or a fatal ethnicity of blood or culture. Another way of making the same point is to notice how strikingly absent egalitarianism has been from modern English culture (though it is fairly prominent in the British periphery). Democratic nationalism and ethnic populism are in a sense only two different articulations of this seminal notion - the very core of modern politics, registering what the English conservative idiom regards as the Original Sin of popular intrusion into civil and State-life. What the familial national identity has done is to canalize and regulate that intrusion and destroy its natural egalitarianism, partly by suppression and (more important in the long run) by the measured compensations of an alternative, if increasingly idiosyncratic, culture.

The same view can also be reached simply by reading the Whig Régime-mythology in reverse. The resolutely Parliamentarist constitution hymned by Edmund Burke refused popular sovereignty in principle, but conceded many of its discrete effects in practice over a suitably immemorial time-scale. Regrouped around the Monarchy and the Crown-in-Parliament mythology, this profoundly élitist structure has simply imitated the later models of democratic polity by an interminably staged and necessarily superficial process of 'modernization'. It has 'opened its doors' to the people, at moments convenient to its own interests and in the largely justified hope that, spiritually chastened by a long wait, the mob would then settle down at each stage and put up with the old mansion. But of course, the very success and longevity of this strategy has *also* held populism permanently at bay. Egalitarianism in the democratic sense was partly absorbed and partly (the more important part) broken. And once politically pulverized in this way, it was then very unlikely to reassert itself in the 'bad sister' shape of folk-nationalism or angry ethnic resentment.

It may be argued that there are some advantages in this, given what popular nationalism has been like in many other cases. However, what this familiar Ukanian stance tends to mean is that the longer-range costs and cramps are forgotten about.

Discussing some ideas I put forward in *The Break-up of Britain* (1977), R.W.Johnson noticed shrewdly how the British Left has so often sought instinctively to have it both ways: complaining about the absurdities of the Old Régime yet counting on its antique rigidities for protection against something worse - the potentially right-wing popular resentment invoked (though mainly as unorganized fantasy) by Enoch Powell, and by the street hooliganism of the far right. Fear of this 'monster' makes the most resolute socialists fall back on dear old Nanny-style liberalism: 'silent comfort in an elitist structure of power which bars the way' to something worse.[47] Having no adequate or Republican alternative to that structure, they are uncomfortably aware of how effective a reactionary anti-Establishment movement might one day prove – an 'uncivilized' populism forced down by the conservative weight of the old order into the sewer-bottom of racial and crypto-Nazi nonsense. In U.K.-speak 'nationalism' is of course automatically identified with this uneasy sense of uncontrollable aggression below decks.

Johnson's observation recalls another made fifty years ago by Kingsley Martin. Editor of the *New Statesman* from the 1930s until the 1950s, Martin also wrote a short book entitled *The Magic of Monarchy* after Edward VIII's abdication in 1936: before Hamilton's *My Queen and I*, the only semi-serious critique of British Monarchism produced in this century. However, it was scarcely a Republican tract. Martin's plea was that the British should try and be more 'sensible' about Royalty. Like the founders of Mass Observation he sensed that decline and crisis were affecting popular attitudes towards it, and believed that one ought to try and keep the institution but do away with the nonsense:

> If we want democracy to work we must be sensible. If we cannot be sensible about Monarchy we had better have a Republic and try to be sensible about a President. At present we still believe that Monarchy best suits our traditions and preserves our liberties...[48]

This would be safer than going for Republicanism. A century before (he admitted) it had taken courage to question the Bible or the Virgin Birth, but outspoken criticism of the Crown had

PORTLAND
BOOK SHOP
1 OXFORD ROAD
MANCHESTER
TEL (0161) 272 6060
VAT 145845155

B
OPEN BOOKS   1.50

Total: 1.50

Paid by: CASH   2.00

CHANGE: 0.50

15-03-2006 07:13   001-01-08764
MIKE   Items: 1

THANK YOU
PLEASE CALL AGAIN
RETAIN RECEIPT FOR REFUNDS

been commonplace; now things were reversed. One could speak fairly freely about Jesus Christ, but 'until the advent of Mrs Simpson no journalist dared to attribute a fault to the King of England, or, indeed, to refer to the character of any royal person except in the whispered undertones of worshippers in a sacred place'. None the less outright opposition wouldn't be sensible, since –

> The advantages of Constitutional Monarchy are...more obvious in the post-war than in the pre-war era. If we drop the trappings of Monarchy in the gutter, Germany has taught us that some gutter-snipe (or house-painter with a mission) may pick them up...

No one of Martin's observations has been more quoted than this. Its comforting implications are exactly those Johnson noticed: because no third way is imaginable for the British between the Old-Régime Constitution and dictatorship, one should stick with the former. Gentlemen before gutter-snipes and house-painters.

'In itself' and in the conditions of 1936-7, such a choice was of course unassailable. But the whole historical puzzle lies in this 'in itself': can it really be true that there is *nothing* in between the world of State Openings, Mr Speaker, Eton and Ramsay Macdonald, and that of Adolf Hitler? No alternative that acknowledges a 'people' down there among the gutters, capable of some uncrowned democratic dignity and initiative? Yet such an alternative is little less than political modernity itself and what the blind spot occludes is normal or Republican national identity – that trouble-making complex of ideas which the Regal-State folklore of the Establishment was invented in order to suppress. A fetishism of both Crown and Institutions was imposed, partly to keep out the toxins of both democratic and ethnic-populist nationality, and partly to substitute for them.

The point at issue here is the fundamental one summarized by Raymond Williams in *The Long Revolution*. After stressing how 'democracy has never established a really deep social image, of a distinct kind, in Britain', he continues:

> Just because...it grew slowly, and by gradual constitutional

amendment and compromise, it has always been difficult, here, to separate the principle of democracy from the habitual loyalty to an establishment. The symbols of democracy, in the English mind, are as likely to be institutions of power and antiquity, such as the Palace of Westminster, as the active process of popular decision, such as a committee or jury.[49]

This 'deep social image, of a distinct kind' is of course the essence of Republicanism, whose absence from Kingsley Martin's musings reflected a similar void in the Labour Party and ultimately (as Williams argues) from the whole historical Left of modern British politics. It's wrong, though – and can even be read as collusive – to suggest that the void was due primarily to Constitutional gradualness. 'Gradualness' is also a totemic Régime-category: the partner of 'Not Too Much', 'Muddling Through' and Queenspeak prose. In fact Republicanism was suppressed by ideological battles, conducted in several recognizable phases: at the State's founding moment, during its battle against the French Revolution, and – as we shall see later - once more when the contemporary public-relations Monarchy was created from the 1870s onwards. Such suppression invariably demanded the inflation of Monarchy as the principal counter-model of Established national values - of that integral anti-Republican world to which a British Member of Parliament's Oath of habitual Loyalty is still sworn.

Why was there no sane democratic alternative to which a Socialist like Martin could turn? Because an anti-egalitarian, Royal-family identity had pre-empted it historically. Nonstandard yet effective in British circumstances, this odd variety of nationalism broke down and contained the second-wave bourgeois ideologies of egalitarianism and individualism. Once the abstract democratic identity had been pulped, there was then little to impede the Old Régime's essential continuance: Romantic-national Royalism had little to fear from a Socialism based on 'class' - quite the contrary, it found a new and secure foundation in that brand of parochial ideology. 'Class' in this sense has been little more than the resentful but ultimately acceptive social anthropology of Royalism. While it dominated Ukania's Left there was no hope of Republicanism reviving; no chance, therefore, of a modern socialist politics.

These demand the 'deep social image of democracy' as a prerequisite, and if it isn't there must try to create it.

The Royal Etiquette-Lesson

One of the chief weaknesses of British sport, writes the outspoken runner Christopher Brasher, has been and still is, the importance which is attached to *style*. In athletics we have the most stylish hurdlers in the world, but unfortunately they can't run fast enough between the hurdles.

As quoted in Rupert Wilkinson, *The Prefects: British Leadership and the Public School Tradition* (1964) p.57.

After the founding moment of Ukanian national identity historians follow a customary route reflecting the self-image of those 'institutions of power and antiquity', and above all of the Palace of Westminster. Sagely gradual reform admits the lower orders into an ever-ampler share of authority; harsh in its earlier stage, the Industrial Revolution then spreads well-being sufficiently to buy off the grumblings of Chartism; the early misdeeds of Empire are compensated (as Kohn insisted) by the export of Westminster and the Law to backward areas and peoples. The anti-route is nowadays almost as well-established: Birnbaum's attribution of everything beneficent to pressure from below, where 'the working class was the dominant force' by 1832 and ensured that thenceforth 'class' would be the healthy ballast of the whole system – weighing its ambiguities consistently (with perhaps a few lapses) in the direction of liberalism, progress and (though perhaps not quite yet) Socialism.

These perspectives are impregnated with an unconscious nationalism - the complacent conviction that all struggles proceed within an ultimately unassailable framework of national identity. But the Old Régime has largely reproduced itself within just that conviction: identity as a fixed form of national assumptions and characteristics, within which political battles can then be fought over matters of content – the axiomatically 'real' issues of economics and social welfare. Of course 'fixed' also means 'flexible' in Ukanian mythology: the only genuine fixture of the Constitution is its unwritten, malleable nature – hence, the possibility of doing absolutely anything with it (even Socialism). Oh yes, 'modernization' is built into Britishism and (as we've seen) vividly conveyed in its own way by the Royal ideology.

But if one looks at history directly from this Royal angle and inquires how such a dense ideological structure was constructed, the picture appears very different. Regal-popular nationalism was unusual in eschewing both the democratic and the ethnic motifs of 19th century popular mobilization. It had to replace these by a less doctrinaire and formal illusion of equality, which could only come from familial community: a cultivated sense of moral oneness derived from other sources than radical individualism or vulgar populism. This national identity minus the 'ism' – Providential Anglo-British nature, as it were – was constructed in a wide variety of ways that I will not attempt to register here. Instead, I will take merely two examples of the process – of the stuff of the English-British way of life, the civil and semi-conscious national identity accreted around the core I have tried to isolate. Firstly (following up some of the observations in Linda Colley's essay) the importance of Royalty in women's reading; and secondly (switching genders) the importance of male games-playing as a social metaphor at once national and implicitly Royal.

One reason why socialist thinkers have balked so unbelievingly at the 'incredible' contrast between poverty and Monarchy in Britain is their long self-confinement in the prison-hulks of 'class'. Had women's magazines been made obligatory reading in hulk libraries, however, the conjuring-trick might appear less indecipherable. For half a century Royal features and gossip have been crucial to British periodical publishing for women. Not a single week passes without a whole range of articles about the Monarchy. For instance, the fairly typical week in which I happen to write this sees five main features, in *Woman's Own* ('From shy young girl to majesty, mystique and magic'), *Woman's Journal* ('Princess Michael - Her Personal Dilemma'), *People's Friend* ('Queen's Story Part 3: the Abdication Crisis'), *Woman* ('Princess Diana

Baby-health Pull-out'), and a newcomer to the market, *Celebrity* ('Princess Diana – the Marriage Problems She Has to Face').

Celebrity's version of Princess Di is specially revealing in relation to some themes noticed earlier. The magazine itself is Dundee firm D.C.Thomson's latest assault on the younger female market. Still impregnable throughout Northern Britain in childrens' comics and the old-style popular 'family' audience represented by the *Sunday Post* and *People's Friend*, Thomson's have recently been trying to expand beyond this shrinking base with frantic colonial expeditions into the quicksands of teenage and rock culture. *Celebrity* ('It's Fabulous, It's Revealing, It's *Dynamite* – Tiaras, Toffs and Tearaways!') again tries to squeeze the cosy old house-style into a forced clinch with modernity.

But the most striking fact here is that *Celebrity*'s staple Royal item is largely indistinguishable from so many others. Minor aspects of style and presentation apart, their (unnamed) 'Royal Correspondent' is getting at the same truth behind the same rumours as every other women's or girls' magazine over the previous year. Both up and down market the conclusions had been identical: yes, the Royal Marriage *is* under strain from her temperament and his oddities, but it will survive as an example to us all. Committed to a diet of indecorous innuendo, in other words, *Celebrity* No.1 has a po-faced decorum-lesson in its centre pages: the girl-slaves and big-star torments were put in their place by this note of reassurance. Mere celebrities may be awful and have awful problems, but *They* (being more and other) transcend such difficulties. *She* will overcome them and learn how to reconcile being Herself with a successful partnership and family.

Whatever else they may be, we saw earlier how modern, publicized Royal events invariably have this aspect: snobby 'lessons in good manners' suggesting a standard of deportment to the audience. Colley noticed that this already appealed strongly to middle-class family women in George III's time – a public model in which some of their own aspirations could be both recognized and justified. Though the Royal spectacle is for everyone, it easily acquires a gender-bias with suitable occupants on the throne. Hence, its messages of 'stability', continuity, moral Nationhood (and so on) come to be transmitted partly via this feminine tangent – through domestic metaphors and imagery notoriously reckoned to be beneath the plane of official or respectable culture. Pastness and loyalty are inculcated on the microscale of custom and familial style, as well as by the resonant (and male) litany of Kingly honour and precedence. Yet this homely ideology – in the literal, rather than the disparaging sense – may be all the more powerful in its effect for such displacement: a concern with 'instinctive' cohesion and emotional acceptance has far more leverage here than in areas touched by intellectual or academic questioning, or by political debate.

The phenomenon may also be related to another, contemporaneous one. Once Victoria was safely on the throne in 1837 respectable opinion was won over to a more steadfast identification with Monarchy: though not yet comparable to today's obsession, this would (as we shall see later) reveal its underlying strength against attempts to revive Republicanism in the 1860s and '70s. And the same mid-century period also witnessed a huge development of interest in questions of etiquette and 'manners', primarily among women.

The 1830s was the decade in which this interest established itself. In earlier times manners had been an exclusive concern of the aristocracy. The 'courtesy books' that multiplied in mid-18th century Britain focused on the provincial or *parvenu* gentry and sought to replace coarse, rustic customs with rather cosmopolitan standards of urbanity and polish. Lord Chesterfield's *Letters to His Son* (1774) was the most famous example. But it was also one of the last: the post-1789 counter-revolution permanently blighted its assumption of a universal (in practice uncomfortably French) code of style. The latter was succeeded by the more indigenous – but also more imitable – model of English-gentlemanly conduct. After 1832, with the epoch of upheavals over and a 'reformed' aristocracy more securely in charge again, this new code soon grew far more influential than its predecessor.

Whereas courtesy books had dealt principally with internal differentiations among the well-born, post-1832 guides to proper behaviour treated the latter as a single unit. That was helped by one central trait of the Anglo-British ruling order.

J.C.D.Clark describes this as its 'autonomous culture', a degree of pre-existent homogeneity that lent itself both to artificial schooling (as in the Public School system) and to social mimesis from below. The ruling class here –

> ...was distinguished from its continental counterparts (by) the equality of all gentlemen. England increasingly possessed a unified, not a stratified, patrician corps. It expressed the solidarity not of a caste or of an economically ill-defined class but, principally, of a culturally-defined élite...(and) From that position of strength they dictated taste, manners and morals.[50]

But the point of 'dictation' was of course its seeming inevitability. It was (Clark goes on) 'an influence which operated via cultural emulation in situations in which no process of coercion from above was conceivable'. 'The most ignorant naturally *look up* for example: the common people will be what their *superiors* are' declared the author of *Virtue in Humble Life* (1774). Because the 'superiors' made up such a cohesive entity unshiftably ensconced in power, emulation grew more and not less habitual after Reform – grew into that familiar inner Ukanian landscape that corresponds to the outer oil-paint 'nature' of village green, squire and stately telephone-box.

In the late 18th and early 19th centuries women emerged as 'the main constituency of good manners'. Within the middle class, influences like religious Dissent and cultural Romanticism also had a part in destroying the old notions of *courtoisie*. But it was their class position within a saved and revived status quo that principally regulated the change. The absence of middle-class hegemony was betrayed by the advent of 'Etiquette': a class-craving to establish social credentials, led and handled by wives and mothers. The older ruling courtesy and Polite Manners had been a mainly masculine concern. But now, as the new social world of class collapsed in stages into the special Ukanian alienation of 'class', this sector of the 'class' struggle was from the outset delegated to women. A great and long-lasting boom in etiquette-manuals started up, depicted by contemporaries as showing 'the unworthy and degrading eagerness of the middle class to learn how lords and ladies ate, dressed and coquetted'. But of course this was a sniffy, external viewpoint; in terms of experience (supposedly crucial for so much English social ideology) the process was a form – increasingly dominant, even inevitable – of self-affirmation and 'getting on':

> Those who wanted to learn aristocratic manners perceived the task not as a craven capitulation to a class enemy but as a worthy emulation of high standards. Aristocratic manners did not appear to contradict economic success but rather to crown it with a diadem of high culture. Etiquette-books were indeed an authentic creation of middle-class civilization: a civilization, however, that expressed some of its deepest and truest urges in the emulation of its class antagonists.[51]

Etiquette was much more external than the old courtesy. This element of mimicry made it both learnable and easy to ridicule. The adoption and display of high-status *moeurs* and belongings (particularly in the home) fostered that parrot-like side of British bourgeois life which is one of the main components of the 'class' psychosis. Fashion and mimicry are of course universal traits of modern society; but nowhere else did the aspiring classes inherit such a solid hierarchy, such authoritative and apparently natural models for emulation.

The emulation was linked from the start to the two other important traits of modern Crown-ideology: the special kind of dominance exerted by its Capital or heartland area, and the peculiar social priority accorded to personal speech (spoken accent) over the written, the formal and the 'bureaucratic'. I mentioned these topics earlier, in Part I. Here it's enough to note how the unified, neo-caste structure of the élite which made it such an imitable model was 'based on the triumph of fashionable London over provincial diversity. London Society had matured - or ossified - and now spoke with a forceful and apparently unanimous voice'. Farthermore –

> This "voice" matured literally as well as figuratively. In the elevation of Received Standard English (above other local dialects) to the national language, London played an important role. Received Standard English had, of course, a bright future as an indicator of social status...

As well as the promotion of the Capital and the fixation of

speech-modes, etiquette presupposed 'the emergence of women into the mainstream of sociability'. This emergence was into a secondary, supportive position still far from the centre of the stream. None the less, a new kind of division of social labour was recognized, based on the combination of privilege and powerlessness that defined the lives of new middle-class women. 'Powerless in most ways' (Michael Curtin points out) 'ladies found in manners a means by which they could assert themselves and create effects in their interests'. Somewhat better than many social historians, they realized that 'manners were more than merely an aesthetic fancy' – that via style and deportment both the family and the class were engaged in an identity-struggle that bore directly on larger issues and values. For the first time, the 'lady-like' (a term generated in etiquette) acquired a pervasive general sense. Those viewing primarily the macro-level of social development often dismiss this as 'passive'; but on the micro-level of most day-to-day social living it is of course quite the opposite – a notoriously (and increasingly) assertive and formative influence.

Within the etiquette-world the Crown family won an obvious new significance. Equally, if it went wrong – failed to 'modernize' and be imitable – it would be a social disaster of a sort unknown to pre-bourgeois dynasties. In Britain, the Old Régime was fortunate enough to get a renewal of Regal personnel at approximately the right historical moment. The breeding competition among George III's heirs put Victoria first past the post; and she found a husband who became the first and immeasurably the most important of Royal impresarios. Together they remade the Royal institution in a new mould that accorded sufficiently with both social and national needs: a matriarchally-inclined symbol-family bringing home (in an ever more literal sense) a traditionalist national identity to ever-wider circles of the population.

Now, these new traditions could not (and can't to this day) avoid an overtly anti-egalitarian side tied to the maintenance of élite rule (one of the things they are about). But in his apology for Monarchy the French counter-revolutionary theorist Joseph de Maistre had noted with satisfaction that –

> It is one of the great advantages of monarchical government
> that there aristocracy loses, as much as the nature of things
> allows, all that can be offensive to the inferior classes.[52]

The reason is that a Crown creates a social fantasy of equality
to compensate for the unavoidable element of offence in rank
(or 'class'). Hence a 'man of the people' can feel that he and a
Lord are both 'subjects'. This submission to the same symbol
of ultimate power and justice constitutes 'a kind of equality
which lulls the inevitable irritation of self-esteem'. Though he
does not say this, a 'woman of the people' devoted to post-1832
etiquette and status-struggle surely had an even stronger need
for such a symbol. Only the Monarch - or better still, the
Monarch's family – could be a 'natural' umpire or final
standard in this anxious world of self-esteem. Snobbery (an
old-time contender for the 'British disease' title before things
got really bad) demanded some ultimate model to give it
structure, to regulate it as a system. And only the Royal
summit could furnish that - a 'balance-wheel' influence at once
all-pervading and yet (as only God, Royalty and Money can
be) mystically different and out of reach.

The preoccupations of etiquette were middle-class, as well as
feminine. However, this did not prevent a farther diffusion of
the same attitudes once material conditions permitted. While
manuals of polite manners could never have become mass
reading, something of their essence could, and did, with the
rise of popular newspapers and magazines towards the close of
last century. These were from the start devoted (in David
Cannadine's phrase) to 'the preservation of anachronism' –

> Of particular importance in promoting this new picture of the
> monarch as head of the nation were developments in the media
> from the 1880s. For with the advent of the yellow press, news
> became increasingly nationalized and sensationalized as the old,
> rational, intellectual, middle-class, provincial Liberal press was
> superseded by the great national dailies: London-based,
> increasingly Conservative, strident, vulgar and working-class in
> their appeal.[53]

Technical developments in photography and printing meant
that illustrations were no longer confined to stately old organs
like the *Illustrated London News*. Hence Royalty could be
conveyed with appealing immediacy to this new public - a

'sentimental, emotional, admiring' mode also relayed by the new and lasting artisanate of Royal Biographers.

Nowhere was such 'worthy emulation of high standards' more noticeable than in the womens' press. Working-class women too pushed forward into the 'mainstream of sociability', above all when, after the Second World War, they came to constitute a significant proportion of the national work-force. And here again the Royal Régime was very fortunate in its personnel: the thoroughly identity-worthy family of the Duke and Duchess of York entered the spotlight after Edward VIII's departure in 1936, and its elder daughter would become a second Victoria in 1952. Her consort was hardly a second Prince Albert; but this did not matter, for the 'traditions' of mass-circulation matriarchy were by now so firmly established that little short of genetic catastrophe could disturb them.

The contrast between etiquette and this less respectable Monarchy-worship is merely one more example of the marked idiom-differences we looked at before: the 'language' of Royalism has to stretch from Received Pronunciation down to the wordless prostration of the full-colour pictorial insert. Also, there is a distinction between what is voiced partially or fragmentarily at each dialect-level, and what is expressed by the language-code as a whole. The former is merely the way 'we' feel (as 'ordinary women', yuppies, teenagers, or whatever) but what the language transmits is a vital part of 'national identity' - the cohesive and apparently ancient structure that reconciles such apparent differences to create the reassurance, an element of warm solidity always sought and found beneath the tittle-tattle and the fun.

Playing the Royal Game

There isn't any power. But there can be influence. The influence is in direct proportion to the respect people have for you... Monarchy is, I do believe, the system mankind has so far evolved which comes nearest to ensuring stable government...

Prince Charles, *In His Own Words* (1981) pp. 99-102.

Intervals between readings from the womens' press could well be filled for the prison-hulk inmates by team-games: and these could easily be made another lesson in the futility of a mental life-sentence to 'class'. What more 'typically English' idea-system is there than that related historically to sport, and to 'playing the game'? Gender-distinction is present here too, since the games metaphor classically fits into a 'man's world' rather than the family and nurture. And just as with other features of the reigning *Geist*, decline has suddenly made its significance clearer. Frederic Raphael noted grimly in 1985 how in today's Europe –

> Exhibitions of *le fairplay* are the last things to be expected of the Union-Jacked...The British were once in the smug position of owning not only the ground and the ball but also the referee's whistle. They also wrote the rule-book. Now, deprived of the privilege of supplying both the officials and the winning side, they are losing their sense of humour and their sense of proportion...Unintimidated by patrician linesmen, our unsporting yobs are indifferent to the reproaches of their flagging betters and substitute brutal facts for playful metaphors. *Faire le Liverpool* may well come to mean going for the kill...[54]

If it does, then we should conclude that the games-model (and with it an important chunk of Britishness) is completely worn out. For historically what it signified was the opposite: not 'going for the kill' but observing certain rules to prevent the old killer-instincts of pre-1688 (Hobbesian) England from ever surfacing again. Just as etiquette and bourgeois decorum were translated into Royal-family mania, so middle-class acceptance of the gentlemanly game-of life was turned into popular sport. The negative 'dulling' of popular political aggressivity after Chartism's decline was a positive embrace of Régime alternatives. As Ross McKibbin has put it:

> The (partial) elimination of corruption from parliamentary elections accompanied the (partial) elimination of corruption from sport, and sport and elections remained consciously linked activities: thus the introduction into political discourses of metaphors borrowed from sport, a passion common to all classes – "fair play" (appropriated by most European languages), "below the belt", "not cricket", "Queensberry's

Rules", etc. - made a breach of the rules additionally unthinkable...[55]

Sports started with gentlemen and were made mass property. For generations a special sort of tournament match between 'Gentlemen and Players' (unimaginable in any other culture) would be a recognized feature of many British sports. Horse-racing and gambling became the British 'Sport of Kings', where populace and élite foregathered in common devotion and excitement (and common mockery of clergymen, teetotallers and other middle-class do-gooders). Ascot and Derby Day were great annual events in the calendar of the London poor, and after Edward VII's accession in 1901 'the races' assumed a permanent Royal colouration. The present ruler and her family have carried equestrian worship to novel heights of intensity and show-jumping, polo and horse-carriage driving have all benefited immeasurably from Royal practice and patronage. While in Britain the manufacture of wheeled motor vehicles has declined or been sold off to foreign companies, Ukania has resounded to the ever-growing clatter of hooves and dizzy applause for 'The Man (or better still, Lady) on Horseback'.[56]

More important within this mighty 'culture of consolation' (in Gareth Stedman Jones' phrase) was the development of popular team games. Cricket, football and the two forms of rugby contributed to what he has called the post-1870 'remaking of the working class'. The analogy between these and the remade British political system was unmistakable –

The effect was twofold: by emphasizing the play-element in politics and the rules of the game the sphere of political action was severely circumscribed; anything outside the rule was necessarily unlawful. The fact that the rules were (on the whole) strictly followed made the need to contemplate alternatives even less pressing...

We noticed earlier how in British ideology the narrow circumscription of 'politics' underlies the supposed powerless-ness of Monarchy. But this is also the definition of political life as a game, made possible by a two-party system following basically 'fair' rules. The parties stand for 'class' in the Anglo-castrate sense, according to shared customs instilled by the State folklore: an Established substratum of identity regulating what is and is not done, as well as the limits of what is said. Corporate cohesion ('team-spirit') and ceremonial fetishization of the game itself ('greater than any one individual, however great') are functional requirements of such a system.

When West Indian Marxist C.L.R.James first came to the U.K. in the 1930s, what most struck him was 'the tenacity of Victorian balance and compromise':

> Cricket served as the functioning moral locus for the English ideology since...the English middle class did not need to formulate a coherent philosophy of political power. Cricket served as a means for the renewal of English life and (with football)...a meeting place for the moral outlook of the dissenting middle classes and the aristocracy.

The ideological 'meeting-place' of such different strata and interests is - and can only be – the nation in the subjacent sense at issue here: an apparently non-'ismic' national identity on no account to be confused with vulgar nationalism. Thus, England originated so many sports during this period because the sporting-field had such national importance: it *was* the Nation, safely symbolized in miniature and linking together bourgeois moralism with the style or formal preoccupations of the gentry. 'Playing the game' came to be felt as and was constantly declared as essentially British, and even more essentially English. It was on the same super- and sub-political plane as Royalty and the Constitution: national and (when foreigners could be got to see the point) universalizable as well, yet always outside and below the other (dubious) game of 'party politics'.

However, like actual games the party-political 'game' also demanded an umpire in the background. With no written constitution, president or supreme court, the Monarch was the only possibility. The political 'game' is played for the wielding of Sovereign power – a power so supreme and untouchable that (according to Régime mythology) no Parliament can ever 'bind its successors'. The only conceivable guarantor for this Absolutism at one remove is the Crown itself: the historic and ideal source whose mystic authority has been historically vouchsafed to the Commons.

The referee of Britishness is essential to its whole game of life and politics. Such an *ideal* umpire of course intervenes rarely or never in the play: the more self-regulating and sports-manlike the conduct on field, the more purely 'ritual' his or her rôle becomes – to the point where (it is tempting to believe) an umpireless contest ought to be quite feasible. Yet that can never be so. Only a Utopian social realm could dispense with rule-book enforcement. The Crown may of course also be considered 20th century Britain's quaint 'substitute' for the rational, written, elected guaranteeing of order - but this merely reinforces the point. As that order is threatened by decline and impotence, and as 'playing the game' deteriorates (both on and off the sports-field), the Royal totem of fairness and game-spirit increases in prominence. The society that so exalted games ends – when the sports-field itself has long been taken over and disgraced by a fighting rabble – united only in ecstasy over the spiritual custodians of gamesmanship. Ever more radiantly They go on standing for 'everything decent about us' while all that *was* decent has turned into electrified fences, racial abuse and the delights of armed 'aggro'.

In his study *Football and the Decline of Britain* James Walvin notes wearily how efforts to understand the problem have regularly encountered 'that anti-intellectualism of British life which raises its head whenever social problems are publicly debated in words of more than two syllables'.[57] Most explanations focus on 'the appalling social and economic state of the nation', linking football riots to those of the inner cities, or to immigration, housing and policing. They directly connect the trouble-spots to a commanding scrutiny of contemporary English society which 'reveals a society in a process of rapid and unmistakable transformation and decline'. But he also reflects that such a direct connection is not entirely convincing:

> If the problems besetting the modern game are related to the economic decline of the country and particularly to the scourge of unemployment, why was this not the case fifty years ago when similar regions were no less afflicted by massive deprivation? Such questions are easily posed, but much less easily answered...

Without (I hope) furnishing too easy an answer, it's worth pointing out how much of what is at stake does not reflect socio-economic issues directly at all. The real stupor arises from the revelation of changes in what is sometimes called 'the moral fabric' (and usually 'of the nation', rather than merely 'of society'). The deterioration of the People's Game - in Walvin's own words – 'raised disturbing questions in the minds of people accustomed to thinking of England as a peaceable, well-ordered and unflappable nation':

> It has become part of the English people's self-perception – and the image they have carefully cultivated abroad - that they are a nation of peaceable people, slow to anger and able to conduct their social lives without the turbulent excesses of others. This is...a caricature which has served a host of social and political purposes, at home and abroad...What adds to the confused response in 1985 is the suspicion that such acts of violence will become more frequent, indeed unavoidable.

The weakening 'self-perception' singled out here is a part of that national identity structure that I have been considering from the angle of its Royal apex rather than from that of football crowds. 'Caricature' here also means 'model', or standard of propriety: modern societies live partly through caricatures of themselves, in that sense, and the familial norms of phlegmatic decency, fair play and willing restraint so prominent between (say) 1850 and 1950 were decisive elements in 'the nation'. They weren't vaguely 'moral' or racially inherited traits (and such diagnoses were only comforting endorsements of the identity-structure itself). Constructed with the help of and in close symbiosis with modern British Monarchism, they were the substance of an Anglo-British nationalism.

But if *this* is what's in decline, then surely it deserves some study in its own right – not only as the somehow automatic reflection of social and economic changes? National-popular identity, the mainframe of national politics, is of course affected by such changes; it could even be destroyed by them. But were this destruction to occur, it would be a highly mediated process within the dense and claustrophobic context of Britishism - a culture of reanimated traditionalism always distinguished in the past by its subcutaneous alertness to threats and its remarkable powers of resistance. Which means in turn, surely, that the national culture needs distinct attention in its own right. It is an autonomous dimension and to some degree self-moving – or at least, far more self-moving than the Royal Estate mentality of socio-economic empiricism concedes.

The Heart of Archaism

'In short,' said Vinson, 'what is not symbolic is emblematic?' 'Except where it is token,' agreed Channing. 'Then, it is stuffed.'

Nigel Dennis, *Cards of Identity* (1955) p.125.

Endeavouring to explain England to the readers of the radical German paper *Vorwärts!* in 1844, Frederick Engels wrote: 'In other words, only England has a *social* history'.[58] He meant, not that other places are without society or history, but that in England the 'social' had acquired a special depth and resonance. Though of course related to both economic and political categories, the social dimension remains distinct and irreducible to either: it is not *only* a manifestation of how one earns or what one owns, or (in political life) of one's relationship to the State or power-structure. As well as possessing its own consistency, 'social' conduct has some shaping or formative influence — it is not an inert residue of societal relationships determined elsewhere but in its own way makes the social order.

'The French and the Germans are gradually attaining a social history too, but they have not got one yet', Engels continued, '...whilst in England the social aspect has gradually prevailed over the political one and has made it subservient. The whole of English politics is fundamentally social in nature...' When he reached the Monarchy in his survey of social England, it was to make the following observations:

If the essence of the state, as of religion, is mankind's fear of itself, this fear reaches its highest point in constitutional, and particularly in the English, monarchy...Everyone knows the real significance of the sovereign king of England, whether male or female. The power of the Crown is reduced in practice to nil...Nevertheless – and in this, fear reaches its climax – the English Constitution cannot exist without the monarchy. Remove the Crown, the "subjective apex", and the whole artificial structure comes tumbling down. The English Constitution is an inverted pyramid; the apex is at the same time the base. And the less important the monarchic element became in reality, the more important did it become for the Englishman. Nowhere is a non-ruling personage more revered than in England. The English press surpasses the German by far in slavish servility. But this loathsome cult of the king as such, the veneration of an empty idea...stripped of all content, is the culmination of monarchy, just as the veneration of the mere *word* "God" is the culmination of religion. The word "King" is the essence of the state, just as the word "God" is the essence of religion, even though neither word has any meaning at all. The essential thing about both of them is to make sure that the essential thing, that is, man, who is behind these words, is not discussed.

The Monarchic apex of the social pyramid – he went on to point out - was closely supported by an aristocracy which had likewise traded formal powers for 'social' ascendancy. The post-1688 oligarchy had let new blood in with the 1832 reforms, but made sure it was poisoned.

If at this point a printer's error had slipped his analysis, written in the summer of 1844, into the pages of Willie Hamilton's *My Queen and I* (1975), would anyone have noticed?:

The aristocracy has risen all the higher in popular esteem the more the political influence of the House of Lords declined. It is not just that the most humiliating formalities of the feudal era have been retained, that the members of the House of Commons, when they appear in an official capacity before the Lords, have to stand cap in hand before the seated and behatted Lords....the worst of it is that all these formalities really are the expression of public opinion, which regards a Lord as a being of a superior kind and harbours a respect for pedigrees, sonorous titles, old family mementoes, etc., which is as repugnant and nauseating as the cult of the Crown.

Yet the shrewdness of Engels's insight did not lead him to a pessimistic overall judgement – quite the contrary. He believed that the dense, 'social' texture of English affairs was a sign of maturity, and indeed of imminent revolution. It seemed to him that the 'merely political's' loss of significance was an indication of how capitalism's advance had brought a realism of outlook to the oppressed. They were no longer so concerned with abstractly constitutional questions - the preoccupations of Republicanism which remained so important for the Chartists, like the issue of rights, legal equality, and getting rid of 'Old Corruption'. Instead, more substantial social and economic matters were coming to the forefront. The new industrial proletariat (which he described at the same time in *The Condition of the English Working Class*) had urgent and collective material demands: this sobriety of outlook would find expression in a class consciousness far more fatal to the Old Régime than any form of Republicanism.

The supposed total revolution towards which things were moving in Britain corresponded (he thought) to that country's new ascendancy in manufacturing. The working class produced by the latter would have to take issue with 'property as such' (rather than wasting time with a thinly political radicalism). Chartism, the great protest movement of the 1830s and '40s, was already this movement in evolution. Within a short time Karl Marx – always strongly influenced by his friend's work of the 1840s – would take over this picture and give it heavier theoretical support. Twenty-five years later, for example, his description of the aims of the newly-founded First International centred on this vision:

> England, being the metropolis of capital, the power which has hitherto ruled the world market, is for the present the most important country for the workers' revolution, and moreover the *only* country in which the material conditions for this revolution have developed up to a certain degree of maturity. Therefore to hasten the social revolution in England is the most important object of the International Working Men's Association.

As his journalism showed, Marx was as conscious as Engels of the old-fashioned oddities of the British State and politics. Only three years before the statement just quoted, a second

Reform Bill had brought mild changes to a Parliament still overwhelmingly aristocratic in composition. And that was only possible thanks to the demise of Lord Palmerston in 1865. Until that date this crusty but popular epitome of the 18th century had made farther political advance unthinkable. When extension of the franchise did come (there was to be a second dose in the 1880s) it was a creeping, nervously responsible business, anything but radical in spirit. At just this moment also (as we shall see later) a Republican revival was under way and seeking, with unfortunate results, to test popular opinion's susceptibility to more radical notions.

However, all this didn't matter to the *social* revolution. That old external forms persisted in this way was of little importance, since the material content of society was in such galvanic change. The 'power of capital', the new bourgeoisie, was really in charge. Marx's judgement was in fact very similar to Walter Bagehot's (as R.H.S.Crossman noticed in his introduction to a modern edition of *The English Constitution*): both men were convinced that middle-class mediocrities from (in Bagehot's phrase) 'the second-class carriage' were really running things, and simply using the old façades (which were therefore by definition 'archaic'). Hence, whether one supported their hegemony or wanted to destroy it, there was no longer much point in denouncing this mere theatre of authority.

The views were similar, and similarly mistaken. What the great progressives saw as ripening maturity for revolution was in point of fact political disablement - first of the middle classes, and then of the workers. Discussing Marx's views, Gareth Stedman Jones has underlined –

> The inadequacies in his attempt to construct a materialist theory of the state and his consequent inability to match up the abstract stateless citizenship of the proletariat with the actual political behaviour of working-class members of a concrete nation state...[59]

The backwardness or non-radical character of political life and aspirations signified permanent *im*maturity: the resigned absence of certain necessary conditions for *any* revolution. Both Marx and Engels knew very well that revolutions have to assume an initially political form, even if their aim is total socio-economic transformation. However, they believed that class conflict and consciousness would itself generate such a form - a politics from the bottom up, translating the proletariat's true statelessness into the natural socialist world-view of Internationalism. It was this mistaken conviction that led them to demote a 'merely bourgeois' democracy and make light of the formal egalitarianism so conspicuously absent from Victorian Britain's public affairs. Republican-minded radicalism had become *passé* – marginalized by the far greater (indeed apocalyptic) potential of working-class development.

There was no such potential. Or not, at least, either in the time-scale they imagined or in the country they wrongly believed to typify industrializing modernity. What they were actually witnessing was a growing retreat from an earlier, bloody-mindedly 'political' revolt that threatened Royal Britain into a socio-economic protest movement which the Old Régime could handle perfectly well (and indeed, derive new life from). The tide was running in the opposite direction. A mounting indifference to 'merely political' considerations did not indicate passage beyond the level of radicalism to something greater – to a real socio-economic transfiguration springing from 'class'. It signposted the contrary – long-term retreat below that level and resigned acceptance of never getting there, to the land of authentic popular sovereignty, equality and freedom (as distinct from estate-liberties).

The submergence of the political into the 'social' Engels espied was a victory and perpetuation of what was by the 1870s clearly the Old Order. The apparently tumultuous forces of early industrialism had been contained within the 'pyramid' of Crown and gentry. As Arno Mayer observes in the book quoted at the beginning of this part, the élite 'tamed the industrialization of England without succumbing to it'. Internal divisions and strata were implicitly reconciled within this commanding, if now 'backward', unity. This feat had involved changes in the commanding circles themselves: in Kitson Clark's phrase, 'they had abandoned what was indefensible in their position and retained what was material for their power', the overall result being that – 'After 1848, the position of the old leaders was stronger than it had been before'. However, this evolution was not (as sometimes believed) a feat of semi-miraculous levitation. It was the the oligarchy's own adaptation to the new national identity first forged and tested earlier in the century. Challenged again by the rise of Chartism, this *sui generis* nationalism responded with vigorous counter-assertion and acquired fresh leverage with the accession of Victoria seven years before the *Vorwärts* article, in 1837. It would be under her and the Prince Consort that 'the less important the monarchic element became in reality, the more important did it become for the Englishman' – as a totem of essential continuity, and of the unity and viability of a Ukanian *Sonderweg*, a 'special way' at once with and against modernity, a national code established and reimposed against all misleading foreign models.

But what Engels did perceive rightly was the Crown's indispensability for this formula. 'Powerlessness' was the precondition of its function as ideological keystone or totem. The apex was also the base, and the primal Word of the Régime, its Royal (and necessarily unwritten) phoneme. What this phonic reality articulates is the (necessarily informal) authority-structure of familial national identity: the 'sense of oneness' by which what Engels saw as the 'artificiality' of the Constitution was rendered natural, and given the semblance of inevitable fate. Thus, a Regal community as immemorial, as constricting and as supportive as the family was collectively 'imagined' by the community in Ben Anderson's sense: a British way or British character-inheritance seemingly as determining as an individual's genes. This is what 'flashes up at a moment of danger' (as Walter Benjamin wrote), the mobilizing myth-memory that national consciousness seizes hold of to face a new threat (and which, he added, has so little to do with 'the way it really was').[60]

Writing nearly a century after Engels, at just such a moment of danger, George Orwell's famous essay 'The Lion and the Unicorn' pointed out how this familial oneness has no discernable rapport with democracy:

England is the most class-ridden country under the sun. It is a land of snobbery and privilege, ruled largely by the old and silly. But in any calculation about it one has got to take into account its emotional unity, the tendency of nearly all its inhabitants to feel alike and act together in moments of supreme crisis...The nation is bound together by an invisible chain.[61]

Its cohesion 'resembles a family, a rather stuffy Victorian family' with the wrong members in control. Abstract democracy and equality are anathema to this as to any real family: concrete hierarchy and a moral, rarely formalized authority are of its essence. It relies at bottom upon 'a code of conduct which is understood by almost everyone, though never formulated'. This furnishes at once an overall 'organic' sense, and an image of individual station or belonging. What makes the system tolerable is that those with the power have shown themselves not *too* bad: they will themselves follow the implicit rules of family good form, if compelled to – re-arranging the accommodation and even redrawing the will when 'popular opinion really makes itself heard':

> As people to live under, and looking at them merely from a liberal, *negative* standpoint, the British ruling class had their points. They were preferable to the truly modern men, the Nazis and Fascists.

The characteristics of England, 'this everlasting animal stretching into the future and the past', are described by Orwell in terms of nature: 'The gentleness, the hypocrisy, the thoughtlessness, the reverence for law and the hatred of uniforms...along with the suet puddings and the misty skies' - inherent familial traits destined to configure any future English socialism as they have all of its past. As against these ascriptions of an almost climatic fate, it is the 'truly modern' that stands condemned.

The values of the Nazi counter-revolution of 1933-45 were in fact a violent, in the end almost an apocalyptic, rejection of modernity. They represented 'Eastern' ethnic or blood-nationalism transformed into a racial imperialism. But for England-Britain's 'invisible chain' this sort of astigmatism is normal: the curse of the modern may come from East or West, left or right, indifferently and still be condemned as 'foreign'. Edmund Burke's original formulation of it was against Jacobinism while Orwell's terser and more urgent rallying-cry was directed first at Fascism then more indiscriminately at 'totalitarianism'. 'The Lion and the Unicorn' was a meditation on 'Socialism and the

English genius'; but its keynote was defence of the latter against *any* imposition of the foreign, the abstract and the anti-communitarian - against 'power' as disembodied entity, a State governed by those querulous, anti-family intellectuals whom he hated above all others. Later this obsession would be projected as the blackly desperate fantasy of *1984* – a vision of all the national family's values (now transformed into Humanity itself) being devoured for good by deracinated sadists.

Forty years on (as Anthony Barnett's *Iron Britannia* has recorded) the old Orwellian identity was still in good working order for the Battle of the South Atlantic. Its author has described elsewhere meeting someone on a London bus as the country went to war again, who said it was all inevitable because of *'noblesse oblige'*. The family owed it to its Falkland kin of 'the island race'. They too have skies, telephone-boxes, a Crown on their stamps, decent chaps in charge, and observe the Estate-principles of muddle-through and 'Not Too Much'. Another moment of danger had flashed up the old image, and invoked the same Royal-familial reflexes - 'instincts' with (as we have seen) a great deal of historical substance to them, quietly nourished from day to day by a conservative and Regalian culture, and thrown into relief only rarely as conscious 'nationalism'.

Not itself an ordinary link in the chain, the Crown serves none the less to complete its charmed circle – the invisible bond of community bestowing a faint halo even upon suet puddings. This nationalist exaltation of the concrete requires a key: the vital formula for transcendence, for the fusion of crass and faery. It must seem to the philistine eye that everything would be exactly the same were that key to be lost. It would of course all be exactly the same – and all utterly different: a world not enchanted in that particular fashion, and unstrung by the loss of whatever cohesion and psychic community the 'illusion' made possible. In the same way – following Baron Stockmar's metaphor, also cited above - it's tempting to think a clock-mechanism could go on turning without its delicate and almost weightless balance-wheel. So it could; however, the time would not be kept for long, and in only a few days all its original sense would have disappeared.

3

THE GLAMOUR
OF BACKWARDNESS

True thoughts are those alone which do not understand themselves.

Theodor Adorno, *Minima Moralia: Reflections from Damaged Life* (1951)

3

The Glamour
of Backwardness

Bustard Identity

The dream is not about the Queen; it is about you.

Brian Masters, *Dreams about Her Majesty the Queen and
other Members of the Royal Family* (1973), p.139.

The three oldest codgers registered at U.N.O. are all (as one
might expect) Monarchies. Given to immemorialist rhetoric
about their own origins, their representatives take an apparently kindly but naturally haughty view of nation-building in
the earnestly constructive sense which has grown so widespread since 1917. Two are Himalayan Kingdoms whose after-
life can be ascribed almost wholly to geographical isolation –
Nepal and Bhutan. But the third occupies most of a European
archipelago under the title 'United Kingdom of Great Britain
and Northern Ireland', and, as we have seen, the reasons for its
survival are a lot more complex. While they and Ethiopia's
Solomonic régime stood at the outer edge of world development, Ukania was one of its prime movers for two and a half
centuries.

But there is a connection between eccentricity and source:
neither have been carried along by the mainstream itself. The
point underlined earlier is not that Great Britain antedates
most nation-states in the League of Nations and U.N.O. : it
andedates nationalism itself, in the sense of that distinctively
modern union of nationality with State which created these
organizations. It was the historical midwife both of contemporary statehood and of modern industrialism; but that very rôle

meant it could never become an example of either. Although it helped modernity to birth, its own genetic codes remain those of an anterior world. The 20th century Monarchic infatuation is Adorno's 'true thought' of this anteriority – the celebration and preservation of older structures reified in an unwritten familial constitution, of 'customs in common' concretized by living cards of identity.

This is why the forms of Anglo-British identity appear so atypical when traced out from the vantage-point of Monarchy – the apex which is also, as Engels put it, the basis of British society. Far from being visibly ancestral to most contemporary forms – even the fairly antique Constitution of the United States – they are almost indecipherably odd: I suggested above they are more like an old evolutionary side-stream which unusual conditions have favoured for an unusually long time. Stripped of that environment, however, Britain has been turning for a generation into something like the duck-billed platypus. Or perhaps more appropriately, into the flightless Great Bustard that once scampered over the English grasslands, and which Edward Thompson was to resurrect as an emblem of the injured-yet-triumphant English national idiom in his *The Poverty of Theory* (1978).

'Glamour' is the old Scottish word for magical enchantment, the spell cast upon humans by fairies, or witches. It was brought into modern English by Sir Walter Scott, who also thought up and organized the first really modern Royal spectacle, George IV's descent upon Scotland in 1822. 'Here', notes J.H.Plumb, 'George had struck the future note of the monarchy....be-kilted, be-sporraned, be-tartaned, riding up Princes Street to Holyrood House to the roaring cheers of the loyal Scots, he was showing the way the monarchy would have to go if it were to survive into an industrial and democratic society'.[1] Glamour had won a new lease of life, in both language and the State. It had become part of modernity.

As for 'backwardness', this was until around the middle of the century the condition attributed by Her Majesty's subjects to most of the rest of the world. It meant those incapable of industry and democracy, or still on the long uphill road of modernization. A summit or advance-party view, it looked back with inevitable condescension to the treacherous lower slopes of picturesque superstition and back-sliding ignorance. The British Empire had done its best but many would, alas, simply never make it. Since then things have changed. Three decades of unconcealable retreat and contraction have fostered a general awareness that the United Kingdom is itself sliding helplessly backwards at an accelerating rate. Neither its industry nor its democracy are quite what they were taken for. Had they been true exemplars of modernity, they could not possibly have succumbed to such a fate. If the Industrial *Revolution* had really been what that title implies, how could Britain have foundered into today's near-catastrophic 'de-industrialization'? Had the Westminster Constitution actually been the 'Mother' *of democracy,* how on earth could it have shrivelled into what we see today: an example of arrogantly centralist and secretive dominion buttressed by a crass and increasingly localized populism, a governmental Court reducing its Country to a nerveless subjection unknown since Charles I's head rolled in the Civil War?

The glamour of this backwardness is its legitimation through icons of continuity and reassurance: the human presence of Royalty with its concrete, familial guarantee of all being well in the longer run. British history since around 1800 is a slow and staged counter-revolution which for long retained the appearance of liberalism because so much of the political world was worse. As decline and failure have corroded this antique liberality the appearance has been shed, but in the same period the Monarchical glass of national identity has constantly brightened and extended its radiant appeal. Originally (we saw) the myth of Monarchy was employed to build up national-popular identity, in the time of George III – a safely anti-Republican nationalism which would keep the spirit of democracy at bay even when democratic forms of government had become inescapable. Now the myth is amplified and diffused in order to rally this same identity, to preserve a national self-image (and the old power-reality it serves) against the greater tensions of a polity in disintegration.

And yet – the Bustard scampers on: the Britannic 'platypus' is a relic in some ways all too much at home in today's world. 'Survival' does not denote the fossil-like persistence of a feudal entity but the constant recuperation of an early-modern one to post-modern times: an identity reanimated by some long-duration link to the altering wider environment. I will go on to try and analyze both that connection and its representation in Monarchy: the real sense of 'anachronism' in Thatcherite Britain. To do so it may help to refocus some of the categories suggested earlier around a specific Royal event. The best thing here (as Goethe remarked) 'would be so to grasp things that everything factual was already theory'.[2] But not even the most indurate of British empiricists can accomplish this, and the point is really a humbler one. Analysis of pathologically concretized or anti-abstract customs and ideology has to take off from what that order itself has consecrated as 'reality': fetishized 'experience' as the incarnation of the human.

Nationalism in Satin Breeches

...May this hour
Reach through its pageantry to the deep reservoir
Whence Britain's heart draws all that is fresh and young.
Over the tuneful land prevails One song, one prayer – God
bless the Prince of Wales.

C.Day Lewis, Poet Laureate, 1969

After contemplating the Investiture of the Prince of Wales at Caernarvon in 1969 Tory journalist Peregrine Worsthorne wrote:

How strange and rather wonderful it is that it should be the role of monarchy today not to act out fantasy but to be the one institution that seems able to be natural and normal!

'Rather wonderful': here Worsthornean languor can be observed performing the primal act of all British media before the Crown. The awe of 'wonderful' is slightly salted by 'rather': yes, for all his worldliness the disabused observer of strange facts has simply had to grovel once more. Meta-grovelling (as it might be called) is the quality worship of those at one remove from the tabloid crowd, with its simple and heartfelt 'God bless you, Ma'am!' Farther up, spurious excuses for prostration are often adduced in this way: they enable the educated to join in – as they know they must – and at the same time exorcise a nagging sense that there may just be something irrevocably suspect and misguided about the whole business.

Many features of both the staging of the Investiture and its history combined to underline Worsthorne's judgement. As I noticed earlier 1969 was also the year of Richard Cawston's famous BBC television documentary *Royal Family*: a moment when, as several historians have shown, the Royal Family was (once more) 're-launched' into mass consciousness. The Queen's Private Secretary Sir William Heseltine recently penned an obituary for Cawston in *The Listener* underlining the close connection between events in Wales and that film:

> In 1968, the decision that the Prince of Wales should be invested at Caernarvon in the following year brought to the Press Office at Buckingham Palace an unsolicited rush of requests from the media for facilities to prepare features about the young Prince...So the idea took shape of a television film designed to show something of the role for which the heir to the Throne was being educated and prepared – shown ultimately to a surprised audience of unprecedented millions as *Royal Family*... (9 Oct. 1986).

We need not dwell farther here on the unctuous details of Cawston's production. By universal consent its success marked a new rapprochement between Crown and People, and the maker has never since then been far from the nation's fireside. On this point the Monarch's own judgement prevailed over that of her nerveless advisers:

> There was in 1969 a small minority who thought the film had gone too far in destroying the mystique which should surround the Throne. But the Queen herself showed her confidence in Dick Cawston by asking him, from 1970 until 1985, to take over the production of Her Majesty's Christmas Message to the Commonwealth.'(ibid.)

Like so many apologists before him Sir William succumbs in his obituary to the delusion that there was anything genuinely novel about such a new step in the intensifying cosiness of Crown and Nation. On the contrary, since Victoria's accession in 1837 relatively few years have passed (specifically, those between Albert's death in 1861 and the end of the same decade) *without* such visible and satisfying manifestation of deepening popular loyalty. Every step has of course had its own new features: fresh developments in technology and social relationships constantly arise and have to be pulped into Ukanian identity. Thus, between the Coronation and the 1969 Investiture the decisive televisualization of Monarchy took place.

In 1953 the decision to televise the Coronation ceremony produced a boom in TV sets (still mostly manufactured in the U.K.). Julian Rathbone's Bosham family in *Nasty, Very* were characteristic:

> It is a large gathering, the largest 263 Goldsmith Drive has ever seen since it was built in the early 'thirties, and the reason for it is the presence of the large box that stands beneath a fringed standard lamp in the corner by the leaded bay window, its screen now dead. It has been made clear that it is the patriotic duty of those who have television sets to invite those of their acquaintance who have not to view the day's events at a Television Party...[3]

The Party continued with words from Winnie, in 'the familiar, measured, patrician yet idiosyncratic tones, the s's slightly lisped', dropping lapidary phrases into the inter-family row which has broken out during the film:

> It ish. Our dearesht hope. That the Queen. Shall be happy. And our resholve unshwerving. That her reign. Will be ash glorioush. Ash her devoted shubjectsh. Can help her to make it...

And finally the National Anthem, jerking all three families from sexual confusion to upright attention:

> What a din as it crescendoes into the second strophe! The men and boys are shiftless for a moment, then see how Elizabeth Bosham has straightened immaculately, head up, hands pressed flat to her box-pleated skirt. Awkwardly they adopt similar poses, then Mr Bosham leans forward, tweaks by the ear fat Anne from her chair and holds her thus upright as the last chords crash into silence.

For many years after that date patriotic duty was recalled by obligatory renditions of 'God Save the Queen' at the end of all public cinema and theatre performances: this particular custom only died away in the later 1960s, and there must now be many who happily know nothing of the old-Ukanian art of the quick exit – a balance of ultra-precise timing, obtrusive glances at one's watch and the discreet yet firm 'Excuse me's' required for pushing past bitter-end patriots. Special weaponry was also needed when the way was blocked. Around the time of my first Labour Party card I remember exiting with a comrade and compatriot from *Kind Hearts and Coronets* in a Birmingham cinema to find both stairways completely choked by would-be fugitives. These had been caught short and petrified by the Royal chords and – as often happened – turned with an exaggerated masochism to honour the scratched screen image of H.M. on horseback. Bolder than I, my companion pushed ruthlessly ahead until asked by one elderly gentleman why folk like us couldn't 'show some respect'. Scorning tales of a train to be caught, he yelled in a naturally broad Scots, 'Damned if I'll stand still for *the Electress of Hanover*' and lead a whole rabble of Jacobites into the safety of the foyer. It was with old clothes like these that closet Republicanism once confessed its misery.

In truth neither cinema nor television ever seriously menaced the mystique: quite the opposite – the elements of apparent 'modernization' have always been required in order to deepen and steady Regal penetration of the hapless body politic. And that process itself has been almost as unaltering as the British climate. By 1969 even more people had TV sets, many of them in colour, a fact solemnly allowed for in Lord Snowdon's designs for the Welsh event.

Continuities were more significant than all his highly visible novelties of staging. In this connection, it's particularly interesting to note that some of the same elements were present in 1969 as on previous such moments, like the return of Queen Victoria from her widowed seclusion in the late 1860s, or the first 20th century Investiture in July 1911. Comparison of the three moments would seem to indicate three vital ingredients for full success in such operations: (1) a 'progressive' or reputedly left-inclined government with really bad identification problems, both within its own party and in the State; (2) a political leader capable of bringing to such dilemmas a mixture of radical bombast and shrewd underlying conservatism; and (3) an able impresario who can be trusted with stageing the event on suitably Cawston-like lines.

Of Victoria's return from mourning I will say more below. As for the 1911 Investiture, one can do no better here than turn to the late Duke of Windsor's *Memoirs*. When his father became George V in 1910, Chancellor of the Exchequer Lloyd George decided it was time to revive 'a ceremony which had been allowed to lapse for centuries'. Thus, the 1911 Coronation would be followed quickly by another great display, at a time when the United Kingdom's self-image seemed to be really in trouble. This was – one must remember – the epoch of the old Liberalism's 'strange death', when aggravated foreign Imperialism and violent domestic class-struggle were threatening the State. Only the previous year George V had reluctantly acquiesced to the Parliament Bill's passage through Parliament amid mutterings of aristocratic mutiny. Farthermore, the menace had assumed the feverishly precise form of an identity-question which (though this could not be known at the time) was to pursue Ukania to within sight of its grave: Ireland. Those conflicts which would lead within a few years to rebellion and an Irish Free State, and then to the civil war of the 1960s and later, were just then approaching a climax. At the same time acute labour unrest threatened to break away from respectable trades unionism and its Parliamentary representatives in a different kind of mutiny. And as if all this weren't enough, Alfred Edwards the Bishop of St Asaph (and later Archbishop of Wales) was nagging Lloyd George for some declaration of Anglo-Welsh unity to heal the wounds left by the recent disestablishment of the Welsh Church.

Lloyd George's own credentials for tackling this symbolic issue-cluster are also interesting. He had been M.P. for Caernarvon since 1890, first of all as an 'advanced Liberal' and active supporter of the Welsh Home Rule movement *Cymru Fydd*. But by 1911 all trace of radical nationalism had subsided into the manipulative skill of a member of the élite. In his case – as in Ramsay MacDonald's later on – the distance of a half-foreign periphery simply furnished a more acute, Faustian awareness of certain realities fogged over by metropolitan complacency. In a State with no democratic-popular identity, democratic-popular individuals end by learning to trade their souls for power and making a ruthless best of the bargain. This is why semi-outsiders can so easily turn into the ablest and most odious servants of any Establishment. The Duke of Windsor goes on:

> David Lloyd George, who only a few years before had shocked my family with his famous Limehouse speech attacking inherited privilege, decided that (the Investiture's) revival would appeal to the national pride of his people. With an eye to what would please his constituents, "L.G." proposed that the ceremony be transformed into a spectacular Welsh pageant. My father agreed. Mr Lloyd George became my coach in the Welsh language, and I still have, written in his own hand, some of the Welsh sentences he taught me to speak at the Investiture. One was "Mor o gan yw Cymru i gyd" meaning, "All Wales is a sea of song". Mr Lloyd George made me repeat it over and over again, saying with a twinkle, "All Welshmen will love you for that". Out of those meetings...grew a friendship that lasted until his death.

After this the Prince suffered the attentions of a tailor commissioned to make 'a fantastic costume designed for the occasion, consisting of white satin breeches and a mantle and surcoat of purple velvet edged with ermine'. It was too much:

> I decided things had gone too far. I had already submitted to the Garter dress and robe, for which there existed a condoning historical precedent; but what would my Navy friends say if they saw me in this preposterous rig? There was a family blow-up that night...

But there was to be no escape from the white satin breeches. As usual in the modern British Monarchy, the decisive vector of ideological affirmation was Mother. Queen Mary 'smoothed things over' by reassuring him that his pals would understand how 'as a Prince you are obliged to do certain things that may seem a little silly. It will only be for this once'.

A So-called English Prince

It was an eerie vision! The Land of the Lion!
Each clear creature, crystal-bright,
Honey-lit with lion-light,
All dreaming together the Dream of the Lion.
...But now the globe's light hardens. The dreams go.
And what is so is so.
The awakened lands look bare.
A Queen's life is hard. Yet a Queen reigns
Over the dream of her people, or nowhere.

Ted Hughes, Poet Laureate, poem for the Queen Mother's 85th
birthday, August 1985.

So the ceremony went ahead on the lines prescribed by Lord
Esher, an adroit impresario and all-purpose *éminence grise* of
that period. On a hot July afternoon the future Edward VIII
heard Winston Churchill as Home Secretary read out his titles
('he told me afterwards that he rehearsed them on the golf
course'), while George V accomplished the main symbolic act:

> Upon my head he put the coronet cap as a token of principality,
> and into my hand the gold verge of government, and on my
> middle finger the gold ring of responsibility. Then, leading me
> by the hand through an archway to one of the towers of the
> battlements, he presented me to the people of Wales. Half-
> fainting with heat and nervousness, I delivered the Welsh
> sentences that Mr Lloyd George, standing close by in the
> ancient garb of Constable, had taught me...[4]

The ideological success of all this was incontestable: Wales
received its gift with delight, Monarchy and Nation benefited
from a 'new start' at a troubled time when deeper unity would
be badly needed. The Duke records how, although it was never
put into so many words, he received the clear impression that
the event's success 'would help Papa in his dealings with the
difficult Mr Lloyd George' – and, more important, George in
his dealings with the Nation.

By the time of the next Investiture in 1969 Lloyd George had
become Harold Wilson, Lord Esher's role was taken by Lord

Snowdon, and Prince Charles (perhaps because Mother was now Queen in her own right) put up far less resistance to a reinvented pantomine drag. Wales, Scotland and Ireland were again challenging the Imperial identity; parts of the working class were once more in mutinous mood; the Labour Party's mid-1960s plans for technocratic modernization were a receding yet still shameful memory, and Wilson's administration was trying to cement them over by behaving like the natural party of government; General de Gaulle had refused Britain entry into the Common Market. It was time for a dose of symbolism.

By a fortunate coincidence some changes were going on at the Palace too. There, a reign of another sort had just ended: that of Sir Richard Colville, who had been Buckingham Palace Press Secretary since 1947. For over twenty years this clam-like figure had defended the Royal dignity by allowing as little as possible to be said about it. 'It was' (sighs Royal biographer Kenneth Rose) 'particularly unfortunate that Colville's costive reserve coincided with a widespread quickening of interest in the Monarchy' –

> He seemed to make no distinction between journalists in search of scandal or sensation and those – the majority – who needed little encouragement to stimulate and strengthen loyalty to the Crown. All were made to feel that their questions were impertinent if not downright vulgar...[5]

But Colville's retiral in 1968 had let in a new public-relations regime, personified by his Australian successor William Heseltine (now Knighted as H.M.'s Private Secretary, and quoted above). Suddenly the whole family, and especially the Prince of Wales, were projected at public attention in the new Cawston way. There occurred what John Pearson in his study *The Ultimate Family* has called 'a hallucinatory few weeks...(when) suddenly it seemed as if real human beings were emerging from behind those familiar public royal masks'. Only a week after the showing of *Royal Family* Prince Charles's human-being side now stood revealed in public interviews and conversations: an apparently diffident, jokey individual who could discuss the approaching Investiture with the BBC's Jack di Manio in these terms:

As long as I don't get covered too much in egg and tomato, I'll be all right. I don't blame people demonstrating like that. They've never seen me before. They don't know what I'm like. I've hardly been to Wales, and you can't expect people to be overzealous about the fact of having a so-called English Prince come amongst them...

Thus, a recognizably ordinary chap was disclosed, ready for the astonishing tinsel and glad rags of Caernarvon. The 'purely human' – with a wart or two – was ready for transubstantiation into the supernal. Pearson continues his mordant description of the Investiture in these terms:

The public myth of monarchy now relied upon its cyclical renewal through grand and elaborately staged ceremonies of state in which the family assumed their charismatic roles before their subjects via the television cameras...[6]

For the charismatic dimension, Snowdon had created a superb television spectacular using Caernarvon Castle – the old symbol of English colonial power over the Welsh – as a stage-set equipped with 'plywood knock-down chairs...slate thrones and a space-age laminated perspex canopy, surmounted with gilded Prince of Wales feathers, built by the ICI Plastics Division and wind-tunnel tested against gusts of sixty miles an hour'.

The 1960s had been in some ways an unsettling era, even in the U.K. Himself a part of that vexing novelty – a trendy outsider who had married the Family's troublesome Bad Sister – Snowdon was from the outset determined that tradition should be overwhelmed by invention. Anthony Holden has described his attitude in *Charles, Prince of Wales* (1979):

The new materials developed in the '60s, the chic new aesthetic brought into middle-class homes by Sunday Colour Supplements, the role Snowdon had won himself as a champion of industrial and commercial design (he had recently provided London Zoo with its controversial aviary) – all were going to play a part...[7]

He was keen above all not to imitate the 1911 ceremony. That had taken place mostly in a striped yellow 'crusader's tent', visible only to a few. The age of mass media by contrast demanded 'the largest perspex object in the world': it was intended to suspend the thing from balloons at first, until it dawned upon the Ministry of Works that a single shot from a Welsh Nationalist marksman might cause sensational havoc.

Such Welsh extremists had been active for some time, and Queen Elizabeth had long fretted over her 1958 vow to 'present' the Prince. Would the new era of violent protest claim its noblest victim at Carnaervon? Yet that era and all the fuss in Wales were of course unassailable arguments *for* going ahead. Government circles appear to have suffered extreme agitation on the question, which was finally resolved by Wilson's new Secretary of State for Wales, George Thomas. Lord Tony-pandy (as he now is) called a meeting of all the parties involved six months before the events and swayed the doubters with his passionate, almost ecstatic Loyalism: 'There should be', he preached, 'no part of the United Kingdom where the Royal Family cannot go'. The necessary omnipresence of the Regal *Geist* would be discredited by retreat before the threat. That settled it: the show was on.

Six members of the Free Wales Army received prison sentences the day before the ceremony at Caernarvon castle. But explosions still punctuated the event: two men were killed when gelignite went off accidentally in the early morning, and a small bomb was detonated near Caernarvon railway station. 'Security precautions became almost frantic', noted the *Guardian*'s local reporter, in a town where there were already 'two uniformed policemen every ten yards' and three at each street corner. Worse still, policemen outnumbered spectators on the processional route', observed Michael Parkin, where 'what were laughably called "crowd control barriers" held at bay only small scattered groups'. Even at the Castle the crowds could only be described as 'Third Division football size', and houses which tried to rent windows with a view of the procession found them untaken.

Though noted and honestly recorded at the time, such facts somehow disappeared the day after – devoured by what was unanimously agreed to have been the blazing success of the event. 'Investiture fever' (as it was called) dutifully peaked in spite of the bangs and missing spectators. Only a few drops of rain fell.

Snowdon had run a special Committee to supervise the production of aesthetic souvenirs fitting in with his castle designs; but by the day itself his tasteful doilies and modernized pie-funnels had been swept aside by the gaudier, less pretentious trash which crowds bent on Royal fun appear to favour.

In fact, the results were even better than those of 1911. 'The Labour government was delighted with the Royal Family', concludes Pearson. It is hardly correct to claim that 'Welsh separatism was...killed stone dead' by the show – a few years later Plaid Cymru was again in the ascendant – but it was certainly affected. Wild tales circulated of ardent nationalists so inebriated by Investiture fever that on the day itself they were heard threatening to brain anyone who touched their Prince. More soberly, the climate did appear to increase the influence of Plaid moderates quite willing to see Wales independent 'under the Crown'. Charles's speeches in Welsh had a similar effect. Whereas his great-uncle had managed only to stammer a few inaudible words, he spoke at least three hundred to the Welsh League of Youth in Aberystwyth before the ceremony. Some of his public remarks about Wales conveyed such sympathy, indeed, that for a time Secretary Thomas was a little suspicious: could there be a mild strain of actual nationalism creeping into the young man's remarks? At the ceremony itself Charles's reply to the Loyal Address from the People of Wales also came first in Welsh – 'which was very much more than respectable' (noted Nesta Roberts on the *Guardian* front page)...The double-l, reputedly impossible to English tongue, was perfectly negotiated, the vowels were broad and clear, the guttural "ch" genuinely Welsh'.

All Manner of Folk

Adaptation requires a hold of the past, of traditional life. The past lives in the tradition of the national community; if it is destroyed no adaptation is possible. Therefore, although they are a radical party which seeks fundamental changes in Wales, nationalists have been conscious of the necessity for roots and continuity in human society and of the importance of identity and community in human life...

Gwynfor Evans, *Wales can Win* (1973).

When viewed in this perspective the Investiture antics make plain something of great significance (and all too little grasped by Welsh, Scottish and Irish nationalists). Through the agency of even such synthetic symbolism as this, endorsement of a deeply conservative British nationalism was obtained *which appeared to have nothing to do* with nationality in that regrettable or demonological sense I discussed above. Thus, Regal Britishry appeared quite unrelated to the Mr Hyde who has stalked through so much of 20th century history – the ogre of 'narrow' ethnic resentment and vexatious or bellicose chauvinism. The glory celebrated at Caernarvon was at once grander, vaguer, *and* more purely human than this: the refulgent symbolism of a State somehow both far above and safely below such things. The arrival of still another Prince of Wales at Caernarvon was the affirmation of England's continuing domination over the Welsh (and Welsh nationalists weren't wrong to insist on this). And yet, that affirmation took the form of a non-ethnic parade from which 'England' was entirely and mysteriously absent, while Welshness was patted on the head by the mystic materialization of *its own* essence. Via the Regal catalyst, the Sea of Song swelled as one to duly gratify itself (and silent or recalcitrant elements found themselves drowned in the tide). He was after all only a 'so-called English Prince': that is, someone at once less (shy young lad, etc.) and vastly more (Civilization, 'decency', George Thomas, etc.) than any such restrictive and merely national category could possibly convey.

Referring to the above account of Welsh cultural nationalism in his study *Devolution* (1979), Vernon Bogdanor points out the significantly close connection of Evans's ideas to 'the mainstream of British conservative thought as represented by, for example, Burke, Scott, and Disraeli'.[8] This list of masterfakers underlines the strange dilemma of peripheral nationalism in the British Isles. It has tended consistently to arrogate community and the mythology of rootedness to itself, counterposing such natural identity to the shallow artifice of Britannic Statehood. But this stereotype bears astonishingly little relationship to the real structures of identity operating in Ukania's force-field. It reflects standard theories of neo-nationalism and internal colonialism evolved in Europe and

North America, rather than the singular reality of Anglo-British identity. Yet the Investiture was a demonstration of the latter's continuing command of the Welsh – a control exerted precisely through a synthetic panoply of 'community', Regal 13th century 'roots', spurious yet psychically effective 'continuity' and portentous 'adaptation' to an (ideologized) 'human life'.

Contesting this formidable apparatus in what are apparently its own terms, a would-be nationalist ideology is (as events have regularly shown in both Wales and Scotland) on very uncertain and limited ground. The main pitch is already occupied. Its stall-holders are seasoned vendors of these ideological wares skilled in the adaptation of their goods to newer tastes and times – so confident, indeed, that they no longer see any reason to stamp out competitors by techniques of intimidation and cultural tyranny. As long as nationalists stick to coconut-shies rather than bombs, a mild, limiting contempt is far more effective. It would be different, of course, were such ethnic upstarts bent on Republican dissidence – not in an Irish-Catholic but in a modernizing sense. Yet the chances of that are small too: for the dominant ideal hegemony focused around the Crown long ago appropriated a distinctive mode of 'modernization' as its own property and this too is rehearsed on State Occasions. As long as peripheral intellectuals remain glamour-struck by it (most often via the sub-ideology of Labourism) and instinctively feel Progress as immutably located 'up there' (rather than being consistently crippled up there) there's unlikely to be much trouble.

Since the Welsh too are grateful for their right to Royalty, Royalty cannot (therefore) be purely or narrowly English. And if the Monarchy inhabits this super-ethnic (or super-national) realm, so surely does the State structure of which it is Crown and essence? Hence, Royalty is at once manifestation and guarantee of the truth by which Lord Tonypandy has lived: 'Britain' isn't just England in white satin breeches, but a supernal realm to which Welsh, Scots, and Irish (and once upon a time Hindus and Xhosas as well) may in good conscience belong. Farthermore the 'human', in the sense of the *ordinary* – Charles' touching self-doubt, his mother's sense of humour, his father's bad temper, and so on – had now been more directly transfused into the magic sphere by public relations. Thus, the a-nationalist patriotism of Monarchy passes directly from individuals ('just like us') straight on to a God-like plane where all narrow group affiliations seem equally irrelevant. In this act of transcendence the entire vulgar and somehow foreign world of mere '-ismic' nationality is somehow annulled. H.M.'s Customs Inspector gives one glance at this dark, fanatical-looking, visa-less alien and turns him back instantly: in the transcendental or Royal-family sense, he could just never 'belong' (and may well be a foe of civilization as such).

There has never been much hope of H.M.'s academic institutions or literary cheer-leaders getting to grips with all this. As one might expect, it is only from non-empiricist, semi-deviant or half-foreign angles that any light has been cast. In a brilliant essay on 'Royalty and Representation' in her *Consuming Passions*, for instance, feminist semiotician Judith Williamson has neatly pointed out the structural difference between Royals and mere Presidents. The former can genuinely be said to 'represent' ordinary folk, only this mode of representation works quite differently. Presidents and M.P.s are 'indexical signs' – locatable and measurable by at least some modern or 'abstract' criteria:

> However, the royal family are neither elected nor replaceable, nor could "we" ever be "them": they represent us by sheer *analogy*, as an *iconic* sign...This way in which the royal family *parallels* our own, but at a distance, is the heart of its representative function. The Queen is a much loved popular figure who, far from being identified with the upper classes...is strongly identified in people's minds with the ordinary population, the average kind of person.[9]

It's also true that this mode of populism depends upon the institution's 'archaism'. As Williamson goes on to underline, it is not a product of modern capitalist social relations, in the sense taken for granted by Marxism and industrial sociology. But *that* is exactly why it has so constantly to be 'modernized' and brought ever closer to the masses by perspex technology, gasping revelations of 'what They're really like' and successive alignments with garden-gnome taste.

The Investiture period produced some striking examples of such iconic-sign refurbishment. On a preparatory visit Snowdon introduced the Prince to his father's boatman, a Mr Evan Lloyd. Holden notes at this point, heart perceptibly in mouth: 'The boatman then simply took the Prince home to meet his wife Nellie. Number 3 Balaclava Road, Caernarvon, thus became the first Welsh household in which the Prince of Wales ever set foot...' A quite ordinary fellow *simply took the Prince home with him*: this is the content of the majority of dreams about H.M. the Queen and her family which Brian Masters has analyzed. It is essential to note also how Wales and ordinariness emerged haloed from this incident, as well as Royalty: reality had been ennobled, while the transcendent had demonstrated its humanity. And to think there were swine about willing to blow all this to pieces!

The fake-mediaeval oath invented for 1911 and repeated by Charles ended by telling his mother he would live and die for her 'against all manner of folk' – the Welsh, Ulstermen, kelpers, coal-miners, immigrants, even Englishfolk, none would be held exempt from either the magic or the wrath of the Crown. Being not quite of this world either in time or mere geography, Monarchy can easily assume a metaphysical equality with each and any folksy bit of it – a charmed and unchallengeable humanity indifferent to exasperating modern quarrels about rights and impersonal powers.

By a similar act of prestidigitation Regal pageantry of course annuls the reality of social class. I mentioned the *Guardian*'s editorial reaction to Caernarvon earlier. Indignant progressives well to the Left of the *Guardian* also fulminate on this point, without seeing quite how the gross deceit is perpetrated. The resultant psychic bloc leads straight into the cul-de-sac of an imaginary mass stupidity or a fiendish media conspiracy. What's wrong here is the direct contraposition of the Monarchic show with 'society' in its curiously Ukanian sense of a socio-economic basis shorn of both nationality and politics (save in the crypto-Regal sense permitted by Westminster): in other and more familiar words, Society as defined principally via the equally odd Ukanianism of 'class' (a category of virtually 100% insular peculiarity having little to do with modern social science). Having forsworn the available means for comprehending either the human truth or the charismatic swindle simultaneously purveyed by Monarchic glamour, this mentality ends merely by intensifying the puzzle of just how such a sensible and notoriously mature populace can so infallibly lose its marbles over fake-feudal buffoonery. And the blankness in turn confirms the whole complex of feelings about the Crown: for the latter (after all) are *experience* – the category so notably foregrounded by the Régime's literary criticism – while intellect has shown itself once more as cankered and futile. The hosts of the bluffly sensible are vindicated once more; while both totem-pole and meaning have been preserved more effectively than they could have been by the most ostentatious metaphysic of Royalty or the State.

The reason why such a stalemate is inescapable is that it leaves out everything essential: all the factors of national identity which constitute the dimension where Monarchy actually functions. The Crown overrides class so easily by its prior appropriation of the Nation; and part of that ease lies in the disguised or surrogate form which Monarchy alone can give to such nationalism. This can be put in another way: Monarchy converts social class into Régime 'class', the British synthetic-folk edition of a universal fact. One thing the Investiture vividly conveys is how this powerful and popular version of national identity is structurally poised against just those 'narrow' ethnic or democratic-populist concepts which elsewhere have found direct expression in the century's typical national ideologies. It is that articulation which enables Royalism to bury the political and ideological dimension of class-struggle virtually without a contest. The Crown stands for a national community-family known and felt to be primary (without a trace of stupidity or 'illusion' on anyone's part); and it does so in a way that simply occludes stratification, by joining the numinous or super-national to the 'ordinary' or sub-national – supra-ethnic spirituality to the instant, polaroid humanity of 'They're just like us!'. However 'odd' this may appear as a variety of national identity – ethereal, archaic, stilted, familial, and so on – it none the less traps and canalizes sufficient of the emotions and impulses associated with nationality in the contemporary world to work. And once these deeper impulses have been surrendered there's only one way out or forward: grovelling (I include in this broad category everything from Tonypandian prostration to those wry, twinkle-eyed, near-imperceptible inclinations of the head characteristic of Neil Kinnock's current 'modernization' of the Labour Party).

The point of the contrived drama of the Investiture lay precisely in the normality of the absurd. That is, it was a guaranteed and popular way of bolstering up the normality of Britishness – of making the increasingly precarious and threatened appear more natural than ever. While power ebbed and one government after another juggled dismally with economic modernization, *this* was ever more splendidly itself. An identity victorious against such odds deserves ever more stylized and emphatic rehearsal in the national theatre of the mind; this is the 'acting out' for which Monarchy provides such superb costumes, actors and props – a familiar pantomine whose 'fantasy' draws the audience together into a single instinctive body, the *union sacrée* always there and (in spite of bloodless intellectual cynics) ever poised to dissolve the future into a mantic past. The amazing 'this' wasn't merely the uniforms, the hushed awe and the gladsome outpourings of so many commentators and watchers: it was the renovated sense of 'who we are' – a nation and a popular identity thus served, symbolized and rewarded. The collectivizing 'fantasy' wasn't (as philistines claim) just a day of light relief or innocent solace from reality. We have already seen how all modern nation-states exist partly but importantly through such collective symbolic representations – a common imagination of who they are and what they mean. That's the sense in which 'fantasy' has become constitutive of political reality. And this happens to be ours. That is, the natural and normal-seeming visage of who we (really) are in terms of our state's prevalent nationality-code: the soul of the Anglo-British State's nationalism.

Like the Scottish Royal Visit described before, the Investiture reminds us that Britons live not in a 'nation-state' but a multi-national grouping of four main tribes and some weird hangers-on like the Falklands and the Isle of Man. But this constitutive fact hasn't meant we Brits cannot have national identity: it has simply meant we require a made-to-measure one which appears simply marvellous or hopelessly deformed depending on the vantage-point. Require, that is, a non-national (even in some degree an anti-national) version of nationalism.

Some other non-ethnic States experience analogous problems – the United States, for example, and the Soviet Union. But there is an all-important distinction here: those newer entities have come into the modern world with paper credentials identifying them as (respectively) products of bourgeois Enlightenment and proletarian Revolution. Windsorite intellectuals love nothing so much as gleeful analyses of the elements of forgery and wish-fulfilment present in both cases – their *Schadenfreude* implying that, for all its lack of modern diplomas, Britain's old Unwritten Constitution must be at least as good as such bragging upstarts. However, to remain stubbornly Unwritten is to remain customary; and habitual observance benefits above all from reminders or tokens of an equivalently old-fashioned kind – concrete talismans, icons capable of magically refocusing the ever-flagging devotional spirit of the tribes without laborious abstract thought or obtrusive philosophy. As Edward Thompson has so often reminded his fellow-subjects, to the 'empirical idiom' all such things are a damned nuisance – abrasive reminders of how, since 1789, foreign importers have been ruining politics with their impossibly abstract demands.

The deeper this vessel's troubles, the greater the need for reinforced national identity: hence each phase of crisis or decline has been accompanied by more exaggerated Royalism, and by the intensification of both glamour and taboo in pantomines like the Investiture. At the same time as 'Welsh hearts were won', the mining of Royalty's underlying seriousness was casting an aura of stolid traditionalism over Wilson's failures: pathos and the beginning of British Socialism's collapse were given the demeanour of paternal authority. As Eric Hobsbawm remarked in *New Society* (not without some satisfaction even then) Labour had begun to look like a 'natural party of government' rather than a movement shaking old truths and risking the unknown for great purposes. Divested of Empire and barred from Europe, Britain could still rejoice – indeed rejoice ever more fervently – in its own soul, in the brilliantly refurbished emblems of a phoenix-like civilization and the ample customs so reassuring to gentlemen toiling in the craft-workshops of old truth.

Royal Family and the Investiture did not in fact keep Wilson in power the following year, any more than they stopped the rot in the Ukanian periphery or allayed the 'economic problem'. But this is because their function was on a different and deeper level. They were national-identity operations designed to consolidate the foundations of the State. While the government responsible for stageing such events derives some instant kudos from them, it is actually the basis of all national government which is at stake. Labourism, for example, though voted out in 1970, was now quite definitely and permanently a 'safer' and more trustworthy party – a party which both Court and country could count on to 'bind up the wounds' after Mr Heath's rash and premature experiment with right-wing radicalism in the early 1970s. Indeed the way was prepared for the whole cycle to be repeated over again, from the 1970s into the '80s. If it is now unlikely to go on being repeated into the Third Millenium, this will be the result of modernizing radicalism from the Right rather than from the left. The wounds have become undressable – not because a reckless Left or rebellious nationalists smashed the old world but because, in the end, that old world become too much itself and then – able no longer to sustain its old vectors of hegemonic identity – ceased to be itself.

The Nerves of Fetishism

Like the soul in the body it acts as all substance, yet it is itself immaterial; it gives motion, yet it cannot be said to exist; it creates forms, yet has itself no form; it is neither quantity nor quality, it has not whereness, or whenness, site or habitat. If I should say it is the essential shadow of something that is not, should I not puzzle the thing rather than explain it, and leave you and myself more in the dark than we were before?

Daniel Defoe, *Essay upon the Public Credit* (1710).

However insignificant 'in itself' (when peered at through the taboo-specs of Loyal Empiricism) I have tried to show how Monarchy grows in importance when seen out of itself – that is, in terms of its meaning, its role as the conscious focal point of a much broader ideological structure. But such interpretation leads to what many will diagnose as foreign blather about both ideas and interconnectedness. And not far behind this arrives the dread accusation of loony idealism. How can anyone but a Hegelian (and probably Tory) crank *seriously* assert the importance, let alone the centrality, of Monarchy in British society today? Doesn't that amount to making ideas, symbols and conscious sentiments like nationalism into a kind of primary or causative force – rather than old friends like the difficulties of the economy, the costs of military (especially nuclear) defence, or the class/'class' struggle? In the end, doesn't it entail believing spirit to be more important than mere matter? Some may be willing enough to concede that the Windsor Monarchy is (in some suitably loose sense) contemporary Britain's 'religion'; but it's something else, surely, to erect that religious *Geist* into a positive and even a controlling force?

This view of the argument is based upon a misunderstanding, which it is probably time to clarify. To take Monarchy with the seriousness which in my view it deserves does certainly mean stressing consciousness, in a sense stretching from 'Isn't she *wonderful!*' to the more episodic and nebulous plane of collective self-awareness and nationhood. My thesis here is that Monarchy has helped, in significant and significantly unacknowledged ways, to constitute one kind of English-British nation – and to suppress other and better historical candidates to the title. Making the argument demands emphasis upon factors like identity and the forms of collective consciousness fostered by nationalism. However, such emphasis upon consciousness and the pervasive emotionality of Ukanian self-regard is only a matter of method: it has nothing to do with fundamental diagnosis. In a culture so hobbled by taboo and a self-neutering empiricism, no attack on the central nervous system can avoid a degree of exaggeration, or even caricature. And when its object also happens to be that system's most visible public-relations image, it becomes difficult at times *not* to suggest or imply that the Crown's 'meaning' is what people consciously think, feel and imagine about it. Both the personality of the Monarchs ('What they're really like', etc.) and how they appear to their subjects have grown over-significant, for deeply-rooted reasons. Before she knows what's happening, any scholar of these phenomena can find herself as 'obsessed' by them as the most befuddled onlooker at a Royal parade.

But one should not confuse the pitfalls of method or the shortcomings of unavoidable polemic with underlying theory. The 'deeply-rooted reasons' behind Monarchic infatuation have nothing directly to do with either the palpitations of Lord Tonypandy or the groans of Willie Hamilton, the flag-waving crowds or the drunken vibrato of Royal hacks. They condition all these things, but are themselves perfectly material. The machinery and operations of what I have often called the '*Geist*' of Royal identity are more interesting and important than generally believed – essential (or so I believe) for grasping the overall cast of British society and State. However, they function as they do in the service of a structure quite independent of them: that is, the long-term structure of the British political economy. 'Capitalism' is the end-explanation of Britain's strange nationalism and over-developed Regal traditionalism; but here the term denotes no standard late-20th century economic system, any more than 'Ukania' describes an ordinary national state-form. For the Crown-mystique is the spiritual breath of a specifically anachronistic and parasitical form of capitalist evolution: a form which though rooted in early-modern times was able to endure through the entire era of primary industrialization and has persisted, finally, into the post-modern universe.

That form's capacity for survival is the underlying cause of Dynastic reanimation and the obtrusively self-conscious arch-aism of contemporary Britain. Important as these neo-Habsburgian ramparts are for politics and in securing the legitimacy of a State which ('in itself') ought to have disappeared – at the very latest – in 1918, the reverse isn't true. This asymmetry is crucial. No number of ideal Monarchs or brilliant Royal impresarios would by themselves have been able to guarantee the Throne's longevity or construct a

bondman's Socialism with such success. Had that been possible, then true or Absolute Monarchy would probably still be
with us, for all the pre-1914 *anciens régimes* made enormous
efforts in that direction – efforts which in their own day
appeared successful enough. But their ideological schemes and
invented traditions foundered for the reasons analyzed in
Gellner's account of nationalism: as we saw, socio-economic
development inevitably incubated nationality as a newly
decisive factor in politics. This led in turn to a situation wildly
different from all liberal and enlightened predictions (and
notably from those of Marx and Engels) where, in Arno J.
Mayer's words:

> By the late 19th century the organized struggle for survival
> between nations overshadowed the orderless conflicts within
> society. This transposition of permanent strife from the
> national to the international sphere coincided with a sea-change
> in the world-view of the ruling and governing classes: from
> confident and flexible traditionalism to pessimistic and rigid
> conservatism, not to say reaction...[10]

Such hardening reaction then plunged Europe and the world
into over thirty years of warfare and counter-revolution. From
around 1850 progressives and socialists had promoted a
hopeful dogma whose main tenet was that Absolute Monarchy
and aristocracy were (or would very soon be) mere façades –
the veils or the instruments of a capitalist bourgeoisie already
in control of events. Hence (the logic continues) capitalism was
solely responsible for the post-1914 catastrophe – a system not
merely mature but 'over-ripe' for revolution and replacement.
This tenacious set of fables is still remarkably popular on
today's Left, and I will return to it later.

One victorious social formation *did* restore and carry on its
'confident and flexible traditionalism', not only after 1918 but
into the 1980s. But as post-1950 development has so cruelly
demonstrated, this could not conceivably have been because of
its generally or inextinguishably progressive character. Every
single serious analysis of Great Britain's age of decline has
concurred in locating the origin of its present maladies far back
in time: pre-World War II, pre-World War I, or even in the
primitive traits of the so-called 'Industrial Revolution'. Without discounting these, another kind of explanation is also

suggested from the Monarchical viewpoint: through the sight-lines of 'Imperialism' a homology is discernible between the Royal sublimation of nationality and the profoundly extra-territorial cast of Southern England's heartland economy.

At Caernarvon the Welsh (and especially their nationalists) were being urged to look upwards and outwards: towards Grandeur, and away from pettifogging or parochial issues. The Crown is a spiritual vector translating souls out of narrowness and into outward-looking light. Indeed, 'outward-looking' has always been a key term of Queen's English: the fact that it is often pronounced with greater feeling and intentness on the Left than on the Right shows its hegemonic value. As ideology, it could only work in Wales because it was still sustained in England and the rest of Ukania. Fringe folk can only be invited into Grandeur as long as the metropolitans – or at least their élite and a decent number of the rest – take it seriously. In 1969 this meant primarily the Commonwealth, whereas in 1911 it had of course signified a vast territorial Empire and the largest navy in the world. By the time Prince William is due for the treatment around the year 2011, it may mean very little indeed.

Yet however much or little Britain's imperium amounts to by then the chances are that Ukanians will still be addicted to Grandeur and proud that the 'Great' is back in their title-deeds, while the Scots, Welsh, Asians and Tynesiders will still be urged to turn away from a narrowly selfish (inward-looking) contemplation of their own misery. This is because what 'outward-looking' (and the Crown) basically manifest has little to do with either territorial dominion or effective military power over the wider world. What it does echo and legitimate may be more accurately defined as historical extra-territoriality. Although this extra-territorial structure was built up by colonialism and consolidated in the extensive direct rule of the later 19th and earlier 20th centuries, it was never identified with them. Again, it is the epoch of decline which has made this much clearer: after Empire had crumbled and turned into its Commonwealth ghost the extra-territorial dimension, far from dwindling, was to grow steadily more important. During the Thatcher years since 1979 both the 'internationaliz-ation' of Britain's economy and the vulgar ostentation of its totemic identity-structure have concordantly reached new peaks of intensity.

This enduring congruence between the symbolism of the British Crown and the enduring economic conditions of British society is the real 'secret' of what will be the Third Millenium's single specimen of late-capitalism encased in an early-modern Monarchic Constitution. That secret derives from the very origins we looked at earlier: from an early or pre-bourgeois revolution which installed Capital and Property in power long before an urban middle class had evolved suffi-ciently to become a national standard-bearer of modernity. Since capitalism 'triumphed' in that sense too soon, it found itself decisively locked into the early-modern forms of com-mercial and financial dominance: a chronic pre-modernity from which there was to be no developmental escape either backwards (with Jacobitism) or forwards (with Republicanism and industrialism). A mercantile city-state economy had turned into a super-Venice and even succeeded for a time in heading the mainstream of global development.

Yet such global reach did not alter the original essence – on the contrary, it systematically confirmed and buttressed it. As in Venice (but now on a far larger and multi-national stage) the aristocratic stamp of the early-modern was nourished and eternalized by colonialism. Though by now an oligarchy – joining landownership to the Southern *grande bourgeoisie* of the City – this élite had both the temporal and the geographical luck to constitute its fortune and its mode of hegemony before the fuller flood of modern economic development brought the rivalries of modern imperialism. Its off-shore and commercial nature remained far more important than either its primitive industrialization or its late-Victorian parade of overseas possessions. A patrician State which had led the way into modernity, it would never become an authentic or inward part of the world which industry and democracy broughtwith them. Its ruling caste adapted to thatworld, naturally, with an energy and confidence derived from their early start and from the great external resources which let them buy off one social threat after another. But 'adapt' here has an eccentric signifi-cance, some of whose cadences I tried to interpret before:

vociferous and mimetic 'modernization' devoted (with unfailing support from a romantic and anti-technological culture) to the domestication of modernity.

In this perspective what the Crown-Constitution stands for is simply the secular or long-term ascendancy of *one sort* of capitalism: while certain features of that *longue durée* may appear as triumphs of spirit or what Martin Wiener has called the 'anti-industrial culture' over crass materialism, the longer trajectory means exactly the contrary.[11] There, all it stands for is the complex reproduction of an earlier mode of crass materialism lodged in unshakeable command of both State and British civil society before either the steam-engine or democracy were invented. The 'fit' between Monarchic myth and its social order is thus located in the homology of an aristocratic symbol with a still patrician economy: 'the City', as Queen's English usually labels it in a kind of unconscious homage to just these pre-nationalist and pre-industrial origins.

Seeking for an epitome of Southern capitalism's historical character and success, Anthony Hilton has found it in this tale:

> There is in New York a large fund of British money deposited by the authorities of Lloyd's, the London insurance market, on the eve of the outbreak of the Second World War. It was moved across the Atlantic as the storm clouds threatened over Europe, to convince the Americans that whatever happened, and even if Hitler's tanks were to roll into the courtyard of the Bank of England, the American clients of Lloyd's would not be affected. The fund...was the City's way of telling them that even defeat in a war would not be allowed to interfere with business...The money is still there, invested in the main in US government bonds, and has grown large over the years.[12]

What this shows (he concludes) is that the City is international in its scope and thinks on a global scale. 'It underlines how the City institutions put their own interests first...The City regards itself as separate from the country at large, and sees the actions of government as somehow not binding on it'.

Since Mrs Thatcher's radical advent, Britain's overseas assets have risen from the equivalent of only 6.5% of national income to 22% – 'an increase roughly equivalent to the £54 billion contribution made by North Sea oil to the U.K. economy in the same period...This is the basis for the allegation that the City shipped the benefits of North Sea oil abroad to employ other nations' workforces, while depriving British manufacturing of its investment lifeblood'.[13] Significantly, such figures are still far below historical norms of economic extra-territorialism: in 1913-14, for example, foreign assets made up the equivalent of about 180% of British national income. Though this level will probably never be attained again, the 'declining' economy is clearly headed in the right direction. After Empire Anglo-Britain did indeed shrink (as so many elegists have said) to 'being herself again': however, the self has turned out to be not a nation but a City-state. The rediscovered origins are not those of an English *Volk* or of the Revolution so travestied and dishonoured in popular recollection and culture: they are the new-old lineaments of a Southern heartland, the metropolitan zone suddenly seen as distinct and alien from 'the North'.

The congruence between these lineaments and Royalism could never have been established for a primarily industrial economic order, or in a new state made or remade by nationalism (as nearly all now in existence have been). But then, neither is the actual trajectory of British industrial capital conceivable under either of these conditions: the long tale of a Prometheus easily Bound and casually gutted by the political hegemony of commercial and financial capital – by a benign State neglect, systematic and finally unarrestable demotion, and at last a guided sell-out to more dynamic foreign industrial capital.

Monarchy is in this sense little more than the popular visage and social cement of Great Britain's unique version of capitalist development: the prolonged and baroquely gilded hegemony of 'early' or commercial capital over all subsequent phases. To its spiritual enwrapment of the British there corresponds on the material side the hegemony of a City-controlled economy for which (as Hilton and others have shown) domestic industrial production was always secondary, and has now become quite peripheral. The apparent detachment of the Ukanian Crown from the social nation – its mystic stratosphere of dignity, the aloofness it requires to irradiate the 'ordinary' – matches the permanent and functional separation of City capital from merely domestic concerns. Both the national Soul and the national Money-bag (so to speak) are located at a safe distance from the merely or grossly national. Both automatically repulse any reprehensibly 'narrow nationalism', whether the latter be focused on the economic protection of 'our industry' or on a forced ethnic definition of Englishness (virtually absent from the Ukanian polity). Equally automatically, both normally function in harmony to promote a more outward-oriented patriotism, the spirit of the Great-British in both free trade and Civilization. National interest finds its natural expression here in ostensibly a-national grandeur – in the anti-narrowness of those born (like all Royalty) to give example to others. Whether as the 'good boys' of the post-war American world, as the soul of the Commonwealth (a role genuinely dear to Queen Elizabeth), or as the moral tutors of a new Europe (forever preaching clammy sermons against crude anti-American narrowness), Crown and City have been perfectly united in this great tradition of sanctimonious but rewarding perfidy.

The *necessary* relationship of such a mercantile or intermediary capitalism is with the 'outside world' in the sense of the global market in both money and commodities. That rapport has altered in Britain's case from centrality to being a secondary but still significant 'service station' of international trade. The only significant modernization of the Thatcher reign has been the drastic reform of City operations to cope with (and fight back from) this displacement: 'Big Bang'. But the essential point is to note how well that transition has worked. The crucial difficulty of the whole 'archaism' hypothesis – whether applied to the Monarchy or to the hereditary deformity of British capitalism – is that both have been so astonishingly successful. Anyone can perceive their reliquary characteristics: yet Royalty is far more alive and genuinely popular than any 'fossil' has a right to be, while capitalism's constantly-advertised 'decline' has led not to a fall but to the election of Mrs Thatcher's ultra-capitalist tyranny.

A way out of the dilemma is suggested by an elementary distinction. Crown and capitalism remain florescent, but the *nation* they are linked to does not: there, the whole world correctly sees collapse, rigor mortis or worse – the 'wasting of the British economy' in Sidney Pollard's phrase:

> The statistics confirm the national consciousness of a staggering relative decline, such as would have been considered utterly unbelievable only a little over thirty years ago...After having led the world for two hundred years, Britain is no longer counted among the economically most advanced nations...[14]

At current rates of growth, he concludes that 'Britain will not have reached the *present* German level until 2051'. And his estimate was worked out before 'the wilful further destruction of British industrial power under Mrs Thatcher's rule'. However, what Pollard and like-minded prophets are talking about is the domestic industry of 'Britain', the United Kingdom traced out (as is normal) from primarily internal coordinates.

Ukania is another story. As we have seen, this Crown-and-Capital land is not really a national state: it is more accurately described as a Southern-lowland hegemonic bloc uniting an hereditary élite to the central processing unit of commercial and financial capital. For the latter, the 'nation' has always been too small: a hinterland of romance and industrially 'spoiled' river-valleys configured precisely in the Home County pronunciation of the word 'provinces'. Those unversed in the Queen's tongue may not appreciate the full sodden misery of the concept. With medecine-pill intensity it evokes all that Crown and Court are not: a *terrain vague* of indeterminate rusticity and toil which chaps enjoy (on holiday) and quite definitely have a duty to help and encourage. This far-flung waste of garden-gnomes and factory-chimneys is in effect an image of nation-state prostration before the City's hegemony. Had either nation-state economics or Republican nationalism ever emerged it would, of course, have signified the reverse: the dominance of the North and industrial capital over exchange-value and trade, and of the manufacturing lower orders over Hyde's Mortimer and its City and Treasury cousinhood. It is the sheer inconceivability of any such reversal which registers in the standard intonation of 'provinces'.

For the old Southern-based hierarchy formal 'Empire' was optional – it came and then, without too much trouble, went – but a 'Greater' Britannic realm naturally extending outwards into the exploitation of someone and somewhere else is not. Maintenance of *this* has been the matrix of London's post-1688

State: the precondition of Civilization, and the ultimate logic of the Crown's wonderful illogicality. Naturally, Ukania made good use of England and Britain while the going was easy (and the modernization of elsewhere proceeded with such agonizing slowness). But now they're beginning to look dispensable – an aggravating burden of unemployment, rot and 'excessive' State expenditure only made tolerable so far by the North Sea oil revenues. The Ukanian South-East, by contrast, has accelerated all its natural advantages over a foundering periphery. The Crown heartland has done well out of the long recession of the 1970s and '80s, and were that to be treated as a statistical entity few of Pollard's strictures would apply. The lamented 'growing abyss' between North and South should not really be a subject for mere figures, nor for moral outrage, nor for futile retreads of Westminster-inspired 'modernization': it can't be tackled within the existing State, because it *is* the existing State, the dominance of the Crown (or 'anti-industrial') culture, the thriving pseudo-nationalism of the Old Régime. Put another way: it is what it always was, the suppression of most of the preconditions of both 'enterprise culture' and democracy – that popular sovereignty of the North through which alone either 'equality', the destruction of 'class', or a nationalist democracy could ever have emerged.

Through this irresolvable and still strengthening cramp, Southern Royalism has consistently aborted any potential Northern Republicanism. With the help of a Royal, distributive form of Socialism it has reduced the North to mainly gestural resentment and kept Scotland in its traditionally apolitical condition. And this Royal manipulation of 'class' has only been possible because it isn't – or isn't just – a spectral triumph of Idea or romantic culture over socio-economic realities. The most effective, dynamic, best-deployed 'reality' happens to be in silent, structural support of the Crown: concentrated for purposes of easy description as 'the City', this consistently successful sector of British capitalism has gone on being quite able – through its command of the State – to buy off trouble in the outer and lower reaches. 'Buying off', as we now see, has the indispensable triple meaning of material (albeit diminishing) compensation, political neutralization via

Labourism, and the Crown-centred reinforcement of a conventional and anti-modernist culture. The degree of emphasis I have placed on the latter in no way implies a metaphysic of determination by ideas or moving spirits, for at bottom the Regal spiritualism of Ukania-Britain is only the elaborate and highly functional tool of an historical materialism – of the metropolitan Southland's ancient and still profitable place in world economic growth.

The results are traced by Geoffrey Ingham in his penetrating decipherment of British capitalist evolution, *Capitalism Divided?* (1984). He points out there how obsession with the Industrial Revolution has led to overall misinterpretation of that development (and hence to consistent failure in locating its cultural and ideal corollaries). This has been most true on the Left, where Marx himself –

> failed to consider in full...(how) these originally "pre-industrial" elements would be required in an expanded form by the world system, and that Britain was prepared to maintain them in positions of relative dominance. In short, it is international commerce and banking which, to a marked extent, have determined the trajectory of British capitalist development as a national economy within the world capitalist system...[15]

Put in another way – Marx's own 'preoccupation with the production process' in *Capital*, while justifiable in relation to 'general capitalist development', could hardly have been more profoundly misleading in his country of adoption. Contrary to many appearances of the 1800-1850 period, the national economy there would remain governed by exactly these 'pre-industrial' elements – in fact, commercial and financial capital was able to contain and eventually utilize industry to bolster its own pre-existent role as world-broker and intermediary. Above all Marx 'underestimated the efficacy (under particular but not "exceptional" circumstances) of the *political* conditions of existence of the non-productive forms – commercial and banking capital'.

The Outward-looking
and the Backward-looking

At a recent press conference in London, the following exchange took place:
Questioner (French): 'After nine years at No 10 Downing Street, do you feel more or less European?'
Prime Minister: 'Precisely the same as I have always felt – thoroughly British with an enormous contribution to make the world over.'

The Independent, 29 Jan. 1988.

U.K. development both stemmed from and has never forsaken this different mounting tide – one which preceded the mainstream of modern growth towards industrialization in which political nationalism has been rooted. Yet it has found it perfectly possible to coexist with and indeed to live off all the later phases of mainstream growth. The emergence of an industrial-capitalist modernity did not blot out all earlier tendencies. On the contrary, its successive periods have afforded one opportunity after another to the single surviving ancestor which resumed all the traits of pre-modern, mercantile culture within itself. Amid all its antagonisms (and partly because of them) global capitalism has always found a useful place for at least one universal entrepôt, clearing-house, middle-man and banker – for one reliable 'off-shore' centre or shopkeeper-facility with institutional resources reasonably distanced from nation-state interference.

This is what I meant earlier by suggesting that extra-territoriality is the true genetic code of Britishness. The deeper reason for the perplexing absence of a narrowly English identity is its affirmation in the permanently broader shape of 'Britishness', a complex range of ideas and customs articulated around the Crown – both as popular totem and as constitutional symbol. This oddly a-national nationalism locates within itself and defuses all the standard *motifs* of nationality and populist resentment – awarding them a place, as it were, in the overarching construction of fakelore tradition – the 'Great Arch' as some socialist redemptionists recently described it.[16]

Such traditionalism is ultimately configured by economic extrusion: the backward-looking has derived both its covert logic and its real dynamism from the outward-looking. And that dynamism in turn has come from successful exploitation of one phase after another of global capitalist evolution: both perennial parasite and functional intermediary of that growth, the Southern-based élite has always needed a domestic strategy aimed against 'Little England' and all that this phrase should have entailed historically, with its dual sense of restricted nationhood (ethnicity) and popular-democratic sovereignty (republicanism). It is these avenues which have been and remain proudly occluded from the Anglo-British *mentalité* – the oldest of existing State-ideologies, yet benefiting (as Thatcherism's success has shown once more) from the ageless 'youth' furnished by its eccentric-exploitative relationship to the main currents of world trade.

Before the steam-engine the Greatness in Britain was an unsavoury power-bloc of mercantile capitalism and efficient big-estate agriculture. Now that the steam-engine has vanished into the railway-enthusiasts' nostalgia of the 1980s, it remains recognizably the same thing: a booming and cosmopolitan City allied to Europe's largest concentration of millionaire farmers, supported by an increasingly rapacious and politically spineless middle class and a subservient urban peasantry. It even looks the same: the old Hanoverian style has been replicated in the upper reaches by Quinlan Terry and Bankers' Georgian, while Prince Charles's anti-modern taste is bestowed upon deserving estate-workers as 'Community Architecture'.

Such is England, and all her Greatness. But then it always has been, since the Stuarts were evicted and the Whig or Venetian class established itself in the saddle with George I. In his historical survey of British wealth, *Men Of Property* (1983), W.D.Rubenstein showed that this élite was always richer than the industrialists. Since his book appeared it has greatly augmented the disproportion: Mrs Thatcher has made Great Britain more herself again, the sole difference being that the renewed hegemony is more blatant and displays the arrogance of a possessing class which has finally liquidated serious opposition and feels able to dispense with niceties. Reversion to first principles was Machiavelli's formula for rejuvenation of the State: hence the giddy rise of a new corruption so disconcertingly like that Old Corruption which all liberals were sure had been Reformed away by post-1832 morality and gentlemanliness.

The old Whig pomposity depicted our Ship of State as the Providentially-appointed vanguard of civilized Progress, a posture providing natural immunity from fundamental critique or reform: this machine is inherently open to all sensible, reasonable change – beyond which there lies but the wilderness of abstract rationality and fanaticism, the 'abroad' sort of thing typical of lands without chaps who know how to run things. In the 1980s the clearest and most consistent denunciation of this suffocating inheritance has come from Neal Ascherson, notably in his *Observer* weekly column.[17] Where so many philistines have seen British decline as the fruit of economic backwardness, Ascherson highlights 'the unreformed political structure':

> It is commonly and comfortingly said that that there is nothing basically wrong with British institutions, "the finest in the world", but that they are not working well at present because the economy is in such a bad state. The reverse is true. The reason that the British economy does not work is that British institutions are in terminal decay.

His verdict is surely far closer to the mark than the quotidian drivel of Westminster and its media echo-chamber. However, if the location of the core State institutions as primitive-modern rather than ancient is accepted, then it too needs much qulification. The point really at issue here is the explanation of the Régime's longevity and (by implication) its prospects of longer survival. For all its candour and imagination, Ascherson's is by no means the first scenting of graveyard decay in the Raj; and past predictions have been exorcised by the onward course of events.

This doubt is powerfully underlined by another facet of Ascherson's writing since 1979. For his column has become a coruscating commentary upon the irrepressible life of the Thatcherite heartland, as well as upon the folly and anachronism of its institutions. What we see there isn't a perambulating

cadaver but a disconcerting mixture of Rip Van Winkle and
Peter Pan: on the one hand Druidic waxworks like the
Gartered Callaghan and the late Earl of Stockton, on the other
the obstreporous newly-rich country of Ernest Saunders,
millionaire window-cleaners and a reanimated servant-class,
where under-stairs cupboards sell for the equivalent of two
years' Northern wages. The great panoply of Gargoyled
Britain and the slavering gnomes uncorked by the City's Big
Bang occupy the same capital, and are seen treading the same
lawns at Conservative Club garden-parties. Frenetic new
blood seems to be pumping through the old hidebound
paralysis, and (as *Sunday Telegraph* Editor Peregrine Worsthorne put it in an immediately famous phrase) has generated
a 'bourgeois triumphalist' resynthesis of kenspeckled 'tradition' with loutish vulgarity.

However, these new schizoid characteristics remain explicable within the trajectory outlined above. From the 1688
Revolution forwards, this is a society which has existed outside
of itself as much as in. Its original formation, the formula of its
world-historical success, and the final solution found for its
20th century decline have all depended largely upon an extra-
territorial centre of gravity. Confirmation of this can be seen
above all in the way age and retreat have rendered the Raj more
outward-looking, not less. 1986's Big Bang, 'de-industrialization', and the carefully-fostered take-over of the old manufacturing river-valleys by foreign multinationals, are no more
than the cumulative slide on a gradient whose contours were
decided centuries ago. Thatcher's increasingly deregulated and
'open' economy has an address-system gabbling out slogans
about modernization and prosperity for all, in brashly populist
accents displeasing to old-timers like Worsthorne. But so in its
day had the preceding instalment of Our Island Story,
'Imperialism'. Before then this populism-from-above may
have been less prominent, but the notion that Britain's
Greatness lay with Free Trade in opium, gold and Birmingham
Small Arms was just as crucial – a notion founded in turn upon
an 18th century commercial pre-eminence already established
as asset-stripping colonialist, general shop-keeper and carrier
to the globe.

As development has proceeded the location of the facility has naturally altered from that of all-purpose prime mover to being simply a parasitic epicentre. This epicentre still has fixed delusions of grandeur and decrepit institutions whose pathos have long been evident to outsiders. Yet these count for little beside the continuing utility of such an off-shore service-station – indeed its hierarchical quaintness and colourful devotion to 'class' are well known to attract both the world's super-rich and intellectual tourists enamoured of the exotic. Hence both Ingham's thesis and Ascherson's vivid renditions of metropolitan grotesquery may suggest an uncomfortable future perspective. Negatively, almost any sceptic might suspect there is no chance whatever of domestic-industrial revival in Britain, or of a principled Republicanism capable of demolishing Hyde's Mortimer and building something more rational. But a more positive suspicion too seems legitimate: why should Ukania *not* derive still another fresh lease of life from whatever capitalist revival follows the nagging depression of the last decade? It has done well enough during it. In which case, a wholly 'unviable' national economy (in Sidney Pollard's sense) may flourish as never before, simply because the demand for its 'outward-looking' services is greater than ever: Royal Ukania *redivivus*, the Third Industrial Revolution's indispensable parasite, will then be well able to bear forward its rotting polity and *kitschig* Monarchy into another century or so of life.

At the same time she will be able finally to put her long-suffering nations and sub-nationalities out of their misery. Never having been able to generate a Republic – either 'British' or their own – they will end up with Heritage Trails, Industrial Museums, time-share complexes and Japanese or American assembly-plants (all consecrated by a Royal Visitor).

The Royal Bomb: Implosions of Greatness

When poison-gas is no longer enough, then in a room somewhere in this world a man just like anybody else will invent an incomparable explosive, something in relation to which the explosives we know today will seem like innocent toys. And some other man just like anybody else, only a little sicker than most, will steal this explosive and climb up into the centre of the earth with it to the point where it can do most damage. There will be an enormous explosion nobody hears and then, turned back into gaseous form, the earth will wander through the heavens free at last from its parasites and illnesses...

Italo Svevo, *La coscienza di Zeno* (1916).

Svevo was another great exponent of Habsburg tomb-humour, writing on its Adriatic fringes only two years before that Empire's final passage into night. The old Middle-European Kingdom had foundered into modern warfare without acquiring the political equipment of modernity (or even a British-style facsimile thereof). Materially it had adapted much better than is now generally allowed: it is (for instance) a myth to think that the Habsburg State was exploded so completely out of existence by economic failure. True, its ruling ethos contained and scorned the entrepreneurial spirit exactly as in Britain; but the dynasty was unhampered by a parliament and could also deploy greater technocratic energy and reforming zeal (through régime families like the Wittgensteins and the Musils). In his *The Economic Rise of the Habsburg Empire*, David Good cautions historians against 'simplistic models of the link between economic and political development', since –

the overwhelming weight of evidence on the performance and structure of the Hapsburg economy leads to a wholesale rejection of the economic failure thesis. Perhaps the Empire's problems were not ones of economic failure but of economic success. In a Marxist sense the malfunctions may not have resided in the economic sub-structure but rather in the ideological superstructure....[18]

Between 1870 and 1914 its rate of economic growth was much

higher than Britain's, for instance; yet this advance simply aggravated the nationalist discontent which impeded any 'social' readjustment to change. If (as in Britain) the régime had been able to reduce aspirations to those of 'class' – the institutionalized safety-valve of conservative rule – all might still have been well. But the strains of war and defeat were to spring apart the less reconcilable elements of national identity. The 'bomb' prefigured in *Zeno* was really the explosive tension which racked the polyglot Trieste of Svevo and convinced him that an unhealably sick mankind was bound for extinction.

The enduring aim of the Habsburgs was (in A.J.P.Taylor's words) 'to exist in greatness' at the heart of Europe.[6] Substitution of 'the world' for 'Europe' translates us into the ideology of Windsordom. But it has a real bomb to help keep it there: a politico-ideological weapon rather than a strictly military one, whose real meaning derives from an appropriately complex grandeur-mentality related to both extra-territoriality and the Crown. Like the Special Relationship to the United States – where nuclear weaponry has always played a key role – Royal Deterrence serves a myth-grandeur whose profane utility rarely if ever surfaces, either in official pronouncements on Our Defence Posture or among the critics of thermonuclear doom and vileness.

In England the Great-British or covertly Royal identity is often carried to the absurd point where *not* being ('merely') English becomes itself a paradoxical rallying-point of national honour and identification (in short, like the Monarchy, a kind of crypto-nationalism). And how deep this perverse structure lies is shown most plainly by its almost unshakeable hold on the English Left. Labour's former Leader Michael Foot has of course long been the most passionate defender of 'Parliamentary Sovereignty' and an immoveable opponent of even meek proposals like a formal Bill of Rights. But a more staggering instance of the same mentality has recently been offered by a champion of English extra-Parliamentary Leftism, E.P.Thompson himself. In an article entitled 'How Britain Could Break the Ice in the Cold War' he wrote:

> I think it is in the power of Britain to break the Cold War stalemate, not because – after two terms of Mrs Thatcher – Britain qualifies as the moral leader of anything, but for other

reasons...because of a weight of inherited history, a history which sometimes seems to smother us with inertia or guilt, but which on this occasion might serve to furnish us with resources in a crisis. History has left us uncertainly at a crossroads, between Europe, the United States (with whom we share a language) and a former empire, which even Mrs Thatcher has been unable to drive out of the Commonwealth. These conjunctions offer a mediating role, in which several of our Commonwealth partners...have more experience than ourselves. And despite Britain's role as an architect of NATO, we might prove to be acceptable...to the Soviet bloc. (*Independent*, 25 Feb. 1987)

On first reading this, I had to pinch myself. But yes, it actually *is* Winston Churchill's old 1948 definition of Great Britain's geo-political destiny at the intersection-point of the 'three circles', Europe, the U.S.A. and Empire. The old hero of Empire outlined Britain's cross-roads destiny for the Tories at their Conference that year, stressing how 'we are the only country which has a great part in every one of these circles' –

We stand, in fact, at the very point of junction, and here in this Island (*sic*) at the centre of the seaways and perhaps of the airways also, we have the opportunity of joining them all together. If we rise to the occasion in the years that are to come it may be found that once again we hold the key to opening a safe and happy future to humanity, and will gain for ourselves gratitude and fame...

Later the same notion was pursued by Eden, with his view of London as essentially 'a balancing influence between the American continent, Europe and the Commonwealth'.[19] Indeed all Foreign Ministers since then have done so: the aim of Greatness in retreat can only be to cling to a 'crossroads' location and status for as long as possible. The Royal Bomb was created for this political purpose alone, like the rest of the post-war U.K.'s relatively huge Defence budget. Modern-minded critics of the latter reason as if Great Britain was a mere middle-sized nation-state like others. Were that true, such expenditure would of course be outrageous under the Conservatives and certifiable with Labour at the helm. But it isn't, that's the whole point (unintentionally betrayed by Thompson's stance).

The Bomb has never 'deterred' the USSR or anyone else for a second, but what it has done is to keep Windsordom out there among the 'Greats' – a posture supremely important for the kind of extruded State and economy I've been trying to depict. Not being a State and nationality vulgarly *comme les autres* may seem like ostentatious criminal indulgence; for a non-nation – an extra-national ('outward-looking') polity dependent upon the retention and reinforcement of its parasitism – it may be quite practical. It may appear at least to retain 'the power of Britain', or something of it – that unctuous, dreamed-of 'influence' as mediator, counsellor, 'acceptable' busybody, and possessor of 'resources in a crisis' which haunts the dreams of both the Foreign Office and even its most fervent native critics. Bomb-Greatness is denounced primarily in terms of an equivalently Great renunciation: the reverse 'enormous contribution' leading Mankind out of the cross-roads in another direction.

British political life exists to service 'Greatness'. This is its origin, the logic of its evolution and the condition of its survival. A functional, mercantile centrality forged the long duration of its history and imagined centrality remains its ideological lifeblood. Wits in the Conservative Central Office labelled Andrew Lloyd-Webber's 1987 electoral theme-tune for Mrs Thatcher 'It's Great to be Great', and her campaign duly concluded with a day of resonant recalls to the theme. Keeping the 'Great' in Britain is no mere exercise in Tory rhetoric, however – it goes to the heart of the matter. It's ultimately a question of structure, rather than of sentiment, banners and daft superiority. The Crown is the totem of Greatness and exchange-value is its living or material nervous system. Both are omnipresent powers lacking 'whereness and whenness, site and habitat' (in Defoe's words); and they fuse into the customs of a polity regulated by the specifically 'vague' or outward-looking nationalism which Monarchy has made possible.

I raised the semantics of 'Great' earlier in discussing Queen's English. Here the point worth emphasizing is that it has two conjoined formal meanings, neither of them covering Ukania. Exploring the cadences of Royal-popular identity the true sense is almost invariably an informal yet determining one. The geographical denotation is of course 'larger', more extensive, as in the Magna Graecia of Antiquity, or today's *Argentina mas grande* (from the South Pole to the River Plate, via the Malvinas). 'Great Britain' was originally a coinage of this kind. 'Britain' is really Greater England, but in curious disguise – boring yet sometimes inescapable, a kind of simulacrum-extension of the real thing. The extensiveness is formally absurd but ideologically and emotionally necessary: an inevitable infra-structure of 'Great', or England-in-the-world. Idiotic or not, the emotive sense of 'grandeur' has also rooted itself in popular awareness and grown more important: glory, exemplary centrality in the destiny of homo sapiens – what Gaullist intellectuals call *rayonnement*.

As a *Times* editorialist wrote after Nasser nationalized the Suez Canal in 1956 –

> Doubtless it is good to have a flourishing tourist trade, to win Test matches and to be regaled by photographs of Diana Dors being pushed into a swimming pool. But nations do not live by circuses alone. The people, in their silent way, know this better than the critics. They still want Britain to be great. (27 August 1956)

Yet this context is also misleading. If the core sense of 'great' was just territorial empire it would by now have vanished from the British ideology. In fact, Mrs Thatcher has just been putting it back there to the sound of impresario's trumpets. The *effective* meaning of 'great' in Anglo-British history is neither definable, claimed territory nor spiritual splendour alone, but a wilfully imprecise amalgam of elements echoing the undefined extra-territoriality I evoked above.

The genuine opposite of 'Great' in the inherited-history or Crown-&-Bomb sense would naturally be small, or smallish: diplomatically resourceless, without a Special Relationship to call one's own, an absence unnoticed at Top Tables, an ordinary country (or collection of countries) comfortably distanced from today's global crossroads and with problems like those of such un-Great nations as Italy, Spain and Holland. Instead, we see how even such a Régime-critic as Thompson exhibits every symptom of chronic anti-smallness – even attachment to the Commonwealth. Out-greatnessing

Thatcher here, he denounces her for tending to abandon the unique emplacement in world affairs it affords – the old-Imperial centrality which may yet be turned to good.

One might have thought it possible for democrats to discern at least a few redeeming features in the Leader's impatience with Commonwealth blarney and her scarcely-veiled hostility towards Elizabeth II. It is unpalatable when a reactionary for her own malign motives does what the Left should itself have done a generation (or a century?) ago. But it's futile merely to wish this sadly recurrent feature of the Thatcher years away. The dreadful truth is that a creeping, hypocritical, unconfessable and right-wing 'Republicanism' may be a little better than none at all (and should at least nudge socialists in the right direction). But no: after episodes like those Thompson is referring to here the Régime Left rose as a single impassioned entity to defend the inherited inertia of Crown, Commonwealth and Consensus. The Kingdom's *fin-de-siècle* dilemma is thus conveyed in a nutshell: while the De'il blunders crassly into the future, the unco' guid are capable of little but pining for the glamour of times past.

Even in the negative-image vestment of disarmament politics, Great in spite of ourselves, we enjoy a weighty patrimony which qualifies us as, ah...well...moral leaders actually, or 'honest brokers' at the very least. This kind of pleading makes the ideological point, and returns us to the historical one: 'Greater England' preceded and irrevocably formed mere modern 'England', deforming both their nationality and our own upon its template of undefined extra-territoriality. Successive tides of expansion then carried this State-form forward in a uniquely distanced ('Island' or off-shore) rapport with general development, projecting its pre-democratic and a-nationalist characteristics across three centuries. Such astonishing survival and adaptation required far more than a merely Royal or State ideology, however – it demanded the formation of a popular Anglo-British identity, the surrogate for both citizenship and nationality (some of whose origins and traits I looked at in Part II). One of its other key aims was to favour energetic and temporary mobilization against outside enemies: the bouts of warfare at a distance inherent in a course of predatory commercialism. I will return to this theme farther on. But it's important also to stress that the 'absences' of Anglo-British identity are never sheer negativity: approaches to it using standard models of nationalism and constitutional statehood always have this drawback. They can't convey how Greater England, or 'Britain' in the morally extensive sense, has built up into an extremely powerful presence.

One way of measuring that presence is by its grip on intellectuals, and especially upon dissidents. Looked at in the comparative sight-line of nationalism, it may appear 'vague' and illogical – the customary emotive palimpsest of ideas ranging from Elizabeth I to the Falklands, and from Royalty to ruralism. When regarded in the sufficiently long perspective of its own evolution, however, these vagaries make their own insular sense. They represent a consistent and staged refusal to 'modernize' into the standard nation-state form – a 'Little England' to match the mainstream of modern nation-building and identity imposed on most peoples by 19th and 20th century history. The results of such systemic anti-modernism may look queer (because of the different evolutionary fossil-layers stuck together in it) yet the conservative-national principle itself doesn't: retention at all costs of an 'England' outside itself or – put another way – of a 'cross-roads' structure capable of exploiting (or at least 'influencing') the outside world.

The example illustrates one aspect of the dilemma with pitiful clarity: intellectuals have rarely been able to resist the appeal of 'Greater'. Historically intellectuals have since the Enlightenment tended towards the Left, and in certain more extreme situations have formed an alienated stratum or 'intelligentsia'. But here is one distinguishing feature of the 'Greater England' identity: both as Imperialism *and* as anti-Imperialism it has helped prevent intellectuals becoming an intelligentsia and secured their basic loyalty to a quite unusual depth and over an unusually wide spectrum. That's how, after Chartism, the real viruses of Little-Englandism and Republicanism were easily kept at bay. The narrower nationalism which these implied was always far more of a threat than the more advertised (and eventually obsessional) foes of 'class' and Socialism. Royal-distributive Socialism, especially, was a fairly straightforward matter of buying off discontent with extra-territorial resources – the surplus product of the Southern economy which remained the nucleus of international exchange until the 1950s, and then (after the collapse of Sterling's pre-eminence) fought its way back into that position again with the Euro-dollar. The last savagely comic round of this process has come in the 1970s and '80s as London has successfully cushioned de-industrialization and mass unemployment with a final 'extra-territorial' dispensation from Providence: North Sea oil.

This dispensation allowed a re-born and more aggressive Conservatism to re-adjust for another round of cross-roads Greatness. The new, colossally-expensive Trident system being bought from the U.S.A. will help guarantee its performance there. It recapitulates all the servile dependency of a 'Special Relationship' with America, of course. But that in turn has become an indispensable way of avoiding being 'merely European': not just the British Isles but the European Community is far too narrow for the City's expanding definition of extra-territorial reality, which since the permanent abolition of foreign exchange controls extends naturally from Hong Kong eastwards to San Francisco.[20]

The Investiture at Caernarvon happened against a backdrop of newly assertive Welsh nationalism. But the nationalist debates of that period (and later in Scotland) were often founded on radical failure to grasp the import of this history. They seemed to imagine 'Britain' as an artificial State-construct clamped on top of four nations whose ethno-cultural identities simply awaited release from this burden. The problem was aggravated by the way one of those, England, employed the all-British apparatus chiefly in its own interest and refused to make the distinction between nation and State. Yet 'England' itself proved damnably difficult to track down in this scenario. Seeking an equivalently English national paradigm to fight and measure themselves against, Welsh and Scottish nationalists were often driven to invent one – projecting suitably narrow or Little-English conspiracies and ambitions where, in truth, none existed or needed to exist.

What they were actually confronting was the historic apparatus of 'Greater' – a combination of formal Statehood, informal authority-structure and ideology soldered together into the formidably powerful identity of Britishness. This is an entity which has no business to exist in the contemporary world, but does. It 'makes no sense' according to the standard concepts of today's nation-state politics (which, naturally, the nationalists imported and applied to their own cause). But that's because it dates from before the formation of these concepts: it is not (as so many fatuous apologists claimed at Caernarvon) 'above that sort of thing', but *before* that sort of thing – an anteriority carried forward into modernity by the peculiar survival-conditions of an a-national economy.

Ascherson's *ancienneté* perspective sees this archaism as weakness, the explanation of decline and backwardness. But the very same factors have also provided strength: however fake, Anglo-Britain's Royal-familial traditionalism has time and again shown its mobilizing force in war-time 'emergencies' like the Falklands War in 1982. As Peter Nettl showed in his rare and important study of *Social Mobilization*, such movements occur more readily in stable, élite-controlled hierarchies than in either democracies or mere bureaucracies. It is those very factors inimical to peacetime change – custom, supposedly 'instinctive' conservatism, the 'tribal' pressure of emotionality upon reason and individual calculation – which also lend themselves to an unquestioning, galvanic response against outside threat and interference. But this is precisely the kind of capacity which a structurally over-extended economy and polity needed, since it could not help facing constant though limited threats to its overseas operations. Its distinctive High-Imperialist ideology was one of 'emergency', or adventurous individual readiness for sacrifice and combat.[21] And there was in any case little other choice for a polity to which the normal forms of democratic and nationalist identity remained consistently alien, and which had since the Civil War maintained such a small and low-prestige land-army.

Here again the 'backward-looking' was the sole way of servicing the outward-looking, whether as peaceful ethos or as emergency response-mechanism. It hampered industrial development, disparaged individualism, stultified the general culture and locked society into the cramp of 'class'. But, though singly deplorable – and routinely deplored for over a century – what did such failings really matter, as long as the

great outgoing machinery of exploitation continued to function, keeping the oligarchy in its place and providing enough
means to buy off discontent? The simulacrum of 'Britishness'
has proved all too functional in this sense. Its grotesquely
exaggerated Royalism, snobbery, familial claustrophobia and
reverence for pastness (including the 'customary freedoms'
hoarded by the Thompsonian left), even its lordly vagueness
and 'flexibility' – all are parts of a psychodrama which has
worked. The audience kept their seats, throwing fewer
tomatoes and rotten eggs than in most other lands. Only in the
later 1960s and early '70s did some get up and try to quit; and
most of these returned after an interval. In the late '80s they're
still there, uncertain of what to do next; while down in the
heartland stalls the most dominant and affluent sector of the
public is applauding as never before.

'Class': the Totem-shadow

The baker's man that no one will see rise
and England made to feel like some dull oaf
is smoke, enough to sting one person's eyes
and ash (not unlike flour) for one small loaf.

Tony Harrison, 'Marked with D.', *The School of Eloquence*
(1978).

Like all other Royal Visitations the Welsh Investiture marked
the displacement of one British obsession by another. The
week-day fixation is 'class', down-staged and temporarily
forgotten during week-end raptures with the Crown. But it
creeps glumly back on Monday morning. P.N.Furbank's
recent essay on social class in British consciousness, *Unholy
Pleasure*, opens with the sentence: 'People in Britain...talk
much too much about "class"'. Not only do we talk too much
about it – the notion has a positively 'evil and anachronistic
hold over our minds' like some English original sin which
continually reinvents itself in both literature and life, forever
finding new publicists like Jilly Cooper and Auberon Waugh
or new caste-marks like those of the Sloane Ranger cult.

Furbank's book is a literary revolt against this universe of shame. Yet, however justified in spirit, the actual diagnosis and escape-route he proffers are almost as absurd as the ramblings of its loopier prison-guards and ideological torturers. There are no actual social or statistical boxes corresponding to these obsessive class-divisions (he goes on): hence, the latter must be seen as essentially 'rhetoric' – mere 'pictures of society taken from a particular angle and...only meaningful from that angle'. 'Class' merely comes into the eye of the beholder, particularly when he or she wants to label and disparage others; but otherwise does not really exist.

Hence his formula for exorcism: this *vice anglais* is due for some appropriate therapy. But the author's collapse into subjectivism produces of necessity a starkly idealist cure. His recommendation turns out to be a stiff course of reading modernist classics like Proust, Joyce, Kafka and Musil, since these reject all the assumptions of the conventional English 'realist' novel. Such a break is psychically indispensable (the author broods insightfully) because –

> One cannot deny the fact, that there are some things about the classic English novels which are wearisome. Their authors often seem to be playing some game, of great if tortuous ingenuity, yet somehow insulting to the reader...[22]

This is really the game of collusion with the alienating consciousness of 'class': that natural-seeming, dense landscape which it is the duty of a mature, responsible creative imagination lovingly to explore rather than (for example) to bomb or to flee from. Such is the great tradition. Such (indeed) are all the Royal custom-codes, which the literary one merely translates and uplifts to a higher imaginative plane. Mr Furbank's sympathetic stance is one of 'principled defiance' towards all that – a plea for cultural revolution oriented to the 'more liberating and optimistic answer' that can can only come from *un*thinking this whole inheritance.

Heartily as I agree with the impulse, it is, surely, hopeless to confine it to literature. In its own way this confinement risks – even invites – collusion with the very anachronism Furbank deplores. It may be true that (as he stresses) the Ukanian Monarchy of Letters has consistently underwritten the slavishness and prostration of Anglo-British observance. But how has it done so? In part, by exiling politics in the grander sense from its societal landscape; or (with the same ultimate effect) by making politics into one variety of the socially picturesque – the interesting antics of Westminster's human nature. The forbidden 'grander sense' is that of the State, or of a national identity still imperilled and to be made. These have been apprehended as essentially immutable – a single, consecrated Centre of things which changes through history only to be ever more itself.[23] From such fixity culture projects a corresponding stability of human nature: all the meaningful cards of identity have been dealt by 'class' and literary art can only shuffle and reshuffle them into variants of the old story.

Failing to tackle the wider political framework, Furbank's reading-course continues to register dissent within the classical terms of British literature and literary criticism: the terms (that is) of a kind of cultural homoeopathy devoted to righting social malaise by the administration of appropriate tinctures. Taking over certain aspects of the State and traditional religion, this substitute has from the period of Matthew Arnold onward sought to –

> ...soften the stridency of self-interest, leaving some leeway for humility and self-control...to replace repressive and restrictive rules, which only invite rebellion, with ennobling examples and models which invited conformity through self-restraint, conscience, and the subordination of a "lower" to a "higher" self...The right kind of deference could more readily be commanded by affective literary works than by an external, alien authority: Arnold used the example of Shakespeare and the Church of England's Thirty-nine Articles – Shakespeare, he insisted, was more "stable"...[24]

This is what Chris Baldick has called the 'Social Mission of English Criticism': the attunement of modernization to a sinuous and informal English nature, via the modelling of mature 'higher selves'.

Furbank's call for dissonance cites other literary works, and questions the missionary method only by implication. However, such cultural homoeopathy in reality subsides before the Régime's Royal principles. The latter has always worked by homoeopathic dosages and the subtle prescription of thoroughly natural (or natural-seeming) antidotes to the rough intrusion of foreign or inorganic bacilli. Indeed the Prince of Wales we saw presented in 1969 has developed into one of the prime practitioners of this stately art – an apostle-in-chief of communitarian salvation and little-by-little treatments, the kind of Bushman wisdom brought on by deep breathing and conversations with Sir Laurens Van Der Post. (Well before the latter arrived, it should also be remembered that medical homoeopathy had been an established element of the Royal life-style since Sir John Weir 'introduced the Royal Family to its folk remedies in the 1920's).[25]

What was really at stake was (as Baldick has pointed out) more like a substitution of literature and its accompanying critical priesthood for the national religion: a secular Anglicanism striving to bind national community together as the Church of England itself had conspicuously failed to do:

> It is less religion as religion than religion as occupant of a privileged 'pinnacle' in relation to other kinds of ideology that Arnold and his followers tried to replace with literary discourse, creating a substitute moral philosophy and a substitute social analysis as much as a substitute religion. Poetry was to become a kind of lynchpin for a whole range of other social habits, moral values, and assumptions, confirming them and reflecting them back in harmonized, self-consistent, and emotionally appealing form. If it could fill the gap vacated by religion, literature could offer its own principles of internal consistency, completeness, and regularity of form as a shaping and governing principle for all the conscious and unconscious affairs of society. The order of the one and the order of the other would fall into an "organic" continuity, a harmonious, rounded, and self-complete development of civilization under the guardianship of literary criticism...

'A kind of lynchpin': this fantasized custodial centrality took for granted a traditional continuity and stability of the State. Its great fear was that lower-class vulgarity and materialism might diminish the stability created by so many 'higher selves' of the past. Hence the panic to get the emergent lower selves (or at least their future school-teachers) reading Jane Austen, George Eliot and Henry James – the man with (in T.S.Eliot's admiring phrase) 'a mind so fine that no idea could violate it'.

But the real lynchpin symbolized by this strategy of cultural conservatism is the Crown: the Royal impersonation of a customary State authority, popularized and projected far more effectively by pulp magazines, pageants and TV than by the reading-courses of the Cambridge English School. Both are ideal buttresses of the Crown-State, widely different in form and in immediate object yet united in the underlying values of civilized motion. As we saw earlier while discussing Popular and Respectable Monarchy, such differences are required by any functioning and comprehensive ideology: how else could it operate to produce 'organic continuity' in a stratified society? It makes no difference that the 'mature' worshippers at George Eliot's shrine regard Windsordom with suitably measured distaste, or that Royal-Wedding addicts have never heard of either her or F.R.Leavis.

From a conservative point of view there is positive value in such 'unbridgeable' distances – provided the strata-gap itself is a stable and reproduceable one, and provided there are sufficient underlying and unifying values to make a bridge in emergencies (mainly against outside threats). 'Class' implies the linguistic chasms noted earlier – the heteroglossia whose most typical habitat is traditional societies –

> Status societies – those rigidly classified worlds that generate all sorts of local and professional jargons, of almost sumptuary distinctions and nuances, of expressive idiosyncracies and arcana of communication...[26]

The opposite is dialogue, the anticlassificatory mode which 'implies equality, spiritual mobility, interchangeability of positions'. Franco Moretti observes the absence of this in England's Great Tradition, and the presence of a comic dominant concerned with expression rather than communication. What it expresses (and confirms) is 'the "peculiar habit"' of a social second nature, those inherited cards of identity regulating one's hand and one's game:

> From Square to Thwackum...from Uncle Toby to Micawber: the great English comic characters are always terribly deaf and irrepressibly talkative. The reason is that they do not speak but rather, so to say, *secrete* language: their words are not signs, abstract entities potentially available to everyone, but "symbols", as integral a part of their nature as their physical features,

their trade, their hobby horses. This endless flow of words is...a status symbol, a caste indicator. "Tell me how you speak and I shall tell you who you are": this disturbing proverb is the most appropriate motto of the realm of heteroglossia...

But that is the whole point of 'class': it has furnished the Ukanian State with an ultra-stable social foundation which has been, none the less, easily mobilizable through the subjacent and more powerful unity of a Royally-defined nationalism – the shared (if often tacit) values of an imaginary and closed familial community. Classes that 'don't talk the same language' will for that very reason constitute a solid conservative framework for society – provided the lower and peripheral idioms stay in their place, and crisis remains capable of fusing them all together at moments of either ecstasy or peril. One can laugh at 'Spitting Image' one day, but angrily defend 'Our Royal Family' the next. For these moments a common national master-tongue is of course rediscovered – in what George Steiner has described as 'the intimate centre...the zone of familial immediacy' where 'the world-picture of the clan' has been reliably hoarded during its periods of civil squabbling and rows over the family inheritance. The group identity's essential 'resources of consciousness' lie in its capacity to remobilize for whatever type of struggle history has made part of this archetypal totemic zone.

In the poem cited above Tony Harrison imagines his dead English working-class father being cremated, and thinks how –

...his cold tongue burst into flame
but only literally, which makes me sorry, sorry for his sake
there's no Heaven to reach.
I get it all from Earth my daily bread
but he hungered for release from mortal speech
that kept him down, the tongue that weighed like lead.

It was not class but 'class' that made him 'feel like some dull oaf': the quasi-caste confinement of an hierarchical culture materialized in tongues, and hence in consciousness – where (as Gareth Stedman Jones has said in a brilliant analysis of working-class cultural forms) 'Class is a life sentence, as inescapable as any caste system.[27]

'True thoughts are those alone which do not understand themselves': truth – in this case, a true faith in Monarchy –

subsists in a kind of structured isolation from doubt, reflection and theory. Hurtful negativity is held instinctively at bay by such plenitude. Thus even in fading sunlight the tree of marvels can go on blindly flourishing, shielded from harm by its taboo-walls and a collusive culture of enchantment. Its language overfills the national consciousness in order to exclude and destroy alternatives. This is a sweet form of politico-spiritual extinction: when stinging insects are drawn helplessly into the sticky interior of certain plants one has to imagine them dying with the last drunken thought: 'So *this* is what happens to wasps!' British Socialism? By all means, just as long as the Royal State Opening of Parliament is left intact. Another dictum from Adorno's *Minima Moralia* comes to mind here. It was quite possible that 'a film that strictly and in all respects satisfied the code of the Hays Office might turn out a great work of art', he admitted: '*but not in a world in which there is a Hays Office*'.

Saying is neither everything nor quite what it appears to be. We looked at some features of Queen's English earlier and noted its homology with the ghost-chart of Ukania: to an attuned ear, all the secrets of 'class' and tradition may be focused within the pronunciation of a single vowel. But though continually voiced in this way, an important part of the realm's articulation is what cannot be said at all: the taboo or self-reinforcing silence which has tied the national tongue for reasons important to the definition of nationhood with which it normally operates. Within the Crown-dream it is allowed to wag only on certain occasions and with a choice of pre-programmed messages. Beyond these silence is normal, and expected; yet this remains a live and pulsating expectation, in its own way eloquent.

The deeper truth here is that nothing is more crucial to language generally than lying and evasion. 'Scarcely anything in human speech is what it sounds', says George Steiner in *After Babel* – where he contends that the possibility of negation and falsehood is just as important to distinctively human communication as the more edifying themes tackled by theories of truth:

In actual speech all but a small class of definitional or "unreflective-response" sentences are surrounded, mutely ramified, blurred by an immeasurably dense, individualized field of intention and withholding...Human speech conceals far more than it confides; it blurs much more than it defines; it distances more than it connects.

It is partly because 'Words are the living eyes of secrecy' that English Royal-speak has been reanimated so successfully. All tongues originally encoded the separate, 'peculiar' reality of some tribal or familial group. A privacy impenetrable to 'foreigners' was one aspect of language's function. It is the nagging, nationalist renewal of such privacy which has given that term its quietly but odiously exclusive edge in contemporary English. From the outset speech-patterns-

> ...encode, preserve, and transmit the knowledge, the shared memories, the metaphorical and pragmatic conjectures on life of a small group...At its intimate centre, in the zone of familial or totemic immediacy, our language is most economic of explanation, most dense with intentionality and compacted implication ...(It) hoards the resources of consciousness, the world-pictures of the clan. Using a simile still deeply entrenched in the language-awareness of Chinese, a language builds a wall around the "middle kingdom" of the group's identity. It is secret towards the outsider and inventive of its own world.

The 'essence' of that world is of course no longer actual Crown rule, but its informal alter ego, the collective Leviathan of *rule from above* by an at least partly hereditary social élite – a class reared to go on functioning as a collective analogue of Royal authority, on a basis independent of *real* control and legitimation from below. One must stress 'real' here because a vital secondary characteristic of the Régime has become its chameleon-like ability to adopt democratic disguise. The formal façade has been set up in measured stages between 1832 and the present, and the process continues: for example, as we approach the tri-centenary of the Glorious and Bloodless Revolution of 1688, there has been some (abortive) debate in recent years about reforming, or even abolishing, the House of Lords. But Mrs Thatcher's revival of hereditary peerage in 1983 (with the ennoblement of Viscount Whitelaw) shows how little danger the mediaeval essence is at present in.

Another more telling example is the last decade of (equally abortive) discussions on State secrecy, with their plaintive demands for 'open government' and free access for the ruled. The very existence of such notions is a symptom of some shakiness in the Old Régime. From the 1680s up until the 1980s the right of those in power to disclose nothing about the exercise of power but what suited them has been a constitutive principle of British tranquillity and decency. The right itself is unlikely to change. However, the increasingly ungentlemanly nature of Mrs Thatcher's reign has led to a marked increase in State phobias on the issue. She has inherited the Leviathan of Ukanian Sovereignty – which makes her a *de facto* tyrant and (as so many commentators have noted) an almost literal Queen in the pre-modern sense – and will obviously never throw away such an instrument. But at the same time she genuinely despises the class which was its historic vehicle. Grasping the lightning without the lightning-rod, she can only wield its power in growing nakedness – with a new, invasive brutality which since 1979 has spread like fire.

Since gentlemanliness won't return, the sole alternative is what should have been enacted many days before yesterday: written constitutional protection and a public right to know. Yet if taken seriously this principle is the sharp end of a wedge which could destroy élite authority and de-legitimate the Unwritten Constitution and the Crown. Hence, heads are now being scratched to find another acceptable simulacrum of modernity: in this case of 'open government'. What's needed is a mimetic formula balancing apparent concessions and the 'scrapping' of some blatant grotesqueries against retention (and reinforcement) of what really matters: the absolute and uncodifiable power of the Mace, that elective Supremacy which no true Westminster politico will ever willingly give up (and least of all the current Mace-holder).

The Monarchy of Letters

Reticence...represents the extremely English concept, wide-spread throughout our society, though most Europeans would call it aristocratically conservative, of appropriateness as an ideal in itself...There is a decorum beyond decorum, beyond convention; its demands are unspoken and its essence is tact. There is a Great Tradition to be strung out along this line (whose chief props would be Jane Austen and Henry James)...

> Russell Davies, review of A.O.J.
> Cockshut's *Man and Woman: a Study*
> *of Love and the Novel,*
> *New Statesman,* 1 July 1977.

In a country where the people above seized the historical opportunity of building up their own safe version of rule from below, a special variety of Royal or non-ethnic nationalism was the most important key to their achievement. However, the affirmations of Investiture needed more than Laureate effusions to implant them in the collective psyche. Royal-institutional patriotism has always needed its own civil means of diffusion – unconscious or semi-conscious vehicles of its magic influence and binding authority. Queen's English speech is the most obvious of these; however, speech in the wider and more stable written form of literature has also been of notorious significance here and it is for this reason that (as we saw) literature and literary criticism have been so centrally important to conserving the statutes of an old régime.

In the survey of the Royal spirit-realm made above it was obvious that a measure of holiness attaches to the latter – something like an almost universally-accepted religion not formally linked to any church or cult, or even to belief in a Deity. Sometimes it's said that Monarchy is in this sense like the lay religion of modern Britain.

But little reflection is needed to show that God alone can hardly be the key to the mystery. True, some survey material indicates persistence of the idea that Heaven takes a special interest in the British Crown. As a test in one investigation, respondents were asked whether they thought that 'God guides this country in times of trouble'. In the mid-'seventies, a majority still did; and it was noticeably higher (about two-thirds) among those also supporting the Monarchy.[28] However, this influence alone does not account for the popularity of the Royal mystique. The survey authors recognize that:

> Religion is often mingled with monarchy...in ceremonial evocations of national unity. In England the relationship between throne and altar is evident upon many occasions, from the Coronation to daily proceedings in Parliament. The monarch is not only Queen "by Grace of God" but also "Defender of the Faith". Sanctions of religion and sanctions of royalty are meant to reinforce one another in a mystical union of symbols of authority...Support for the monarchy thus appears to encourage irrational and mystical confidence in political authority.

But (they conclude) any direct divine sanction of this sort has become secondary in a predominantly secular system.

Though treated to some extent like holy signs, the wrappers of the Queen's after-dinner mints, Princess Diana's nappies and her husband's bald spot remain something less than telegrams from On High. They are not (for example) like similar trivia associated with the Pope. Here, it is scarcely surprising that each tiny trace of the Divinity embodied on earth should fascinate and move. The Vatican manicurist pares His toe-nails; the embroidered handkerchief – a gift from the loyal worshippers of Krakow – is in a sense blowing His nose. Minor wonders, but no more miraculous than the transubstantiation itself. For the British Monarchs, however, the line to the transcendent is a good deal less direct. They are of course heads of the Church of England, and more austerely and distantly acknowledged as Christian rulers by the Church of Scotland. But few would attribute whatever magic they wield solely to these functions.

Organized Christianity in Britain is both too weak and too divided to furnish any direct explanation. The Monarchical cult has a sacred dimension with an accompanying taboo. And its being 'religion' only in some derived or secondary sense does not imply it is now socially weaker than formal church-going observance. But still (to take another contrasting example) it can hardly be compared to the Royal and national Japanese cult of Shintoism.

This version of theocracy was imposed as part of the Meiji Restoration after 1868. Prince Ito, the architect of the great upheaval that set out to modernize Japan under Emperor Meiji, chose Shinto as the most suitable belief-system for the new régime. It was supposed to replace the host of traditional local deities and demons most Japanese previously worshipped, and it put the restored Imperial Throne at the heart of things. The Emperor now united heaven and earth (rather as if the Pope had been made Absolute ruler of Europe). 'The Emperor is heaven descended, divine and sacred', reads Prince Ito's *Commentary on the Constitution*, 'He is pre-eminent above all his subjects. He must be reverenced and is inviolable. He has indeed to pay respect to the law, but the law has no power to hold him accountable to it. Not only shall there be no irreverence to the Emperor's person, but also He shall not be made a topic of derogatory comment nor one of discussion...'[29] The Imperial edicts assumed a sacred character, unalterable axioms of duty and subservience, and until 1945 images of the Ruler were bowed to and wept before in classroom, office and home.

This is all very distinct from the treatment given the icons of Queen Elizabeth II which decorate British wall-surfaces, particularly offices and public spaces. The distinctively modern exaltation of British Monarchy began about the same time as that of Japan – around 1870. But the end-product is remarkably different. In Britain portraits of the symbolic Ruler are a gesture supporting some kind of civility and style, a certain order and niceness; reverence is still there but appears mildly diffused into social appearances, as if the divine and the ordinary had become one and emphasis now lay upon the latter category. British subjects feel lumps in the throat at significant moments – crownings, weddings, etc. – but nobody would expect even pillars of the Monarchist Press Association to literally grovel before Royal portraits, or faint at the sound of the Ruler's voice. But my own knowledge of religion is far too limited to let me try to trace or estimate just how Christian faith has been translated into today's State folklore of Royalty

– how Anglicanism has been turned into Arthur Marwick's 'secular anglicanism' and made a feature of Royal-national identity. I gladly leave the topic to other inquirers.

In a heroic attempt at cultural cartography some years ago Perry Anderson claimed that the crucial fact about modern British culture is its 'absent centre'.* This is the only major national culture which, whether through incapacity or indifference, failed to produce its own version of *either* grand modern system of social ideas – sociology or marxism. Its main philosophical tradition, empiricism, was of course anti-system in orientation: an organized and habitual scepticism about 'grand ideas' as such, which underwent a renaissance from the Edwardian period onwards. Bertrand Russell's *Problems of Philosophy* (1911) was a lordly dose of native salts which evacuated what was left of Hegelian and other speculation in the academies, leaving the way clear for Wittgenstein. Around the latter was created those peculiar mystiques of linguistic philosophy which functioned as a kind of blank cheque to Ukanian conservatism. The cults of common sense and common language were administered by a university intelligentsia, whose traits Ernest Gellner observed in the 1950s:

> We have here a sub-group consisting of people who belong to, or emulate, the upper class in manner; who differentiate themselves from the heartier rest of the upper class by a kind of heightened sensibility and preciousness, *and*, at the same time, from the non-U kind of intelligentsia by a lack of interest in ideas, argument, fundamentals or reform. *Both* of these *differentiae* are essential to such a group...[30]

Protected by this formidable flood-barrier against foreign toxins, Windsorite culture had no need for an intellectual 'centre' in the sense of its own commanding theory, or official gun-battery of notions. It had what Noel Annan called an actual 'intellectual aristocracy' ('secure, established and, like the rest of English society, accustomed to responsible and judicious utterance and sceptical of iconoclastic speculation'): hence, it could largely dispense with speculation itself (and all the attendant risks).[31]

Such retrenched traditionalism and cultivated smallness of outlook did carry penalties – most notable an inertia leaving

*'Components of the National Culture', *New Left Review* 50 (1968).

the culture exposed (paradoxically) to certain outside influences. It screened out dangerous abstractions and their bearers; however, proponents of conservatism and anti-Marxism were another matter. Intellectuals in flight from the doctrinaire revolutions and counter-revolutions of post-1914 found a safe haven here – a 'white' immigration which in turn contributed notably to maintaining the lineaments of tradition and hierarchy. Since Wittgenstein's day Namier, Popper, Berlin, Gombrich, Eysenck and many others have ably contributed to this fortification – and so to the curious basic structure Anderson describes with heavily underlined indignation. Thus securely inoculated against both classical sociology and Marxism –

> *British culture was consequently characterized by an absent centre..* (and) *has for more than fifty years lacked any form whatever of such thought. The whole configuration of its culture has been determined – and dislocated – by this void at its centre.*

But the deliberate intellectual 'void' was partly filled up by literature – here viewed as an evocation of society's inner worthiness and cumulative wisdom. A tradition of poetic and novelistic revelation had constituted the spiritual 'centre of things', requiring only exegesis and commentary by literary criticism. The latter should not be confused with the short-winded build-ups and put-downs of Sunday-paper and weekly reviewing: as exemplified by F.R.Leavis and his Cambridge school it was conceived as a priestly calling rather like commentary on the Constitution – exalted tutelage of the national community-soul, the very 'essence of civilization'. Saved from vulgar 'ologies' and 'isms' this soul found more humane nourishment in a kind of imaginative-moral culture – fantasy educatively modelled to society's needs and supplying ineffably concrete answers to all the deeper questions.

The epitome of this ineffability is given in Leavis's critical method, wholly aimed at wringing a sort of inevitable moral consent out of his readers or listeners: all literary critique, as René Wellek put it, narrows down on to the question – 'This is so, is it not?' Farther probing of this unvoiceable intuition produced only farther evocation: the idea of 'Life', as found in his hero D.H.Lawrence. In the latter's novels 'Life' is victorious over 'class' – a natural, spontaneous something-or-other obliterates the insufferable constriction and deadly artificiality of society. The social order reverts to nature (i.e. Ukania's poisoned modernity is 'cured' by impossible flight inwards and backwards). One can only point at Life, not define it in arid categories. As Leavis wrote of Lawrence's *The Daughters of the Vicar*, Life has to be creatively presented, or exemplified:

> The phrase gets its force in the tale, the movement and sum of which define 'life' in the only way in which it *can* be defined for the purposes of the critic: he has the tale – its developing significance and the concrete particulars of its organization – to point to.

However, as Anderson points out, for the audience to understand such a gesture demands in reality 'a shared, stable system of beliefs...a morally and culturally unified audience'. Placing this kind of literary evocation at the centre of national civilization assumed that its prayers would at least make sense – that an answer was possible. Hence, though Leavis's guiding notion was that the ideal 'organic community' of England had perished and was due for reconstitution by such spiritual means, he could only preach that idea at all to an actually (if tacitly) existing organic culture – an intellectual class whose pulse would respond to the exaltations of Life and Community.

But this has an odd implication for Anderson's own thesis too. He argues that the structure of national culture has an absent centre filled (unsatisfactorily) by this kind of literary sermonizing. The absence is an intellectual one – that of 'a total theory of itself', the conceptual self-imagery derived from the usual sources of classical philosophy, sociology or Marxism. Yet as his own acute analysis of Leavis shows, such a 'vacuum' corresponds in fact to – and only makes sense in – a powerfully unified and stable cultural field. It follows that unity must have been attained by means other than the conceptual ones which concern him. The 'absent totality' is made possible by a social order which has – perhaps more effectively than its competitors – forged an underlying cultural cohesion owing nothing to (indeed opposed to) the 'typical' modern apparatus of social understanding.

That absent centre so ably exploited by the conservative immigrés in fact presupposes an entirely solid, if intellectually tacit, central *presence* capable of dispensing with theoretical toys. This centre has been maintained over the last century by assiduous, increasingly inventive cultivation of Ukania's pre-modern cultural inheritance: the rediscovery of presentable variants of national 'community' and 'tradition' capable of furnishing the necessary social cement – and, above all, of maintaining a sufficiently strong bond between the intellectuals and the masses. And in this generally successful project, the Monarchy has played a crucial rôle. The mysteriously missing focus of intellectual self-awareness is simply the other side of that success: a non-conceptual, emotional burning-glass through which social sentiments are consistently concentrated upon an effective symbol of (national) 'Life' – the concrete exemplification of a natural moral decorum transcending 'class', which can in the end only be pointed at and adored as a self-image unbrutalized by abstract notions.

This is surely the context within which England's Monarchy of Letters should be placed. The decorum of an essentially Royal literature imposed parameters rather like those Anderson observes on the plane of theory: traditionalism, conventionality and hierarchy disguised as family. The mixture was steadying but crippling, above all to the rebellious and emancipatory drive of an *avant-garde*. Hence Modernism was to have less long-term impact on English than on most other contemporary literatures. Above all after World War II its influence dwindled into that of the quiet counter-revolution more appropriate to the rediscovered domesticity of the New Elizabethan Age.

What New Elizabethanism called for was 'an enlightened literary class dealing with average beings...a poetical élite preoccupied with the trivialities of daily life.' In his study of Philip Larkin – the most significant member of that élite – Andrew Motion describes the context of his work like this:

> As well as stimulating a resilient and protective love for England and its traditions, the war significantly narrowed the country's social divisions and cleared the way for interest and pride in what had previously been condemned as "ordinary"...[32]

However, he falls into myth almost at once with an explanation of 'ordinariness' (a *Leitmotif* of the Movement Larkin headed) as produced by 'the levelling democratizing process which has gathered strength throughout this century'. The Movement's main ideological plank was in truth one of many *substitutes* for democratic levelling generated in those post-war circumstances – in the conditions of a democracy once more stalemated and stuffed back into the corsets of 'class'. The true contrary of 'ordinary' is 'extraordinary', and what made it poetical was the latter's constant, lurking presence: banality transfigured by the numinous. This corresponds exactly with the categories of Royal-national identity. Regal-spiritual equality metamorphosed into conservative nationalism, or 'resilient and protective love' for traditions. This is in turn the source of what Motion concedes to be 'revealing paradoxes' of the tendency's 'democratic manner': resentment of 'class' was accompanied by an intense class-consciousness which poetry alone transcends – that of their words and (by analogy) that of the English-British Word, the family which solves the aggravation as well as creating it. Later on all these apostles were to assume aggressively right-wing postures and Larkin especially – the true if formally unacknowledged Laureate of post-1945 Ukania – ended as an admiring supporter of Mrs Thatcher.

The Royally-grounded trajectory of Ukanian Letters had another significant feature underlined by Terry Eagleton in his essay *Exiles and Emigrés*:

> The paradox is...that with the exception of D.H.Lawrence the heights of modern English literature have been dominated by foreigners and émigrés: Conrad, James, Eliot, Pound, Yeats, Joyce...The unchallenged sway of non-English poets and novelists in contemporary English literature points to certain flaws and impoverishments in conventional English culture itself. That culture was unable, of its own impetus, to produce great literary art: the outstanding art which it achieved has been, on the whole, the product of the exile and the alien.[33]

Also, the exception turns out to be more than proof of the rule. Leavis's idol D.H.Lawrence was ultra-English all right. But his irrefutable stature lay in the total, Nietzschean rejection of everything existing English society meant. This impulse drove him in exactly the opposite direction to that seen in Eagleton's other names: whereas they colonized the corpus of England's literary culture from without (like Anderson's 'White' intellectual immigration), Lawrence was ejected from that culture's bowels and turned into a hopeless alien. This is why he ended in the 'Byronic' exile of Australia and New Mexico, scanning primitive life for clues to absolute truth. Had fate taken him to Southern Africa Prince Charles's Kalahari Bushmen would have been just as appropriate.

Speech and Silence of the Crown: Spectrogram of Greatness

It is easy to see that when the republican virtue fails, slavery ensues. Why is the constitution of England sickly, but because monarchy hath poisoned the republic, the crown hath engrossed the commons?

Tom Paine, *Common Sense* (1776)

To invent one world is, in modern times, to deny or suppress others. Individual and social cultures are in part defined by what they fail to look at, or flinch away from. Also, while such absences may be made to look accidental, they are rarely random or unconnected. Closer examination may show how they tend to support one another and form a pattern – the profile of an alternative character which it is necessary to keep at a safe distance.

What alternative is distanced by the official tongue and symbolism of Ukania? We have now drawn out some of its elements more than once, but it may help to attempt a brief overview here. The Crown ideology is earthed in modern Britain as a surrogate nationalism: the sole possible ideal vehicle for a State at once extra-territorial in its economy and multi-national in its ethnic basis. Monarchy offers a way of intensifying social bonds without raising the awkward definitional questions of political nationality: both 'community' and 'tradition' have been reinvented under its aegis. The former merges individuality into a moral or familial myth-entity, 'society' as second nature; the latter legitimates and gilds the infantile aspects of this bond as 'immemorial'. Were such a structure merely one of imposed reaction it would rapidly fail; but we have seen how it encompasses its own sub-mythology of adaptation – an ideologized 'flexibility' or openness to change. Since the 1830s that has been represented at Throne-level by regular 'modernization' and popularization: a message of 'appropriate' and dignified evolution, the 'really necessary' shifts by which authority is best upheld.

The Throne-level in itself would accomplish little. But (not for the first time) I must underline the pitfall of 'in itself'. The Monarchy is nothing in itself, but everything as part of a Monarchic Constitution. We will look at some features of the political Constitution in *it*self later. For the moment it's enough to point out how Royalism has persuaded people they live under the quite different system of Constitutional Monarchy, that is, a system whose precondition is exactly what Royal Ukania has steered the polity away from – a written Constitution embodying the Sovereignty of the People. This steering-course was made possible by the formation of an insular national identity: a conservative-popular simulacrum of nationality which made 'Britain' into a temporarily viable entity – the 'community' of an unusually protracted historical experience in common where ethnic differences were overlaid by the joint ventures of mercantile and colonial exploitation. That is (incidentally) the root explanation of the pathological over-exploitation of 'community' in Ukanian dialogue: whether uttered by the local Anglican Vicar or by Arthur Scargill, the sacral emphasis accompanying the concept alerts listeners to passage of a Regal *Geist*. When fused with 'class' its power of mental paralysis traditionally attained a devastating maximum – a sticky interior capable of drowning even the most noxious of intrusive abstractions.

Royalty has been essential to this 'overlay', to the crypto-Regal power which is the core of Anglo-British Statehood and its dense penumbra of customs and ritualized beliefs. What has been 'distanced' by it comports *both* democracy and nationalism in the senses characteristic of mainstream political development since 1776. It forged its own curiously early-modern substitutes for these. Although pock-marked by both wilful anachronism and a grotesque mimicry of modern forms, Ukania not only survived but occasionally led the developing 'mainstream' until the middle of the 20th century. For long what now appears the odd man out remained easily abreast of its more 'typical' competitors and descendants. There were both internal and external reasons for this and I shall return to the question below. But here let's concentrate on the underlying taxonomy of Monarchy and its occluded alternatives – that other Republican route which was not to re-emerge until well after 1950, when the political stabilization of Europe, the end of Empire, and the exhaustion of Royal Socialism have at last combined to replace it on the political agenda.

Regal Britain is the Capital: no mere central or administrative venue, but the spiritual defeat and annullment of its 'Provinces' in that voided sense I mentioned above. It stands for 'this country', the great estate: that is, the eclipse of 'the nation' in any sense either democratic or folkish – either a more popular or a more ethnic totality. The Crown-focused institutions of the estate have become all, the romantic concentrate flashed up as 'this small country of ours' where those beneath or in the outer margins can only define themselves by either open or covert dependency. In 1909 H.G.Wells noticed how London was really Hyde's Mortimer, or the 'Bladesover' of his novel *Tono Bungay*:

> Bladesover is the clue to all of England...There have been no revolutions, no deliberate restatements or abandonments of opinion in England since the days of the fine gentry, since 1688 or thereabouts, the days when Bladesover was built.

He points out how London's West End reflected 'the very spirit and architectural texture of the Bladesover passages and yards', and how the area's museums and libraries (for all their general utility) were also like 'the little assemblage of cases of stuffed birds and animals upon the Bladesover staircase grown enormous', so that –

> It is this idea of escaping parts from the 17th century system of Bladesover, of proliferating and overgrowing elements from the estates, that to this day seems to me the best explanation...

The epoch depicted in *Tono Bungay* is that where the

totemization of Queen Victoria coincided exactly with London's definitive take-over of provincial Britain and the fabrication of a High Imperialist variant of 'Greatness'. Until then the situation had been potentially quite different. Largely independent of Southern finance and culture, the lower orders of Britain's uplands and Northern river-valleys had at least maintained a self-respecting presence. The overweening dominance of European capital cities can be traced originally to the influence of Absolute Monarchy. Its supreme concentration of authority demanded an appropriately superb urban centre, the focal point for administration, military force, large-scale venality, and the symbolic display of architecture and other cultural forms. In England and Scotland, however, the defeat of Absolutism had initially opened the way to a much less centralized and Statified culture. In spite of the incipient tyranny of Parliamentary Sovereignty, what John Carswell calls 'old-fashioned particularism' fused with the tissue of English privilege and produced 'a durable pluralism that gave first place to personal and corporate rights'.[34] That was what Paine identified as the 'Republican part' of the Constitution a century later. Had the State been broken in a subsequent upheaval (or 'second bourgeois revolution') then of course such factors could have emerged to produce a political defeat of the South. The factors themselves persisted long after the political defeat the North's conscious agents in the earlier 19th century; yet the defeat itself was in the long run decisive.

In the later 18th century, for instance, the intellectual centre of British culture was not London but Edinburgh. Even in the mid-19th century, writes Krishan Kumar –.

> One of the outstanding facts about British society was its *provinciality*...It was in the tension between the metropolis – London – and the other great cities of the Kingdom that, in all the activities that concerned its health and vitality, Victorian society found its greatest resources of creativity and growth.[35]

This was true above all of social and political movements. Owing little or nothing to metropolitan influence, the public opinion they generated was usually anti-central, identifying London principally as the centre of Old Corruption and organized resistance to progress – the core of a slow counter-revolution in command of the State but not yet enjoying a hegemony of all social existence. This is why (as Kumar continues) – 'The major social movements, and a good deal of the social philosophy of the 19th century, had an unequivocally provincial origin'.

But it is precisely these bourgeois and radical tendencies which were sat upon and suffocated by the great Monarchic revival towards the century's end. The rediscovery and popularization of the Crown was simultaneously a reassertion of metropolitan all-importance. In his *Victorian Cities* Asa Briggs points out how –

> The story of Victorian cities in the 19th century is the story of the development of separate provincial cultures which during the last ten years of Queen Victoria's reign were increasingly "nationalized".

'Nationalization' here is given its true, inward sense: not just ownership by 'public' entity but expropriation by the national identity, subservience to a now organic social culture defensively regrouped about the Throne. The recastellated grandeur of an Imperial capital could no longer tolerate raw, potentially indigestible impulses from without (notably those of Republicanism).

Like Republicanism, radicalism and its 'Little England' creed of opposition to Empire and foreign involvement were mainly provincial in origin and now found themselves redefined by the new central glamour as narrow, second-best, somehow incomplete. They were unworthy of the centre's rediscovered glory, *passé* notions no longer measuring up to either the new depth of the Royal spirit or the imperial spread of British responsibilities. From being lively sources of innovation and opposition the provinces turned by degrees into pitiable annexes defined primarily in terms of what they no longer were or – worse still – in terms of an unexpected liveliness occasionally descried from the watch-towers of the South. It was during this same period that the centre expanded into its present location: no longer merely London but 'the South East' or metropolitan region, one colossal heartland suburb defined by proximity to the centre of things.

In his brilliant 1983 essay 'The British Monarchy and the "Invention of Tradition"', David Cannadine too has noted the prominence of Imperialist mythology in this shift, and its relationship to the Capital-provinces theme:

> During the first three-quarters of the 19th century, no royal ceremonial occasion could plausibly have been called an imperial event. But, from 1877, when Disraeli made Victoria Empress of India, and 1897, when Joseph Chamberlain brought the colonial premiers and troops to parade in the Diamond Jubilee procession, every great Royal occasion was also an *imperial* occasion...[36]

The new mass enjoyment and popularity of the Crown was in that context *also* imperial – 'An emblem of the British race, to encourage its expansion over the face of the globe', a perpetual 'family festival of the British Empire', and so on. The festival required an appropriate setting, which could only be an aggrandized Capital capable of holding its own in the new 'environment of extreme international competition'.

But it was never only this. As Eric Hobsbawm warns in an accompanying essay on the general topic of 'Inventing Traditions', the invariable real focus for such exercises was the Nation. The British synthetic Monarchism of post-1870 was only one of a broad range of comparable developments in late 19th century Europe – new ideological strategies aimed at containing and contesting democracy and socialism, by bolstering up or reanimating the old, the customary, the formal and the élite or noble. These trends sought to reanimate the world of honour and status, against that of equality, acquisitive individuality and contract. And it was precisely through that contrast that 'tradition' in the new, more self-conscious sense was elaborated – success being attained where (as in Britain) people grew convinced in a short time that such contrived harking back was the real thing. That (in the terms familiar to all Royal-watchers) there actually was a throbbing 'thousand years of continuity' behind each wave of the Lord Great Chamberlain's wand.

Britain was soon prostrate beneath the technicolor immemoriality and 'taste for pageantry' we know today. Yet as Cannadine and others have observed, this change was in decided contrast with what had been the actual customs of Victoria's Kingdom until then. The new, phoney Hapsburgism was imposed upon a country hitherto notorious for the squalor and incompetence of its public ritual. At least until the later 1860s the keynote of most public Royal occasions had been (as Cannadine puts it) somewhere between farce and fiasco. The Tudor and Stuart public displays of Absolute Monarchy mentioned earlier were one thing; so is our own intense and well-rehearsed theatre of decline. But in between these, under the Hanoverians, Royal ritual and public relations had sunk to the wretched level shown at William IV's funeral in 1837, and at Victoria's own coronation ceremony shortly afterwards.

Like his brother George IV (1820-30), William had also strained the patience of even the most resolutely sensible of subjects between 1830 and 1837. He is memorably described in Lytton Strachey's *Victoria*:

> A bursting, bubbling old gentleman, with quarter-deck ges-tures, round rolling eyes, and a head like a pineapple, whose sudden elevation to the throne after fifty-six years of utter insignificance had almost sent him crazy....He rushed about doing preposterous things in an extraordinary manner, spread-ing amusement and terror in every direction, and talking all the time.

It was in his reign that the Great Reform Bill became law. Missiles were thrown at the Royal carriage by Reform mobs in 1831-32, making the elderly sailor think Revolution was near. 'I feel the Crown tottering on my head', he is supposed to have said. He had consequently to be bullied into passing the Bill (and later tried, feebly and unsuccessfully, to get his own back by dismissing Lord Grey's reforming Whig government).

Like 'Prinny' before him 'Sailor Billy' was by contemporary standards a hopelessly cracked vessel of Royal authority. The former's vagaries were known to everyone, and not forgiven even by *The Times*. Though less of an occasion for open rejoicing, William IV's funeral produced mainly crocodile tears. The best that could then be said of him was that he had not wholly fulfilled his youthful promise as 'The worst kind of Hanoverian princeling: arrogant, insensitive; half buffoon, half bully.'[37] Apart from Queen Adelaide, the long faces round the death-bed were chiefly those of his bastards, worried about their final pickings from the Throne. Afterwards, the Lying in

State was the usual improvised British shambles, a 'wretched mockery' distinguished by constant sniggering and loud conversation on unrelated topics by the 'mourners'.

Yet somehow or other, a transition was accomplished from this to 'the finest pageantry in the world' – from a time when the new mass opposition of Chartism was automatically Republican, to the country of Victoria's Golden Jubilee in 1887, where a diarist noted gloomily in the wake of the delirium: 'I have made socialist speeches for years...and the last two days have shown me how useless they have been, and always must be, in this country.' In a comparatively short period, the insubstantial pageant of Royalty had acquired social body and psychic strength. What had happened? One of the few historians to concern themseles with the subject has offered the following diagnosis. Between the 1830s and the 1880s –

> The purpose for which ceremonial events were mounted underwent a subtle though crucial change. Traditionally these functions had been arranged as courtly pageants, in which the bulk of the nation neither expected nor wanted to participate. At best, people were meant to be passive spectators content with the merest glimpse of gorgeous trappings. In such circumstances mistakes were relatively unimportant, however annoying, since few people would know about them and even fewer care. But with the development of a widely read and influential national press, a sense of actual presence and participation could be imparted to everyone no matter how far removed from the scene. Moreover, with the introduction and development of Prince Albert's concept of a sovereign above party and of the crown as the representative not of a faction but of the entire nation, mystically embodying the national will, pageantry as the symbolic image of monarchy took on an enhanced significance.[38]

Thus, the reason why continental Monarchy put on better shows than the Hanoverians was simply that, with the exception of post-1789 France, the 'court' in the relevant sense remained far stronger and more extensive. Before the revolutionary wars and again after 1815, Europe was dominated by true *anciens régimes* where Kingship was the focus and self-reflection of unregenerate aristocracy, of a landed and military caste still far from extinction. By contrast, the English post-Revolution régime put up with a weak and historically illegitimate dynasty, predominantly for those negative motives mentioned earlier – as the sole way of keeping its legitimate Stuart rulers out, without risking another round of civil war and popular insubordination.

We saw previously how the crisis conditions of the 1790s and early 1800s had none the less produced a marked and exemplary change in both Royal public relations and popular attitudes – a new orientation related to the British national identity then called into being. Although in the middle of the century pressures in that sense had slackened (when Britain enjoyed pre-eminence) they returned once more in the last third: the 'extreme international competition' of Imperialism and the first symptoms of British industrial backwardness. But whereas the earlier epoch of challenge in George III's day ended with British victory, the second one never would: it was permanent. In that sense the 'crisis' was also to be permanent, knowing only brief moments of respite after the two World Wars (when a shadow of United Kingdom hegemony was restored by the military destruction of competitors). And it is of course in this period of enduring tension and relative decline that Monarchy has been consistently aggrandized and made something 'mystically embodying the national will' – the reinforcement of a threatened conservative-national identity by a kind of spiritual Absolutism.

The resultant Ukanian mystique is both pervasive and placeless, a Regal fog of all-purpose management and belonging within which are distributed 'chaps', who 'run' things. By far the most incisive description of this order of thing has been provided by Jim Bulpitt in his *Territory and Power in the United Kingdom* (1984). He describes there how Ukania's 'Constitution' bears the same sort of weird relationship to modern constitutions as 'class' does to normal social or sociological class. It has been 'run' by the Crown, or Crown-class, in a *sui generis* fashion impossible to pin down employing standard theories of the State (composed, inevitably, mainly from Continental or American models).

The fact is that until recently the Centre sought not to govern the United Kingdom, but to manage it; the code of an absentee

landlord with reasonably efficient local agents. Yet, paradoxically, the Centre provided one of the few sources of Unionist
sentiment in the system. It was prepared to brandish the
symbol of the Crown (the regal Union) when needed and, at all
times, it attempted to relate to (or distance itself from) *all* parts
of the periphery in similar fashion....Or, in terms more
appropriate to the country's history, territorial politics was
based on a court/country dichotomy. The joke, however, is
that this bias was facilitated by the advent of electoral
democracy...[39]

Thus, hovering loosely above the Home Counties, the 'Centre'
of Ukania guides the periphery with the support of like-
minded chaps 'out there' (occasionally also 'up there' or 'down
there'). 'We live', as Sidney Low wrote over half a century ago,
in *The Governance of England*, 'under a system of tacit
understandings, But the understandings themselves are not
always understood...' Courtly authority functions far better
without such pedantry.

Hence internal articulation of Great Britain is neither
federal, confederal, nor 'unitary' in the formal and bureaucratic sense of (say) France or Sweden. Unusually unified in
certain respects, it none the less allows different nations, legal
and school systems to persist. It sanctions even different
legislatures: weird self-governing and self-taxing anomalies
like the Isle of Man and the Channel Islands. Attempts have
been made to show that behind this informality lies a structure
of 'internal colonialism'. But, while there are certainly elements of this in the relationship, it cannot be made to stick as a
theory either: there has been too much accident, and far too
much mass and élite collaboration over long periods.

When (for instance) there was agitation for more self-rule in
Wales (of the sort that punctuated proceedings at the 1969
Investiture), the Régime did not reply with a dose of the
'colonial' repression so familiar from the history of its overseas
possessions. The Welsh, and later the Scots, were invaded by
chaps: vexed Professors, precautionary Conferences, Royal
Commissions, sermonizing Ministers of the Crown, responsible Party Leaders keen for compromise followed up – once the
subject had thoroughly sunk into these quicksands of ver-
bosity – with two Parliamentary Acts which totally defied

Republican comprehension. By that time a combination of economic slump and Ukanian boredom had so blunted the wish of the subject-peoples to be free, that nothing could safely be allowed to happen.

What counts here is *culture*, in the broader sense. The Centre radiates Received Pronunciation: knowing how to speak, amplified into knowledge of how chaps behave. Jim Bulpitt's penetrating diagnosis goes on:

> The British....resolved the contradiction of local self-govern-ment and "partnership" within the unitary system by manufac-turing a common culture at both the Centre and the periphery; a culture in which the "chaps" involved (both bureaucrats and politicians) would behave themselves, would not overstep the mark. In short, everything depended on an elaborate system of compromise and mutual deference between political and administrative elites...

This text is remarkable for its key use of a term normally absent from established political science: 'chap'. Bulpitt obviously found no alternative, yet he does not define it properly. Foreign readers are liable to be completely bewildered by its use, and would get worse than no help from an expedition into the *Oxford English Dictionary* ('lower jaw', 'buyer or custo-mer', 'cause a fissure', 'fellow or lad, once contemptuous', etc.). At such moments the *Geist* is always in the offing: a spectral guiding hand from the Upper Spheres, bearing tinctures of Royal plasma to the most humdrum of committees and the angriest of opponents.

Even this mode of hegemony requires one location, however: one non-ethnic, non-regional and non-popular focus for its transcendent articulation of civilized unity. And this can only be the court-location of the Crown – the *capital* in a sense at once civil and irresistibly or naturally supreme. Small it may be, but this is a Country that makes sense only in relation to a Court. The civil and ideological hegemony characteristic of Britain's Royal – or élite-charismatic – authority has both the advantage and the disadvantage of being 'placeable', non-abstract: a national reverence for the concrete, abbreviated into the bright colours and individual physiogn-omy of Royalty. One aspect of this was an inevitable localization of the Word: as a polysemic or depth-charge word, 'England' assumed the courtly estate-resonance of the South or 'Home Counties'. Though able to extend itself by sheer expansive grandeur to Jarrow and Polynesia, the taproot of Monarchy's revived glamour was really fixated here.

Both the provincial and the lower-class counter-movements silenced by metropolitan magic were, inevitably, couched in more abstract terms. The advance and the advantages of abstraction are inseparable from real modernization (as distinct from the crab-like displays of its Britannic simulacrum). Modernity demands a degree of radicalism; but there is no radicalism (whether of the Left or the Right) not driven on by some degree of faith in ideas, in an imaginative vision vigorously counterposed to the (all too concrete) status quo of experience. The story of the modern British Ideology pivoted on Royalism is one of how this status quo has again and again broken the political teeth of opposition by inducing the metropolitan Word – ultimately, the Word of Regal Constitutionalism – down its throat.

After its initial triumph over the Scots and the provinces, the Word has defended itself successfully first against a castrate national Left and then since 1979 (much less successfully) against the overdue assault of a *petit-bourgeois* Right. What is specially interesting in the present context is to look back at the fate of Ukania's Metropolitan Socialism – the official 'alternative' allowed house-room in the downstairs parlour (with occasional use of the conservatory and library). Labourism has never been (as so often depicted) merely a matter of the ascendancy of (wise, moderate) 'reform' over (crazed, foreign) 'revolution'. These are labels stuck on Ukanian conflicts mainly to conceal their true character. What counts is Brit-Soc's *Royal* character – the secure domination of a Crowned head over the confused moral volition of its provincial limbs. And at bottom what this reflects is no more than (as Perry Anderson put it) 'the spatial map of British capitalism', where the old mercantile South never lost its political and ideal grip over the new industrial North – retaining it so well, indeed, that it ended by fostering a working-class movement in exactly the same mould:

In effect, the cold economic fact that London remained

throughout the 19th century largely a rentier, commercial and bureaucratic capital, dominated by court and city – closer in some ways to Vienna or Madrid than to Paris, Berlin or St Petersburg – was to be a major obstacle to the emergence of a politically aggressive labour movement in England. A capital without heavy industry helped to separate a factory proletariat from an instinct for power...It might be said that London ended by bureaucratizing Northern moderation into a municipal-national system, in the age of Morrison.[40]

Yet it is exaggerated to describe the South's hegemony over the Left as mainly a matter of administration. The Labour Party, in particular, has conducted repeated anxious inquiries of its own on the subject, all revealing only a pathetic travesty of 'bureaucracy': Lord Wilson's famous 'penny-farthing bicycle'. Rather than from bureaucracy, its reforming achievements have been inseparable from a Royal-paternalist centralism requiring the structural suppression of more democratic or populist alternatives. And this process has always been far more that of an ideological Court over its well-meaning but ill-formed Country cousins: National presence implies assuming one's ('rightful') place within the historic Palace-framework of the South, duly attuned to the latter's antique but responsible *moeurs*. Bureaucracy in a more genuine sense ought – like educative and cultural effort – to be among the strengths of the Left. The virtual absence of both things from Labour Party history simply reflects the strength of what has taken their place: a Royal spiritual concrete consistently poured out to reaffirm the hold of Civilization over troublemakers from the bush, making 'promising' backwoodsmen of them and smoothing their path upwards into the light. The 'spatial map' of capitalist evolution in Britain is one of human and social geography, rather than of a simply territorial North and South: and it carries the Royal coat-of-arms. Westminster's courtly institutions furnished both the spine for an entirely Parliament-oriented opposition, and an encompassing culture within which all essential questions of democratic and national identity had been forever resolved.

It was not (for example) even necessary for Labourism itself to be formally democratic: in spite of occasional bouts of half-hearted reform (the most recent in 1980-82) it remains governed by a typically informal, familial *entente* – or occasionally *mésentente* – between Parliamentarians and the trade-union leaderships. Its key organizational nexus is not undemocratic but anti-democratic: the plebeian obverse of patrician familiarity, vehicled through a pseudo-proletarian rhetoric of 'Unity'. What 'unity' in this castrate sense denotes is class solidarity minus formal democracy and individual rights – the totemic or anthropological allegiance of 'class', rather than the political transcendence of genuine class struggle. This is why, as Anderson was later to write, events which anywhere else would have led to either revolution or counter-revolution produced in Ukania a strengthening of conservatism. The 1974 miners' strike was 'the most spectacular single victory of labour over capital since the beginning of working-class organization in Britain' and 'the only time in modern European history that an economic strike has precipitated the political collapse of a government'.[41] And yet, all it produced was a Labour government bent on healing the wounds to 'consensus', on the restoration rather than the radical reform of the old Crown-State.

Such was the claustrophobic definition of civilization into which British Socialism grew up. Potentially the most subversive of provincial forces, based on the working classes of South Wales and the Northern and Scottish river-valleys, its representatives were taken over and thoroughly transmogrified by the customs of the new Imperial Cathedral. The latter's institutional nationalism relegates both State (vulgar bureaucracy, pen-pushers) and People (sturdy fellows, football hooligans) to an attendant stance: the former as instrument, the latter as subjects. The Royal-national identity rests upon Parliament, instead of democracy; flexible customary software rather than the democratic hardware of a defined constitution; the great-estate bunkum of community, class and 'compromise' in preference to nation, equality and principle – and so on: those sentiments of an eternally preservable national Life which have from our own mid-century decayed into today's fitful death-march. It is in this fuller semantic context (the field of its meaning, rather than of its separate existence as a sign) that Monarchy may be said to have actually *become* that sniffy suspicion of 'success' and of humourless principle, that contempt for not knowing how to behave and for straight lines which (as estate visitors learn from their guide-books) makes up the way of life.

Kitsch Identity: Sinuosity of the Truly Royal

Whereby her beauty reigns remote from Time
Blooming untouched as on a branch...sublime.
> Adrian Bury, poem '*On Seeing Pietro Annigoni's Portrait of Her Majesty Queen Elizabeth the Second*'.

Farther clues to the concrete and the curvaceous may be obtained from certain modes of depiction of Royalty. In everyday life the Royal Family is of course represented in many different ways: photographs both 'live' and posed, T.V. and filmed images, cartoons and satirical drawings, and the impressions of artists. We have tended to deal with radio and T.V. above, since they represent the most obvious symptoms of 'modernization' between the 1920s and the present day. The definitive icon of the reign has not been provided by these, however. Old-fashioned portraiture was responsible – indeed, the most old-fashioned and aggressively anachronistic style of depiction at that time on offer in the art markets of the world. This is of course (as it has so often been described) the 'image of the reign' given by Annigoni's 1955 State Portrait painted for the Worshipful Company of Fishmongers.

Created soon after the Coronation, it was meant to convey the spirit of the 'New Elizabethan Age' and rapidly became by far the most familiar and most frequently reproduced view of Elizabeth II. It shows her in three-quarter length wearing the dark blue cape and star of the Order of the Garter, gazing to the left with a kind of imperious innocence: youth and beauty uplifted into a Sovereign trance, Royal courage enhanced by the cold light of the early spring scene evoked below. In the Royal iconographical tradition this picture enjoys a distinct place. That tradition passed from the portrayal of Absolutist grandeur – as in Rigaud and Van Dyke – to one of family intimacy, the apparent union of dynasty with domesticity.

As Simon Schama has put it in a rare study of the process:.

> Once the means of mass production and distribution of images
> was available, allegiance (or at least the sentimental bond forged
> between monarch and subjects) depended on a steady flow of
> appealing images. Beside the continuing importance of military
> uniform and coronation robe portraits, the genre of nursery
> album pictures and conjugal portraits became the stock-in-
> trade of the monarchy-mongering business.[42]

The pseudo-domestic style is best represented in recent times
(e.g.) by James Gunn's conversation piece of George VI and his
family at tea in Windsor Lodge, displaying the Royals round
the table 'just like us' with a single empty place to which the
spectator is implicitly invited. Annigoni's depiction, however,
introduced another dimension appropriate to the age actually
dawning in the 1950s: for though in obvious ways the
Fishmongers' portrait comes within the category of formal or
'coronation robe' depictions, it also belongs unmistakably to
the world of *Kitsch*.

Its cold, waxy texture and contrived enigma of pose and
expression, and the association of a 'mysterious' cloaked
femininity with the weak, frondy lyricism of the ultra-English
landscape (Windsor Castle itself shadowed in the right-hand
boscage) brought the Royal Estate finally into line with
Tretchikoff and the Mona Lisa cult: a frankly popular icon
whose real content is stereotyped sentiment. Both the open
and the latent contents are frankly expressed in Annigoni's
own memoirs. On one hand he felt the episode was like an
affair of State: 'Looking back it is like a half-dream in which I
took part in a light opera, with a military band playing off-
stage for the Changing of the Guard ceremony and a Real
Queen as the heroine'; but on the other hand his initial absence
of inspiration was really solved by a fleeting glimpse of Her
Majesty in the Palace corridors, as off-guard and sylph-like as a
Mills & Boon heroine: 'I glimpsed her eager young profile
against the autumn evening light...' and by this mildly erotic
shock 'she was momentarily transported in my
imagination...etc.'[43]

This painter was already established as a master of up-
market *Kitsch*, and had been promoted in Britain as such by Sir

Alfred Munnings and other champions of anti-modernism. After initial failure Annigoni was ushered through the portals of British culture by Munnings in the famous speech where he said of Picasso: 'Don't you think if we could meet him somewhere in the dark we should kick him in the pants?' He was rapidly established as '*the* painter of beautiful women' in Britain, though still continuing to churn out religiose images back in Florence. It was one of the latter which had a prodigious triumph at Wildenstein's gallery some time before the Royal commission. The *Times* critic found himself a little non-plussed by this story-picture, reporting:

> He has a large painting of what appears to be a headless stuffed dummy on a table with three figures contemplating it; this is entitled 'Sayest Thou This is Man?' and evidently it has some deep message.

But the message turned out to be one which registered with the inner self of the host culture. It is eloquently conveyed by the ghost-writer of the painter's memoirs:

> In the foreground on a wooden stretcher lies a straw-stuffed dummy – the artist's "lay figure". Behind it to the left is the *maestro*'s self-portrait: with his index-finger he points accusingly at the dummy, a symbol of modern man, inert and debased, a spiritual corpse stricken by his own godless despair. To the right stands his model, a lithe lovely figure almost nude, fair-haired and also wrapt in the *maestro*'s teaching...Behind the figures, all life size, broods a storm-racked sky with massy clouds, and a single blaze of lightning illuminating the stern face of the master.

Crowds flocked to gaze at this object's lurid charm in Wildenstein's window, and Annigoni was deeply touched by 'the love and reverence evinced by the less wealthy, by the humblest of London's citizens who came thronging to see his works'. The stage was set for the great post-Coronation picture.

In accordance with the rules of *Kitsch*, the Fishmonger portrait's formal invocation of reverie invites each viewer to his or her own 'personal' interpretation of the message. But the same rules ensure all such interpretations will coincide on a lowest common denominator of taste. The image's brilliant success lay in its perfect reconciliation of Sovereignty with trash: State Portraiture had become now implicitly yet utterly at one with the universe of souvenir-mugs and soap-opera – hence the unprecedented success of the picture in reproduction and popular esteem. As the painter Laura Knight said, perhaps with a touch of envy: 'This was their Queen as the British people had always wanted to see her portrayed – at once the natural, human girl they loved, and the Sovereign they honoured and revered'.[44]

What that successful union suggested was a people basically at one: joined at one crucial neuralgic point of identity (however wildly they differ in other respects). One image magically acceptable both to Barbara Cartland readers and Academicians, to the out-of-work and the aristocracy, at home in Offices of State and the humblest of parlours, in classrooms and dentists' waiting-rooms – a single icon turning almost anywhere into 'Home' in that Stately sense essential to the Monarchic Constitution. A true icon of Royalty (as Judith Williamson observed in the essay referred to earlier) has to be polysemic or multi-meaning: it packs together a wide range of significance into single emblems which can then be 'read' from differing social angles. Men, women, children and different social classes all have their own Monarchy: 'Our own dear Queen', in Piers Brendon's phrase. And yet this varying spectrum of emphases can also be *one* – reconciled at some deeper level by one enchanted glass.

The nature of that enchantment, incidentally, was to be cruelly underlined by the fate of one of Annigoni's later efforts. This is the far less familiar picture in the National Portrait Gallery commissioned by Roy Strong. It attempted to portray pure Sovereignty through an austere image undefiled by charm; the result was something like a fuzzy Russian wooden doll, quite devoid of polysemic or other appeal. But H.M. and the Tory critics loathed it. The *Daily Telegraph* art correspondent said it 'failed to catch the magic that has touched millions...No nuance of character is conveyed, no intimation either of a vital human being or of a symbol of majesty' (February 1970). It was in fact curiously like the straw-stuffed dummy which had first impacted on mass sensibility twenty years earlier: the spiritual cadaver of a Monarchy which, once denuded of its 'They're just like us' glamour, has nowhere to retreat to.

But the lapse had little effect upon the broadening tide of Royally sponsored anti-modernism. In 1984 Prince Charles delivered some interesting thoughts upon this question of national life-style, in a speech to the Royal Institute of British Architects. He began with family reflections about his great great great grandfather. Queen Victoria's husband Albert had involved himself heavily in architectural matters, and bequeathed us 'a series of buildings which never fail to fascinate and which display great individuality – though always inspired originally by some earlier style of architecture'.* Balmoral and Osborne House are of course prominent in this perspective: gloomy displays of mediocre revivalism.

But much more striking is what the Prince of Wales left out. As well as the 'farm buildings and interiors' to which he also refers, his ancestor played a decisive part in something else altogether. His real significance in this field – surely worthy of mention in any address to architects – lay in his close connection with the most modern building of the 19th century. This structure displayed no 'individuality' in the romantic sense, and owed nothing whatever to any earlier style of architecture. It was designed by a gardener, gave powerfully functionalist expression to the high-tech engineering of the day, and reduced many traditionalists to apoplexy. Joseph Paxton's Crystal Palace was put up in Hyde Park to house 'The Great Exhibition of the Works of Industry of all Nations', and advance the cause of Free Trade. In his speech inaugurating the show's fund-raising campaign, Albert stressed its international aims:

> We are living at a period of most wonderful transition, which tends rapidly to accomplish that great end, to which, indeed, all history points – the realization of the unity of mankind...Gentlemen – the Exhibition of 1851 is to give us a true test and a living picture of the point of development at which the whole of mankind has arrived in this great task, and a new starting-point from which all nations will be able to direct their further exertions.[45]

Albert's rôle in encouraging and securing the approval of

Paxton's plan has been documented by biographers and historians. Indeed, his attitude towards this prodigious piece of (in today's language) 'anti-architecture' was the diametric opposite of what was to be disclosed to the R.I.B.A. audience by his great great great grandson. The Prince Consort and his supporters found themselves assailed by fogeys both old and young, from John Ruskin ('a cucumber frame between two chimneys') to the notorious Colonel Waldo Sibthorp, M.P., who prophesied 'the desecration of the Sabbath, the demoralization of the people, a disunion of parties, and increasing poverty to a most serious extent'. In a sardonic letter to the King of Prussia (who had urged his own family to boycott the Official Opening of the Exhibition), Albert commented on the inflamed mood of orthodoxy:

> Mathematicians have calculated that the Crystal Palace will blow down in the first strong gale, Engineers that the galleries would crash in and destroy the visitors; Political Economists have prophesied a scarcity of food in London owing to the vast concourse of people; Doctors that owing to so many races coming into contact with each other the Black Death of the Middle Ages would make its appearance as it did after the Crusades; Moralists that England would be infected by all the scourges of the civilized and uncivilized world; Theologians that this second Tower of Babel would draw upon it the vengeance of an offended God. I can give no guarantee against these perils, nor am I in a position to assume responsibility for the possibly menaced lives of your Royal relatives.

Prince Charles by contrast chose to voice the characteristic contracting fogeyism of the 1980s Kingdom: that of 'welcome reaction to the modern movement which seems to be taking place in our society', a sanely romantic nativism reflecting 'the feelings and wishes of the mass of ordinary people in this country'. Much of his time was devoted to the universally approvable maxims and admonitions found in any Royal speech: help for the disabled, and good news about community (in this case, 'Community Architecture'). But then came the famous 'giant glass stump' (a contemporary version of Ruskin's 'cucumber-frame'): his denunciation of the redevelopment plan for the City's Mansion House Square. This envisaged a Mies van der Rohe tower on one side: something 'better suited to downtown Chicago than the City of London', in the Prince's obviously heart-felt opinion. He continued with a eulogy of what he imagines to have been the 'Venetian' character of the pre-stump metropolis, where – 'the affinity between buildings and the earth, in spite of the city's immense size, was so close and organic that the houses looked almost as though they had grown out of the earth and not been imposed upon it'. This is the old low-level townscape originally praised (and turned into permanent ideology) by Steen Eiler Rasmussen's *London: the Unique City* in 1934.

One denunciation led to another. What, he asked, was modernism now about to do to Trafalgar Square?

> What is proposed is like a monstrous carbuncle on the face of a much loved and elegant friend...it looks as if we may be presented with a kind of vast municipal fire station, complete with the sort of tower that contains the siren.

He was referring to Peter Ahrend's design for an extension to the National gallery. Not long after this Royal complaint the plan was rejected (as was the Mansion House project). And in both cases a search was begun for safer alternatives more in tune with the nervous insipidity of most of the capital's other Windsor-period monuments. Had Charles been addressing the architects of the later Habsburg Empire, one can imagine how much he would have found to praise in the decorous pomposity of the *Ringsstrasse*, and the malicious mockery he would certainly have aimed at the carbuncles of Otto Wagner, Adolf Loos and the young Ludwig Wittgenstein.

Berthold Lubetkin commented at the time upon the curious, almost totalitarian reflexes which the Prince's address had both revealed and exploited. These emerge at its climatic moment, a Crown clarion-call for the organic and the familiar, eerily reminiscent of Stalin's 'The proletariat has acquired the right to its own Corinthian columns':

> Why can't we have those curves and arches that express feeling in design? What is wrong with them? Why has everything got to be vertical, straight, unbending, only at right angles – and functional?...The present day school of Romantic Pragmatism could at least provide an alternative.

Thus, the curvaceous or undulant conveys feeling: straight

lines and right angles do not. Bending with due humanity is the essence of taste, or more exactly (as Charles went on to underline) the opposite of 'imagination without taste'. The latter – fantasy divorced from 'the mass of ordinary people in the country' – leads straight into what Stalin called 'the bog of reactionary cosmopolitan opinion'. Romantic-national pragmatism by contrast bends with a self-conscious grace before the wind from the past, and knows how to make smiling allusions to its own second-hand nature: it inclines to the close and organic, the spirit of a Royal earth – all those features we saw earlier displayed in the Karl Kraus-like story of the Advanced Passenger Train

There too, all things maturely considered, humourless direct lines melted back into the ineffacable contours of the Royal terrain: not just the land of great estates where roads curve discreetly round field-ends to avoid disturbing the view from the terrace but also the home of Mr Michael Foot, John Betjeman, F.R.Leavis and Archbishop Runcie, whose politics cling to the past as intently as its culture grows from the pragmatic earth. Again we perceive how the Royal nature which resisted Jacobinism must surely resist over-abstract engineering barbarism too. Don't both of these problematics centre upon brutal interference with all our natural affinities – those noble and inbred impulses rendered elective by a national identity chosen and honed against the onslaught of modern times?

Estates of the Realm

> *To Captain*
> Knowst thou this shore, sir?
> *Capt.*: Your sir is pleasing in my ears; no sound
> Has quite the sweetness of the bending spine.
>
> *The Prince of Antioch: or, An Old Way to New Identity*,
> by William Shakespeare (Nigel Dennis), in *Cards
> of Identity* (1955), p.238.

I suggested earlier that in the Royal-family sense 'class' has very little to do with the wider and more typical concept evolved by Marxism and academic sociology to explain the general process of industrialization. British class-in-inverted-commas represents an historical pathology of stratification, and not (as once so widely and piously believed) its standard anatomy. In terms of this study, what it stands for could be called the Royal Wound: the holy ailment both constitutive of and inseparable from all the strengths and the weaknesses of a powerful but anachronistic identity. A deviant category every bit as peculiar as the Windsor Monarchy and the Unwritten Constitution, the social anthropology of Britain's obsession with 'class' has since the demise of Chartism signified little but a special double-edged mode of corporate adhesion to all the national status codes. Such acceptance is often grumbling and may even find expression in the cultivation of life-long resentments. But so what? That's what stable family life has always been for some. As parents have always been quick to point out, in a shop-soiled phrase which Mrs Thatcher infused with new life in the 1980s, 'There Is No Alternative'. Also, this familial existence traditionally had at hand a host of pretty reliable rewards and potent tranquillizers to compensate for all the frustration, immobility and claustrophobia.

It is worth recalling too that Ukanian pseudo-familiarity reconnects at a few points with a genuinely immemorial inheritance. Dynastic and aristocratic States accounted for most of man's history until the later 18th century, and their hegemony over the Old World did not end until 1918. By contemporary, nationalist standards they paid relatively little attention to whom they reigned over. It was (sometimes) important to keep their peoples happy, but of little significance what tongues they spoke, which songs they liked, or how their 'customs' related to others. Priests were supposed to take more interest in all that, as part of the care of souls; but even their concern was not ethnic in the sense of anxiety for (say) the Finns or the Irish *as* Finns and Irish. Universal religions had their primary investment in the souls of all God's children, and hence in an uplift transcending the minutiae of nationality.

Thus, literate ruling castes and clerics typically presided (or 'lorded it') over illiterate and usually ethnically mixed populations with different languages, who normally either disliked or were indifferent to one another: fairly unimportant facts, when set against the everlasting verities of Throne and Altar. In 'agro-literate societies' (as Gellner calls them):

> Thanks to the relative stability...sharp separations of the population into estates or castes or millets can be established and maintained without creating intolerable frictions. On the contrary, by externalizing, making absolute and underwriting inequalities, it fortifies them and makes them palatable, by endowing them with the aura of inevitability, permanence and naturalness. That which is inscribed into the nature of things and is perennial, is consequently not personally, individually offensive, nor psychically intolerable.[46]

However, that era began to give way to another in the 17th century. What the Dutch and English 17th century Revolutions launched was in that sense a three-century-long disintegration of the universe of estates and millets. Although Absolutism fought back to preserve honour and servitude it could do no more than slow down the spread of the new age's main characteristic: a relative but chronic *in*stability. Under agro-literacy the urban middle classes had been secondary; now, capitalism propelled them into inevitable prominence and influence. Above all, moves towards the creation of mass manufacturing (and then later, machine-industry) tended to unsettle or even upset the old order. They undermined the landlords' revenues and pulled away their labour-force; and – equally important – they demanded the constitution of a new and at least minimally literate working class. Early industries could make do with unlettered and innumerate people straight from a rural background. But the kind of consistent development implied by industrialization needed a degree of education. In the terminology of our own epoch – when development has become a global problem – it required the 'mobilization' of all available resources: and the principal resource everywhere was people.

This elevation from field-folk to 'workers' brought in its train an unfolding chain of consequences, and certain crucial ones related to nationality. As Ukania still suggests in a ghostly subcutaneous tracery, nationality had been of small account to true *anciens régimes*; but as these now plunged forward into modernization, they encountered a fatal contradiction. The reason was that no true dynastic régime could undertake the necessary 'mobilization' of its human resources without putting at risk all forms of traditional authority. 'Development' could not avoid shaking Throne and Altar, and eroding 'inevitability, permanence and naturalness': hence, the authority-structure of dynasty was bound to be challenged. Literacy and urbanization sprang apart the social universe of 'estates or castes or millets', and made the ethnic-linguistic more central: for the question of *which* language (or more widely, which culture of identity) one was educated into became crucial. People liberated from their estates commonly faced this dilemma.

In the vital area of central Europe (for example) should a South Slav or a Bohemian try to 'become' German, since German culture had (inevitably, in the first instance) become the vehicle of industrialization? The choice was a hazardous one, given the natural advantages enjoyed by ethnic German speakers and the limits of assimilation. He might try his best and still end up as a stoker or a ticket-collector. The alternative was to remain proudly himself, and work for the modernization of the Slav countries or Bohemia 'in their own terms'- with the different perils of repression and defeat inherent in nationalist politics. Assimilation – presented by the ruling, courtly culture as the sensible course for all moderate folk – entailed the long-term erosion or even disappearance of a culture; but resistance promised agonising, long-term conflict on every front from the factory-floor to the concert-hall.

Had 'Progress' been a purely economic matter, something to be calmly run from above – as old élites from the Venetian Doge's Council down to Sir Robert Armstrong have invariably prayed for it to remain – then history's course would have been different. But fortunately, the second or nationalist alternative was most often pursued. Progress through trade and industrialization invariably released political demons, a class consciousness and varieties of ethnic-national consciousness: and in one combination or another, these always proved fatal to continued dynastic rule. *On the whole* the demons were beneficent, although their very force also held the potential (in extreme circumstances) for unheard-of new malignancy.

Until the 1970s the Ukanian attitude towards this dominant theme of modern history was: nothing to do with us. The Crown's harmony betokened a civilized nation's triumph over such rude and damnable dilemmas. With the exception of Ireland – shrouded in decent forgetfulness until around 1970 – the realm appeared to have exchanged them for the single, stable and universal embarassment of 'class'. In this way a unique feat seemed to have been achieved. The fixity and almost unalterable status-system of agro-literacy had some-how been carried forward into a modern and reputedly industrialized society. At least a degree of inevitability, permanance and naturalness still attached to that system, which in Britain continued to externalize inequalities through vocation, education, speech, dress and 'manners' and also provided an appropriate variety of social punishments and rewards meant to stiffen the hierarchy against headstrong individualism ('bounders', 'counter-jumpers', those thinking money is everything, chaps who won't play the game, etc.). While often psychically intolerable to intellectual bounders who had let foreign bees get under their bonnets, the evidence suggests this hybrid social order remained quite palatable to most of its inhabitants: the majority consciousness of confine-ment within a 'class' was palliated by material betterment during most of the century from Victorian times until the 1980s. Psychically it was if anything over-compensated by the regularly victorious and increasingly picturesque patriotism of Crown extra-territoriality: the refulgent glamour of Empire and Greatness.

The resultant national identity can be approached from different angles but focus on its curiosities may be helped by looking backwards from the present day. An acute recent analysis is worth citing here. Modern societies rest on 'a shared view of the world', suggests L.A.Siedentop, 'a way of looking at things which makes it possible to have stable expectations and which provides channels for both cooperation and peace-ful conflict'. This is of course substantially the point made a number of times above, vis-à-vis nationalism and modern development. Without it (he continues) people will be 'thrown into the world merely with fragments of identity. Lacking a viewpoint or *core* of identity, they find it difficult to pursue any consistent course in life...' So he concludes:

> Does British society provide its members with such a viewpoint? I think not. Whereas most developed Western societies reflect adherence to what can be called, very broadly, liberal principles, British society has for several centuries sought unity in manners rather than in ideas. It has, *de facto*, discouraged discussion of what Marxists would call ideology, preferring to rely on shared manners or civility as the cement of society. "Decency" and "commonsense" have been the undoctrinaire watchwords...[47]

This has been accompanied by a mode of 'gradualist politics' which actually fitted the 'early achievement of representative government in Britain' – the 18th century order in which different patrician cliques manoeuvred and compromised with one another for power. Though very advanced in its own time (by contrast with a still Absolutist Europe) the extension of such a system to first the middle class and then the 20th century working class has turned it into a cramping stranglehold on change. It was a way of 'making possible a *limited* amount of social mobility', by permitting limited shifts of direction among the élite and keeping the upper stratum 'open' (though never wide open) to new blood. However, first industrialization and then (more acutely) the difficulties and decline of British industry made much larger shifts necessary; and an apparatus constructed for the management of inhibition has been congenitally unable to cope with this. Its supporting corset of decent manners and gentlemanliness has become an inescapable tourniquet, the cause of consistently ebbing circulation, inertia and (finally) of gangrene.

Pointed as it is, this sociological portrait too has an interesting blank at the centre. Siedentop sees national failure as linked to an *absence* of comprehensive viewpoint or 'shared beliefs'. The theme is echoed in many other theories of British decline. What the notion seems to imply is that there is an absence of *respectable* or rational ideology. In other words, there is no 'bourgeois ideology' in the canonical sense prescribed by the various 'isms' which intellectuals have elaborated and to which all liberal statesmen have given at least formal allegiance over the last century and a half. Also – and presumably related to the void – there is a consonant lack of philosophical vexation about the ideas behind these 'isms' – what Siedentop calls 'The traditional embarassment of the British when faced with general ideas – that embarassment which has contributed so much to comical writing and the theatre'.

The analogy with Perry Anderson's argument is very striking. In both cases what cannot seriously be admitted is any absence of shared beliefs *as such*. However unrespectable, anti-intellectual, mawkish or eccentric, the socially dominant belief in Monarchy as a mascot of 'the British way' is far too palpable and important to be dismissed. It is simply and blatantly not the case that H.M.'s subjects find themselves thrown into their distinctive culture-world equipped with mere fragments of identity. The truth is closer to this: few (and perhaps no) other States in the industrialized part of the globe offer such a distinct, popular and technicolor 'core of identity' as Ukania. Set in the fuller context we are considering bit by bit – the sheer institutional weight of Westminster, Law and shamanic Constitution, as well as their dense cultural side-growths – the structure is overwhelming. Far from suffering *anomie*, no other modern collection of peoples has been so helplessly over-identified for so long.

The reason Royalty doesn't count in the Siedentop or Anderson perspective is presumably its 'irrational' nature: being 'instinctive' it has to be beneath serious notice. The very popularity of Monarchy is made to count against it. The atmosphere of tabloid Monarchy, with its chimpanzee antics and drugged hysteria, may be seen as evoking the zoology of an under-class like George Orwell's 'proles' rather than the respectable working-class psychology of a 'modern industrial nation'. Beneath contempt, such manufactured delirium therefore disappears from these sober diagnoses of 'what's wrong with Britain'. The author's new version of this sempiternal issue is that –

> The chief characteristic of an aristocratic society remains – that is, a fairly strong sense of being fixed in a social position. The typical English conception of society remains a corporate one, the image of a hierarchy of classes essentially different from one another...

While all this may 'provide stability and keep anxiety at bay', its true significance lies in having kept healthy individualism at bay: it prevented the middle classes from being the effective bearers of 'an individualist conception of society'. This is why enterprise culture is doomed in Britain and industry flounders. No *rational* bourgeois world-view was generalized by the bourgeoisie. Instead, a sinister combination of aristocratic embrace and Imperialism led to 'a partial collapse or failure of middle-class values and ideology which is basic to an understanding of the condition of Britain today'.

As a negative diagnosis this is wholly justified. Yet it side-steps the whole problem of what the national identity of this former Great Power really was: of just how and why such an archaic and class-ridden State dominated the world for a century and a half. After all, that long success keeps it going now, in spite of whatever elements of 'collapse and failure' may also be present. Ukanian ideology may indeed be an embarassing and retrograde guest at the feast of ideal modernity. However, it sat (and occasionally seemed to sit almost alone) at the head of that table for a very long time; and – as we noticed – it's still run by people who more than half-consciously feel it belongs there for ever. The 'proles' feel the same way. Only a formidable and very positive identity-structure, surely, could have lasted so long and resisted 'decline' so effectively?

In part the significant confusion arises from a false and over-rational model of national identity itself. Though of course it must hang together in order to function, such a structure does not have to cohere like an intellectual construction or theory. Also, it is never present as one entity in experience – being a set of conditions *of* communal experience, it can't be 'held in the mind' like an image or the gist of some theory. Its disparate elements are experienced separately, and the way in which these support or reinforce one another may be unknown to (or only obscurely felt by) the subjects of the identity. The less reflectively or philosophically formed an identity is (as in the Ukanian example) the more important this broader and less conscious dimension is likely to be. 'Nationalism' usually evokes a posture of alert self-awareness: *our* values aggressively asserted against someone else's. But of course this kind of definition occupies a relatively small amount of individual or social time. For the rest people are 'being themselves', normally without worrying just how their behaviour constitutes the 'Britishness', 'Frenchness', etc. which has sometimes been asserted by force of arms or through political and cultural contestation. The overall pattern of any national identity can only be discerned by viewing these different dimensions in relationship to one another. In the British case the Monarchy provides the best view-point for doing so, and we now have some clues as to what they are.

In this context, what becomes of Gellner's supposedly fatal contradiction between estate inertia or caste-outlook and industrial modernization? How *can* 'class' have been reconciled with industry, and quasi-feudal manners have survived into the age of the third industrial revolution? The answer to this is in one way simple: it hasn't, and they haven't. Such things survived in amended form all right; but not into 'an industrialized society', for the good reason that the industrial modernization *of society* has never occurred or indeed been seriously attempted in Great Britain. Ukanian State and civil society have remained mercantile-capitalist in structure, not industrial-capitalist. They represent not an industrialized social order hiding behind early-modern or neo-feudal façades, but an early-modern reality which became part-industrialized and then (afraid of the results) sought stability at that point. Eventually – after the decisive failure of British Socialism's re-industrialization project in 1964-67 – it began to retreat from industry altogether. After 1979 slow retreat turned into a race: breakneck reverse 'modernization' aimed at restoring British capital's ancient parasitic or 'outward-looking' function rather than 'national industry' in the previously obligatory sense.

The historical fact is that in Her Majesty's domains categories like 'modernization' and 'remodernization' have only ever applied in what one might call a rhetorical or Parliamentary sense (and that sense is itself regularly employed to occlude the fact – nowhere more notably than on the political Left). In his classic account of technological history, *The Unbound Prometheus*, David Landes explains how the rise of capitalist-governed technology has had –

..explicit consequences for the values and structure of the economy and society, consequences that centre in the principle of selection by achievement....This universalistic standard of selection contrasts sharply with the so-called "particularistic" criteria of the preindustrial society, dominated by agriculture, landed property, and an Establishment resting on interlaced family ties and hereditary privileges. Men are chosen, not for who they are or whom they know, but for what they can do....The logical concomitant of such selection is mobility: otherwise, how make the choice effective? A competitive industrial system will therefore place a premium on easy movement of labour power, technical skills and managerial talent. It will encourage people to move from their ancestral homes and families to work in strange places; and it will increase social mobility, raising the gifted, ambitious, and lucky, and lowering the inept, lazy, and ill-informed... Industrialization is, in short, a universal solvent, and its effects are the more drastic the greater the contrast between the old order and the new...[48]

A marked impersonality usually attaches to economists' descriptions of these changes ('The dissolution of all bonds', as Marx put it in the *Communist Manifesto*). Populations are reconstituted like ants at the bottom of a box, and the agent is 'it' (Capitalism or Modernization). In reality 'mobilization' was also self-improvement, choice, conscious adjustment, making new starts or the best of awful circumstances. Culture and literacy did not only claim people; people claimed them, and to some extent re-made them to fit.

That side of the story has been told most famously by Edward Thompson's *The Making of the English Working Class* (1963). However, as his title indicates, such redemptive history has focused overwhelmingly upon people as class – more exactly, as class tending towards the self-obliteration of 'class'. This might not matter but for the tacit exclusion of something more important: people as nation or – at that moment in social history – people also on the move from mere nationality to 'nationhood' in the sense of conscious participation in national community through literacy and citizenship. Only in English conditions was the particular progress and the special bias of Thompson's approach possible. That is, in an island where a single ethnic mass had already attained relatively easy and uncontested hegemony – both isolated from broader and more typical dilemmas in Europe, *and* spared them at home.

Elsewhere, the bias could not help ending up the other way. National *ethnos* rather than social class became the primary factor in popular emergence and self-definition – in that 'making' which Thompson rightly stresses. In Central and Eastern Europe above all the impact of capitalist industry, literacy and mounting social mobility was to generate the characteristic forms of aspiration and conflict determining the historical mainstream until after World War II. Within that area, one domain was crucial in every sense. The Habsburg Empire embraced Germans, Hungarians, Italians and a variety of Slav peoples under a single dynastic Crown – a Europe in miniature, and often seen as such by both its defenders and its foes. Like their Windsor successors the intelligentsia satirized in *The Man Without Qualities* imagined the Crownlands as forever imparting crossroads-messages about harmony and reconciled contradiction, but enemies had a soberer and more truthful vision of the Hapsburg 'prison-house of nations' – of an archetypal Old Régime struggling with long-accumulated cunning to preserve dynasty, caste, religion and Baroque grandeur against the national liberation of its peoples. There one could of course also say that the old order was sitting on 'democracy' and the class-emancipation of Czech, Slovak, Croat and many other workers. But in Austria-Hungary, as in most of Europe (and most of the world thereafter) social liberation *could* only take the form of national struggles.

In the Windsor domains where the class-nation bias ran another way, there arose that marked tendency already commented upon to assimilate nationality to mere emblems or not-quite-serious display: definitely the kind of thing foreigners go in for. This conservative misreading sees national 'identity' as dissociable from the substance of a nation's *culture*, in the broad or anthropological sense (not the high-brow sense). Chaps who know all too well 'who they are' don't need that kind of display. Hence the regulative understanding of identity is perceived as moral, religious, or even as literary and literary-critical. The Crown-culture's identification codes inherit this a-national cast, and what is really the communication-system of a nation-state existence assumes a virtually Japanese impregnability.

The system also transmits its characteristic set of birthmarks, however. These have become better and better known during Britain's decline, as the port-wine stains have turned into inescapable death-marks. One can read them off (so to speak) in the negative by simply referring back to Landes's general formulae. 'Selection by achievement' is supposed to take over from the 'particularistic criteria' linked to 'an Establishment resting on interlaced family ties and hereditary privileges'. In Britain, it never has. This fact has been the burden of so many complaints, polemics, despairing analyses and flights into exile that a chapter would be required merely to list them. For half a century (until Mrs Thatcher) British domestic politics consisted in little but crocodile tears about this beloved burden, followed by (at best) footling rearrangements of its weight to keep the victim staggering forward.

'Geographical and social mobility'? Modern British society has been stamped by chronic *im*mobility on both fronts. Unwillingness to move and inability to rise have anchylosed the social structure. This anchylosis is manifested in the Régime's literary self-image as well as in apartheid-like housing policies to cage off the under-class. Triumph over the industrial pseudo-revolution and Chartism turned British society into 'by far the most stable in Europe', notes Franco Moretti in a study of the social novel:

> In this framework, the notion of social mobility cannot evoke the certainly ambiguous but fascinating and vital figures of Julien Sorel, Rastignac, or Bel-Ami. It has rather the bestial and slimy face of Uriah Heep, the feeble and snobbish behaviour of Pip in *Great Expectations*...Here is a solid world, sure of itself and at ease in a continuity that fuses together "tradition" and "progress"...a world that cannot and does not want to identify with the spirit of adventure of modern youth.[49]

Thus the 'universal solvent' has here been neutralized, or turned into a kind of ideological glue. The profound arrest entailed by this path (Moretti goes on to observe) brought an exaltation of childhood or youth in a contrary sense to Sorel's spirit of enterprise and adventure: the fabular world of a perennial, somehow inescapable youngness – at once prison-cell and arcadia – which resonates through all the later confinements of society's rigid 'second nature'. The result was to be a thousand 'Public School' novels and plays, so many tearful exacerbations of 'class's' suppurating wound. 'The term "second nature" is just what we need' (Moretti goes on cruelly) – 'for isn't an English plot a sort of visit to the zoo, where countless and amazing exemplars are offered to our eyes, each one tightly locked in his cage...keeping alive the taxonomical rigidity of "traditional-feudal" thought even *after* the erosion of its material bases?'

Landes's attention is forced back to this queer dénouement: how on earth did the strong right arm of Prometheus Unbound end up with Harold Wilson, Blue Streak, the A.P.T. and *Upstairs, Downstairs*? 'How much' (he asks) 'have objective principles of selection really governed the assignment of position and responsibility in societies like England, where higher education has been the prerogative of a favoured few, and where personal connections have been an open sesame to success, in business as well as in social intercourse and politics?' Unfortunately, his answer is vague: 'No economic and social system...has ever been pushed to its extreme logical consequences'.

Actually, the point is not a general (and dubious) one about humanity's non-extremism. It concerns a social order deliber-ately reined back and – inexplicably, in Landes's own terms – guided away from the 'logical consequences' of massive industrialization: a long and slow counter-revolution within which non-objective principles were reanimated and all the illogical consequences of a pre-industrial world were given new authority. 'Man is too perverse a creature to admit of absolute systematization', he sighs, '(and)...vested interests have ways and means to preserve something of their advan-tages'. Truisms apart, *what* ways and means?

The Monarchy was one of these ways, and an especially crucial one in the sense that it functioned as cynosure or catalyst for so many others – the reference-point of a general renovated traditionalism now made over into national-popular identity. Cultivated anachronism was necessary to this new dynamic, which was like nationalism in its effects yet had to avoid so much of the standard content of that 'ism': it strove to assimilate the consequences of industrialization to the hierarchy of an older version of capitalism – the mercantile-landed élite whose 'collective Monarchy' had reigned since 1689. But an assimilation *without* surrender to equality and generalized individualism could only assume a compromise or corporate form – the synthetic estate-psychology of 'class' and social place.

This was how a new kind of what Gellner (above) called 'relative stability' was made possible: the pseudo-estates of an industrialization limited and de-natured by a unique range of older societal pressures. Though not formal or 'sharp separations' in the genuine *ancien régime* sense, these to some degree compensated for their fluidity by high ideological profile – by an exaggerated conscious externalization, propagated (like the rest of Ukanian folklore) from above yet ultimately accepted and reproduced as identity below. By later Victorian times these were indeed 'endowed with the aura of inevitability, permanence and naturalness' although never (of course) really as 'psychically tolerable' or 'inoffensive' as serfdom and slavery had once been. In the modern world they have had an equally inevitable (but generally harmless) accompaniment of disseminated resentment and festering personal grudges, particularly among those escaping from the system or crossing its partitions. Such ideological acne accounts for a good deal of 'class' in its distinctively Ukanian-deviant sense.

The national bending spine also has a familiar corset to help its curve stay in place: the Honours System – another of those Ukanian Courtly phenomena which 'serious' minds tend to flinch away from or dismiss as trivial. As well as the daily media spectacle and nightly communion, Monarchy also refracts a more direct beam of ennoblement into every sector of the social body through it. 'The most carefully preserved status game in the world', commented Andrew Duncan, fully understandable only by 'a virtuoso of hierarchical jigsaws'.[50] Twice yearly the refulgence is distributed, in Honours Lists of those reckoned to have served the public weal sufficiently well.

In a panegyric in his *Review* (1707), Daniel Defoe described money thus:

> Mighty *Neuter*! Thou great *Jack-a-both sides* of the World,
> how hast Thou brought all Things into Bondage to thy
> Tyranny? How art Thou the mighty WORD of this War, the
> great Wheel in the vast Machine of Politick Motion, the Vehicle
> of providence, the great *Medium* of Conveyance, in which all
> the Physick of the secret Dispensation in human Affairs is
> administred, and by the Quantity of which it operates to
> Blessing or Cursing? Well art thou call'd *the God of this
> World*...

But 'Honour' is only the spiritual money of Monarchy: a
coinage which, though now distributed by governments, owes
all its real value to the Royal source. Distribution is regulated
by the Ukanian chart: a single status-system knitting together
the social order into one accepted and constantly renewed
hierarchy – all 'merely symbolic' of course, like the Crown
itself. The only defect of the argument is (as usual) that the
'merely' is Crownspeak. A five-pound note or a cheque is a
wholly 'symbolic' artefact: does it follow that the existing
social order would easily survive the sudden disappearance of
such tokens?

Some honours are distributed by rote, notably to Civil
Servants and other cogs of the State armature. But in the larger
arena where this does not apply, for months beforehand the
general dream-life of grace and order is intensified to fever-
pitch in the thousands of homes and offices where at a given
moment 'recognition' is just possible, and half-awaited. But
which precise quality of recognition? In what gallery of the
vast edifice is one's contribution to be hung for public view?
How visible will it be? Cosiness and *Angst* grapple daily as the
postman approaches, either with or without the Letter from
Downing Street. Far below the five categories and five degrees
of the real peerage, beneath even the ephemeral 'Life Peers'
confined to a single generation of Lordship, there is the
anguishing problem of exactly where in the Most Excellent
Order of the British Empire or the Royal Victorian Order the
long overdue thanks for service will be lodged. A Knight or
Dame Grand Cross, a Commander, an Officer – or down amid
the barely-distinguishable mob of 'Members 5th Class', an
M.V.O. or M.B.E. eternally and helplessly exposed (after the
inevitable praise) to deflating comment?

Reveries of improbable heights like The Order of Merit (limited to twenty-four) or The Order of the Companions of Honour (restricted to sixty-five), vie with fear of an acknowledgement 'hardly worth while' (yet virtually impossible to turn down). 'The boardrooms of England, the green rooms of theatres, the ostensibly blasé headquarters of television executives, reek with the scramble for honours', observes Duncan. For most the pinnacle remains the genuine, mediaeval Royal Touch of the sword in Sovereign hands: 'Deftly, carefully, the Queen taps the recipient on his right shoulder, then with an elegant flick of the wrist, hits the other shoulder' to convey Knighthood. Ennobled or bemedalled, he or she then shuffles backwards (generally to the accompaniment of the Royal Marine band playing thoroughly bourgeois muzak like *If I Were a Rich Man* or *I Love Paris in the Spring*, rather than Handel or Vaughan Williams).

Other governments and states bestow symbolic rewards for public service, sometimes with titles or medals attached; and there too a degree of snobbery and social utility may go with such distinctions. Even Socialist states have their own accolades, also designed to support the status quo and also pined for by possible recipients who have 'done their bit'. It is often argued that our Royal apparatus is merely another example of a universal tendency, by implication neither much better nor much worse than others.

But this ignores two features which together do render it unique. First, its sheer mediaeval complication, and its intimate links to an already powerful Royal ideology and Establishment. No other system of official recognitions constitutes such a huge and integral social universe extending from *Burke's Dormant and Extinct Peerages* (1978) to West Indian fast bowlers and village postmistresses. It crosses and cushions those class boundaries otherwise so prominent in British life – by endorsing society's spiritual regulator valve, it effectively confirms the principle of hierarchy upon which these rest (even in disgruntlement). Second, no other system is sustained and informed by the single principle of Royal gift and patronage: it may be governmental and Parliamentary committees who select the fortunate, but they do so only as conducting rods for the Crown's lightning. No other system ranges and locates moral-spiritual authority so completely, or – as I shall try to show – in such unison with the long-term needs of a governing élite.

As Michael De-la-Noy puts it in a recent examination of the whole system:

> If Great Britain became a republic, an honours system could still exist, but without the Queen and the Ball Room, the debonair members of the Household, the fabulous china in glass cases, the baroque and the gilt, the sense of having wandered into the home of someone who is better off than you but really just the same, it would all be seen as far less fun and far less glamorous...far less unreal, part of that seemingly necessary fantasy world of pantomines and soap opera.[51]

So, when recipients say they feel 'society' has acknowledged their efforts, in practice this means a social order given savour and beneficence by the Royal element. It is not the abstract 'society' of sociological theory which has blessed them, but England-Britain. However many the intermediaries, the benison of regal grace has furnished the essential glow, a spark of binding mystery. Without the 'visit to the Palace' the whole antiquated and cumbersome system would not stand up for a single session without revision. As things are, it is with the rarest exceptions accepted unquestioningly, and indeed gratefully, as one of the advantages of Ukania. Through ennoblement or recognition the symbol-world constantly re-penetrates reality, re-transforming it into the spiritual commodity of 'place'. A sort of cosiness is radiated through alienation: a warmth of belonging and self-regard which no mere reality could bestow. While it lasts this adhesion to the organic whole will, like Monarchy itself, continue to eclipse all the attendant absurdity, brazen anachronism and belligerent snobbery.

The Royal Prerogative

Authority is a characteristic of social organizations as general as society itself...It is in this sense more general than, for example, property, or even status.

Ralf Dahrendorf, *Class and Class Conflict in Industrial Society*.

Contrary to P.N.Furbank's diagnosis above, there is nothing whatever subjective or arbitrary about 'class' in the sense he is so anxious to denounce. He made the mistake of assuming that because British 'class' doesn't exist in terms of its own myth, it doesn't exist at all (except 'in the mind' of grudge-laden beholders). The point is surely that (as the Marxist historian R.S.Neale has written) – 'The first thing to do is to cease visualizing or conceptualizing social strata or social classes as separate boxes'. This box-consciousness, and the barbed wire and sentry-posts of inclusion-exclusion, suppress the central nerve of the social process: power. 'It appears to me' (Neale wrote previously in his introduction to *Class and Ideology in the 19th Century*) 'that social class seen merely as social strata is a dead thing, useful as a background for description but lacking that element of movement over time which is the essence of history.'[52] When made a foreground – as in the distinctive rigidity of speech-obsession – the effect is of course just this: deadening of the 'element of movement', or containment of those aspects of the 'essence of history' inconvenient to Royal tradition and community. Or in other words, the sapient cramping and diversion of that underlying movement Marx in the Manifesto believed to be inseparable from 'the giant, Modern Industry..(and)..the industrial millionaires, the leaders of whole industrial armies, the modern bourgeois...'

Dahrendorf's view of power as the real essence of class defined authority as operative within 'imperatively co-ordinated associations'. And as Neale points out, the nation is the most significant such association. In *Languages of Class* Gareth Stedman Jones has minutely described the post-Chartist subordination of class-consciousness in that sense. Once the earlier Republican struggles had been defeated –

315

A second formative layer of historical experience was superimposed upon the first...The struggles of the first half of the century were not forgotten..(but)..the solidarity and organizational strength achieved in social struggles were channelled into trade union activity and eventually into a political party based on that activity and its goals. The distinctiveness of a working-class way of life was enormously accentuated. Its separateness and impermeability were now reflected in a dense and inward-looking culture, whose effect was both to emphasize the distance of the working class from the classes above it and to articulate its position within an apparently permanent social hierarchy...[53]

'Class' in this modern British sense was 'a culture of consolation' which now 'sang *Jerusalem* not as a battle-cry but as a hymn' and 'accepted not only capitalism but monarchy, Empire, aristocracy and established religion as well'. It was built around the pickled and fermenting memory of past political defeat. The first working class had been the first to be defeated and incorporated into a still strongly developing capitalist nation-state. It was this experience of containment and frustration which produced subordination and maximum social *apartheid* – the 'apartness' and those resolute caste-marks celebrated (as we saw earlier) by Norman Birnbaum and so many others.

The real blood from King Charles's neck gurgled through the planks of the Whitehall scaffold in 1649 and mourners crowded round to mop it up with handkerchiefs as a Christly symbol of the departed age. From the ever-open Regal wound of English 'class' there flows a cultural blood to which similar properties are attributed: as long as it can be sniffed hope remains for the salvation of an older and more humane world, a wholesome progress unscarred by vicious abstraction, anomie or impersonality. The pathology of 'class' is not a manifestation of separate and unconquerable will, but of acceptance. This acceptance was forced, but became conscious and – in a key term of the Old Régime's English – 'deferential'. Deference may also be resentful: but this is the rankling, nostalgic and repetitive resentment which subsists after losing a war, not incipient revolt. Far from being opposed to the Shils-Young sociological *Schmalz* about integration and consensus, such marks have themselves become perverse ways of belonging to the national community: the social anthropology of a separate 'place' and life-style within ('against', yet also defined by) a larger traditional unity. Class in the broader or epochal sense is a contradiction generated by industrial capitalism and urbanization: a secular transformation of the tides and of the greater human shoreline. 'Class', in contrast, is like a parochial tide-pool deposited by one particular mode of failed modernization: the stagnant waters of an 'industrial revolution' doomed to containment and then dehydration within an older and more specialized capitalist polity.

That polity's triumphs as an authority-system rested upon such contained passivity. As I noticed earlier, to say that Estate-Royalism was a 'surrogate' or deviant kind of nationalism doesn't imply that it was weak, or ineffective. On the contrary, its mobilizing power was always formidable: what may appear as deformations or forms of backwardness in the broad comparative perspective of modernity were linked to remarkable internal strengths. Again employing terms from classical sociology, Ukania is a variety of synthetic (and often preposterously phoney) *Gemeinschaft* – instinctive, customary, or pre-rational community. Although conspicuously (and in a sense deliberately) lacking in the alternative characteristics of *Gesellschaft* – rational, contractual and individualistic society – such absences also fostered astonishing coherence and solidarity against the barrage of external threats to which extra-territorialism was inherently prone.

The strengths of this odd national identity – collective Monarchy harnessing 'class' loyalism – nurtured what Keith Middlemass has called the 'corporate bias' typical of the system's self-regulation. The inertia of this sedulously preserved estate mentality lent itself well to an informal corporatism of outlook. Working-class institutions turned into 'estates of the realm', committed to cooperation with the State, even if they retained the customary habit of opposition to specific party governments. But while the opposition was theatrical ('adversarial') and intermittent, the deeper will for consensus was tacit but continuing. It worked by exploitation of the all-important inner, informal authority-structure rather than through formal bureaucracy. As Middlemass observes –

> In direct contrast to the rigid linkages lain down...in the Fascist constitutions of Italy or Portugal, or the totalitarian systems of Hitler's Germany and Stalin's Russia, the British system in the half-century after 1916 depended on a multiple bargaining process at all levels...even though its aims of social harmony, economic well-being and the avoidance of crisis were not dissimilar.[54]

This informality absorbed some of the strength of the traditional élite structure which it contested. Under the thrice-blessed title of 'consensus', its categories of 'fair play', reasonableness and customary rights (vocalized in trade-union ideology as 'free collective bargaining') proved effective most of the time. Break-downs like the General Strike of 1926 and the miners' strike of 1973-4 had little effect on underlying attitudes save to strengthen them. As a consequence, 'the harmony which was achieved enabled governments of the 1930s and '40s to maintain order and consent and to survive the Second World War as no other European State did'. The self-regulating, informal Royal polity –

> ...ensured a uniquely low level of class conflict compared with countries of comparable social and economic development in Western Europe. Britain was the one society to survive the collapse of political values in the 1900s...without lapsing into authoritarian rule or political decay. It is reasonable to assume a relationship between internal political harmony and national survival, if only to explain the absence in the 1930s of effective revolutionary discontent, and in the 1940s of opposition to the rigours of war: Dunkirk, after all, was the symbol of national reconciliation, not its cause.

Up until 1979 the greater Estate was regulated by an historic machinery designed to suppress conflict through an ever-growing jumble of corporate compromises and balances: Ukania's enchanted forest of Royal Commissions, Boards, Councils, Inquiries, admonitory Reports and impartial Arbitrators of this and that. The most incisive recent sketch of this terrain is the one provided by Raphael Samuel, in a 1985 polemic on the miners' strike. Contrasting Britain to the ideas expressed in John Rawls's *A Theory of Justice* (1971), he pointed out that the latter – like any theory drawn from

post-1950 society in either Western Europe or North America
– simply took for granted a whole range of non-Ukanian
factors. It assumed, for instance –

> The political practices of a society where citizen powers are
> written into the constitution, where controversial items of
> public expenditure are the subject of referendums, and where
> there is a Supreme Court to arbitrate on the moral legitimacy of
> social claims. It presupposes freedom of information, highly
> visible interest groups, a written constitution to serve as a
> charter of rights...[55]

But this is why a translation of Rawlsism and similar creeds
into the Queen's English is bound to generate gibberish-laden
confusion. The reason is that modern concepts are being
squeezed into reluctant copulation with the Burkean pho-
nemes of emotive custom and personalized reasonableness. Its
hybrid results may appeal to academics but (like Marxism) are
precluded from any real effects upon the non-Republican
polity:

> None of these conditions obtain in Britain, a society hon-
> eycombed with invisible powers. Here government is typically
> – even obsessively – secretive. The system of representation is
> not transparent but opaque; decision-making is not an event
> but a process. Judges do not make law in Britain, they only
> follow precedent. Policy emerges from administrative neces-
> sity, rather than from legislative enactment. Nobody is respon-
> sible in Britain for anything...[56]

It is quite true that metaphors are indispensable for the mode of
argument I have adopted in this book; and true also that
metaphor can mislead as well as illustrate. However, it may
also be worth recalling that the official Ukanian identity-charts
themselves consist of little else. The 'Industrial Revolution' in
particular has been the largest and most lying of metaphors,
indicating a supposedly total transformation of British society
by the prime mover of modernity, industrialization. This
transmutation was unique because peaceful: the managed
miracle of Britishness. It seems to follow that a State and class
equipped with such secrets must be capable of resurrection.
Failure of the second miracle to occur so far is explicable solely

in terms of policy (preferably economic): the managers are out of practice and despite some decades of honest trial and error haven't pulled it off yet. Their ability to do so is indubitable, however: after all, 'getting the economy right' seems quite a minor feat compared to that of leading the whole of humanity into modern times.

So, a perverse metaphorical perspective is bound to suggest itself from any point of view putting Royalty first. In this disreputable sight-line there was no such event or process as the 'industrial revolution' (and hence no call for the customary upper-case letters). There was of course rapid primary industrialization in certain upland areas of the Kingdom, generating plenty of unsavoury problems. But the *revolution* associated with these occurred elsewhere, when an imitative industrialization was promoted by more backward States in less homogeneous societies. In the United Kingdom itself an over-developed form of mercantile capitalism already existed (after an earlier revolution) and had achieved what was to be permanent expression in a natural élite-management State. Such venerable entities were neither averse to nor particularly interested in river-valley industrialization, machinery, manufactured exports, 'G.N.P.' and other fetishes of the new age: they simply learned to manage its problems, and prevent these doing too much damage to their established interests and way of life. It was especially important to limit the corrosive spread of vulgar creeds like individualism and egalitarianism: that was why the grosser features of aristocratic rule summed up in 'Old Corruption' had to be got rid of after 1830. As part of the same movement a more popular style of conservative nationalism was (as we saw) constructed around the synthetic institutional cults of Crown, Westminster and the customary Law.

This stiff and hampering folklore-from-above discouraged the more rampant excesses of industrial capital: its cultivated rigidities of status and culture naturally impeded the 'freedom' of economic man so trumpeted by *petit-bourgeois* ideologists. But by keeping that middle class firmly in its place, reactions to such excesses could also be in their turn muted and contained. All the extra-oligarchic strata were held 'in their place' by the same degree of immobility, deference, spine-curvature and consciousness of 'class'. As long as external and colonial dominance was upheld – that is, the conditions inherently favourable to the prosperity of the 'upper class' Southern commercial and financial nexus – there were no insuperable problems in maintaining this cramping yet beneficent 'backwardness'. The semblance of contradiction arises only from treating 'capitalism' as a single dark room full of black cats – from thinking with Marx that the bourgeoisie *as such* stood for a revolution which has 'put an end to all feudal, patriarchal, idyllic relations (and)...pitilessly torn asunder the motley feudal ties that bound man to his "natural superiors"'.* Had it really and with iron inevitability 'stripped of its halo every occupation hitherto honoured and looked up to with reverent awe', then the occupation of Monarchy could never have become decked with new awe under the later Queen Victoria, Ramsay Macdonald would have remained a clerk, and Eton might now be retraining workers to write software for a booming native electronic industry.

In reality (as Marx's own broader historical studies suggested) capitalism was a multi-phased transformation, the early-modern stage of which was not only compatible with, but dependent upon, the retention of some 'patriarchal' relations and motley feudal (or at least élitist) ties of dependence, hierarchy, and pre-egalitarian grovelling. True, only exceptional circumstances could have allowed the indefinite persistence of this stage. But these are precisely what the Anglo-British oligarchy enjoyed after its defeat of France: an unmatchable political strength giving it far greater purchase over the development of civil society than that enjoyed either by struggling *anciens régimes* or (until well into the present century) by the precarious new-bourgeois States that took over from them. 'Class' is nothing but the internal fossilization – wondrous yet wounding – deposited by the resultant long historical fixity of British power. It is the congealed, scab-like social memory of democratic defeat and containment, and of the rich culture of consolation evolved for and by the prisoners once the lock had turned and the key been thrown away. Only an authority so continually and irrefutably deployed from above could have constituted the crippling yet reliable psychosis of 'class consciousness', which has ended with today's accumulation of political apologies and literary *Doppelgängers* haunting a unique physiognomy of decay: phosphorescent populism presided over by high-cultural gloom, fake rusticity and an almost Viennese nostalgia for the days of yore.

4

QUIET REPUBLICANISM

'The project of modernity, the hope of Enlightenment thinkers, is not a bitter illusion, not a naïve
ideology that turns into violence and terror, but a
practical task which has not yet been realized and
which can still orient and guide our actions'.

Richard J. Bernstein, 'Introduction' to
Habermas and Modernity (1985).

4

Quiet Republicanism

From Bang to Whimper

When I speak of Ancient Britons, I am suggesting that we live in an archaic political society...It is commonly and comfortably said that there is nothing basically wrong with British Institutions – 'the finest in the world' – but that they are not working well because the economy is in such a bad state. The reverse is true. The reason that the British economy does not work is that British Institutions are in terminal decay.

> Neal Ascherson, *Radical Scotland*
> October-November 1986.

In this comment on the tragi-comic inversion of Ukanian politics, Neal Ascherson has recently pointed out one way of answering the identity-question: what Monarchy actually means is that we decide every day to remain 'Ancient Britons'. 'Like an animal' (he wrote earlier in *The Observer*) the existing Ancient-Brit identity 'cannot think about itself'.[1] 'True thoughts are those alone which do not understand themselves'. The truth is the fact of being constitutionally incapable of understanding itself – signalled through the taboo around the Crown. What that taboo *means* is (as he goes on) the whole works: our settled, indefeasible place in front of Nigel Dennis's 'Hyde's Mortimer', the family home –

> We are gazing from the terrace of a country house down carefully-landscaped perspectives of barbered lawns and positioned trees. The eye is masterfully led down a vista of elements

325

(this battle, that Cabinet) chosen to combine with one another into a single artistic experience. You could say: "Prune back that Reform bush and make the Tolpuddlia bed twice as big". But you would feel a bit of a vandal...

Modern U.K. Republicanism has been unfortunately little more than this vandalizing impulse, taboo-shrunk to mere naughtiness: unable to upset the landscape, rebels are reduced to stealing Papa's stamp-album or carving their initials on the ancestral furniture. During the 1964-66 Labour government its most radical Minister was reduced to a campaign to remove the Queen's profile from some of our postage-stamps. His efforts were neatly foiled.[2] But of course real Republicanism would have by contrast paradoxically little to do with the Monarchy *as such*. It can only acquire sense and public dignity as a refutation of what the Crown *means*: that is, as a refusal of the whole estate and a demand for the new constitutional habitat which must one day replace it.

It may be useful here to look backwards again, to the fate of the main historic foe silenced in the 19th century by the restored ascendancy of the Royal Word – to unjustly ignored battles fought and lost generations ago. Though I have touched on the subject a number of times, there are still some important lessons in the later decline and fall of Republicanism worth considering. The old Chartist question had been: How can Old Corruption ever be overthrown without getting rid of its most blatant and odious symbol? How can a new, democratic nation ever arise without destroying this bloated embodiment of the old one – the hoary, false 'nation' of the Norman Yoke, Lordship, the Rotten Boroughs, and Property? Though defeated by the long counter-revolutionary struggle which ended at Waterloo in 1815, and farther circumscribed and defused by the dismantling of 'Old Corruption', such attitudes were by no means extinct after Chartism's decline in the later 1840s. This was proved by the way in which they were revived in the 1860s and early 1870s. However, it must be conceded that over that period Republicanism had dwindled from Chartism's big drum down to a virtual whimper.

That was the era when Victoria practically vanished from public life after Albert's death in 1861. She appears to have been spiritually felled by the Prince Consort's departure, and for some time thought in terms of passing the rest of her life mourning for him. 'To speak in rude and general terms', wrote Gladstone at this time, 'the Queen is invisible, and the Prince of Wales is not respected'. It began to look as if Albert's previous and highly successful efforts to modernize the Monarchy might have been in vain. If the Queen were to pass another twenty years in such seclusion and then be succeeded by another George IV, the institution might not be salvageable. It was in this stale and ominous atmosphere that the foreign events of 1870 suddenly impacted.

In his study of *Victoria's Heir* (1940) George Dangerfield describes how –

> The fall of Napoleon III, the subsequent declaration of a French Republic, shook the English monarchy as a minor earthquake shakes a house. The floors heaved, the plaster pattered down from the ceilings, here a picture crashed to the ground, there a statue fell upon its nose; and people began to wonder whether the whole picturesque edifice would not come down in ruins...[3]

Within a short time, in fact, Britain witnessed an outburst of Republican enthusiasm: more than fifty Republican clubs sprang up all over the place. A large trade-union-based demonstration against the monarchy was staged in Hyde Park, in April 1871. In July of the same year (Dangerfield goes on) –

> The public resentment at length came to a head, when a great mass meeting submerged the fountains and the lions in Trafalgar Square and flowed from the steps of St Martin's Church to the entrance to the barracks. Here Charles Bradlaugh – it was just a week after the Queen had asked Parliament for some provision for her son Arthur – protested against "any more grants to princely paupers" and shouted that the House of Brunswick should take warning, for the patience of the English public was almost exhausted.

Even more seriously, 'democracy in fine linen' (Dangerfield's ironic phrase) emerged from its closet to support the mobs. Personalities later to be important in political and cultural life, like Joseph Chamberlain and G.O. Trevelyan, played leading parts in the renewed agitation.

And yet, this movement was very short-lived. It turned out to be only the last flickering of a flame, rather than a true revival of tradition. How weak the latter had already become – and how recognizable the situation is to us today – may be gauged from the tragi-comedy of the young Charles Dilke's flirtation with Republicanism. Dilke was an up-and-coming young Liberal of the 1860s, enjoying his first parliamentary seat as Member for Chelsea and possessed (according to his modern biographer) of 'an instinctive and deep-seated loyalty to the left'. In 1871 he decided that the mounting dissatisfaction with Queen Victoria and her heir might be harnessed. Very cautiously, he raised the question of Monarchy in a series of speeches in the provinces. These were mainly devoted to the perennial Ukanian theme of reforming the electoral system. In Newcastle-upon-Tyne, however, Dilke abruptly woke his audience up with an assault upon Royal waste and corruption, listing the grotesque and well-paid sinecures still within the Court's control and condemning such servility as a blight at the heart of the national life. Encouraged by the enthusiastic response from his Tyneside public, he ended with something of a peroration:

> Now, history and experience show that you cannot have a republic unless you possess at the same time the republican virtues. But you answer: Have we not public spirit? Have we not the practice of self-government? Are we not gaining general education? Well, if you can show me a fair chance that a republic here will be free from the political corruption which hangs about a monarchy, I say, for my part – and I believe that the middle classes in general will say – let it come![4]

This outburst proved nearly fatal to a budding career. 'Recklessness bordering on criminality', snarled *The Times*, 'These are eminently improper points, to be handled, and that with little candour or delicacy, before an assembly of working men...' The rest of the metropolitan press caught the scent and joined in. At Cambridge, Dilke's old university, tutors swooned and old rowing companions vowed never again to enter the same boat with him. Lord Chelsea vented the general opinion of clubland by regretting publicly that the days of duelling were over. The provincial speaking tour soon disintegrated into chaos as Tory hoodlums turned up to disrupt meetings and local Liberal Associations withdrew support. Dilke back-pedalled from his first fairly mild remarks, saying at Leeds for example:

> To say these things is not to condemn the monarchy, because they are no necessary part of the monarchy, although the opposite idea – that of promotion by merit alone and of the non-recognition of any claims fonded upon birth – is commonly accepted as republican. I care not whether you call it republican or whether you do not, but I say that it is the only principle upon which, if we are to keep our place among the nations, we can for the future act.

But even this wasn't enough. As the furore intensified, he was compelled to retreat altogether, into what he himself called 'ineffably dry orations' on reforming themes, in order to pacify the public.

Yet Dilke's main point in his brief campaign had been a simple one – exactly the same as that made by Joseph Chamberlain around the same time. No genuine Republic was possible without 'the Republican virtues'. The issue was put more strongly by Chamberlain in an 1872 speech at his power-base, Birmingham. After earlier exploratory dabblings with Republicanism, he too was forced to come clean on the subject (he had found no escape from proposing Queen Victoria's health at a dinner, and the Prince of Wales was shortly to pay the town a visit). Republicanism, he observed, was undoubtedly 'the form of government to which the nations of Europe are surely and not very slowly tending'. However – warned by recent events – he too had absolutely no intention of putting his career on the line for it. 'I do not consider the name of the titular ruler of this country a matter of the slightest importance', he went on, 'What is of real importance is the spread of a real Republican spirit among the people. The idea, to my mind, that underlies Republicanism is this: that in all cases merit should have a fair chance, that it should not be handicapped in the race by any accident of birth or privilege; that all men should have equal rights before the law, equal chances of serving their country'.

Circumstances had driven him back into the same corner as Dilke (the corner inhabited by Republicanism to this day).

This last refuge for those who acknowledge Republican principle but don't want to be crucified upon it, consists in saying that society can quite well be republican in essence even though a 'titular' Crown is retained. An implication quickly follows (or can be thought to follow): we *already have* these 'republican virtues', the 'real Republican spirit' is already diffused among the people. The *national* identity-codes where the Crown looms so prominently don't matter: more symbolism. No real necessity, therefore, to get worked up about a symbol: one is free to toast the Queen, and welcome the Prince of Wales for a harmless bit of colourful pageantry. If pressed farther, a reference to Bagehot's *English Constitution* will satisfy the academics, while a few ineffably dry reforms can always be suggested to spread democratic virtue more evenly.

Now, when Chamberlain used the argument, it was in staggeringly bad faith – all the more staggering, one must add, for having nothing of Bagehot's blinkered philistinism about it. An audience of his Birmingham radicals could swallow it, persuaded as they then were that their city was a great energy-source for transforming the political scene. But in any wider view, the notion was indefensible. 'Real Republican spirit', the aggressive levelling urge against 'birth or privilege', had steadily weakened among the middle classes, leaving most of their backbones in chronic and (by this time) fairly complacent curvature. The Republican revival found some popular resonance lower down the scale, but 'responsible public opinion' (in that sense observed earlier) now closed ranks against it. Nor was the new grass-roots radicalism Chamberlain captained going to make much difference. Its rise – like that of British Socialism a few decades later – could not help coinciding with the New Imperialism: he himself became an outspoken leader of the latter as well, and strove in later years to combine Empire and social reform in a new ideological mix.

Returning to Dilke, this is the point at which the Royal Family itself retaliated with an historically significant illness – the one mentioned earlier, which prompted Alfred Austin's 'He is not better; He is much the same'. The heir to the throne contracted typhoid fever on one of his country-house expeditions, and for some time his life appeared in danger (Prince Albert had died of the same disease ten years previously).

Then, after almost expiring, the Prince of Wales unexpectedly and dramatically rallied on the anniversary of his father's death in December 1871.

'Getting Rid of it Altogether'

Victoria's retreat from public life was initially unpopular. In 1864 posters appeared outside Buckingham Palace that read "These commanding premises to be let or sold in consequence of the late occupant's declining business". In retrospect, however, it can be seen that her withdrawal was a chrysalis of sorts from which emerged a transformed monarchy more mysterious and more popular than ever before.

> Ilse Hayden, *Symbol and Privilege:*
> *the Ritual Context of British Royalty*
> (Arizona, 1987), p.69.

The result was a significant and too little-known moment of Ukanian history. 'The Republicans say their chances are up – Thank God for this! Heaven has sent this dispensation to save us,' rumbled the Duke of Cambridge. The Commander-in-Chief of the British Army was not mistaken – as one of the few commentators on these events writes: 'No monarchist needed to be told to what use the Prince of Wales's illness could be put'.[5]

The drama of near-death and last-minute recovery did indeed have remarkable impact. The miasma of unpopularity which had dogged the throne was dispelled by a solid wave of sympathy and commiseration. At the National Thanksgiving Service in St Paul's after the Prince's recovery, there were scenes of mass rejoicing unknown for many years (and suggesting, in retrospect, something of the more famous popular celebrations to come in the 1880s and 1890s).

These later events (above all the Jubilees of 1887 and 1897) have always been recognized as signalling the revival of Royal popularity in Britain: vast, fervent Imperial circuses in which both the plebs and the aristocrats of the New Rome affirmed the Crown's global leadership. In the same vein Disraeli – the most self-consciously Imperialist politician of the period – has been given the main credit for restoring Queen Victoria's charisma. However, more careful research has shown that the new popularity was soundly established well before the 1880s. Farthermore, it was based on national factors rather than the simple exploitation of Empire (though the latter certainly intensified its appeal); while W.E.Gladstone's role in building up the new cult was probably far more significant than that of Disraeli.

For instance, it was Gladstone who (Freda Harcourt notes) saw just as quickly as the Duke of Cambridge how the Prince's illness and 'miraculous' recovery provided a perfect chance to strike back against the Republican threat:

> (He) recognized it as an incomparable opportunity to turn the thanksgiving into a "great public act" through which he could impress his new vision of the nation on the public...Gladstone believed a public thanksgiving would bring about a moral purification, not only of the Prince himself who would surely be a better man for having been so close to death, but of society as a whole so that class harmony could be restored.

However, the Grand Old Man's aim was a good deal more precise than these cloudy perspectives of moral uplift and class harmony. In a memoir of one visit to the Queen (Windsor, December 21st 1871) where he tried to persuade her to let the Thanksgiving be as spectacular as possible, the notes read –

> What we should look to...was not merely meeting (republicanism) by a more powerful display of opposite opinion, but to getting rid of it altogether, *for it could never be satisfactory that there should exist even a fraction of the nation republican in its views*. To do this it would be requisite to consider every mode in which this great occasion could be turned to account, & if possible to take away the causes which had led to the late manifestations.

The reactionary shrewdness of this 'Liberal' judgement deserves underlining, and underlining again. Gladstone understood that it wasn't simply a question of augmenting Monarchy's popularity but of rendering it henceforth *invulnerable*. And what that goal implied was not just the defeat but the cultural *obliteration* of Republicanism. If even a fraction of 'serious' opinion remained anti-Royal then Royalty would be less than omnipotent; no effective taboo on the subject would work; opposition to the State (as distinct from a 'flexible' and responsibly sinuous 'Her Majesty's Opposition' within the State) would always end by seeking out a leverage at this weak yet strategic point of the apparatus of authority. Hence, the only real security lay in making what had again become a weak point of the élite's hegemony appear immensely strong – so radiantly popular that in future noone but self-evident eccentrics would ever dare attack it (and display their own futile isolation in doing so). The Crown's obvious elements of fragility had to be turned into something like a magic, untouchable fungus: only if the overground 'symbol' was rendered inviolable would its underground spore-system – the traditional identity-code conveyed in Gladstone's short-hand as 'class harmony' – be truly safe from subversion.

The trouble was that even in the 1870s noone was quite sure how such a great magic act should be staged. The same problems arose as we noticed before, with the sudden deification of George III at the beginning of the century. The 'well-oiled machine' of 20th century British Pageantry still lay rusting and forgotten in assorted Southern stable-yards and attics. Its blueprint had to be part reconstructed from old ledgers and long-unread memoirs, and part invented to suit the new conditions – above all, to appeal to the metropolitan lower orders, what Gareth Stedman Jones calls in a memorable phrase 'the vast limbo of semi-employed labourers, casualized semi-skilled artisans, "sweated" home workers, despised foreigners, tramps and beggars'.[6] To this end, much patient preparation and argument with the old lady was required: she was still living in the past and wanted 'a quiet and simple service' with the minimum of display. But Gladstone gradually coaxed her out into accepting the new limelight, and was rewarded with a public relations triumph.

February 27th 1872 was declared a Public Holiday, and great crowds assembled to applaud the Sovereign and her heir: they were 'doing homage' (a phrase which now entered popular parlance). Fifty tickets were set aside for 'selected workmen' to join the service at St. Paul's. And mother and son appeared later on the balcony of Buckingham Palace to wave and 'acknowledge' the cheering. One onlooker later wrote that the capital 'looked quite mediaeval again...like a scene out of one of Sir Walter's novels of ancient English life'. Next day the papers rejoiced in such a spontaneous show of 'ideal nationality', and such a decisive rejection of 'the cold-blooded theories...and soulless philosophies of English Republicans'.* Bagehot's editorial in the *Economist* declared (more pointedly than the better-known passages of *The English Constitution*) that Monarchy was 'the most national thing in the nation...the standard to which the eyes of the people perpetually turn to keep them all together'.[7]

Such was the counter-offensive mounted by the anti-Republican majority (Disraeli had merely to exploit it in his famous 'great speeches' on Empire and Throne later in 1872). For his part, Dilke now faced almost complete social ostracism, and rumours of a move to get him out of his Chelsea seat at the next election. Former radical colleagues deserted him in the House of Commons, and in a vote on the Civil List only one other Member, Auberon Herbert, was willing to give support. Gladstone delivered a characteristic put-down, overflowing with the milk of sadistic righteousness. If the Member for Chelsea wished to become promising once more, he had no option but to give up his insane notions about a Republic.

Give them up publicly, that is. There is no indication that he ever altered his private views about the Monarchy and its influence. But for the public view and record, they had now to be dismissed as youthful, hot-headed notions; forgiveness had to be begged, and begged forever with permanent uncertainty as to the outcome. Over thirty years later, notes his biographer, 'The Court never wavered in its hostility, despite a series of attempts by the old Republican to circumnavigate the excluding barriers'. In 1689 Edmund Ludlow was expelled from the country; two centuries later Dilke was only banned from the Court – and from responsible public opinion. In that way the 'closet Republicanism' so familiar today arose as part of the same movement: it was the private, forcibly internalized reflex of the public invulnerability so cleverly sought by Gladstone, and so instinctively backed up by all those with the new national identity at heart.

Only with the accession of Edward VII in 1901 did the barriers begin to come down. The verdict of this biographer (Mr Roy Jenkins) underlines the essential continuity between Dilke's dilemma and our own times. 'Dilke, in his first Parliament, had learnt a number of important lessons', he observes with the deep self-satisfaction of one who has himself avoided such obvious traps –

> He was not again to be diverted from more important radical purposes by hurling his strength against the British monarchy, an institution which, even at one of its weakest moments, had shown surprisingly rock-like characteristics...

It is important to notice that Dilke's downfall unfolded in its entirety *before* the Imperial moment usually taken as the start of the Monarchy's revival. I suggested earlier that Empire has been over-rated and the rôle of nationalism downplayed in interpretations of that phenomenon. Here is another illustration of this, surely. We saw also that this problem is confused by another fact: the Ukanian 'national identity' functioning by mid-Victorian times was itself a weirdly atypical formation adapted to the early-modern multi-national structure of the British Isles. Its disguised and overloaded Englishness – rendered 'British' by the Crown – already incorporated a smaller-scale domestic empire. But with this significant proviso, it remains true that the national prevailed over the Imperial in the reaffirmation of Monarchy – over 'Empire' in the showy, novel but also short-lived sense which took the centre of the stage from the 1880s onwards.

It was this Anglo-British national *Geist* which was given a new articulation and force by Monarchy, both before and while the 'New Imperialism' was being superimposed. Hence (Freda Harcourt concludes):

> To the extent that monarchism appealed almost without exception to everyone in the middle classes, it functioned far more successfully than imperialism in reassuring them that all was well and that the social hierarchy and the constitution were secure despite the rapid transformation then in process. By the time Gladstone left office in 1874, a modernized national ideology had emerged...In its propagation, the language of patriotism had come much more firmly under the control of the

governing classes, while the rhetoric of imperialism had become familiar and readily available for political purposes whenever circumstances should make its use expedient.

Republicanism did not pass away. Already in a seriously weakened condition, it was clubbed and then smothered to death. That this was its likely fate was still not quite obvious around 1870 – or else alert young politicians like Dilke and Chamberlain would not even have flirted with it – but the speed and ease of Gladstone's assassination left no room for farther doubt. The cause was abandoned to irreconcilable individuals like Charles Bradlaugh and Auberon Herbert, or to sectarian movements increasingly self-defined by their isolation from popular feeling and the political mainstream. There have been one or two stirrings in the intervening century, but none capable of reconstituting anti-monarchism as a plausible presence.

One side-effect of this national-popular Monarchism was that Republicanism acquired an automatic connotation of being 'middle-class' or 'intellectual' in some deranged and suspect sense. As such it soon merited contempt from socialists as well as from proletarian Tories. It was of course just this dual pressure – from below as well as above – which fulfilled Gladstone's design to the letter. Grinding in unison, the two mill-stones of Nation and 'class' did have the permanent effect of preventing 'even a fraction' of the nation from holding to Republicanism. Working from below, 'class' consciousness now found itself with two alternative (in reality complementary) judgements to deliver on the subject: 'trivial' when set against the mighty engine of an All-British, Working-class Socialism, the Monarchy was 'everything decent about us' (as well as a load of fun) to those less enamoured of the mighty engine, and even to Socialists on their off-duty days. But Left and Right could now both agree whole-heartedly that *anyone* bothering about the Crown as such was only a nut.

It is such nodes of agreement (often tacit, or taken for granted) which define the structure and the real, subterranean workings of an ideology: less the momentary flashes of belief or assent than the shaping, circumambient conditions of consciousness. George Dangerfield's verdict on the after-effects of the Prince of Wales' timely illness conveys brilliantly how the conditions had been established in this case:

> A movement so dynamic and so prophetic could not fail to have its effect; and its immediate effect upon England was to reduce by degrees the enthusiasm of the working classes for the republican movement. An instinct, an intuition, informed them that they would gain little by the substitution of, shall we say, Mr Joseph Chamberlain for Queen Victoria; that conditions would probably remain pretty much as before, only with a group of rather less picturesque people at the head of affairs; that, in short, one can get rid of one's monarchs, and still retain one's masters...The voice of the people, rising spontaneously, is one of the voices of history. As the crowds cheered Queen Victoria, driving to St Paul's, they were expressing a decent English sympathy for a mother who had almost lost a son; but they were also giving vent to a profound, unconscious distaste for middle-class republicanism. There was, no doubt, a great deal of good sense in the arguments of Mr Joseph Chamberlain and Sir Charles Dilke and Professor Fawcett and Mr Taylor. But the people had the last word.

Dangerfield himself endorses the attitude so memorably described here. But the fact is, that the people's 'instinct' was wrong: Chamberlain's early Birmingham Radicalism would have been vastly preferable to Gladstonian (let alone Disraelian) conservatism – and preferable, above all, from the viewpoint of the socialist tendencies which were also emerging in the 1880s and '90s. As things turned out, the 'last word' which rewarded such wonderful intuition about Monarchs and masters was to be the Labour Party of Ramsay Macdonald and Lord Wilson. Nor was there really much 'spontaneous' about the new adulation: conditions were to some extent prepared for it, then cleverly exploited.

The whole point of that exploitation was to foster a profound, unthinking distaste for *some* bourgeois ideas like Republicanism – so that other more cringing, blinkered and romantic bourgeois ideas could gather force to the point of uncontestability. The approaching 20th century was forestalled, so that the essence of the 18th should survive. Following a template now well established, the rational and permanent bourgeois concepts of citizenship, equality and statutory right were again being repruned to their empirical

English size – to make more room for the reanimated cadavers of subjecthood, loyalty and 'class'. Once these had been implanted and fused with decent sympathy for a mother (etc.) – then naturally 'good sense' could appear only as a malady of the cerebral classes, somehow divorced by bookish posturings from the common pulse of humanity which so strongly united the House of Lords with the lowest denizens of the 'vast limbo', the Highest in the Land with the cheerfully apolitical good nature of music-hall and sports-field, and the warmth of the ordinary hearth.

The real trajectory implicit in this new spiral of counter-revolution was illustrated by the later career of personages like Dilke, Chamberlain or John Morley. Ukania now had an immutable trajectory prepared for all such misfits: the progress of brainy upstart from radical firecracker to ennobled (but still grumbling) old codger. Thus, influenced by the Republican stirrings of the early 1870s, Morley wrote to his radical pal Frederic Harrison after an especially dreadful Ministerial visit to the Queen's Highland Home –

> That great dull Coburg at Balmoral. In the presence of the grinding sorrows of real life, I hate the very notion of feeling about such a pampered woman as that, whose sorrows are sentimental, selfish, undignified, gross. She is an anachronism, I tell you, a fat sybaritic solecism. What time and what heart have we for sympathy for such a creature as that, lapped, like a sorrowful poodle with indigestion, in cotton wool and silks when the mass of men and women have to toil through pressing misery, squalor, horror, with their aching hearts, and without a word of sympathy. Let them keep their royal fools' play as long as they like – only don't ask me to waste the shadow of an emotion upon their misfortune.[8]

Even this outburst displayed all the emerging symptoms of contemporary pseudo-Republicanism: the 'fools' play' definition, the saving bad faith of 'Let them keep it', and the retreat towards the closet of 'don't ask *me*' to join in all the sentiment. The note of unpleasant vituperation is equally characteristic: unable to find a rational (or genuinely Republican) motive for objecting to the charade, the great ex-radical essayist – biographer of Rousseau and Voltaire, and historian of the

Enlightenment – resorts to over-personalized abuse and empty rhetoric. This is only another, earlier version of that impotent fury we noticed before in Chapter One: unable to stand the universal sycophancy, baffled critics react by 'discovering' that the Royal totems have in reality all been pampered cretins who pick their noses, mistreat servants and roll about in silk sheets at the public expense.

Pseudo-Feudal Socialism

> Count Leinsdorf was wondering whether what he was about to reveal was not after all too audacious for the inexperienced younger man. "Well, you see", he began cautiously...."Practical politics means not doing the very thing one would like to do. On the other hand, one can win people over by granting some of their minor wishes". His listener gazed at him, evidently awe-struck...."Very well then, what I was just saying is this – practical politics must on no account be based on the power of ideas, they must be determined by practical needs. Everybody, of course, would like to make all the beautiful ideas come true. And so one must not do the very thing one would like to do! Kant himself said so...."

> Robert Musil, *The Man Without Qualities* Vol.2 Ch.81

In Windsordom the reforming side of politics above all has been conspicuous for its broad, unquestioning acceptance of the 'framework' provided by national history. Through the unique alchemy of Westminster 'class' stands revealed as covert politics – the faith-filled acknowledgement that all desirable changes are (eventually) possible without the soul-searching and fuss over constitutions which foreigners go in for. Power as such is no problem; neither is the Nation. Hence reform-mided Britishers are Providentially at liberty to cope with the *real problems* (Gross National Product, the unions, housing, and so on). This almost sublime good fortune brings true Windsorites into implicit agreement with Musil's 'Count Leinsdorf', the nobleman in charge of Franz Josef's 70th Jubilee Festivity.

Dumbfounded by Leinsdorf's cunning, Ulrich then learns that the general goal of greatness and mightiness is enough, along with proper attention to the nation's feet:

> We have four years ahead of us yet (went on the Count). All sorts of things may happen in these four years. One can put a nation on its feet, but it must walk by itself. You see what I mean? Put it on its feet – that's what we must do! And a nation's feet are its established institutions, its parties, its associations and so forth, and not just the talk that goes on...
>
> "Your Highness! Even though it may not sound exactly so, that is a truly democratic thought!"
>
> "Well, well, it may be aristocratic too, though my fellow-peers don't see what I mean....So let us set to work wih caution".

A comic Utopia in Austro-Hungarian conditions, Leinsdorf's 'practical politics' have been like second nature under the Saxe-Coburg/Windsors. Here, to dispute the meaning of the Nation has indeed meant proper care of the national bunions and walking-gear, leaving uniform and soul strictly alone. But – as far as Monarchy is concerned – this attitude is bound to consign it to the sphere of the inscrutable – up among John Buchan's 'ultimate sanctities', those untouchable verities which permeate the social fabric, are endured in consciousness each day, dreamed of each night, told to children, sent to relatives for Christmas, and recollected (as the Shils-Young essay points out) like 'VE-Day' and 'VJ-Day', while remaining – as sensible men know (though women may not be so sure) – of not the slightest real importance whatever.

In *My Queen and I* Mr Hamilton states that his party has never even debated the problem of Monarchy at an Annual Conference. This is not accurate (though a Republican can be forgiven for preferring to ignore the event). There has been one debate on the Crown in the 'Parliament of the Labour Movement' (as this Conference is often and all too accurately called). It took place fifty-three years ago, in the 1920s. This is a fact of small significance: as far as the content goes it could just as well have been in the 1980s.

In 1923 J.Vipond of the Stockton and Thornby Labour Party moved the following Resolution:

> 'That the Royal Family is no longer necessary as part of the British Constitution, and that the Labour Party is therefore

asked to state definitely its view of this matter.

Even though progress was slow and in Britain superstition died very hard (he argued), 'was it not *time* this resolution was passed?' Seconding the motion 'as a Democrat and consequently a Republican', Ernest Thurtle of the Shoreditch Trades Council said he knew that the leaders feared that 'the great bulk of the people would not support them if they came out as true Democrats'. However, if only they faced up to the question boldly, people would come round.

Left-winger George Lansbury replied on behalf of the National Executive. He *personally* was a Republican (he began) but it was clear the Party was divided on the subject. So, why should they 'fool about with a question which was of no vital importance?' The subject of *real importance* was the capitalist system which (Hyndman and William Morris had taught him) made the workers poor. Get rid of that and the question of Monarchy would answer itself. Until then –

> He wished to remind them that every member of the Parliamentary Labour Party...took the same oath at the Table in the House of Commons and when Mr Thurtle got there he would do the same thing. They swore they would uphold the Constitution. One of those days, by law-established principles they would not have a King or Queen, but what was the use of bothering about that just now?

Then came the joking aside intended to clinch the argument: Royalty were *just ordinary people* about whom no such fuss needed to be made. Why, Lansbury himself had 'sat behind two Princes at a football match' and delegates could take his word for it 'they were just ordinary common people like themselves'.[9]

The Chairman declared the resolution lost by an overwhelming majority, and pointed out that a second motion demanding the 'abolition of the hereditary principle in the British Constitution' was really covered by the same vote, and should be dropped too. Thus, symbolism and spiritual principles vanished from Labour's agenda for good. The Movement was now free to concentrate on the Social Revolution undistracted by trivia.

Returning to *My Queen and I* half a century into that revolution one notes little change in essential attitudes. The gist of Hamilton's theory is that: 'Internally, the story of our democracy has been – certainly over the past century – a story of capital against labour, of wealth and privilege against poverty and deprivation. Essentially our two-party system has grown out of that very clash of economic interests....' Monarchy is a weapon in the hands of capital and privilege, regrettably popular through its appeal to the lower instincts. But in the long run the 'class struggle in Parliament' (as Eric Heffer has described it in a book of that name) is bound to win through. From such a hopeless country and people only the most wonderful political system can redeem us.

Fortunately, we possess such a system. Its ultimate meaning and potential are demonstrated by the very presence of oath-swearers like Mr Hamilton and Mr Heffer at Westminster (as by that of George Lansbury fifty years before). In time – with more like them elected to prosecute the Class Struggle, more moral will and patient attention to all that *really matters* – the Monarchic and other fevers and delusions will grow less.

Little now needs to be added about these alibis for bankruptcy, but *My Queen and I* does contain one Leinsdorfian tale which, though unnoticed by reviewers and rampant Royalists (who all tended to concentrate on the author's squibs about Princess Margaret and the Civil List), does at least add to our knowledge of the fevers and delusions. It should not be forgotten that in spite of its Leader's almost total prostration before the Siamese-twin fetishes of Throne and Sterling, the Wilson government of 1964-70 did accomplish one anti-Monarchic gesture. This was so unique, so pitiable, and Mr Hamilton devotes so much space to it that any thoughtful reader ought at least to pause before it – rather as during an English cemetery walk one might halt and gaze at some specially eccentric or evocative tombstone.

In the year 1133 King Henry I appointed Aubrey de Vere as his Lord Great Chamberlain. This important high office – which remained in the de Vere family until it ran out of male heirs in 1626 – numbered among its perquisites control of the Royal Palace of Westminster, where in Mr Hamilton's time the United Kingdom's Parliament still assembles. The post also embraces some high ceremonial functions: he walks backwards at State Openings of Parliament, and bears the Royal apparel to and fro during Coronations and Investitures.

'On no intelligible principle' (according to *The Complete Peerage*) the House of Lords subsequently partitioned these duties among the three female lines descended from the de Veres. The families went on angrily disputing the right until matters reached a climax around the time Edward VII's Coronation in 1902. Then, the Committee of Privileges called on to settle this vexed question discovered that the de Veres should never have had the title in their family at all. Lords Great Chamberlain had only become hereditary in the first place through a mixture of well-aimed graft and Palace insouciance. The mixture was so deplorable that even at eight centuries distance the Committee felt obliged to condemn it.

And yet, there was nothing to be done. Having settled in to the Constitution, confusion was now best left alone. Later in our own century natural processes had narrowed the claimants down to two, who arrived at a deal: one would serve in each alternative reign. Thus, the Heathcote-Drummond-Willoughby line glided backwards before George VI, and the Cholmondleys (received pronunciation: 'Chumleys') continue to do so before Elizabeth II. During State Openings of Parliament Cholmondley can be seen bearing his slim white wand, the perfect emblem of the Faery transformation regularly wrought by this event. 'The astonishing thing', comments Mr Hamilton, 'is that it still went on exactly as before until 1964', the year when Labour regained control of the Palace filled with fresh zeal for modernization.

Now, while many judgements may wait to be made on this tiny footnote of the great story, only one is certain: there was nothing astonishing about it. By page 114 of *My Queen and I* there is no possible element of surprise in the fact that in 1964 a Lord Great Chamberlain went on managing Westminster in the Queen's name. That is, while in session the Commons were allowed in between 2.30 on Mondays and 4.30 on Fridays but outside these prescribed hours were liable to be treated like squatters. 'He could, and did on occasion, prevent M.P.s from entering the House on a Saturday or a Sunday. Once he actually stopped Mrs Marcia Williams (now Lady Falkender) from going to Harold Wilson's office....' Presumably in revenge for this slight, Wilson 'decided the time had come to shed this piece of historical nonsense' and nationalize the Palace of Westminster. It was time for British democracy to come of age: a Socialist free-holder rather than the Grace-and-Favour tenant of an improperly-obtained 12th century Royal decree. Realization of this sturdy purpose was, *My Queen and I* insists, mainly due to the obduracy of Charles Pannell, Minister of Public Building and Works. This Cockney sparrow won a partial victory against the Court Establishment's inevitable counter-thrust in defence of the ancient grace and order.

All decent logic (it had better be admitted) lay on the latter side. Why, the Court faction demanded, in a ceremony-encrusted State-order where the stiff brocade holds up the tottering humanity within, should anyone draw the line at *this* minor relic? The Crown regulates the Constitution, employs thousands, represents the British soul to the rest of the world and millions of thrilled tourists, and owns vast tracts of British land. Why on earth should it not hold on to one glorified janitor and relic-bearer at Westminster? There may be a case for unwrapping the Mummy altogether, or sending him off to the crematorium; what point could there be in snipping off just one of his mouldering bandages?

However, Labour's fit of petulance proved incurable. The House of Commons was brutally sundered from its mediaeval roots and given over to the Ministry of Public Works (now modernized as 'the Environment'). In the Lords a healthier sense of pastness prevailed (largely, Hamilton notes, 'due to entrenched opposition from Labour peers'), and Marquess Cholmondley continues today to look after the fixtures and fittings of a televised Chamber. The Prime Minister and Baron-to-be, though as a rule diligently silent on all matters Monarchical, 'announced the victory in the Commons with no word of praise' for Pannell's persistence. The episode seems to have had no effect upon his popularity at Court. A forgiving Monarch has never lost what one biographer calls her 'special, and unexpected, personal empathy with Harold Wilson'. In fact both then and later in the 1970s –

Westminster feeling has, if anything, suspected the Monarch of bias towards her Labour rather than Conservative governments – though not without a little friction over the traditional socialist shibboleths...[10]

Such is the class struggle in Parliament. It is perhaps in this light that Hamilton's verdict should be re-read: 'In Britain, a radical party faces a largely hostile press and a people innately conservative; and also instinctively monarchist....The Labour Party must therefore be seen as basically, if not too enthusiastically, pro-monarchist'. In 1975 it seemed to Hamilton that 'too much nepotism and feudalism' remained. It can now be added that in the 1980s hereditary peerage has been revived in one of the superbly inconsequent gestures which have typified Mrs Thatcher's radicalism – perhaps the most sparkling example thus far of Stuart Hall's 'regressive modernization'. As for the breaker of feudal shackles himself, soon after *My Queen and I* appeared Mr Wilson made his move – not, as Hamilton predicted, straight to 'Earl of Huyton' but first to a simple Knighthood and then, after the 1979 Parliament, to the more sonorous 'Baron of Rievaulx' in his native Yorkshire.

T.S.Eliot and Clap-trap: Fathomable Givenness

Egalitarianism is the death of community.

Peregrine Worsthorne, *Sunday Telegraph*
Feb. 7 1988.

Since Gladstone and Disraeli spoke, and Queen Victoria gave in, there has been no lack of Royalists to register and voice the new climate of High Ukania. Each year, each great hieratic event, each addition to the dynastic household has produced its unfailing crop of glassy-eyed comment and discreet revelation. Yet this ever-growing mass of celebrants has also remained largely unsalted by inquiry or analysis. Left-wing genuflexions at the altar of Crowned Whiggery have been accompanied by a more sapient and satisfied silence on the Right. As

J.H.Grainger has noted in an interesting article on the subject, after Bolingbroke's *The Patriot King* (1740) barrel-scraping is almost instantly imposed upon explorers into this domain. Hugh Cecil, Hilaire Belloc, J.M. Petrie and T.S.Eliot are among the names he offers up.[11]

Eliot is by far the most interesting of these: an outsider who had fervently adopted Anglo-British culture but believed it required support and purification from the Right. However, as regards the Monarchy, he too was able in the end to give it astonishingly little. In the Preface to his essay-collection *For Lancelot Andrewes* (1928) Eliot described his general standpoint as 'classicist in literature, royalist in politics, and anglo-catholic in religion.' The second of these terms (he went on with undeniable prescience) 'is at present without definition, and easily lends itself to what is almost worse than clap-trap, I mean temperate conservatism....' This was to be set right, he assures the reader, by a forthcoming 'small volume' to be titled *The Outline of Royalism*. Regrettably, it never appeared. Commentators on his later work have noted how impressed he was by the popularity of George V in the 1930s, as exhibited in the Silver Jubilee festivities and the mourning after his death in January 1936. He may also have seen some hope in Edward VIII as a possible Patriot King (and was certainly not alone in this).

But such indices of the renewed significance of Royalty had no real effect on his thinking. Like the 18th century's Henry St. John, Viscount Bolingbroke, he was too much of a nostalgic reactionary to have enough purchase on the subject. Coping with the new Monarchy meant trying to perceive its relationship to new social and economic trends – those vital changes which had, since the 1870s, led to the invention of such a formidable and many-sided tradition. It meant looking for a *rationale* of Kingship within contemporary conditions: that is, intensifying urbanism and Britain's queer, constricted industrialism and Caliban-like socialism.

But like Bolingbroke Eliot detested all these 'isms' too much to wrestle effectively with them. His 'theory' of élite Christian community-culture has sometimes been praised for its subtlety and anti-bourgeois nuances. It was in fact little but the exorcism of modern culture as such, deriving from the absurd historic location he had (from early on) selected as the fount of all virtue: the early 17th century. The Jacobean Bishop Lancelot Andrewes epitomized salvation from the long blight of modernity: that exquisite blend of Royalism, Religion and quotation from Antiquity which was the heart of the Great Tradition. Then Revolution destroyed it. The fall of King Charles's head brought the 'dissociation of sensibility' from which Culture (and therefore Man) have yet to recover.

Had *The Outline of Royalism* ever been written its aim would have been part of Eliot's broader ambition – that of 'expressing a unifying conservative vision in his religious verse and in his social and literary criticism...a cultural consensus where the English people are at last united "in the strife which divided them".[12] He would effectively have crowned the British 'Monarchy of Letters'. But in a sense there was no need. The consensus existed and had a real Crown to rally it: a farther coronation would have been superfluous. As Tom Paulin notes in his *Political Verse* collection, the Republican tradition of Milton and Harrington was already subordinated in national memory. The 'poignant vision' and the 'experience grounded in the British people's profound sense of national solidarity during the Second World War' leaned towards King Charles rather than to these reprobates. That inclination was based in turn upon a now deeply entrenched national identity, a received articulation of memory going back to Edmund Burke – who was himself only giving new form to the patrician inheritance of 1688. But this is only the literary manifestation of a perennial problem: *all* questions lead back to the nation and (since Britain is a State-nation rather than a nation-state) to the tri-secular trajectory of her form of State. Nothing was really 'grounded' in the experience of World War II, any more than in British Socialism, the rise of class-struggle, the industrial revolution or Burkean romanticism.

For all his dithering Bolingbroke hadn't been more than a century or so behind the times. The actual wreckage of the world he had lost was all about him, some of its rooms still inhabited, apparently still recuperable. Eliot's nostalgia, by contrast, was of the modern, wilful kind: one episode in that wider and longer-lasting counter-revolution which, from 1914 to 1945, accompanied the agonizing collapse of the European

Old Régimes. This is shown most evidently in the influence which the French thinker Charles Maurras never ceased to exert on him (and notably on his notions of Monarchy).

'The Toryism which Eliot adopted in the 1930s was neither directly related to the traditions of English conservatism nor to the British Conservative Party of his own day', writes Cairns Craig, 'it was an English version of Maurras's, with heavier emphasis on religion than on nationalism.[13] It may seem remarkable that France should be the inspiration for the most significant literary apologist of modern British Monarchism. But the key is provided by that observation from *For Lancelot Andrewes:* however practically important Monarchy in Britain might be, its justification in ideas was indeed (as it has remained) 'worse than clap-trap'. Temperate conservatism was omnipresent – at least until 1979. In France, by contrast, the very force and propagandist success of the Republican tradition had engendered an intemperate and high-profile opposition. From his part in the anti-Dreyfus campaign around 1900 till his death in 1952, Maurras represented a highly articulate and virulent form of Monarchist nationalism: restoration of a popular Patriot King to sweep away the corruption of bourgeois rule. Nor should it be overlooked that those two uncrowned General-Kings, Pétain and De Gaulle (the former strongly supported by Maurras), have come much closer to the reassertion of Monarchic practice than any British King since George III.

But Eliot's understandable fascination with this phenomenon simply underlines the futility of his own Royalist philosophy: the sole alternative reference-point to Bishop Andrewes is found in a foreign and drastically different State-tradition. Neither provided any real antidote to clap-trap. The social power of the British Monarchy was – as George V had demonstrated – huge and growing. However, this was a power which rested on two formidable supports, both inimical to the kind of theoretical justification Eliot hankered after.

One was the Crown's degree of integration with both State and society: contrary to many appearances the United Kingdom Monarchy is not decorative icing on the socio-political cake. It is an important ingredient of the whole mixture – important enough to render both justification and critique of the institution remarkably difficult *in isolation*. It was necessary to tackle general national conservatism and all the claptrap head on, in order to make any sense of it. The great renaissance of Monarchy in Victoria's later years was achieved partly by this remarkable diffusion: the Crown was more effectively transformed from distant symbol to daily sentiment and presence. The new mass media, working in a society constituted to allow them maximum effect, had successfully introjected Royalty to popular culture, 'nationalizing' it into the status of an omnipresent household god – a cosy fetish of the State domiciled like a garden-gnome in everyone's front conscience. Added to this was a second ideological factor. Ever since the resurrection of Victoria in the 1870s the strong taboo we noticed had been carefully nurtured around the Throne. It had grown alongside the new National-Imperial shrine of Monarchy, making an already feeble Republicanism progressively more unthinkable. The smiling gnome became untouchable, as well as omnipresent. Yet one by-product of this success was to make it almost as difficult to frame any new or resonant apology for the Crown. It was not merely unnecessary, but a bit dangerous. Not only should Monarchy be left mainly to the realm of sentiment and ritually articulated feeling: it ought to be positively fenced in there, and anyone breaking down the fence should have his ears boxed.

As regards Eliot, this is why (as J.M.Cameron noticed) 'No-one wholly English in culture could have brought himself in the 1920s to confess to "Royalism" as a political creed...'[14] One aspect of the cohesion reinforced by the Windsor cult was tacit limitation of discourse: the allowable expression was a self-fertilizing and self-reproducing torrent of banality – the conceptual cloning process we know so well today, capable of endless expansion and repetition precisely through its almost total lack of content. Beyond that silence is preferred, and indeed culturally imposed by the deeper language-conditions in question. A few anguished shrieks from somewhere under the shroud are of no significance. In fact they are quite useful, serving if anything to amplify the grandeur of quietude, the reassuring comfort of the Received Idea.

More recent times have seen little theoretic intrusion on the Royal taboo-peace. The neo-liberal New Right has understandably had nothing to say, although there have been symptoms of mounting suspicion there about certain aspects of Royal backwardness. After some years of grumbling on the subject its Sunday newspaper finally came (relatively) clean in January 1988 with a demand to 'Modernise the Monarchy'. 'The new royal baby' (from the Duke and Duchess of York) 'will grow up in a country more intolerant than ever of historical hangovers which have no relevance to contemporary lifestyle' wrote the editorialist, clearly hankering to follow the honest style of Australian Republicanism expounded elsewhere in the same issue by Malcolm Turnbull – the lawyer who had impaled Sir Robert Armstrong in a Melbourne court over *Spycatcher*. But such bluntness is not yet possible in the Thatcher Court. After denunciation of the sexism and bigotry enshrined in Protestant Succession, he delivered a few warnings to the Commonwealth and E.P.Thompson:

> If Australia were to become a republic it would undoubtedly upset loyalist sentiment in Britain...But there would be some advantages. The Queen's personal role in Commonwealth affairs reinforces the myth that Britain has a special obligation to pay heed to what the Commonwealth, particularly its more vociferous Third World members, think...but propping up an imperial heritage is no way to foster relationships which need to be based on contemporary realities.

However, a native sleekit caution prevents this editorial voice from saying what it longs to: 'get rid of the damned thing!'.He ends merely with 'modernization', a truism rendered all the more numbing for earlier recognition that 'the strength of the Monarchy has been its ability to move gracefully but shrewdly with the times' – i.e. to 'modernize' in just that sense I was concerned with above.

The caution is legitimate, and unlikely to be thrown to any wind from that quarter. The reason for this is located in the very heart of 'Thatcherism'. That is, in the apparent paradox of a radicalism little concerned with reforming political and State institutions as such. But this is surely a disinterest with its own powerful logic. After all, Mrs Thatcher has simply inherited the naked supremacy bestowed by the British Old Régime – inherited and deployed it with more ruthless vigour than any other modern Premier in peacetime. Why should she or her camp bother reforming an instrument whose 'historical hangovers' hide and legitimate that sort of power? No conceivable 'rational' or written Constitution would do the same. So, to go over the top and turn against the whole Crown-in-Parliament mythology would (paradoxically) threaten her ambiguous counter-revolution. An actual right-wing Republicanism would threaten all that a tacit, hypocritical, sidling anti-Monarchism has achieved. The former would pose the whole question of a different State, and an alternative national identity; the latter allows her to foster these growths – the sort she wants – under the cover of pantomine appeals to old institutions and last century's sense of being 'British'.

It needed a special storm like the Falkland conflict to reveal the new contours of the old Ukanian topography more clearly. Listening to the House of Commons debate at the outbreak of that war, Anthony Barnett wrote–

> ...was to enter into a kind of collective inanity, in which each speaker held up a distorting mirror for the others to admire themselves in – it was a self-consciously historic occasion.

The Leader of H.M.'s Opposition, Michael Foot, out-gunned the government in reconstitution of the National Will. Parliament reforged its pseudo-ancient credentials as the snarling lion on the Royal Standard of National Identity –

> Its frothing and raging were all the purer for being brought about by an object as insignificant as the Falklands... Each party rallied in its own way to the call of history and the nation's "honour". Some leapt for joy, others scurried, many panted to catch up, plenty caught the whiff of intimidation, the job was done: the MPs had rallied to the flag...The real judgement of such a collective is revealed precisely in adversity, when its response to a crisis matters. The combination of instinct, collaboration and procedure defined the true methods of British parliamentary rule...[15]

It also redefined the National tongue-identity for Mrs Thatcher, in precisely that way acutely noted by Tom Paulin in his essay on 'The Language Question'. The real fulcrum of 'good English' lies not in academies or dictionaries but here, in the 'actual location...of the British House of Commons' where –

> In moments of profound crisis people speak exclusively "for England". On such occasions all dialect words are the subject of an invisible exclusion-order and archaic Anglo-Norman words like "treason" and "vouch" are suddenly dunted into a kind of life...[16]

All that these rhetorical methods reflect is the inmost nature of the Old Régime, where national identity is far stronger than supposedly 'fundamental' divisions of class or party. This identity is deeply past-oriented, and projects an underlying continuity of development. The process may be registered either from above (Throne, Lords and Commons, sea-victories, etc.) or from below, by Foot's counter-traditionalism of Dissent, moral radicalism, 'This Great Movement of Ours', and so on. But such contrasting angles have to end reconciled in the more commanding perspective of Parliamentary Sovereignty and the sword of honour. Barnett calls this 'Churchillism', emphasizing its continuity with the 'formative moment' of May 1940 when Churchill rallied the nation against Hitler. Churchill*ism* (he suggests) –

> is essentially the political flesh of national life: its skin, muscle tonality and arthritis. Churchillism combined the contradictions of capital and the workforce, as well as the desires for freedom with those of imperial grandeur. Furthermore, it wedded these two distinct sets of opposites into a single enveloping universe of demagogy...It ensured the preservation of the Parliamentary Nation and thus Westminster's allegiance to a moment of *world* greatness that was actually the moment when the greatness ceased. Churchill's National Coalition ensured an astonishing recuperation, one that left the patient structurally disabled for the future and obsessed with magical resurrection from the dead.

However, Churchillian demagogy – like its Footian echo forty years later – was itself only the recovery of an underlying national-identity syndrome whose history returns us to Burke.

In 1982 it was Mrs Thatcher's turn. Unlike Churchill and Foot she is in many ways contemptuous of central parts of that syndrome and her version of 'modernization' has corroded it more than any other modern government. This has created an increasingly visible misfit between the old Royal mantle and what's happening on the ground – and hence the ditherings of the *Sunday Times* and (in Worsthorne's phrase) other 'discontinuity men' hostile to tradition – but the idioms of Greatness and Pastness are, still, very unlikely to be discarded. Some 'arthritis' will have to be put up with; for the loss of too much of the 'skin and muscle tonality' might leave the skeleton of elective despotism uncomfortably naked.

This dilemma seems likely to keep radical-right Republicanism within bounds; but what about the neo-Tory New Right, with its devotion to historical hangovers and spiritualistic community? Roger Scruton's *Salisbury Review* has had a little to say on that front. At least it has published one piece of theoretical Monarchism arguing (in the editor's words) that –

> One of the virtues of monarchy is to align our perception of legitimate government with the unfathomable given-ness of human life, and so to abolish that fruitless quest for abstract principles which inspires and embitters the constitutional theorists of liberalism.[17]

Peter Levy's article 'The Real and the Royal' admits at the start that conservatives have had strong motives for keeping the Crown away from 'the corrosion of destructive criticism'. Silence is the best way to that end. Admirable as it is, this has also led to 'complacency of a high order', typified in the stuffiness which finds any sort of Monarchism by conviction (like Eliot's) 'curious and even eccentric' – and hence more appropriate 'to those whom destiny has chosen to live beyond the narrow seas'.

But even the English need not fear to sprinkle a little theory over their given-ness. They have tended to be too defensive about Monarchy merely because it is not 'representative' in an electoral sense. Yet people do feel the Queen stands for them, or for something about them; and what this feeling denotes is another, deeper mode of representation – something like the way a work of art 'represents' its subject. Judith Williamson analyzed representation (we saw earlier) as in that sense an 'iconic sign' summing up a variety of meanings or projections in one image. Such high-falutin theory finds no echo in the *Salisbury Review*, naturally. The deeper mode of representation is more obviously at home beyond the narrow seas:

> Though the liberal constitutionalist in each of us rebels at the thought, people have ofen preferred representation through the acts of a Führer, a Caudillo or an Ayatollah than through the niceties of a carefully balanced electoral process...

And yet, Anglo-Britain's taste for such niceties derives from illiberal 'representation' too: for Westminster and the puppet-melodrama of our elections are secondary matters 'rooted in the experience that has given us our identity'. This experience and identity relate to *the nation* – the 'political unity which is a more fundamental achievement in the face of potential disorder and conquest than the thrust and counter-thrust of electoral struggles'.

This is all both interesting and true (though haunted by an odd nervous pomposity, as if the author feared some kind of retribution). But one wants to know more. What is the 'national identity' focused through Monarchy? How was it formed, and how does it actually work? Hushed awe normally suppresses this kind of inquiry (rather as, in Mr Levy's analogy, it is difficult to think in the presence of an art gallery masterpiece). So it is quite exciting to have such a *terra incognita* suddenly exposed.

Alas, the curtains have been drawn back merely for another episode of grovelling. Both author and editor drop on to their knees at this point, and the rest is messages from the Scrutonian deep. We can't help being born into one nation or another, Levy observes: a near-miraculous truth –

> Life is not chosen by the one who enjoys and endures it...we are subject to the conditions of time and place which precede birth and accompany us through earthly existence...(and) Hereditary monarchy represents the chance and necessity inseparable from life and carries the thread of continuity in visible form across the chasms of birth and death...

Thus, Queen Elizabeth represents Life. Or at least Life in its

British quiddity, already dourly familiar to any voyager in the Monarchy of Letters – that inscrutable nexus of chance and necessity which has given *us* 'a system good in itself...generally encouraging to the fulfilment of man's potentialities for positive achievement'.

The taboo has not really been analyzed at all – merely reintroduced at another level. The question has been posed only as an excuse for deeper piety and more arduous prayer. A new layer of mystique has been added, this time with professorial authority. Farther search is quite definitely a fruitless quest, for (Scruton continues his editorial theme) – 'We must all recognize, in the end, that "political obligation" is *sui generis*, not only in its structure, but also in its value' – one aspect of the kind of national given-ness which occupies the attention of H.M.'s subjects in between chasms. Conservative intellectualism exists to exalt this marvel (after thrashing shoddy abstractionists); not to analyze it.

In reality the 'argument' rests on a sleight-of-hand. The 'Nation' is elided into sub-Churchillian quaverings about Life and Death. What the subjects of Her Majesty have actually been given by their national history is transformed into an untouchable Grace – a glamour evoked in theory only to be farther endorsed and then quickly rubbed up with metaphysical polish. A recognition that the 'secret' lies in the dimension of national identity becomes mere emphasis upon the latter's magic inviolability – as if the latter were a Tibet forever closed to explorers (but known of course to healthy popular instinct, and in our collective dream-culture).

The answer to these chalice-bearers of a new wisdom is, surely, that there is nothing essentially mysterious about English, British or any other national identity. Nationalities and national states have arisen and developed – or more often failed to do so – like other aspects of history. They have imposed their cultural marks (by definition 'peculiar') like religion, language or climate before them. The difficulty which surrounds the subject in Britain is one of practice, not of principle: we happen to be afflicted with a hermetic, custom-laden and self-protective traditional 'identity' now in less gradual dissolution. That is what the Crown mystery is about (and why it now needs a little help from the *Salisbury Review* medecine-men). That the British system is not quite so 'good in itself' and rather less encouraging to fulfilment of man's potential is now a matter of daily inter-chasm experience: millions of continuity-threads have been stretched to breaking point on the dole, and (except when some Royal occasion is on) few news bulletin pass without their dose of decline and humiliation, or a reference to some prophecy of doom. A chorus of 'J'accuse' has been directed at this creaking social order and stifling state for a generation now – not by maniacal foreigners or constitution-mongers but (on the whole) by rather staid economists and somewhat over-empirical political and social analysts.

Hence this turbulence in the barrel-dregs: no longer allowed to snore in its traditional theoretic peace, a New Toryism is forced to defend the principle of somnolence itself in Christmas-cracker prose about the ineffable beauties of dreamland.

Bagehot: Dressing up the Mace

Mace, n., A staff of office signifying authority. Its form, that of a heavy club, indicates its original purpose and use in dissuading from dissent.

Ambrose Bierce, *The Devil's Dictionary*

People were abruptly reminded of the original purpose of this symbol of transplanted Royal authorityin 1977 when, after a particularly exasperating and long-drawn-out debate, the Conservative M.P. Michael Heseltine suddenly picked it up and mockingly threatened members of Her Majesty's Opposition with instant punishment. But before that political scientists less hypnotized by Bagehot have recognized that there is something more than flummery here. In one notable attempt at decipherment of the Régime, Richard Rose points out that –

In a political system that lacks both a sense of the state and a Constitution, the Mace is the appropriate symbol of political authority. The mediaeval origin of the Mace is a reminder of the long historical process that created the United Kingdom. In

physical form the mace is a five-foot-long silver gilt representation of prepotent power...(and) only when it is in position on
the table of the House of Commons is it deemed to be in
session.[18]

Its significance lies in the curious substitution which seems to
inform United Kingdom affairs. We enjoy a five-foot-long
ornamental club in lieu of a State – a piece of fetishized
Monarchy instead of the humdrum bourgeois abstraction
informing the governmental affairs of so many other societies.
'The idea of the state' (Rose explains) –

> ...as a thing in itself, an institution independent of and superior to
> members of society, can be found in most parts of Europe for
> most of the modern era. But it is alien to British political
> thinking...(and) To describe the United Kingdom thus would
> require the translation of a continental idea into English, a
> translation in which something important and distinctive is lost...

This distinctive nature lies in the bicorporeal reality of the
Crown – at once sovereign and singular, the totality of powers
and a concrete emblem. An often feebly articulated 'maze' of
administrative institutions is somehow both resumed and
presided over by the Mace. This conjuring trick (as Rose
comments bitterly) 'substitutes mysticism for meaning' – and
yet the mystic surrogate works. It establishes a double range of
what he calls 'asymmetrical commitments' between the geographical heart (Southern or Home-County England) and the
U.K.'s territories or provinces; and between the social apex or
élite and its subordinate classes.

Such a dual hierarchy or 'oligopoly' concentrates real power
into a staggeringly narrow compass: an élitism simply without
comparison amongst other modern and supposedly comparable States. Thus for example–

> Although in population it is one-quarter the size of the United
> States, the United Kingdom has something like one-hundredth
> the number of government organizations. By comparison with
> continental countries with similar populations, the U.K. has
> about one-sixth the number of government organizations of Italy,
> one-twentieth the number of Germany and about one-thirty-fifth
> the number of France.

Whitehall's 'oligopoly' is also defined by an elusive yet essential distinction between 'high' and 'low' politics: the former is a preserve of the apex, articulated via the 'profound monotheism' of Prime Minister, Cabinet and their supporting élite. 'Low' politics is the rest: the 'subjects' of the Mace stranded amid the humble undergrowth of an enervated 'local government' or non-Mandarin administration, forever (and increasingly) liable to blunt dissuasion from malpractice by the great staff of office.

Rose's title is *Understanding the United Kingdom* – a process which if pursued to the bitter end invariably brings one back to some analogy with Monarchy. Here the Professor is like some obstinate *garagiste* determined once and for all to get at what makes this old monster tick. Nothing – one can't help feeling – would please him more than triumphantly to uncover a tiny modern engine purring away beneath the awesomely rusting pipe-work and primeval valve-gear. Instead of which – after chapterfuls of adroit tinkering interspersed with many a curse and joking aside – he finds himself staring at an inescapable five feet of crypto-mediaeval junk. His key category of 'oligopoly' is of course derived from economics, where it means 'near-monopoly'. But there is no real escape: 'The basic idea of oligopoly' (he has to admit) 'is indicated by its root term *oligo*, "a few"'. However, the few in question obviously don't compete like great firms. On the country, they stick together as in no other modern society: they constitute the Small yet commanding Country of High Politics devoted to (in his own words) 'foreign affairs, defence, the Bank of England, the law, the monarchy and the Church...as determined by traditional status, reflecting origins in government by aristocrats'. Tiny yet imperial in reach, this is the domain now given a visage for TV viewers by 'Sir Humphrey Appleby'. And its impenetrable and stylish unity derives less from the Official Secrets Act (1911) than from the historic 'secret' of incorporated Monarchy – from the transubstantiation of a unitary *Geist* not merely into silver gilt but into the control-codes of a ruling caste.

Professor Rose's long wrestling-match with the Devil is all the more admirable for its stark contrast with some earlier conclusions he reached on the subject. In a paper on 'The

Monarchy in Contemporary Political Culture' (1976), he and co-author Dennis Kavanagh had shown an almost ultra-Bagehotian complacency. There, it was claimed that Kingship today has an 'epiphenomenal character' still quite explicable within the great Victorian's terms of reference. But comfortingly, the mass of people has become more educated since then and the accompanying theatre of Royalty grows ever less important. This is why 'The characteristic European monarch of today is a "bicycling monarch"'. Now, even Kingsley Martin understood very well that the British Monarch is nothing of the kind: he could only argue with dwindling conviction that this more sensible age will arrive, eventually. But Rose and Kavanagh went still farther. The 'superficiality' of today's Royalism has become such that-

> The Queen is like a colour photograph covering a large box of chocolates. The photograph gives pleasure to some, while others hardly think about it. Only a deviant few would refuse a box of chocolates because they were emotionally upset by such a photograph...[19]

The contrast between this Ultima Thule of philistinism and *Understanding the United Kingdom* is astonishing. But then by 1982 noone – not even a Royal biographer – could have envisaged life in Great Britain as 'a box of chocolates' without being destroyed by universal ridicule. The emotional qualms of the 'deviant few' also appear in a different light, once it has been grasped – against all the resistances of caste-culture – that the old computer actually does run on *noblesse oblige* and has re-coded Monarchy as its central processing unit.

Chief Malefactor:
'The English Constitution'

There has ever been a *structure* in English political society and every man has not walked by the light of his own eyes...the many have subordinated their judgement to that of a few – opinions have always *settled down* from the higher classes to the lower, and in that manner a decision that is really national has been formed...

Walter Bagehot, 'The History of the Unreformed Parliament and its Lessons', *National Review*, January 1860.

For Bagehot, Democracy – men and women trying to walk by the light of their own eyes and exert authority from below – was the premature rashness of modern times. He did concede that it might work when the lower orders had all become as well educated as himself, but declared this state of affairs to be centuries away. That is (in classical constitutional terminology) 'popular sovereignty' was a menace which, happily, the bovinely deferential English nation could by its well-tried and flexible Constitutional arrangements hold at bay and prevent becoming a curse. Associated with 'the solid clay of the English apathetic nature' (as he described it) was an equally fortunate antipathy to abstract concepts. Frenchmen, Americans and other Republicans are naturally plagued by these, while the English – or more accurately the Anglo-British – prefer the concreteness and colour of a pleasing nation-state theatre where always 'The climax of the play is the Queen'.

The Right has its historic reasons for failure to think much about Monarchy. But we have seen that the Left does too: faith in national community far stronger than mere principle. Mere ethnic nationalism could never have supplied such loyalty; but the mystic super-nationality of Crown and Constitution is another matter. These have been apprehended as runes of Civilization itself, which first Liberals then Socialists persuaded themselves could be read in a sense favourable to their own designs. This is why Martin, Hamilton and other 'anti-monarchists' appear so crotchety and ungrateful: happy to live in the Palace yet keen to smash up the Throne for firewood.

The State-community is basically wonderful, but *this* (the major emblem of wondrousness) will really have to go. Dignified Republicanism is impossible; so one ends up as a House of Commons 'character'.

Where does the conviction come from? In the domain of such theory as there is the source is not hard to find. The guilty party is Walter Bagehot, and the 'disguised republic' notion so lethal to progressive British thinking has normally been taken straight from the pages of his *The English Constitution* (1867). A hundred and twenty years after its first publication, this study remains the first, almost automatic reference-point for political discussion of the British Monarchy.

The first, and usually the last. What Bagehot provided was indeed less a theorization of Monarchy than exactly what British conditions required: an alibi for not bothering to think farther about it. And since 1867 almost everyone has picked up this alibi and used it. 'The use of the Queen, in a dignified capacity, is incalculable....' begins the famous section –

> Without her in England, the present English Government would fail and pass away. Most people when they read that the Queen walked on the slopes at Windsor – that the Prince of wales went to the Derby – have imagined that too much thought and prominence were given to little things. But they have been in error; and it is nice to trace how the actions of a retired widow and an unemployed youth become of such importance....

The apparent cynicism of this last phrase has been greatly relished. It indicates a disrespectful, journalistic urge to pry behind solemn façades and expose what's really going on. Taken in by the posture, even anti-monarchists have felt that this is probably what he was doing.

In a relative sense, it was. Bagehot did to some extent debunk older notions about the Constitution, including its Monarchical elements. But it should be remembered that he did so at a moment when the prevailing ideology of British politics had grown almost as myth-laden and out-dated as it is again today. R.H.S. Crossman points out in a modern edition of *The English Constitution* how in the 1860s constitutional thinking had failed to keep pace even with the modest reforms of 1832 and remained fixed in an 18th century groove.[20]

The whole trade of commentary upon the Constitution is in any case a realm of quasi-legal necromancy in Britain. It is performed on a mist-shrouded academic plateau by a specially-evolved breed of academic lawyer-philosophers, whose totemic lore is remote from everyday politics. An ancient goat-track connects it with Westminster, and ends there; mutual exchanges of gifts do take place (customarily in the shape of finely-wrought footnotes rather than tomes), but rarely more than once in each generation. The task of these upland shamans (it should be recalled) is to 'interpret' an historical transubstantiation almost as miraculous as the one patented in Palestine: how the Sovereign authority of the English Monarchy was conveyed to Parliament, and thence bestowed in wisely reluctant doses upon the people. God's descent into History is recorded in no written Constitution. How could it be? This was an unique advent, which since then others have merely sought to copy with their abortive revolutions, bureaucrats and batteries of pathetic 'principles'.

Hence, the eternal problem is that of reading and re-reading the 'conventions' of constitutional practice – those rules which (as one authority puts it) 'have by their antiquity and utility acquired a normative, a binding quality'. But this quality is also elusive. It radiates nuances and fine gradations of inclusion and exclusion (uncomfortably like the famed texture of English social class and speech). Meditation on these is always needed, and a generation or so can easily slip by while it proceeds. In Bagehot's day several had. This gave an air of novel ruthlessness to his celebrated verdict that the Constitution was no more than a veiled and secretive élite tyranny:

> The efficient secret of the English Constitution may be described as the close union, the nearly complete fusion, of the executive and legislative powers...The connecting link is *the Cabinet*.

This concentrated instrument of authority expresses the 'despotic power' of the dominant class, and can only function as it does because of 'deference': there are '*deferential* nations' of which England is of course the prototype, where the mass actually want and expect to be ruled by a stratum that 'knows how'. In such profoundly un-republican countries –

The numerical majority – whether by custom or by choice , is immaterial – is ready, is eager to delegate its power of choosing its ruler to a certain select minority. It abdicates in favour of its *élite*, and consents to obey whoever that *élite* may confide in....It has a kind of loyalty to some superior persons who are fit to choose a good government, and whom no other class opposes.

Within the select minority there may be different strategic views, organized as parties and it may even matter who is 'in' and who 'out' at any given time. However, a vital part of the 'efficient secret' lies in keeping such oscillations 'tolerable' (to the core concerns of the ruling class, or 'national interest').

Who did Bagehot think the 'select minority' were? He asserted they were, simply, 'the middle classes'. He was writing in an England which had just lost Lord Palmerston. This crusty epitome of the pre-1832 régime had passed fifty-eight years in Parliament, forty-eight of them in one office or another. In later years he presided over governments consisting almost entirely of landlords, and while he endured there had not been the slightest chance of farther reform. Only after his death in 1865 could change be thought of; and that only on the basis of a Parliament where, two-thirds of the way through the century, three-quarters of the Members represented the 'territorial class'. This social character, points out Richard Shannon, 'corresponded precisely to the ascendancy of the traditional ruling class. The classes enfranchised in 1832 had made no serious inroads into positions of place, power or influence'.[21]

Neither would the new lower classes enfranchised in the electoral reforms of 1867 (as he proceeds to explain). So what did Bagehot mean by 'the middle classes' being in charge? Not that they had deposed and taken over from the old élite, plainly. This would not be attempted until far into the next century's decay – not until Empire had gone, 'deference' had withered and British Socialism had humbly done its work. Or did he mean that the old gang now had to rule in conformity with middle-class interests? Taken in a strong sense, this was (and has remained) quite false: a hundred inquiries and reports have shown that no comparable modern State has demonstrated such consistent indifference and incompetence towards

– for example – manufacturing industry and technology. In a weaker sense the phrase was true, but somewhat truistic: of course no British government could hope to act for long *against* the interests *of the dominant sector* of the 'middle class', located in trade and finance rather than in industry, in London rather than in Manchester and the North. However, there was nothing new about that in 1867: it had been so since Walpole's period, in the early 18th century.

Bagehot himself did not represent 'the middle classes' in some broad or indeterminate sense. Indeed few commentators can be more precisely located in terms of 'interest'. He was (literally) born in a bank and became a life-long creature of the City. Professionally he moved from managing a London bank to being editor of the City's main organ, the weekly *Economist*. Before *The English Constitution* his most important work had been a brilliant analysis of the mid-century financial system, *Lombard Street* (in every respect a more valuable work). When he claimed Britain was really controlled by the famous 'bald-headed man at the back of the omnibus', therefore, we should imagine a City gent on his way up Fleet Street towards Westminster – rather than (for instance) a small spring-manufacturer on his way from West Bromwich into Birmingham.

What he stood for was the part of bourgeois opinion which had the most marked influence on governments, and the strongest motive for imagining itself in control. But of course, his self-congratulatory myth could also be read as flattering to the provincial manufacturing middle class: it too read the *Economist* and aspired (though now only tamely) to a greater say in affairs of State and Empire. 'Middle class' was a label confusing these two fractions of the British bourgeoisie: its old, Southern mercantile élite locked into State power and the social hegemony of the gentry, and its new and politically supine Northern industrialists convinced that gradual reform would bring them the new State they wanted. The desperate political nullity of the latter was (admittedly) not yet fully defined. That too would not happen until much later (one is tempted to say, not until the establishment of the Confederation of British Industry in 1965).

Within a short time – at any rate – Bagehot's myth was unchallenged. The essence of the Constitution was to admit change and control from below – not to arrest change and maintain control from above. If the 'middle classes' had got into real (if rather 'secret') charge of the State, then it seemed to follow that the working classes could do the same. The 'external show' of State, notably the Monarchy, were of no importance set beside this internal magic: where the bourgeoisie had led the way, the Labour Party could certainly follow.

Many other parts of *The English Constitution* in fact contradict such an interpretation. Bagehot was an unashamed and complacent élitist who thought things had gone far enough. He was furiously hostile to farther reform of the franchise, and convinced that it would take centuries to make the majority fit for democracy. However, these interesting aspects of his theory were to be eclipsed by a more digestible legend. The worthless elements in his theory were mythicized, while its anti-democratic thrust (which did reflect the real Constitutional values) was ignored or apologized for. Farthermore, as Crossman sadly notes, Tory apologists did not have to foist the Bagehotian ideology upon the Left: the 'radicals' were only too keen to fool themselves –

It was a long line of radical theorists and left-wing reformers who wilfully misunderstood the lessons of *The English Constitution*, seeing it not as a model of how to pry behind the façade and observe the technique of power, but as the classical account of how a British democracy does work and ought to work...

Harold Laski and Lord Morrison are accused by Crossman, but of course Kingsley Martin, Willie Hamilton and a legion of Parliamentarians and Professors also deserve their seats in this capacious and multi-generational dock.

They fell into it all the more easily since Bagehot compounded the 'middle class' delusion with another necessary piece of journalistic flattery: the idea that there was something deeply *modern* about the British Constitution. We have seen already how remarkably pervasive this piece of blarney is: sure enough, here is its source.

Monarchy and aristocracy were merely the 'theatrical show' of society, a way of beguiling the rude multitude:

The climax of the play is the Queen....There is in England a certain charmed spectacle which imposes on the many, and guides their fancies as it wills.

This spectacle is bound up with 'the dignified parts' of the Constitution, 'very complicated and somewhat imposing, very old and rather venerable'. Lords Great Chamberlain, Ladies-in-Waiting, Royal Processions, Beefeaters and so on, all cultivating an awesome sense of the past. Then, inside and hidden by the show, we find what Professor Rose and Mr Bulpitt have been unable to locate today for all their efforts: 'the efficient part....which is decidedly simple and rather modern':

> Its essence is strong with the strength of modern simplicity; its exterior is august with the Gothic grandeur of a more imposing age...

How many thousand times has this bit of self-congratulatory twaddle been quoted and sagely endorsed? Modern machinery propelling antique coachwork; up-to-the-minute engineering encased (but not hampered) by Gothic decor and fine pageantry; modernization with dignity?

He was quite right in seeing something strong and simple at work. But there was nothing whatever *modern* about it. On the contrary, *it* was the real antique – the authentic heart of England-Britain's post-1688 Old Regime. It was the ritual and flummery that were 'modern', in the sense of being deliberately revived and constantly added to (a process due for dramatic expansion in the decades after *The English Constitution* came out). The only evidence of political modernization Bagehot can point to is that the Monarchy had less influence upon elective dictatorship after George III's time: however, the curtailment of that influence was inscribed in the Tablets of 1688 – George had merely tried to re-interpret them, and failed. The inner system itself remained the essence of oligarchic hegemony: patrician and imperial, the expression of a complex political culture hammered out over a century of tumultuous trial and error from the 1620s to the 1720s.

Far from 'broadening' over time, this system has invariably tended to narrow under threat, or in periods of enforced retrenchment. Since Churchill's time, Crossman shows how Cabinet rule has become 'Prime-Ministerial rule' – the dependence and concentration of the entire machinery of power upon one man, or woman. Originally founded upon a purloining of the Divine Right of Kings, 'Parliamentary Sovereignty' has with the passage of time gravitated back from the Parliamentary class to an 'executive committee' of that class, and then to one individual again – an elected tyrant with the whole State upon his or her shoulders. Crossman indicates how Lord Avon handled the Suez crisis in 1956 as an example of what this means – the Prime Minister could run a war without Cabinet consultation, helped only by 'a handful of colleagues and advisers'. We now have the more forceful example of Mrs Thatcher's 1982 'War Cabinet' to underline his message.

The most significant post-World War II re-analysis of the Constitution, John P. Mackintosh's *The British Cabinet*, bore exactly the same message: far from broadening out in a democratic direction, U.K. government was contracting under the pressures of decline. Its 'first principle' (in Machiavelli's sense) is sublimated Monarchical authority, not popular sovereignty. 'Sometimes the British system is called constitutional or limited monarchy', notes another academic commentator –

> ...but these terms are unrealistic. We have not had limited monarchy since the days of Queen Victoria or earlier. Monarchy and royalty are totally different things. Monarchy is a term of political analysis meaning government by a single person. Royalty refers to status and is a matter of inheritance and blood. The Queen is royal but she does not govern and therefore she cannot properly be called a monarch....The British Prime Minister combines the powers of the single man and of the elected assembly, and that is why I see nothing for it but to call him a monarch...[22]

The theatrical 'show' of Monarchy and Westminster archaism is not in any sort of contradiction with this real tendency of power. On the contrary, it expresses the genuine, inward nature of élite government – the national, anti-democratic populism of an inherently aristocratic power. In his comparative survey of European administrative practice C.H.Sisson has noted that –

> However strong one's native conviction that foreigners are
> queer a glance at Europe makes it plain that it is we who are
> odd. Constitution-making, and the passion for legal precisions
> and codifications which go with it, are normal in the western
> world...No doubt if we were starting from scratch we should
> have to have some such stuff but, more through luck than
> judgement, we have hitherto avoided the disasters which would
> make that necessary. And so it is not necessary.[23]

But of course (he sighs) this lucky oddity has nowadays to be
concealed. In a constitution-mad world, chaps just have to put
on the best show they can –

> 'It is not to be denied that the requirements of international
> negotiation and – what is sometimes much the same thing – of
> international publicity, make it necessary to approximate, at
> any rate superficially, to foreign habits. The Atlantic Charter
> was a most un-English document, derived from the French
> revolutionary streak in the American tradition...These are
> games we have to play if we are not to be left out in the cold'.

The same exasperating necessity forces one to try and define
the quiddity of Anglo-British governance for foreign con-
sumption. Since the effortless presence of hegemony is (so to
speak) the sole definition required in its natural habitat,
Mandarin-culture is ill-suited to this kind of contortion. A
liberal-humanist formation brings commanding style – the
charisma of good form, rather than a pedantic concern with
formal rules and pinning down Life's natural poetic flow.

However, if define one must, then it had better be admitted
that the Crown is at the heart of administrative darkness – not
the party battles at Westminster or the five-yearly electoral
pantomine. This is not merely because officials run Ministers:
the world of *Yes, Minister* is itself made possible by the
immanent spirit of British rule. This is the 'Spirit of British
Administration' (Sisson's title) which derives from the Monarch, whose 'one inalienable function...is to secure the
coherence of her country'. She or He provides the 'national
entity' (or the focus of underlying national identity) which this
old and continuous hegemony exists to serve. Non-inter-
ference in mere 'politics' is the precondition of that decisive

focus – or as Sisson puts it, 'Her quiescence is the very principle of order'. By it the centre of things is really maintained – the 'thing itself' or *res publica* (in precisely that sense we saw described by R.W.Johnson earlier).

Thus, the notion that the Crown is an ornamental headpiece to sober political reality is sheer Freudian inversion: the British truth is that 'politics' are the dispensable ancillary of the informal, personalized and charismatic *res publica*. Parties, Governments and Civil Servants alike serve the myth of the Crown; yes, but the 'myth' is historically far stronger than they are – the emblematic display of a 'deep' or structural national continuity and cohesion which has so far easily transcended the meddling of Ministers and occasional modernization tantrums.

Casting a sour backward gaze across the prayerful folklore and penny nostrums of British constitutionalism from Walter Bagehot up to Sir Ivor Jennings, Sisson concludes:

> Popular institutions are – to use a word which Jennings misapplies to the Head of State – ancillary. It would be perfectly possible to govern England without Parliament or elections though it would certainly not be possible to govern it in this way for long with any efficiency...

Thus, when set in proper comparative view, 'British democracy' is in a real and not token sense the servant of the Crown; the converse is not true. Representation of the People exists to promote the efficiency of the old State (alas, with markedly diminishing effect in recent times). While Great Britain is unthinkable without its Sovereignty-apparatus, it has actually existed for over two decades of the present century with the Will of the People in abeyance. These were the periods of war and economic crisis in which elections became too much trouble. So-called 'National' Coalitions or Governments then took over, relinquishing control only when stability had returned sufficiently for the Crown-State to tolerate the nuisance. From 1915 until 1922, and again from 1931 until 1945, 'Popular institutions' were indeed shown the door of the officers' club and told to bide their time in the homely squalor of the Public Bar.

Another broad comparative survey reaches similar conclusions. This Constitution is actually one where democracy has been 'poured into an antique mediaeval mould...still stuffed with officials, terminology and procedures that originated in the Middle Ages'. Nor (Samuel Finer's study of *Comparative Government* goes on) is that just a question of vestments –

> The importance of this tradition is that it has preserved not only mediaeval forms but the mediaeval essence: this was that the king governed – but conditionally, not absolutely...The form taken by an Act of Parliament links the present to the past and attests the underlying continuity of the mediaeval conception of government: "Be it enacted by the Queen's most Excellent Majesty, by and with the advice and consent of the Lords Spiritual and Temporal, and Commons, in this present Parliament assembled, and by the authority of the same..."[24]

The political system rests on a core of officialdom, conceived as nobly 'impartial' – above and beneath mere politics in the same sense as the Crown itself. Anglo-British constitutional history has never been anything but 'a continuous struggle for the control of this executive machinery'. Alas, the Crown's 'machinery' possesses a grandeur, a social cohesion and (through its City cousinhood) an economic rationale incomparably stronger than that of would-be controllers. If this formidable historic apparatus was no more than a hereditary cadre of rulers, then its grip would long ago have slackened. But thanks to the Monarchy and its associated battery of civil control-mechanisms, it has been able to 'run' nationalism too. It is these assorted fuses and voltage-regulators which have given the State a controlling interest in popular national identity – to the point that 'State' and society have gone on seeming at one, and most of society's instincts can still be channelled upwards into adoration of the Crown.

Sooner Than One Thinks

'The current amazement that the things we are experiencing are "still" possible in the twentieth century is *not* philosophical. This amazement is not the beginning of knowledge – unless it is the knowledge that the view of history which gives rise to it is untenable'.

Walter Benjamin, 'Theses on the Philosophy of History', VIII, *Illuminations* (1955).

I have assumed throughout this book that the Crown's 'closeness to the hearts of the people' means something, as distinct from the deplorable nothing of idiot-theory. Archaism, trash, quaintness and a burdensome family *Schmalz* are trimmings or accessories, not the garment itself. Ukania may be (as George Orwell put it) a family with the wrong members in control; or a family in which, sooner or later, the historically right members inevitably gain control (the Whig Interpretation, also popular among Labourites); or a family whose decent elements are being ousted by greedy young swine bent on a second mortgage and selling off the heirlooms (a popular old-timers' theory of Thatcherism). But the point always is: it's a family, and not a modern State. Both the glamour and the 'backwardness' of the modern Monarchy are features of the family alibi, customary cramps which may enable society in some ways and disable it in others but are – in any case – indispensable to what it has become. And both represent an underlying consensus lodged from above (and too long accepted from below) as the mainframe of a national identity.

That self-image is linked in turn to a wider Liberal perspective on modern historical development. It is in this sense only an insular variety of liberal historicism – that general view laying primary emphasis upon emancipation, novelty and advance as the keynote of historical experience. 'For too long', writes Arno Mayer-

...historians have focused excessively on the advance of science and technology, of industrial and world capitalism, of the bourgeois and professional middle class, of liberal civil society, of democratic political society, and of cultural modernism.

They have been far more preoccupied with these forces of innovation and the making of the new society than with the forces of inertia and resistance that slowed the waning of the old order. Although on one level Western historians and social scientists have repudiated the idea of progress, on another they continue to believe in it, albeit in qualified terms.[25]

It is the Left, the principal inheritors of the Enlightenment, who have structured the historical view in this way. Their optimism has commanded a general perspective of advance, and read the expectation of progress back into the past. The result (as Mayer convincingly argues) is that for about two centuries it has always been far sooner than most intellectuals have thought.

After the American and French Revolutions, the rapid disappearance of Europe's *Anciens Régimes* seemed 'inevitable'. Inevitable, perhaps: but there has been nothing rapid about it. In France it took three more revolutions and the 1870-71 war with Prussia to establish a shaky 'bourgeois republic' on lines recognizably like those of the Enlightenment plan. While even in the United States – free from feudalism, with no antique State – the conquering 'triumph' of middle-class values and industrialism would not take place until the defeat and absorption of the South after the so-called Civil War. In both cases a century of struggle and a major war were needed to bring about the partial 'ascendancy' of ideas supposedly borne forwards by the irresistible tide of modernity.

The failure of the Year of Revolutions, 1848, demonstrated how powerful, resistant and adaptable the old régimes were. Often dismissed as inert 'relics' by the ideologists of the middle class, they then embarked upon a second round of restoration. The first had followed Napoleon's final defeat in 1815, when the Congress of Vienna attempted to reorganize and consolidate the old Monarchical States. This counter-revolution had lasted for thirty years but – as 1848 made clear – required new initiatives and momentum in order to keep going. In the second half of the century there took place what Mayer calls the 'remobilization' of the *Anciens Régimes*:

Though losing ground to the forces of industrial capitalism, the forces of the old order were still sufficiently willful and powerful to resist and slow down the course of history, if necessary by recourse to violence. The Great War was an expression of the decline and fall of the old order fighting to prolong its life rather than of the explosive rise of industrial capitalism bent on imposing its primacy...

Capitalism and its accompaniment, 'bourgeois society', have made their way into the historical mainstream far more hesitantly, unevenly and incompletely than either the prophets or the historians of the process have imagined. It was a bedraggled shuffle occasionally going into reverse, rather than a legendary 'march'. In this more realistic perspective, surely, the 'survival' of the U.K. Monarchy and all its accompanying State-oddities appears less amazing. I suggested earlier that – in spite of what so many sour critics have thought – no peculiar foolishness or strain of atavism need be imputed to the British peoples to explain their Royalism. Their anachronisms derive from developmental location; and that location can in turn only be explained by reference to a mainstream itself retarded, contradictory and (at least in the classical prophetic terms) belated.

Lurking behind the misplacement of the U.K. in developmental time is a larger and more fatal assumption. To locate the *ancien régime*-set up as pre-1789 can imply that it ended at that date – or if not ended (a progressive qualifying cough at this point) that it was at least 'fatally undermined', on the slide. Monarchy, aristocracy, religion and rural servitude survived only with the auctioneer's ticket on them, relics to be knocked down at some soon-forthcoming event and made over to the irresistibly rising middle classes. This is the mode of optimism found in the youthful Marx and Engels, for example: around 1850 they were convinced that a Europe almost devoid of political democracy would soon be ripe for Socialism. What remained of the ancien-régime world was already just façade or superstructure, material for antiquarians, ready for the rational new forces to (another old favourite) 'sweep away'.

Later the great men weren't quite so sure. When they died the British aristocracy was still in the Parliamentary saddle, the industrial middle classes were more abject than ever, and the workers had forgotten all about Chartism. By 1889 Engels indeeed 'could see in its typical failure to abolish the anachronistic superstructures of the old order, "the political decline and abdication of the English bourgeoisie"'.* However, such perceptive comments from the later years failed to cancel or even seriously qualify the earlier image – by now influential on the broader Left and mandatory among Marx's direct political heirs. That image bestowed quasi-scientific certainty upon an erroneous paradigm of historical development – at both the U.K. and the global level.

In reality the late-feudal world continued to do far more than survive: it fought back, turned capitalist industrialization to its own ends by often adroit modernization-from-above, and poisoned the emergent civil society of the middle classes with ideologies of race and military conquest. The Habsburgs, Hohenzollerns and Romanovs secured Absolutist domination of the European land-mass until 1917. South of them the Ottoman Sultanate kept its grip on the Middle East; West of them other Monarchies had given some ground to political reform but still held back society in a prevalently conservative and agrarian mould. In his great revaluation of this pre-1914 world, *The Persistence of the Old Regime*, Mayer points out how 'in its prime as well as in its perdurable extension into modern times, the *ancien régime* was a distinctly pan-European phenomenon'. To understand it –

> It may be necessary to reconceive and perhaps even totally reverse the picture of a modern world commanding a recessive and crumbling old order...the "premodern" elements were not the decaying and fragile remnants of an all but vanished past but the very essence of Europe's incumbent civil and political societies.

This is shown by what became of them after the World War they had inflicted upon humanity in 1914: a fall which almost destroyed civilization. Progressivism had imagined the death of such dodo-States as releasing the naked machinery of capitalism and a bourgeois social order. When they did at last crash down, the ruins of these Regal façades filled at once not with peaceable bourgeois bent on contracts and votes but with a vile and nearly fatal mixture of excrement, blood and delirium: the European counter-revolutions of the 1920s and '30s, in which the toxins of the old world's putrefaction turned upon and nearly defeated the Enlightenment modernity whose advance had once been deemed irresistible. Judged by Mayer's paradigm, the 1914-45 era was a single 'Thirty Years War' of dissolution and revenge. In other words, the European Ancien Régime still isn't ancient, and is only just history: the thunder of its collapse is still in our ears, the most characteristic sound of the century, and the dust has only really settled since the 1950s.

By the mid-19th century the optimistic left-wing imagination thought that Europe would soon all be like a misconceived England (Bagehot's England): Monarchy and Aristocracy (if they survived at all) would be transformed everywhere into theatre for the masses, with middle-class shareholders, producers and script-writers. Capitalism would cease being the secret ferment of change and come into open control of the European State-world, with governments everywhere mere 'executive committees of the bourgeoisie'. Grey, loung-suited Utility would take over from Honour as the philosophy of rule, the only 'national spirit' which really mattered.

Now, this may be a recognizable caricature of the present day in Western Europe and it can be made to fit (e.g.) any regular summit-meeting of EEC or NATO leaders. The problem is that it has only been the case *since about 1950*. In other words, about a century 'late' judged by the repeated past prognostications of both Liberals and Socialists. Even then, it would really be safer and more accurate to say 'since the 1960s' or 'the 1970s', to allow for France's last fling with the quasi-Monarchy of General de Gaulle, and the end of military dictatorship in Spain, Portugal and Greece. If the 'triumph' of the bourgeois class and industrial-capitalist values is taken to mean the formation of a number of fairly homogeneous societies regulated by these norms – a stable and pacific state-*system* at approximately the same level of development – then it has only just come about. We would appear therefore to be living in the first decades of true capitalist ascendancy, and not (as so many left-wing and communist theorists have insisted) in its 'last days' – in something like the full flood of capitalism's social evolution, rather than in an effete 'late bourgeois world' already crumbling into its Socialist nemesis.

'Where are we in history?': this is the grand question so ably confronted in Mayer's revision of Marxism. His answer is that now (just as in 1848) it is a great deal sooner than many have tended to think – particularly on the Left, and most of all perhaps among his fellow-Marxists. But the same alteration of perspective, surely, permits a different judgement on the overall character of Britain's Monarchy and Old Régime. The problem has always been that formation's profound ambiguity: a structural 'anachronism' which was nevertheless – and for so long – in the vanguard of liberalism.

Apologists of the Ukanian State still retrieve its honour by stressing how comparatively progressive the British formula was. And their point is historically sound enough to go on convincing. But what they omit to point out is that that small, antiquely Liberal light shone so brightly and for so long almost entirely because of the Stygian surrounding darkness – that is, Absolutism's overlong persistence and the regression brought by its death-throes. The climax of all this was 1940: led into its finest hour by a shifty and 'colourful' nobilitarian anachronism, Imperial Britain's profound ambivalence remained none the less preferable to Pétain, Franco, Stalin and the Nazis.

The converse of the argument is then also omitted. Once Western Europe had been (at last) stably and generally modernized by the 1960s, the old light was blotted out for good: it has in fact been relative and growing darkness for a generation – a fact well known (e.g.) at the European Court of Human Rights though still unacknowledged in the faith of most natives. The ambiguity derived (again) from developmental location: in spite of both intensifying conservatism and its Imperialist phase, an early-modern configuration stably ahead of a continent which could not shake off political feudality; yet immediately, massively and irremediably left behind once that continent did. For two hundred years the advantages of an early-modern, transitional Kingdom at least balanced its narrowness, its defects and its élitist absurdities. In a world of late-feudal monstrosity and the dictatorships which took it over, they still stood for something (even if their survival had become dependent upon American support).

Once it went, they stood for nothing. Or – in the new post-1979 Régime – a great deal worse than nothing: a hideous, drunken combination of Viennese nostalgia, porcine parochialism and tourist vulgarity where Benjamin's famous 'Angel of History' (who was supposed to be blown backwards into the future by the storm of Progress) has turned into a bustling hand-bagged gnome Royally convinced that she is herself the storm, and that the 'wreckage piled upon wreckage' is a stairway to renewed Greatness.

Endless Dream-time?

It is well: it works well: let well alone. Cupbearer, fill. It was half rotten when I was born, and that is a conclusive reason why it should be three parts rotten when I die...

Thomas Love Peacock,
The Misfortunes of Elphin (1829).

We saw above how the Republican spirit was driven underground for over a hundred years. Overground, in the public arena of a reconstructed Old Regime, various substitutes and simulacra for it were developed and accepted: the fulsome tributes of the constitutional counter-revolution to those social and economic advances which proved unavoidable. The Labour Party, above all, was the Greek Gift of Royal England to recurrent democratic pressure among its subject peoples. The gift has been accepted and (on the whole) turned into the second nature of Ted Hughes's 85th Birthday Poem for the Queen Mother, 'Lion's Dream':

And on Standard and Icon a Lion. And Lion
The name our longship island bore
Through the night-seas of the war
Till dawn seemed to rise on the Tribe of the Lion.

The downhill route from this false dawn has shaken that second nature loose, but there still isn't much sign of real desire to cast it off. What we can be sure of is that the emergence of such a wish will be measurable in terms of Chamberlain's 'real republican spirit'. Put in another way, in terms of formal

377

democracy and advanced constitutionalism rather than of 'class' incantation and island-longship sea-shanties. It's often observed that the new or revolutionary can only emerge in the vestments of a past – from a placenta giving modernity birth as concrete reality rather than idea. However, from this very truth there arises at least the possibility of abnormal situations where the vestments have grown too heavy and unadaptable – where the placenta constricts or smothers birth itself.

There is an old argument surfacing here whose barnacled head some addicts will already have recognized. In a recent *Socialist Anatomy of Britain* Laurence Harris observes how in various ways –

> The entry of the industrialists to the national political scene was contained within the shell of the old ideas of deference and *noblesse oblige*. The bonds of patronage were subtly transformed into a structure of sponsorship organized through the major public schools and Oxbridge colleges. Access to top positions depended not so much on who you knew as on attendance at the "right" school or college. The Establishment remained at the heart of the state until well into the 20th century...

Apart from the awkward problem of just what 'well into' should (in 1988) be taken to imply, the thesis accords with the positions taken above; and Harris is generous enough to cite my *The Break-up of Britain* (1977) among the sources for the Marxist notion that –

> The unbalanced development of the British economy since the 1870s – its dependence on overseas investment and the role of the City in international trade – is integrally linked with the position of the Establishment as the dominant power bloc in British society. This is the key to the claim that British economic decline is to be related to the archaic features of the British state.

That claim actually went back fifteen years or so to some articles of the early 1960s in *New Left Review*, of which the most important was Perry Anderson's 'Origins of the Present Crisis' (No.23, Jan-Feb, 1964). The 'crisis' was perceived as the generally critical condition of post-1950 Great Britain, and its origins were traced to distinctive political and economic deformations in the earlier history of a national State which had allowed famously 'archaic features' like Monarchy and a synthetic aristocracy or 'Establishment' to survive. Though winning an arcane and spurious dignity under the title of the'Nairn-Anderson theses', these views were thoroughly worked over in the socialist ring by traditionalist heavy-weight E.P.Thompson and condemned for many years to a suitably furtive and spectral existence amid the revolutionary poltergeists of Ukania's attics and stables. The Establishment ignored them, naturally.[26]

Gazing back over the strange wreckage years later, another more succinct Thompsonian critic pointed out that the distinctive feature of the essays had been –

> The writing of history from a stand-point in the present. In practice all history does this (usually pretending not to), but these were emphatically political-historical essays... (reflecting)... the theme of failure suggested by the immediate context of post-Macmillan Britain and the Wilson electoral campaign of 1964 with its modernising, technocratic rhetoric.

However (he went on) our reflections on this theme were poisoned by 'a rather self-indulgent Anglophobia' which wilfully insisted that the British *always* got it wrong and things were ordered better abroad.

The regrettable Nairn-Anderson streak of national nihilism was rendered still more noxious by another error: over-emphasis on the merely political – on the State and ideology rather than *real* things like 'the forms of civil society and the mode and social relations of production'. This is of course the code for social class (or 'class'): the empirical idiom's prescription of reality. As a result of our hopelessly 'un-Marx-like method' we had been drawn into equally hopeless political exhortations – drawn indeed into a thoroughly outmoded style of radicalism which long-ship Marxism has (fortunately) never taken seriously. As if scarcely able to credit such naiveté the author (Richard Johnson) went on:

> Their main explanatory notion (aristocratic hegemony) *turns out to be nothing more than the principal theme of English liberal ideology*...(for which) the root of evils has been seen

precisely as "feudal", "aristocratic" or "military" residues in an industrial-democratic world.[27]

We saw how Engels and Marx too had seen through such old-fashioned political nonsense – over a century *earlier*. *They* also knew by around 1850 that the backward appearances of British Monarchy and Lordly rule were but expressions of 'aristocratic powerlessness in an industrial world'. So, although it may have looked to smart-alecs like us as if the old U.K. State had contained and crippled industrial capital around 1964 – when Lord Home had just been Prime Minister and the symptoms of chronic de-industrialization could no longer be ignored – real Marxists knew (and had always known) better. Unlike us they were capable of perceiving the 'real trends' and class forces beneath such tinsel. Although Factory-owners and the long-suffering members of the C.B.I. – British capitalism's 'regimental mascot-sheep' as Ascherson has aptly called them – may have seemed to be victims of government economic policy and going bankrupt they were, as always, really in charge; and the only struggle which mattered was the one between them and the *'determining'* presence of the organized industrial working class. This was scarcely surprising, however, since the latter had been (though often in roundabout ways) determining everything decent about Britain since around 1832.

'National nihilism' is the settled conviction that all is hopeless in one's own country. Its converse is subliminal nationalism: a belief that, in spite of so much disgrace, history reassures us everything can and *must* yet be well there. The subliminality derives from those very absences so often commented upon above. Having neither an ethnic nor an affirmed democratic-national identity to fall back on, progressive nationalism substitutes a moral fable: the special inheritance of a popular soul by definition undefeated and forever struggling towards the light. By the very existence of that struggle society is redeemed. No 'ism', and certainly no paper charter, can describe or codify it – national-popular Life itself in an endless quiddity of 'facts', like elusive sacred fish which pass through all nets. A particular rage is reserved for denigrators of that Life – for Orwell's diseased intellectuals, wilful aliens who have refused the national communion. At worst they're a kind of traitor; at best, to decry 'class' and put 'politics' first (as we were supposed to have done) was no more than a laughable reversion to the sort of Liberal illusion so 'astonishingly persistent and pervasive in English political life'. As to thinking that the *Monarchy* was important – well, here the laughter must give way to outright scorn: class-consciousness has always had far weightier matters on its agenda than an out-dated 'republican spirit'.

As regards the interpretation of history there were mistakes on both sides of this old debate. But it is surely more important now to recognize them as complementary antitheses forced by a particular historical situation: a quarrel among the intellec-tuals of an empire in a special sort of dissolution, where no vehicle of political redemption – no alternative national identity – had been bequeathed by a conquering past and a State which had so long been 'Authority itself' and created a 'national character' to suit. Some turned away from the monster; the majority (naturally) continued to embrace it as the kind of fate a nation is, something which will and imagination must make the best of (however much special pleading is required). There was no possibility of winning or losing such a dilemma. It has merely been altered by the farther evolution of the crisis to which it addressed itself.

Looking back from that 'stand-point in the present' what does our weary old 'liberal ideology' and democratic Republicanism now mean in the perspective of the middle 1980s? This perspective is easily defined by a summary of what most observers have counted as the most obvious 'problems' or crises afflicting the realm during Mrs Thatcher's years in office.

The very mode and results of the 1979, 1983 and 1987 elections themselves – where an antique voting system designed for the maintenance of 'consensus' has ended by legitimating right-wing radicalism. Having facilitated a coun-ter-revolution (far more easily than it ever tolerated Labour's brief 'social revolution' of the 1940s) the Constitution has voided the old political mould to expose a true elective tyranny. In mild Régime-prose this can be presented as 'a broad package of interventions and centralization outstripping that carried out by any previous government'. But since the 'central issue in British politics' has always been capturing elective dictatorship (rather than curbing it), this merely 'provides pretexts for a future Labour government' to carry out its own radical plans.[28] Public ownership of the banking system, perhaps, and the abolition of private education? Nationalization of land and the replacement of home-ownership by rental within a reconstructed public sector? An engineered halving of property prices in the Southern heartland to reverse the North-South divide? One need only evoke such prospects to understand that no real 'pretext' whatever has been provided for Her Majesty's Opposition of the future. Post-1987, these are all 'loony left' Utopias renounced by responsible Socialism.

Any temptation to resurrect them has been in any case thwarted by the failure of Labourism's timid and abortive efforts at internal democratization between 1980 and 1982 – which ended in endorsement of its traditional corporate structure and the vassalization of a farther generation of socialist militants. There was never the remotest chance of the British Constitution being democratized by a non-democratic opposition. In typical style, token moves towards 'one person, one vote' were used to foreclose all farther movement in that direction.

In the same period, a struggle between the government and the trade unions over new union legislation was won by the State *imposing democracy* on a protesting union movement. Mounting authoritarianism was victorious by deployment of what were supposed to be its enemy's historic strengths. How victorious can be estimated from Dennis Kavanagh's widely-echoed judgement: 'It is difficult to imagine that there will be a return to the status quo ante regarding the closed shop, trade union immunities and ballots before strikes or for the election of officers...'[29] Yet how contingent and manipulative the new Régime's use of democracy is was forcefully underlined by the other conflict at its espionage headquarters, 'G.C.H.Q.' – where both individual and collective rights were permanently suppressed. However, the full import of that was soon obscured by the nature and outcome of the main socio-economic struggle of the decade, the miners' strike of 1984-5. Here, the N.U.M's travesty of democracy under Scargill was rewarded by absence of wider support, crushing defeat and the foundation of a breakaway Union of Democratic Mine-workers.

The single location which displayed a significant democratic-popular challenge to the 'high politics' of the Régime was big-city local government. That defiance was countered simply and decisively: by liquidation. The London and other metropolitan authorities were dissolved by governmental fiat, and replaced by a weird new undergrowth of powerless Ukanian bodies and committees. Thus, the long saga of Conservatism's local-government 'modernization' was concluded by frank reassertion of the central power: reappropriation of authority from Country to the Court. Throughout the same period, the Court itself was repeatedly shaken by interminable scandals concerning State secrecy which culminated in episodes like the banning of the BBC's 'Zircon' films and Sir Robert Armstrong's stardom in an Australian court-room over *Spycatcher*. Concentrating elective dictatorship ever more crassly within the Mace – in other words – the Court naturally grew more, not less, obsessed by all its traditions of élite prerogative and discretion. Losing the gentlemanly conventions which once operated such codes (and the rendered them supportable), the Centre of Things has thought only of reinforcing them by hysterical and violent means. And yet, this crazed caricature of the patrician culture has generally found support and collusion from an Opposition anxious above all else to accomodate to the new models of responsibility.

Throughout the same era race relations deteriorated to the point of provoking major riots in several English cities, leaving in their wake a festering train of civil-rights issues and complaints about the police and the courts. In a defence of Britain's potential for democratic change, A.H. Halsey has written:

The effectiveness of the deliberate pursuit of equality through governmental action in the 20th century has been severely limited in respect of the relative chances of the working class. In so far as the integration of Africans and Asians is thought of as a recapitulation of the gradual admission of the working class to full citizenship, the task calls for much more politically forceful action than is embodied in the Race Relations Act of 1968 or 1976, or mild gestures towards "positive discrimination"...[30]

But if 'recapitulation' is what's needed, these calls will remain unanswered. There has never been an apparatus of 'full citizenship' in the Old Régime, and what were severe limits for a native proletariat must surely become crippling ones for ethnic newcomers. By definition unprovided (and in some respects unprovidable) with the physical and cultural codes of familial 'belonging' which Royal nationality substituted for formal rights, how can they ever more than half escape from the Ukanian equivalent of racism – 'being one of us'? The dilemma has been spelt out in the convoluted hypocrisies of the Nationality Act and the inhumanities of its administration.

There Ain't No Black in the Union Jack, and Paul Gilroy comments in his well-titled book that 'studying the potency of racism and nationalism and observing the capability of movements formed around "racial" subjectivities involves an examination of the social relations within which people act and their junctions with forms of politics which articulate themselves through historical memory's "traditional roots..."[31] But if both hosts and immigrants are thrown back mainly upon their respective customs in common, what is likely to emerge except romantic stalemate punctuated by riot? The most significant 'social relation' remains nationhood, articulated by the State. Constitutional law should work by rescuing people from their roots and historical memory, not sealing them up there. Its formally enforceable equalities ought to counter-balance ethnicities, not endorse them. The structure enabling 'multiculturalism' can't itself be cultural: but in a Régime of Regally-disguised particularism, without even a modern Bill of Rights, how can such a structure be set up or believed in?

Unfortunately, this list of wounds and humiliations could be continued practically indefinitely. But I leave the reader to compile his or her own. They have of course been given different sorts of definition from both Right and Left. Mrs Thatcher's New Right depicts them as episodes in the liberation of an enterprise culture from the deadweight of State control. The Labourite Old Left (and to an increasing extent a dissident old-style Toryism also) views them as the Satanically-inspired destruction of traditional consensus and 'decency' – as a reactionary dissolution of 'class', and so (by implication) of all the sacrosanct customs of the old national game.

I have mentioned only socio-economic and minority issues, not territorial ones like Ulster and Scotland where the constitutional problem is manifestly central. Yet in all the former the Republican view-point, by contrast, can't help perceiving all these crucial post-1979 episodes as so many illustrations of a single deficiency: the absence of elementary democracy and effective popular sovereignty not merely from Parliament and State but from their principal opposition as well – the organized labour movement and the Labour Party. Every one of them has turned either upon the grotesquely anti-democratic character of the English Constitution itself, or upon the even more disconcerting absence of democratic spirit and structures within its institutional opposition. More lethal still, because of that oppositional paralysis, an ever more arrogant and centralized 'elective tyranny' has been able time and time again to advance behind a screen of democratization – forcing the Left to advance in a grisly recapitulation of everything back-to-front about Ukanian history and customs. The difference, of course, is that while a non-Republican character suits the State perfectly it has become a form of suicide for an opposition which (consciously or uncon-sciously) has colluded with that State for so long and remains regulated by the pieties of 'class' corporatism and commu-nitarian dementia rather than the plain demands of formal democracy.

The puzzle of how such a radical Régime can have been so uninterested in institutional or high-political reform – the normal staples of all radicalism in the past – has the simplest solution. Mrs Thatcher's indifference to it derives from the virtually perfect armoury placed in her hands by the Crown: that is, by the metomorphosed traditions of Supremacy enshrined in a merely conventional constitution. Her con-tempt for its archaism has been effaced by her enjoyment of its powers. All the 'rational' reforms conceivable by a *political* radicalism would in one way or another limit, qualify or sometimes completely remove its magically-founded hegemony. With a Régime-opposition itself entranced, why on earth should she be interested in altering the old mainframe (as distinct from upbraiding butlers and equerries who are insufficiently 'one of us')?

So, twenty years on, what has become of those pathetic infantile fixations we had about modernity and dear old 'liberal ideology'? Their continued absence has largely destroyed the Left, in that interesting way Gramsci described in his *Prison Notebooks.* The 'Fable of the Beaver' (1930) relates how this intelligent animal –

> ...pursued by trappers who want his testicles from which medicinal drugs can be extracted, to save his life tears off his own testicles. Why was there no defence? Because the parties had little sense of human or political dignity? But such factors are not natural phenomena, deficiencies inherent in a people as permanent characteristics. They are "historical facts" whose explanation is to be found in past history and in the social conditions of the present.[32]

To be found (one might also say) in our customs in common and rich memory-stores of popular struggle and defeat. In the (recent) present, Labour's nativist subjection to Ukanian folklore forced the whole thematic of political and constitutional revision into the centre-ground of the Westminster arena – and hence, into alliance with parties more attached to a middle-of-the-road stance than to 'old-fashioned' radical reform. This had a regrettable consequence. The sacred terrain of central consensus was at that very moment being broken down by the success of the Thatcherite onslaught. Hence, elements of the Republican case achieved a fugitive prominence in Alliance programmes only to be swept aside in the rubble of the Alliance's post-1987 disintegration.

What is really at stake was well expressed in an election-day article preceding this débâcle by Matthew Hoffman:

> In Britain...there is a split personality in the electorate that echoes a different history and constitution from those of the USA. The persistence of the hereditary element in the House of Lords illustrates the extent to which ancient, pre-democratic theories of government still permeate the nation's self-image. Only a habit of deference by the populace, and a mirror-image of self-confident authority in the government, makes it possible for Mrs Thatcher to deny the kind of investigation into the MI5 revelations that is *de*

rigueur for less serious infringements of law by officials in the
United States... *(Independent,* 11/VI/87)

However, pre-democratic theory and the deferential self-
image are not confined in their effects to these particular
revelations and the Official Secrets Act (1911). He goes on to
argue that the U.K. political agenda ought now to be mainly
about 'changing the habits of the citizenry, their sense of their
own relationship to the State'.

That is, it ought to be about changing our historical sense of
'who we are' – the British identity-structure. 'Monarchy', in
the sense I have tried to consider it above, is a substantial part
of that identity; while 'Republicanism' is a proposed revolution of national identity, *as a precondition* of any imaginable set
of feasible programmes or socio-economic policies.

But it's also a precondition of restructuring within the Left
itself. Contemplating with due dismay the role of Loyal
Opposition in this continuing saga, Neal Ascherson has high-
lighted the parcel of reliquary bones it goes on clutching within
the Great Tradition:

> The orthodoxy of Labour, transmitted down the Tribunite line
> from Bevan to Foot, has remained a sort of debased economic
> Jacobinism. One day, the unreformed electoral system will
> deliver another huge Labour majority in Parliament, which will
> use centralized State power to redistribute wealth... [33]

All that misplaced 'Jacobinism' of this sort reflects is the
suppression of the real thing from English and Scottish
political development. In the essays now collected as *Games
With Shadows* (1988) he argues consistently that dealing
directly with this unfinished business has become the only
hope of reassembling any viable democratic alternative to the
new Conservative régime.

In a sense the living debate on the Left has been about
nothing else for most of the period in question: the interminable dilemma reposed in a thousand different ways of 'forming
new alliances' or 'coalitions' of popular forces and new or
dispossessed movements and campaigns around this or that
new banner or principle. Perhaps the most brilliant and
influential single contribution to that debate offered the
womens' movement as a model for this kind of advance. 'Ever

since the growth of CND and then the movements which grew up in the late '60s and early '70s among students, trade unionists, women, blacks, gays, and, more recently, youth, there has been a growing force of people...who are impatient with fruitless reliance on a Labour goverment', wrote Hilary Wainwright in *Beyond the Fragments*.

That was in 1979. Throughout the experience of Ken Livingstone's G.L.C. this list of the politically willing-and-able became extremely familiar: few of Red Ken's speeches omitted it, and whether viewed as an alternative to Labour or as a way of rejuvenating the corpse, the same litany of dispossession conjured up an untiring vision of democratic novelty in arms.

In London, the vision was obliterated. Elsewhere, it has remained a vision. Pursuing her argument, Wainwright notes certain lineaments of the 1980s situation:

> When a dominant theory of socialist change collapses in the face of economic and social problems that it can no longer explain or resolve, and when no alternative has matured in previous contestation with the dominant view, then there is likely to be tremendous variety in the attempts to fill the vacuum...Out of this diversity can then come new solutions, greater agreement, and greater strength. But only if we create a new way of organizing...[34]

However, the new way ends by resembling Gilroy's in its evocation of group values and the subjectivity of struggle: in this case, womens' rather than blacks'.

This cul-de-sac is inescapable as long as 'the dominant view' retains its hegemony: a 'mature alternative' is a replacement for the State, in its specifically swollen and constitutional-national (or Royal) sense. Without agreement on some Republican replacement for *that* how can there be any common terrain for the ragged regiment to assemble upon? What armature of purpose can lift the variety of such a list of *Sans-culottes* from dispersed (or 'loony') Leftism into the dignity of an army? What but the 'unfinished business' so often referred to here will ever bring it to a new Valmy (wearing Labourism's old uniforms or not)?

In an 1872 article on Monarchy in the *Fortnightly Review* the radical Frederic Harrison said –

> The Republican Club...is really engaged, not in encouraging the day after tomorrow, *but in accelerating the day before yesterday*.

This was of course the source of that outrage about the apparent exhumation of old liberal ideology quoted above: it was supposedly futile to demand we catch up with such *dépassé* issues when, obviously, Socialism is bound naturally to incorporate them within some all-encompassing triumph yet to come. Only a totally un-Marx-like methodology could see them as necessary conditions of any forward motion at all: the plaintive and shallow creed of those unable to grasp the fact that 'class' consciousness is essentially a redemptive plenitude of (occasionally hidden) heroic virtues from which British Socialism will one day bounce forth Popeye-like to reclaim cross-roads exemplarity by sheer force of arms.

But in fact there is nothing out-of-date about Ascherson's thesis, or our original ones of the 1960s – nothing, that is, except what the prescribed customs of an imperial élite and its Regal Court-dress (left sleeve included) once decreed irrelevant to the British Way. Neither he nor we have ever imagined that political modernization meant simply reversion to what 'Republicanism' meant in the 19th century. It goes without saying that today any movement towards the radical overhaul of State institutions can only take the most advanced as a model, and not what a 'written constitution' stood for in 1776, in the Chartist era, or in Harrison's time. The business which is unfinished is political modernization, not grave-robbery. To act in the spirit of Thomas Paine today must mean (for example) establishing the constitutional rights of both women and ethnic minorities in some new way – a way ahead of what the recent experience of womens' liberation and black struggle have promoted to the agenda, not behind it in a fustily 'bourgeois' tomb. 'Constitution-mongering' is the Régime-left's revealing term for all that: a flea-market where only the soiled and cast-off (and almost certainly foreign) is on display, to be fingered and rejected by lucky islanders sporting a timeless wardrobe. How agreeable to return instead to one's own 'ancient liberties' and comfortably worn customs!

The over-emphasis upon the 'merely political' of which Republicanism often stands accused also rests upon misunderstanding. It is quite true that this involves stressing what in the debates of the 1970s was called (sometimes rather foggily) 'the autonomy of the political'. But behind that there can now surely be seen a very material and historical theory – or, an explanation of just why it is that the specially lop-sided and extruded development of British capitalism has now begun to thrust these questions into the foreground. In decline, the system's economic struggles have at last begun to tear apart an older mode of national identity and 'consensus' – the synthetic totem-world of Royal observance and community described in this book. As that identity has become a deadly shroud the fundamental circumstances of political opposition have altered. Westminster and the system once seemed to offer a possible vehicle for the left; but now it looks more like a hearse every day. One may of course choose to stay in this queer fag-end world where 'Conservatism' has come to mean tampering with the historic plumbing and selling off appartments to squatters, and 'Socialism' a determination to restore the old Palace for posterity. But if not, then the only way out or forward is via constitutional reform.

This perspective on recent history will make no difference to the old argument. In his new rehabilitation of our theses Anderson has described how critics concentrated on supposed historical errors and 'foreign' sources of inspiration because none of them had anything to say on the main issue: what was occurring 'from the standpoint of the present' – the grotesqueries of national decline and British Socialist bankruptcy. This is why it is 'the contemporary pattern of events' from the 1960s into the 1980s which remains 'the real testing-bed for a review of our surmises'. But actually they have always had plenty to say about the present, and will go on saying it: an Anglocentric nativism which, because the national identity has been stolen from it so completely, will be more determined than ever to restore what it feels to be its national credentials and repute.

The quiet Republicanism argued for here is by its own definition 'no answer' to economic and social problems: it won't cure the structural ailments of Thomas Love Peacock's

'Old Embankment' in *The Misfortunes of Elphin* (he was talking about the pre-1832 Constitution and Old Corruption). There is no argument so beloved of true Ukanians as this: isn't the world full of 'advanced constitutions' not worth the vellum used to write them down, and phoney Bills of Rights betrayed by vicious dictators and unscrupulous ruling cliques? Why should our own new Corruption be any different?

But this style of complacency is becoming daily more an argument of despair than of justification. And the counter-stance of a new Republicanism can only be that while statutory and institutional development may 'change nothing' in itself, without it nothing of significance can now be changed. Beyond that, it may certainly be true that (as Anderson continues) – 'The British crisis has no solution in sight; and perhaps the time in which one was possible, as a national recovery, has passed.' The history of modernity offers neither examples nor pros-pects of any 'solution' to nation-building in reverse – to the attempt at a re-definition of national identity under conditions of chronic 'decline' and unarrestable de-industrialization.

In which case, it may be that the break-up of Britain will be accompanied by the dissolution of its heartland or Southern nationalism into a larger European entity. This would simply be the continuation of the extra-territorialism which has been for so long the life-blood of both Crown and Capital. If Republicanism can't now forge and impose a new national identity to replace the old, then varieties of ultra-Europeanism may take over from that 'Greatness' to which Mrs Thatcher's stewardship of the Crown has still clung. The counter-hegemony of North over South will never come about. As the very possibility of it recedes (even from the Parliamentary back-benches of the Labour Party), and the Court reconciles itself to Europe as a substitute for the globe, its Countries will no doubt go their own way at last: discarded provinces beyond a 'divide' past any economic or political cure. I hope at least they are Republics.

NOTES

1: The Mystery

1. *British Social Attitudes: the 1984 Report,* edited by R. Jowell and C. Airey (Social and Community Planning Research, London), p.30.

2. 'The Renascence of Monarchy', in *Twentieth Century,* vol.CLIII (Jan.-June 1953), pp.414-24.

3. See *Speak for Yourself: a Mass-Observation Anthology, 1937-1949,* edited by Angus Calder and D.Sheridan (1985), 'Introduction', p.3.

4. *The Uses of Literacy* (1957), pp.85-7.

5. See *The Sun Book of Royalty: Royal Front Pages from the Sun* (Invincible Press Ltd., n.d.), p.34. 'The Royal Family has always been close to the hearts of the *Sun* and its readers...'

6. Fenton Bresler, 'Royalty and the Law', *Woman's Journal,* Nov.1984.

7. Ernst H. Kantorowicz, *The King's Two Bodies* (1957), pp.382, 447-50.

8. Diana Simmonds, *Princess Di, the National Dish: the Making of a Media Star* (1984): see especially Ch.3, 'And sister Diana can carry the banner...'

9. Roland Barthes, *Système de la Mode* (1967), Ch.18 'Rhétorique du signifié: le monde de la Mode', pp.263-4, 'La femme de Mode'.

10. Colin McDowell, *100 Years of Royal Style* (1985), p.61.

11. 'The Dresser' (reporting on a Royal Visit to Italy), *Observer,* 5 May 1985.

12. Elizabeth Wilson, *Adorned in Dreams* (1985), pp.122, 196-7.

13. Kenneth Rose, *King George V* (1983), p.80. 14. See Christopher Warwick, *Princess Margaret* (1983) 'Having eaten sparingly, the Princess lit a cigarette in a gold holder and recalled..."I was with some of my fellow Sea Rangers in a boat on the lake at Frogmore. And *what* do you think appeared in the newspapers? They said I had pulled the bung from the bottom of the boat! That made me frightfully cross. I was part of a *team* and very proud of it. I might tell you"...Thus began the first of may frank conversations', etc. ('Prologue').

15. David Cannadine, 'From Ptarmigan to Tum-tum', *New Society,* 20-27 December, 1984.

16. See J.L.Clifford, *Biography as an Art: Selected Criticism 1560-1960* (1962), pp.203-4.

17. Princess Marie Louise, *My Memories of Six Reigns* (1956), pp.156-9.

18. Neal Ascherson, *The King Incorporated: Leopold II in the Age of Trusts* (1963).

19. Clancy Sigal, 'America's Favourite Soap', in *The Queen Observed,* edited by Trevor Groves (1986), pp.144-50.

20. Henry Fairlie, 'On the Monarchy: a Reply to Malcolm Muggeridge', *Encounter*, vol.17 (Oct. 1961).

21. Comments selected from calls following 'Borderlive', 24 January 1986, by courtesy of Lis Howell and Paul Baird, Border television, Carlisle. I am grateful also to Anna Coote and Diverse Productions (London) for reports of a similar 'phone-in' and correspondence following her film 'Daylight on Monarchy' (Jan. 23, 1985).

22. Ernest Gellner, *Nations and Nationalism* (1983), pp.37-8.

23. *National and English Review*, vol.149, Nos. 894 and 895 (Aug.-Sept. 1957).

24. *The Reith Diaries*, edited by Charles Stuart (1975), Ch.3, 'John Reith and the Monarchy'.

25. Alice Goldfarb Marquis, 'Written on the Wind: the Impact of Radio during the 1930s', *Journal of Contemporary History*, vol.19, No.3 (July 1984), pp.398-99.

26. Robert Lacey, *Majesty* (1977), pp.265-68.

27. A.C.Gimson, 'The R.p.Accent', in *Language in the British Isles*, edited by Peter Trudgill (1984), pp.45-6.

28. As seen on 'English Accents', BBC2 (Producer, Judi Connor) 17 January 1985.

29. Ralph Miliband, *Capitalist Democracy in Britain* (1982), pp.38-9.

30. Lacey, op.cit., p.259.

31. Tony Harrison, 'Marked with D', *Selected Poems* (1984), p.153.

32. Clifford Geertz, 'Centers, Kings and Charisma', in *Culture and its Creators* (1977), pp.152-53.

33. Keith Thomas, *Religion and the Decline of Magic* (1971), pp.227-35.

34. Philip Ziegler, *Crown and People* (1978), p.183.

35. Malcolm Spaven *Fortress Scotland: a Guide to the Military Presence* (1983).

36. Martin Green, *A Mirror for Anglo-Saxons* (1957), pp.17-18.

37. Paul Theroux, *Kingdom by the Sea* (1983), pp.254-57.

38. Percy Black, *The Mystique of Modern Monarchy: with Special Reference to the British Commonwealth* (1953), pp.26-7.

39. Roger Fulford, *Hanover to Windsor* (1960), p.25.

40. *Chips: the Diary of Sir Henry Channon*, edited by Robert Rhodes James (1967).

41. The classical source here is Ernest Jones's essay 'The Psychology of Constitutional Monarchy', in *Essays in Applied Psycho-analysis* (1951). This complacent study depicted constitutional monarchy as 'an index of a highly civilized relation...between rulers and ruled', unobtainable save in 'a state that has attained the highest level of civilization' (p.230).

42. Ziegler, op.cit., p.192.

43. Philip Magnus, *King Edward the Seventh* (1964), p.114.

44. Emma Tennant, *Hotel de Dream* (1976), pp.22-9.

45. Gustave Le Bon, *The Crowd* (trans.1896), p.149.

46. Ziegler, op.cit., pp.163-64.

47. R.W.Johnson, *The Politics of Recession* (1985), 'The Authoritative State', pp.227-30.

48. Walter Benjamin, 'Theses on the Philosophy of History: VI', in *Illuminations* (1970), p.257.

49. On this see P.Gowan, 'The Origins of the Administrative Elite', *New Left Review* No.162 (March-April 1987). The article deals with Coleridge's influence on political and administrative reform in the 19th century, as the main theorist of non-democratic consent (or 'consensus').

50. *The Times,* 29 January, 1985.

51. Here see especially P.Kellner and Lord Crowther-Hunt, *The Civil Servants* (1980), the best recent study of the administrative élite and its formation.

2: The Nation

1. Haffner, *Twentieth Century,* op.cit.

2. Ziegler, op.cit., Ch. 7, pp.138-54.

3. Fairlie, *Encounter,* op.cit.

4. Franz Steiner, *Taboo* (1967), Ch. XII, 'The Problems of Taboo'.

5. John Weightman, *Twentieth Century,* op.cit., pp.406-14: an attempt to make Monarchism more acceptable to those 'more educated and active people who tend to be less Royalist' than others, especially in the North and the working class.

6. Nigel Dennis, *Cards of Identity* (1955), p.100.

7. Neal Ascherson, 'Stonehenge and its Power Struggles', in *Games with Shadows* (1988), p.71.

8. Theodor Adorno, *Minima Moralia* (1951, English translation 1974), p.72.

9. 'Fetishism' (1927), republished in vol.7 of the Pelican Freud Library, *On Sexuality* (1977), pp.351-57.

10. Peter Nettl, *Political Mobilization* (1967), p.22-4.

11. Shils & Young, 'The Meaning of the Coronation', *Sociological Review,* Vol.I, No.2 (1956); republished in Shils, *Centre and Periphery: Essays in Macrosociology* (1975).

12. *The Coronation in History* (Historical Association, 1953). A review in *History* (vol.XXXIX, 1954) objected that it was 'going too far' to claim as Wilkinson did that 'The democratic element in the ceremony can hardly be

said to be conspicuous, nor is there any conceivable reason why it should be...'

13. Shils, 'British Intellectuals in the Mid-Twentieth Century', in *The Intellectuals and the Powers* (1972), p.137.

14. Republished as 'Monarchs and Sociologists: a Reply', in *Towards a Critical Sociology* (1971).

15. G.Wilson Knight, 'This Sceptred Isle: a Study of Shakespeare's Kings', *The Sovereign Flower* (1958), p.88.

16. Ernest Gellner, op.cit., p.138.

17. See here the debate on pre-nationalist modernization in the Scottish Enlightenment by Hobsbawm, Wallerstein and Smout, summarized in 'Dr.Jekyll's Case', *Bulletin of Scottish Politics* No.1 (Autumn 1980); also Smout and Istvan Hont in *Wealth and Virtue: Political Economy in the Scottish Enlightenment* (1983).

18. Gellner, op.cit., p.11

19. Hans Kohn, 'The Genesis and Character of English Nationalism', in *Journal of the History of Ideas*, Vol.I (1940). See also *The Rise of English Nationalism: a Cultural History 1740-1830* (1987), an extensive study of the contrasting factors in 18th century English national identity which (title notwithstanding) still fails to focus adequately on the post-1789 'ism' – the counter-revolution that decided *which* factors were to emerge as decisively 'English' or 'British'.

20. Gellner. op.cit., p.55.

21. E.P.Thompson, *The Poverty of Theory* (1978).

22. J.N.Figgis, *The Divine Right of Kings* (1914), pp.263-66.

23. G.Sabine, *A History of Political Theory* (1948), pp.397-98.

24. C.B.Macpherson, *Democratic Theory: Essays in Retrieval* (1973), p.241.

25. L.Trotsky, *History of the Russian Revolution*, 1967 edition, Vol.1, pp.101-08.

26. See N.Mackenzie, 'Sir Thomas Herbert of Tintern: a Parliamentary "Royalist"', *Bulletin* of the Institute for Historical Research (London), vol.XXIX (1956). The author points out that the Herbert *Memoirs* are essentially 'a skilful re-shaping of facts' to ingratiate Herbert with Charles II.

27. *Memoirs of Edmund Ludlow, 1625-1672*, edited by C.H.Firth (1894), Vol.I, p.221.

28. Christopher Hill, 'God and the English Revolution', *History Workshop Journal*, Spring 1984.

29. Tom Paulin, *The Faber Book of Political Verse* (1986), pp.24-8.

30. Macaulay, *History of England*, Henderson Edition (1908), Vol.III, pp.436-39.

31. Ludlow, op.cit., vol.II, Appendix VII, 'Papers illustrating Ludlow's visit to England in 1689', pp.509-17.

32. Pieter Geyl, *History of the Low Countries: Episodes and Problems*

(1964), Ch. VII, 'Historical Appreciations of the Regent Regime'.

33. Ryszard Kapuśiński, *The Emperor* (1983), p.43.

34. Musil, *Man Without Qualities*, Vol.1, pp.255-56.

35. *Daily Telegraph, Times* and *Sunday Times*, Feb. 1979 to April 1983.

36. J.N.Figgis, *The Divine Right of Kings* (1914), pp.263-66.

37. C. Von Clausewitz, *On War*, 1968 edition, introduced by A.Rapoport, pp.385-88.

38. G.Newman, 'Anti-French Propaganda and British Liberal Nationalism in the Early 19th Century', *Victorian Studies*, vol.XVIII (1974-5), section 1.

39. C.B.Macpherson, *Burke* (1980), p.69.

40. J.L.Lant, *Insubstantial Pageant: Ceremony and Confusion at Queen Victoria's Court*, pp.168-69.

41. Linda Colley, 'The Apotheosis of George IIIrd: Loyalty, Royalty and the British Nation, 1760-1820', *Past & Present* No.102 (1984); also 'Whose Nation? Class and National Consciousness in Britain 1750-1830', *Past & Present* No.113 (1985).

42. Boswell, *Life of Johnson*, Everyman edition (1958), vol.I, April 7 1775, pp.347-48.

43. A.J.P.Taylor, *The Habsburg Monarchy, 1809-1918* (1948), p.12.

44. *English Today*, 'An ABC of World English', Nos.1-4, Jan.-Oct. 1985.

45. J.Plamenatz, 'Two Types of Nationalism', in *Nationalism: the Nature and Evolution of an Idea*, edited by E.Kamenka (1973).

46. George Steiner, 'A Kind of Survivor', in the *George Steiner Reader* (1984), p.232.

47. R.W.Johnson, op.cit., pp.117-22.

48. Kingsley Martin, *The Magic of Monarchy* (1937), pp.102-04.

49. Raymond Williams, *The Long Revolution* (1961), pp.104-05.

50. J.C.D.Clark, *English Society 1688-1832* (1985), pp.93-103.

51. Michael Curtin, 'A Question of Manners: Status and Gender in Etiquette and Courtesy', *Journal of Modern History* vol.57 (Sept. 1985), p.143.

52. R.A.Lebrun, *Throne and Altar: the Thought of Joseph de Maistre* (1965), p.85.

53. D.A.Cannadine, 'The British Monarchy and the "Invention of Tradition", c.1820-1977', in *The Invention of Tradition*, edited by E.J.Hobsbawm and T. Ranger (1983), pp.122-23.

54. *New Society*, 23 August, 1985, 'Not So Fair Play'.

55. R.McKibbin, 'Why was there no Marxism in Great Britain?', *English Historical Review*, vol.99 (1984), pp.314-15.

56. Samuel Finer, *The Man on Horseback: the Role of the Military in Politics* (1976).

57. James Walvin, *Football and the Decline of Britain* (1986), p.124.

58. F.Engels, 'The Condition of England', in Marx & Engels *Collected Works*, Vol.3, 1843-4.

59. Gareth Stedman Jones, 'Some Notes on Karl Marx and the English Labour Movement', *History Workshop Journal* No.18 (Autumn 1984), p.135.

60. Benjamin, op.cit., p.257.

61. Orwell, *The Lion and the Unicorn: Socialism and the English Genius* (1941 & 1982), p.52.

3: The Glamour of Backwardness

1. J.H.Plumb, *The First Four Georges* (1956), p.175.

2. Goethe, *Maximen und Reflexionen* (Stuttgart, 1949), p.167.

3. Julian Rathbone, *Nasty, Very* (1984), Part 1, Ch.2.

4. *A King's Story: the Memoirs of HRH the Duke of Windsor*, (1951), pp.78-9.

5. Kenneth Rose, *Kings, Queens & Courtiers: Intimate Portraits of the Royal House of Windsor from its Foundation to the Present Day*, pp.52-3.

6. John Pearson, *The Ultimate Family: The Making of the Royal House of Windsor* (1986), Part III, 'Revival', Chapter 9, 'God Bless the Prince of Wales'.

7. Anthony Holden, *Charles, Prince of Wales* (1979), pp.149-50.

8. V.Bogdanor, *Devolution* (1979), p.129.

9. Judith Williamson, *Consuming Passion* (1986), pp.76-7.

10. A.J.Mayer, *The Persistence of the Old Regime* (1981), p.284.

11. Martin J. Wiener, *English Culture and the Decline of the Industrial Spirit 1850-1980* (1981), presents an extensive and lively tableau of British anti-industrialism from the mid-Victorian era to Thatcher, yet (like many others) the analysis is ultimately confined by his chosen time-scale: whether treating of the State or of its underlying political economy, the last century and a half is too short a perspective to permit judgement. Only a longer perspective allows the economic rationale of anti-industrialism (and hence of de-industrialization) to emerge, as an organic strategy of the dominant fraction of British capital.

12. Anthony Hilton, *City Within a State* (1987), pp.1-2

13. Hilton, ibid., pp.166-7.

14. Sidney Pollard, *The Wasting of the British Economy* (1982), Ch.1, 'The Facts – And Do They Matter?', pp.1-18.

15. Geoffrey Ingham, *Capitalism Divided? The City and Industry in British Social Development* (1984), p.38, and 'Concluding Remarks', pp.225-35.

16. See P.Corrigan and D.Sayer, *The Great Arch: English State Formation as Cultural Revolution* (1985): the British 'bourgeois revolution' never having

satisfactorily occurred, this vein of nativist analysis reasons that it must really always have been occurring, in small and easily-overlooked dosages which extend from (at least) Tudor days up to Mrs Thatcher. What British Socialists need, therefore, is a matching homoeopathic programme for the next half-millenium which can be grafted on to Albion's never-ending Cultural Revolution. We want none of these deplorable 'short-cuts' foreigners have gone in for (p.207), and no unseemly fuss about 'abstract, insubstantial Rights' (p.206), since around A.D.2400 it will certainly be realized that (like its predecessor) the Socialist Revolution will have been with us incognito for centuries.

17. See Neal Ascherson, *Games with Shadows* (Radius 1988).

18. David F.Good, *The Economic Rise of the Habsburg Empire* (1984), Ch. VIII, 'The Habsburg Economy in Perspective', pp.237-256.

19. Robert Blake, *The Decline of Power, 1915-1964*, pp.348-9.

20. The best analysis is John Barry's two-hour political history *Our Bomb: the Inside Story*, a London Weekend Television documentary shown in 1986.

21. See John M. MacKenzie, *Propaganda and Empire: the Manipulation of British Public Opinion, 1880-1960* (1984), for a survey of the main 'vehicles of imperial propaganda' which combined to create this psychological climate.

22. P.N.Furbank, *Unholy Pleasure: the Idea of Social Class* (1985), p.126.

23. Christopher Harvie's forthcoming study *The Centre of Things* deals thoroughly with the treatment of Parliament in the British novel from Disraeli to Douglas Hird.

24. C.Baldick, *The Social Mission of English Criticism, 1848-1932* (1983), p.229.

25. See for instance *Champion of Homoeopathy: the Life of Margery Blackie*, by C.B.Smith (1986), Ch.10, 'Royal Physician'.

26. Franco Moretti, *The Way of the World* (1987), pp.194-5.

27. Gareth Stedman Jones, *Languages of Class: Studies in English Working Class History, 1832-1982* (1983), p.228.

28. Richard Rose and Dennis Kavanagh, 'The Monarchy in Contemporary Political Culture', *Comparative Politics*, vol. VIII (1976), Section III and Table 4.

29. Jon Halliday, *A Political History of Japanese Capitalism* (1975), 'The Meiji State', pp.34-42.

30. Ernest Gellner, *Words and Things* (revised edition, 1979), pp.263-4.

31. Noel Annan, 'The Intellectual Aristocracy', *Essay in Social History*, edited J.H.Plumb (1956).

32. A.Motion, *Philip Larkin* (1982), pp.30-31.

33. Terry Eagleton, *Exiles and Emigrés: Studies in Modern Literature* (1970), 'Introduction'.

34. John Carswell, *The Descent on England: a Study of the English*

Revolution of 1688 and its European Background (1969), 'Conclusion', p.235.

35. Krishan Kumar, 'The Nationalization of British Culture', in *Culture and Society in Contemporary Europe: a Casebook*, edited by S.Hoffman and P.Kitromilides (1981), pp.122-3.

36. In *The Invention of Tradition*, op.cit., pp.124-5.

37. Philip Ziegler, *William IVth* (1971), pp.290-4.

38. Jeffrey L.Lant, *Insubstantial Pageant: Ceremony and Confusion at Queen Victoria's Court* (1979), pp.168-9.

39. Jim Bulpitt, *Territory and Power in the United Kingdom* (1983), pp.238-9.

40. P.Anderson, *Arguments Within English Marxism* (1980), pp.35-6.

41. P.Anderson, 'The Figures of Descent', *New Left Review* No.161 (Jan-Feb. 1987), pp.64-5.

42. Simon Schama, 'The Domestication of Majesty: Royal Family Portraiture, 1500-1850', *Journal of Interdisciplinary History*, vol.XVII, No.1 (1986).

43. *An Artist's Life* (1977), ghost-written by Robert Wraight, pp.85-6.

44. Ibid., p.104. Dame Laura's own portrait of Princess Margaret surrounded by strangely Hobbitt-like burghers inaugurating the rebuilt Coventry Cathedral had met with a very different reception.

45. Robert Rhodes James, *Albert, Prince Consort* (1983), pp.194-208.

46. Gellner, op.cit., p.11.

47. L.A.Siedentop, 'The Impotence of the British Middle Classes', *Spectator*, December 30, 1978; 'Viewpoint: the Strange Life of Liberal England', *Times Literary Supplement*, August 16, 1985.

48. David Landes, *Prometheus Unbound*, pp.546-7.

49. Moretti, op.cit., p.185.

50. Duncan, op.cit., pp.152-3.

51. Michael De-La-Noy, *The Honours System* (1985), p.165.

52. R.S.Neale, *Class and Ideology in the 19th Century* (1972), 'Introduction'.

53. Gareth Stedman Jones, op.cit., pp.236-7

54. Keith Middlemas, *Politics in Industrial Society: the Experience of the British System since 1911* (1979), Ch.13, 'Corporate Bias'.

55. Raphael Samuel, 'Ethics and the Strike', *New Society*, 28 February 1985.

56. Ibid.

4: Quiet Republicanism

1. Neal Ascherson, *Games With Shadows* (1988).

2. Tony Benn, *Out of the Wilderness: Diaries 1963-67* (1987). At the start of Wilson's 'modernization' adventure in 1963-4 Benn records how he 'tried to open up the whole question of the monarchy' and put forward 'mood-changing measures – like no dinner jackets for Labour Ministers at Buckingham Palace, mini-cars for official business and postage stamps without the Queen's head on them...' (p.14). What happened to the postage-stamp idea is described with admirable frankness in 'Postmaster General', Ch.3, pp.160-313.

3. George Dangerfield, *Victoria's Heir* (1940), pp.184-191.

4. Roy Jenkins, *Sir Charles Dilke: a Victorian Tragedy* (revised edition, 1965), Ch.4, 'An English Republican', p.70.

5. Freda Harcourt, 'Gladstone, Monarchism and the "New" Imperialism, 1868-74', *Journal of Imperial & Commonwealth History* Vol.XIV, No.1 (Oct.1985), pp.30-33.

6. Gareth Stedman Jones, *Languages of Class*, op.cit., p.235.

7. Walter Bagehot, 'The Thanksgiving' (Feb.24, 1872), in *Collected Works* (1974-), ed. Stévas pp.439-442.

8. I am grateful to Christopher Harvie for showing me a copy of this letter from the unpublished correspondence of John Marley.

9. Labour Party, *Report* of Annual Conference Proceedings, 1923, pp.250-1.

10. Lacey, op.cit., p.290.

11. J.H.Grainger, 'The Activity of Monarchy', *Cambridge Quarterly*, vol.VII, No.4 (1977).

12. Tom Paulin, 'Introduction' to *Political Verse*, op.cit., (1986).

13. Cairns Craig, *Yeats, Eliot, Pound and the Politics of Poetry* (1982) pp.282-9.

14. J.M.Cameron, 'T.S.Eliot as a Political Writer', *The Night Battle* (1962), p.19.

15. Anthony Barnett, *Iron Britannia: Why Parliament Waged its Falkland War* (1982), pp.18-23.

16. Tom Paulin, *Ireland & the English Crisis* (1984), 'A New Look at the Language Question', pp.178-193.

17. *Salisbury Review*, No.3 (Spring 1983).

18. Richard Rose, *Understanding the United Kingdom: the Territorial Dimension in Government* (1982), Ch.4, 'the Institutions of the Mace', pp.86-7 and pp.94-104, 'The Cabinet as Custodian of the Mace'.

19. Richard Rose & Dennis Kavanagh, 'The Monarchy in Contemporary Political Culture', op.cit., p.573.

20. R.H.S.Crossman, 'Introduction' to *The English Constitution*, 1967 Centenary edition.

21. Richard Shannon, *The Crisis of Imperialism, 1865-1915* (1976), Part I, Ch.3, 'The Politics of Reform, 1866-8', pp.52-75.

22. R.W.K.Hinton, 'The Prime Minister as an Elected Monarch', *Parliamentary Affairs*, vol.XIII (1959-60).

23. C.H.Sisson, *The Spirit of British Administration: and Some European Comparisons* (1959)m Ch.XI, 'Reform and Imitations', p.148.

24. Samuel Finer, *Comparative Government* (1970), pp.139 & 146-7.

25. A.J.Mayer, *The Persistence of the Old Régime*, op.cit., 'Introduction', pp.4-5.

26. For a bibliography of the dispute, see Perry Anderson, 'The Figures of Descent', *New Left Review* No.161 (Jan-Feb.1987), p.21.

27. 'Barrington Moore, Perry Anderson and English Social Development', in *Cultural Studies* No.9 (Birmingham Centre for Contemporary Cultural Studies, Spring 1976).

28. Dennis Kavanagh, *Thatcherism and British Politics: the End of Consensus?* (1987), pp.284-292.

29. Kavanagh, ibid., pp.298-9.

30. A.H.Halsey, *Change in British Society* (new edition, 1986), pp.75-6.

31. Gilroy(1987), pp.246-7.

32. Antonio Gramsci, *Selections from Prison Notebooks* (1971), ed. Hoare and Nowell Smith, pp.223-6.

33. Neal Ascherson, *Games With Shadows*.

34. Wainwright, 'Moving Beyond the Fragments', in *Beyond the Fragments: Feminism and the Making of Socialism*, S.Rowbotham, L.Segal and Hilary Wainwright (1979).